W9-BVU-778

READINGS IN INTERNATIONAL ACCOUNTING

Edited by

John Blake

PROFESSOR OF ACCOUNTING, UNIVERSITY OF CENTRAL LANCASHIRE, ENGLAND

and

Mahmud Hossain

LECTURER IN ACCOUNTING, MASSEY UNIVERSITY, PALMERSTON NORTH, NEW ZEALAND

INTERNATIONAL THOMSON BUSINESS PRESS

I(T)P An International Thomson Publishing Company

London • Bonn • Boston • Johannesburg • Madrid • Melbourne • Mexico City • New York • Paris
Singapore • Tokyo • Toronto • Albany, NY • Belmont, CA • Cincinnati, OH • Detroit, MI

Readings in International Accounting

First published 1996 by International Thomson Business Press

A division of International Thomson Publishing Inc.
The ITP logo is a trademark under licence

British Library Cataloguing-in-Publication Data
A catalogue record for this book is available from the British Library

---

First edition 1996

Typeset in the UK by WestKey Ltd, Falmouth, Cornwall
Printed in the UK by TJ Press (Padstow)Ltd, Padstow, Cornwall

---

ISBN 0-415-13685-7(hb)
0-415-13686-5 (pb)

International Thomson Business Press
Berkshire House
168–173 High Holborn
London WC1V 7AA
UK

International Thomson Business Press
20 Park Plaza
14th Floor
Boston MA 02116
USA

CONTENTS

Part I The International Accounting Environment

Part V International Financial Markets and International Financial Analysis

Part I

THE INTERNATIONAL ACCOUNTING ENVIRONMENT

In this section we present some articles that cover the broad environment of international accounting.

Chandler (1992) offers an overview of the various professional bodies seeking to promote international accounting harmonisation and assesses some recent developments in this field.

Van Hulle (1993), a senior official at the European Community (EC), offers an authoritative view of the EC's efforts to achieve harmonisation. Of particular note is his suggestion that the European Court of Justice may become involved in making these efforts more effective.

Three papers raise some interesting questions as to the role of international organisations in pursuing international accounting harmonisation:

a Meek (1984) argues that lack of enforcement powers for international accounting standards may be compensated for by market forces.

b Goeltz (1991) questions both the practicality of achieving, and the necessity for, international standards, arguing that efficient markets can cope with international accounting diversity.

c Chevalier (1977) applies a methodology not normally found in accounting research to provide evidence that different types of accounting data may best serve the needs of different cultures.

By contrast Aitken & Islam (1984) offer a vigorous rebuttal to a range of arguments against international accounting harmonisation.

Agrawal, Jensen, Meador, & Sellers (1989) provide a review of differences between the conceptual frameworks that underlie the development of accounting principles in different countries.

The 'big 6' international accounting firms are a major factor in the international accounting environment:

a Briston (1989) discusses the impact of the internationalisation of the accounting profession.
b Soeters & Schreuder (1988) use a methodology developed from the literature on distinctive patterns of national culture to identify significant contrasts between multinational and national accounting firms in the Netherlands.

Hove considers the implications of international accounting harmonisation for developing countries, and argues that, particularly in the field of accounting education and professional organisation, developing countries need to develop their own approach.

1

THE INTERNATIONAL HARMONIZATION OF ACCOUNTING

In search of influence

Roy A. Chandler

INTRODUCTION

The purpose of this paper is to describe in general terms the various moves towards international harmonization and in particular the progress which has been made to that end and to review the influence of agencies outside the accounting profession in the setting and enforcement of international standards.

HISTORICAL BACKGROUND

The move towards greater harmonization of professional accounting practices has been traced back to 1904 and the first international accounting congress in St. Louis, Missouri (Samuels and Piper, 1985, p. 59, Mueller, 1979 p. 7). Subsequent congresses were held at approximately five-yearly intervals. The issues discussed in the earlier congresses appear to be largely practice oriented. Views differ on the relative importance of international issues: Samuels and Piper (1985) report that 'international issues were not important' (p. 59), whereas Mueller (1979) states 'Attention to international harmonization (in later years standardization) established itself from the beginning as a central purpose of these Congresses' (p. 7). In any event by the 1950s calls for greater efforts towards harmonization were becoming more frequent.

In a tripartite move, Canada, the United Kingdom, and the United States

From International Journal of Accounting (1992 vol 27) pp 222–233.

formed the Accountants International Study Group (AISG) in 1966. The stated purpose of the AISG was 'to institute comparative studies as to accounting thought and practice in participating countries, to make reports from time to time which, subject to the prior approval of the sponsoring institutes, would be issued to members of those institutes' (Thomas, 1970, p. 60). The group produced more than 20 reports on both accounting and auditing issues. These reports are evidence that professional agreement through international discussion could be reached even on issues which had vexed national standard-setters. Whether any action at a national level resulted from the recommendations in the reports is another matter.

It was not until the 10th International Congress in Sydney in 1972 that firm proposals were put forward (and accepted) for means to achieve real progress in international harmonization. Plans were laid to establish an organization to develop accounting standards for a worldwide audience of accountants. The International Accounting Standards Committee (IASC), with headquarters in London, had its first meeting in June 1973.

In 1977, just before the next international congress, the AISG was disbanded and the International Federation of Accountants (IFAC) was formed, operating from New York City. The broad objective of IFAC is 'the development and enhancement of a coordinated worldwide accountancy profession with harmonized standards', (*IFAC Constitution*, paragraph 2). Its mission is to develop international guidance in areas other than financial accounting.

The first standing committees of IFAC were charged with the responsibility to develop guidance on auditing, education, ethics, and management accounting. IFAC was also to assume responsibility for organizing future world congresses. (For contemporary descriptions of the objectives and operations of IFAC, see Chetkovich (1979) and Sempier (1979)). Later IFAC was to add another committee to cover public sector issues.

IFAC and IASC have continued to lead separate existences. Under a statement of mutual commitment, agreed between the two bodies in 1982, their relationship has been clarified:

1 they have a common membership;
2 the IFAC Council nominates as many as 13 members of the Board of IASC;
3 IASC reports annually to the IFAC Council;
4 IFAC recognizes the autonomy of IASC in setting international accounting standards;
5 IFAC supports the work of IASC and requires its member bodies to do the same;
6 IFAC contributes 10% of the annual IASC budget;
7 the President of IFAC is entitled to attend and to speak at IASC meetings

but not to vote, and likewise the Chairman of IASC Board has a similar entitlement in regard to the IFAC Council meetings.

These arrangements ensure that there is a close working relationship between IFAC and IASC while maintaining the autonomy of both bodies. Nevertheless there have been calls for the two to be more closely linked and even merged. A recent review, commissioned by the eight countries which provide the bulk of IFAC/IASC funding into the IFAC/IASC organizational arrangements, accepted the status quo while urging IFAC and IASC to seek the long-term objective of becoming one body.

ADVANTAGES OF INTERNATIONAL STANDARDS

The increasing internationalization of the capital markets provides important opportunities for multinational corporations. Tondkar et al. (1989) describe a number of financial, strategic, and commercial advantages motivating large corporations to seek equity listings on a foreign stock exchange. However, they also report that 'one of the major problems faced by companies seeking foreign listing is the difference in regulations and listing requirements of various stock exchanges around the world. Compliance with the regulations prescribed by the various stock exchanges . . . may require major modifications or even restatement of financial statements' (p. 147). International harmonization in accounting (and auditing) would clearly provide a solution to this problem.

Both Samuels and Piper (1985, p. 56) and Nobes (1991, p. 70) distinguish between *standardization* and *harmonization*, the former giving an impression of uniformity and rigidity, the latter containing the idea of narrowing areas of difference but stopping short of uniformity. Whatever the outcome of the present developments on the international scene, it is clear that for progress to be made some countries will have to abandon some of their existing practices.

Those countries may be persuaded that the advantages of compliance with international pronouncements outweigh the loss of sovereignty in the setting of national standards. In addition to multinational companies, other beneficiaries of greater harmonization/standardization include (based on Samuels and Piper, 1985, pp. 75–82):

1 International investors – comparison of investment opportunities will be facilitated if financial statements globally are drawn up on a consistent and uniform basis.
2 International accounting firms – the recruitment and transfer of staff across international boundaries would be assisted if the required training and possession of skills and knowledge were similar in different countries.
3 Individual accounting practitioners – if training requirements and tech-

nical standards were harmonized, job opportunities would be created or expanded both in terms of the possibility of relocation and work referred from abroad.

4 Accounting institutes (especially in developing countries) – institutes may avoid duplication of research and standard-setting efforts by adopting nationally the standards developed and accepted at the international level. Many already do so.
5 Regulatory agencies – both tax authorities and securities regulators would find their supervisory and enforcement roles eased if national differences in financial reporting and auditing were reduced.

CRITICISMS OF THE STANDARDIZATION/HARMONIZATION PROCESS

Accounting Imperialism

The influence of major countries, especially the United Kingdom and the United States, is certainly clear in the pronouncements of both IFAC and IASC. Resistance can be expected in countries where the national adoption of international pronouncements or standards developed by leading countries may be perceived as being the imposition of standards by economically superior countries on developing countries, – a form of accounting colonialism (e.g., Hove, 1986; Francalanza, 1988).

Both IFAC and IASC have tried to allay fears that their pronouncements are the product of debate between only leading countries. Under the mutual commitments, IFAC is required to nominate at least three developing countries to the IASC Board. IFAC includes in its own Council and committees representatives from developing countries, though there is no constitutional requirement to do so. Nevertheless, since discussions are always in English (the official language of the IFAC and IASC pronouncements), committee members from non-Anglo countries must be at a disadvantage.

Compliance with international standards, however, may not be costless even for those countries which may be regarded as leading the accountancy profession. For example, under the IASC's E32, *Comparability of Financial Statements* (IASC, 1989) the required or preferred methods of inventory valuation were FIFO and weighted average cost; LIFO (the generally accepted method in the United States) was an allowed alternative but US corporations wishing to comply with International Accounting Standards (IASs) would have been required to disclose a reconciliation of their (LIFO-based) income and shareholders' interests to the amounts that would have been determined using the preferred method. A more recent exposure draft, E38, *Inventories* (IASC, 1991) seeks to ban LIFO altogether.

Following the revision to International Auditing Guideline (IAG) 13, *The*

Auditor's Report on Financial Statements, the current UK practice of qualifying audit reports for uncertainty is no longer in conformity with the IAG, and the UK Auditing Practices Board is having to reconsider its guidance on this matter (*Accountancy Age*, April 11, 1991, p. 3).

Inappropriate Standards

Other criticisms of the harmonization process center around the fact that standards set internationally cannot possibly cater for the wide range of national circumstances, legal systems, stages of economic development, and cultural differences (e.g., Samuels and Piper, 1985, pp. 100–109). However, such arguments are effectively refuted by Aitken and Islam (1983) on the grounds that the nature of economic transactions and the accounting for them do not vary in essence.

Low Response Rates to Exposure Drafts

Proposed pronouncements of both IASC and IFAC are exposed for comment. This exposure process gives outsiders the chance to contribute to the standard-setting process (provided the standard-setters are responsive to the letters of comment they receive). However, in general the response rate to international exposure drafts tends to be relatively low. Letters of comment received by IASC are now a matter of public record but IFAC has yet to follow this course, so the nature of the comments can only be gauged from the press releases issued by IFAC on completion of a project.

Compromises

On relatively straightforward and uncontroversial issues it may not be difficult for a committee of standard-setters to reach unanimous agreement on the preferred position. On other issues compromise may have to be struck in order for a proposed standard to be accepted. In addition forceful submissions (even if few in number) in response to exposure drafts may compel the standard-setters to relax the requirements contained in a proposed standard to avoid its being rejected on publication.

This is true even at a national level. In the United Kingdom the former Accounting Standards Committee (ASC) attracted criticism for issuing standards which were considered to be inadequate or permissive. It is not difficult to imagine that seeking a consensus in the international arena would require standard-setters to do more 'deals' and to be more inclined to incorporate permitted alternatives in the standards.

Rivera (1989) comments 'most of the IAS issued probably have been made deliberately flexible so as not to upset any of the leading accounting countries' (p. 328).

The IASC admits as much in E32 (IASC, 1989), the purpose of which is 'to set out proposals for the removal of free choices of accounting treatments presently permitted in International Accounting Standards. Such free choices were necessary in the past to gain acceptance of certain Standards', (paragraph 3).

COMPLIANCE WITH INTERNATIONAL ACCOUNTING STANDARDS

In an early review of the progress of harmonization from the establishment of the IASC to 1979, Nair and Frank (1981) noted an increased level of harmonization during the period.

From a study of the compliance of financial reporting in five countries represented on IASC with five of the IASs issued by IASC, Evans and Taylor (1982) concluded that 'the IASC has had very little impact on the accounting practices of the countries surveyed. Except for a few instances, a country following a particular method prior to the promulgation of an IASC standard continued to follow the same practice after the standard's issuance' (p. 126). They accept, however, that in some of the countries this may have been due to the fact that the extant national standard already was in compliance with the subsequent pronouncement of the IASC.

In a later survey of large firm practitioners in 40 countries (all with IFAC member bodies), Taylor et al. (1986) concluded that the IASC 'appears to be succeeding in improving the comparability and consistency of international accounting reports and thereby reducing the diversity of international reporting practices' (p. 9).

McKinnon and Janell (1983) examine compliance with three IASs and conclude that 'the IASC has not succeeded in changing existing standards or setting new standards. [However,] it has succeeded in codifying generally accepted practice, in serving as a neutral source for standards, and in influencing groups with enforcement powers' (p. 33).

Doupnik (1987) examines 70 financial reporting practices (including 47 issues covered by IASs) in 46 countries. He compares his results with those of a similar survey performed by Price Waterhouse (PW) in 1975. From a statistical analysis of the two data sets he concludes that compliance with IASs improved over the period 1975–1983.

Nobes (1981) criticizes the methodology and results of such studies on the grounds, *inter alia*, that the original PW survey data contained errors. Further criticism comes from Tay and Parker (1990) who claim that a lack of clarity of the concepts at issue may explain the conflicting results of the various studies. They indicate that some of the studies attempted to measure *de jure* harmonization while others sought to measure *de facto* harmonization.

The same confusion of terms is evident in a survey conducted by the

IASC (1988) of member bodies' compliance with all its standards. The result of this survey was that 'in the majority of countries, national requirements or practice conform with 23 out of 25 IASs. The exceptions are IAS 14. Reporting Financial Information by Segment, and IAS 15, Information Reflecting the Effects of Changing Prices' (p. 3). The high level of self-assessed compliance is boosted by the inclusion of national *practice* as well as national *requirements*, so that while a country's national standards may not cover the subject of an IAS, the generally accepted practice in that country may be largely in conformity with that IAS. Another reason for the apparently high level of compliance could be the permissiveness of the original IASs.

COMPLIANCE WITH IFAC PRONOUNCEMENTS

The results of IFAC surveys, conducted every three years, of member bodies show a similarly high level of compliance with most of the IFAC guidance (IFAC, 1987), though the results are not presented or analyzed in the same detail as those of the IASC.

AUTHORITY OF INTERNATIONAL AUDITING PRONOUNCEMENTS

According to the *Preface to International Auditing Guidelines*, IAGs apply whenever an independent audit is performed. However, it is recognized that IAGs do not override local regulations in a particular country. Nevertheless, under the IFAC Constitution, member bodies should use their best endeavours:

i to work towards implementation, when and to the extent possible under local conditions, of [IFAC] guidelines and
ii specifically to incorporate in their national auditing standards the principles on which are based International Auditing Guidelines. (para. 6 (c)).

This obligation is clearly phrased in permissive terms to avoid causing member bodies difficulties in complying when local conditions or laws conflict with international guidance, although the drafting leaves some doubt as to whether the permissiveness extends to auditing guidelines.

The obligation is neither enforced nor enforceable. No penalty is incurred for non-compliance; the power to suspend or expel a member body from IFAC membership can be exercised only in the case of non-payment of financial contribution or acts bringing the international accounting profession into disrepute.

A close reading of the above section of the IFAC Constitution also raises the question of whether the obligation is met when member bodies incorporate the IAG principles in national auditing *guidelines* rather than auditing *standards*. Different professional bodies have different terms for describing the authoritative auditing statements which they produce; Campbell (1985) does not let the diverse terminology distract his comparative study of the auditing guidance in nine countries. What is likely to be more important for the purposes of IFAC (and for that matter IASC) is that national pronouncements (whatever they may be called) carry authority and some means of enforcement at the national level.

ENFORCING COMPLIANCE WITH INTERNATIONAL STANDARDS

Both IFAC and IASC are effectively powerless to enforce compliance by their own member bodies. Both must rely on the moral obligation which membership of IFAC imposes. It should be noted that for the IASC this obligation has, in fact, been diluted over the years (Rivera, 1989, p. 326; Nobes, 1991, p. 77).

Recently, 'In a very significant move, just after year-end the [IAPC] agreed that [international auditing] guidelines would be renamed "International Standards on Auditing". The committee felt that the term "Standard" more appropriately describes IFAC's authority as an international standard-setting body and should improve the perception of users as to the status of the documents and encourage their wider use' (IFAC, 1991, p. 5). The move is 'significant' for a number of reasons, not least because, under IFAC's own Constitution which can only be amended by the Assembly, the IAPC has no authority to issue *Standards*.

In countries where accounting and auditing practices are dictated by a governmental body, international pronouncements (whatever their designation) can be no more than persuasive at best. Dunn (1991) points to the fact that 'the lack of a strong accountancy profession can make it difficult to exert influence in some countries. . . . Any attempt to introduce new standards through the professional body would be hampered by [a] relative lack of influence' (p. 73). Fitzgerald (1981) calls for the IASC to obtain more authoritative support in such countries and to 'broaden its base to encourage involvement of business, government, and other sectors in its work' (p. 26). This call has been heeded.

More generally, the lack of authority attaching to international pronouncements has caused several commentators to question the ability of the accounting profession to achieve harmonization unaided (Samuels and Piper, 1985, p. 87; McKinnon and Janell, 1983, p. 32; Nobes, 1991, p. 78).

Taylor (1987) uses the lack of enforcement powers as one indication that harmonization itself is not 'adequate justification for the activities of the IASC' (p. 161). He advances an alternative rationale for efforts aimed at international harmonization, one premise of which is that the accounting profession is protecting its self-interest by taking action to pre-empt government intervention. Taylor specifies neither the source nor the form of this possible government intervention, though several supra-national governmental bodies have been involved in international accounting matters for several years. The United Nations (UN), through its Centre on Transnational Corporations, and the Organization for Economic Cooperation and Development (OECD) have been active, though relatively ineffective, in furthering the cause of international harmonization in financial reporting, (Fitzgerald, 1981). Both organizations are now represented on the Consultative Group of the IASC, on which wider interest groups other than accountants are represented. It would appear therefore that while both the UN and the OECD remain actively interested in international financial reporting, they are prepared to allow the IASC to lead the way.

The EC Commission is also represented on the IASC's Consultative Group but is certainly no passive bystander. The EC directives on company reporting are seen by some (e.g., Nobes, 1991, p. 89) as the most effective way of harmonizing accounting practices (in Europe, at least). Outside Europe, real progress towards international harmonization is most likely to occur through the IASC but only if it can obtain the necessary authority with which to ensure enforcement of its Standards.

Some outside agencies which have expressed an interest in *using* rather than *setting* international standards include the World Bank and the Regional Development Banks, for example the Asian Development Bank. These agencies have stipulated compliance with the international accounting and auditing pronouncements of IFAC and IASC as one of the conditions for the granting of financial aid for development projects (a practice which Hove (1986, pp. 91–92) views as the best example of accounting imperialism).

CONSISTENCY OF UK AND INTERNATIONAL AUDITING GUIDANCE

Despite the lack of authority of international pronouncements, some countries do appear to honor their moral obligation to incorporate the international guidance into their national guidance. For example, the case of Australia is well documented (Campbell, 1985, pp. 34–36). In the United Kingdom, Chandler (1991) reports that 'a great number of the basic principles and essential procedures contained in the IAGs/RSs are adequately covered by the existing UK guidance. Indeed the wording of some of the UK guidelines bears a very close resemblance to that of the IAGs. This is not surprising given the significant contribution of the UK bodies in the development of new IAGs (the United Kingdom has been represented on the IAPC since its inception) and the recognition given to existing IAGs when the APC is developing new UK guidance' (p. 8).

The major areas of difference appear to be those where the IAPC has recently moved ahead of the UK in developing guidance, for example on components of audit risk, the audit of accounting estimates, audit-related services, and the examination of prospective financial information.

A WHITE KNIGHT APPEARS ON THE SCENE

The International Organization of Securities Commissions (IOSCO) is an affiliation of nearly 50 national securities regulators. One of its aims is to assist the continued growth of the international capital markets by seeking to reduce the diversity of securities regulations. It thus has expressed a legitimate interest in the harmonization efforts of the accounting profession.

IOSCO has encouraged IASC 'to improve International Accounting Standards and to ensure that they are sufficiently detailed and complete, contain adequate disclosure requirements, and are prepared with the visible commitment to the needs of users of financial statements' (IFAC, 1990, p. 19).

To appease IOSCO both IASC and IFAC have been forced to reconsider their existing standards, in particular those which embody permitted alternatives. The IASC, in a major initiative, E32, proposed amendments to nearly half of the existing IASs in order to remove the 'free choices of alternative accounting treatments for like transactions and events' (IASC, 1989, para. 1).

On auditing and ethical issues, IFAC reports that it 'has stepped up its efforts to win [IOSCO's] acceptance of IFAC auditing and ethics pronouncements for multinational securities offering; the differences that existed have been minimized and both IFAC and IOSCO have an objective of a mutually acceptable set of standards, to be reached in October 1992' (IFAC, 1991, p. 1). Some significant revisions to the IAGs have been made since these discussions first took place. IFAC acknowledges too that the ethics guidance had to be modified in response to IOSCO concerns (IFAC, 1991, p. 4).

The term 'regulatory capture' has been used to describe the exertion of influence by one vested interest group over the activities of a governmental or quasi-governmental agency with regulatory powers (e.g., Walker, 1987). There is no evidence that regulatory capture has occurred at an international level, in fact almost the opposite is happening. IOSCO, with no regulatory powers over the accountancy profession, has 'captured' the international standard-setting bodies (which have ineffective enforcement powers) and is essentially setting their policy direction.

IFAC and IASC clearly seem keen to explore the possibilities of close cooperation with IOSCO and have already expended significant amounts of resources (staff and committee time) to upgrading existing guidance so as to meet the IOSCO objections. The *quid pro quo* for this acquiescence from IFAC and IASC is the promise of high level recognition of their international pronouncements and the potential for enforcement of such pronouncements (albeit indirectly through the stock exchanges which are IOSCO members). Whether IOSCO have sufficient influence over *their* members to deliver on this promise remains uncertain. The most that IOSCO can do is to make recommendations to its members; like IFAC and IASC, it has no powers of enforcement.

IMPLICATIONS FOR ACCOUNTABILITY AND STANDARD SETTING

Looking to the future, if the current cooperation between IFAC/IASC and IOSCO produces the hoped for results, a number of consequences, apart from increased harmonization, will follow. The fact that accounting and auditing standards would be set at international level and imposed on national accounting bodies would redirect criticism (e.g., in the UK, Sikka et al., 1989) of the accountability of the standard-setting process away from national standard-setters to those responsible for the international standards.

It would be difficult to defend the procedures currently used by IFAC and IASC against accusations of having unrepresentative and unelected committee memberships, of secrecy regarding committee agendas and voting patterns, and lack of public access to agenda material and (in the case of IFAC) responses to exposure drafts.

CONCLUSION

The advantage of the cooperation for IOSCO is that standards developed by the accounting profession are likely to be more acceptable to preparers and auditors of financial statements intended for multinational use than IOSCO-imposed standards (even if IOSCO were to have both the resources to develop and the powers to enforce such standards).

For IASC and especially IFAC, the recognition by IOSCO of their statements will enhance their standing in the world commercial, financial, and accounting circles. Given the potential powers of IOSCO (via its members), this would also provide a means of ensuring compliance with international statements (initially, at least, in relation to multinational filings).

The down-side of this cooperation with IOSCO is the surrender of some autonomy over the setting of international standards and even over committee agendas and priorities. Other difficulties likely to be encountered are more strident calls for the process of international standard setting to be, and to be seen to be, more accountable.

ACKNOWLEDGEMENT

The author would like to acknowledge the support and helpful comments of the editor and an anonymous reviewer.

REFERENCES

Aitken, M. J., Islam, N. A. (1983) 'Dispelling Arguments against International Accounting Standards' *International Journal of Accounting Education and Research*, 19, (2), 35–46.

Campbell, I. (1985) *International Auditing*, London: MacMillan.

Chandler, R. A. (1991) *A comparison of UK and international auditing guidance*, London: APC.

Chetkovlch, M. N. (1979) 'The International Federation of Accountants: Its Organization and Goals,' *International Journal of Accounting Education and Research*, 15, (1), 13–20.

Doupnik, T. S. (1987) 'Evidence of International Harmonization of Financial Reporting,' *International Journal of Accounting Education and Research*, 23, (1), 47–67.

Dunn, J. (1991) Auditing: Theory and Practice, Hemel Hempstead: Prentice Hall.

Evans, T. G., Taylor, M. E. (1982) ' "Bottom Line Compliance" with the IASC: A Comparative Analysis.' *International Journal of Accounting*, 18, (1), 115–128.

Fitzgerald, R. D. (1981) 'International Harmonization and Reporting,' *International Journal of Accounting Education and Research*, 17, (1), 21–32.

Francalanza, C. A. (1988) 'Setting Accounting Standards for Malta,' *International Journal of Accounting Education and Research*, 23, (2), 163–178.

Hove, M. F. (1986) 'Accounting Practices in Developing Countries: Colonialism's Legacy of Inappropriate Technologies,' *International Journal of Accounting Education and Research*, 22, (1), 81–100.

IASC (1988) *Survey of the use and application of International Accounting Standards 1988*, London: IASC.

IASC (1989) *E32: Comparability of Financial Statements*, London: IASC.

IASC (1991) *E38 – Inventories*, London: IASC.

IFAC (1987) *Newsletter*, June, New York: IFAC, September/December.

IFAC (1990) *Annual Report 1990*, New York: IFAC.

IFAC (1991) *Annual Report 1991*, New York: IFAC.

McKinnon, S. N., Janell, P. (1983) 'The International Accounting Standards Committee: A Performance Evaluation.' *International Journal of Accounting Education and Research*, 19, (2), 19–34.

Mueller, G. G. (1979) 'St. Louis to Munich: The Odyssey of the International Congresses of Accountants.' *International Journal of Accounting Education and Research*, 15, (1), 1–12.

Nair, R. D., Frank, W. D. (1981) 'The Harmonization of International Accounting Standards.' 1973–1979, *International Journal of Accounting*, 17, (1), 61–77.

Nobes, C. (1981) 'An Empirical Analysis of International Accounting Principles: A Comment.' *Journal of Accounting Research*, Spring, 268–270

Nobes, C. (1991) '*Harmonization of Financial Reporting in Comparative International Accounting* (3rd Edn). C. Nodes and R. Parker (eds) Hemel Hempstead: Prentice Hall International, 70–91.

Rivera, J. M. (1989) 'The Internationalization of Accounting Standards: Past Problems and Current Prospects' *International Journal of Accounting*, 24, (4), 320–341.

Samuels, J. M., Piper, A. G. (1985) *International Accounting: A Survey*, Beckenham: Croom Helm.

Sempier, R. N. (1979) 'The International Federation of Accountants: Operating Procedures and Current Progress' *International Journal of Accounting Education and Research*, 15, (1), 24–31.

Sikka, P., Willmott, H., Lowe, T. (1989) 'Guardians of Knowledge and Public Interest Evidence and Issues of Accountability in the UK Accountancy Profession,' *Accounting, Auditing and Accountability Journal*, 2, (2), 47–71.

Tay, J. S. N., Parker, R. H. (1990) 'Measuring International Harmonization and Standardisation'. *Abacus*, 6, (1), 71–88.

Taylor, M. E., Evans, T. G., Joy, A. C. (1986) 'The Impact of IASC Accounting Standards on Comparability and Consistency of International Accounting Reporting Practices.' *International Journal of Accounting Education and Research*, 22, (1), 1–9.

Taylor, S. I. (1987) 'International Accounting Standards: An Alternative Rationale.' *Abacus*, 23, (2), 157–171.

Thomas, R. D. (1970) 'The Accountants International Study Group – The First Three Years.' *International Journal of Accounting Education and Research*, 6, (1), 59–65.

Tondkar, R. H., Adhikari, A., Coffman, E. N. (1989) 'The Internationalization of Equity Markets: Motivations for Foreign Corporate Listing and Filing and Listing Requirements of Five Major Stock Exchanges.' *International Journal of Accounting*, 24, (2), 143–163.

Walker, R. G. (1987) 'Australia's ASRB. A Case Study of Political Activity and Regulatory "Capture",' *Accounting and Business Research*, 17, (67), 269–286.

QUESTIONS

1 Analyse the potential benefits and limitations of the IOSCO initiative to support IASC.

2

HARMONIZATION OF ACCOUNTING STANDARDS IN THE EC

Is it the beginning or is it the end?

*K. Van Hulle**

WHAT IS HARMONIZATION?

It is fair to say that accounting standards still differ quite extensively from country to country. It is also interesting to see how proud people are about their own accounting rules. In fact, they may not like them, but they still believe that they are so much better than those which exist in other countries. This is the challenge of harmonization.

This challenge can be taken up in different ways. One way is the development of uniform rules. Because the objective of harmonization is the comparability of accounts, some people believe that it is necessary that all entities concerned apply the same rules. Such an approach is not very different from standard setting in a homogeneous environment. Another way is the one followed in the EC. It is believed that it is not necessary to develop uniform rules.

Options are perfectly acceptable as long as they can be considered equivalent and are supplemented by appropriate disclosures in the notes. This approach is based upon the establishment of a modus vivendi. Within certain limits, the remaining differences are mutually recognized.

A third approach is the one advocated by the IASC. Options are not totally ruled out. They are, however, labelled as good ones (preferred) and bad ones (alternative). Those undertakings which apply the alternative treatment must reconcile to the preferred method. The IASC approach is

*The views expressed in this article are attributable only to the author.
From European Accounting Review 1993, 2, 387–396.
Reprinted by permission of the European Accounting Review.

somewhat between the first and the second approach described above. It is however closer to the first approach because the ultimate objective is the abolition of all accounting options.

HOW TO HARMONIZE?

Harmonization of accounting standards is not the privilege of the EC. Many organizations are active in the world in this field: the United Nations (UN), the Organization for Economic Co-operation and Development (OECD), the International Accounting Standards Committee (IASC) and the EC.

Some people believe that these organizations are not really doing a good job. Other suggestions have therefore been made. One is the Smith Kline Beecham option as presented by its chief financial officer, Mr Hugh Collum, at the World Congress of Accountants in Washington, DC (11–14 October 1992). In his view there are only two major stock exchanges in the world: London and New York. The accounting standard-setting bodies of the UK and the US should therefore get together and develop *the* accounting standards. The rest of the world should merely follow their lead.

Another suggestion was advanced by Daimler-Benz. It was stated by its chief financial officer, Mr Gerhard Liener, when he announced the listing of the shares of Daimler-Benz at the New York Stock Exchange before the end of 1993. I quote from his speech (30 March 1993): 'During the last few decades the English language has become the world language without a resolution of the UN or any other institution. It just happened. Well, something very similar is happening in international accounting. The Anglo-Saxon principles are gaining more and more ground and thus getting nearer and nearer to become the world's accounting language.' The expression 'Anglo-Saxon' might be misleading in this case. As used by Mr Liener it clearly does not include the UK. The option by Daimler-Benz is clearly an option for US GAAP.

So far, for the latest newcomers on the accounting harmonization scene!

Let us, however, return to the organizations which I have mentioned before. The United Nations have established an Intergovernmental Working Group of Experts on Standards of Accounting and Reporting (ISAR). This is the only international body in which the developing countries and the formerly centrally planned economies meet with representatives from the developed countries in order to discuss questions of harmonization and financial reporting. ISAR has developed a number of conclusions on accounting and financial reporting. It also publishes a yearly *Review on International Accounting and Reporting Issues*, as a result of its annual sessions. ISAR is not a standard-setting body.

The OECD have also set up a Working Group on Accounting Standards. As with the UN, the OECD Working Group came about within the context of the work of the organization on multinational enterprises (which are referred to as transnational corporations in the UN language). In the OECD Accounting Working Group, government experts from the developed world discuss accounting subjects. The group has developed a number of clarifications of the accounting terms in the disclosure chapter of the *Guidelines on Multinational Enterprises*.

It has also addressed a number of accounting topics which are particularly relevant to accounting standard setters of the member countries, such as consolidation, intangibles, leasing, financial instruments, foreign currency translation, etc. The Working Group is not an accounting standard setting body.

The IASC is a private organization representing the accounting profession. Although it has tried to broaden its base (by including financial analysts as members of the Board and by inviting the FASB and the EC Commission to sit on the Board in an observer capacity) and to open the debate by setting up a consultative committee, it remains the only accounting standard-setting body at international level which is so strongly dominated by the accounting profession. The IASC has developed a number of International Accounting Standards. It has been asked by the International Organization of Securities Commissions (IOSCO) to come up with a set of standards which could be accepted by all major stock exchanges in the world, in order to facilitate multinational securities offerings. A number of multinational companies (for instance, SAS) prepare their accounts in conformity with International Accounting Standards.

Some countries (for instance, Zimbabwe) have adopted all the International Accounting Standards and made them into national standards. Although the IASC is an accounting standard-setting body, its standards are not mandatory and compliance is purely voluntary.

In the EC, accounting harmonization is part of the harmonization of company law. It should contribute to the creation of a truly internal market between the twelve Member States. The instrument used in the harmonization process is the directive. It is a legal instrument adopted by the Council of Ministers after a proposal from the Commission. It is addressed to the Member States which must transpose the directive into national law within a given period of time.

I will not describe the harmonization programme in detail. It deals with both annual accounts and consolidated accounts and contains special rules for financial reporting by banks and by insurance companies. An important feature of the harmonization in the EC is that the accounting standards which are included in the directives are incorporated into the law of each Member State. This should render their enforcement easier. Some people have criticized this legal approach as too static. As a lawyer, I disagree, of course, because the law can be drafted in such a way that there is room for interpretation. In addition, the law can be changed relatively easily, especially if the rules are not included in an Act of Parliament but in a government decree. The use of the law as a means of standard setting can also be an interesting mechanism against too frequent (and sometimes unnecessary) changes.

WHAT SHOULD BE HARMONIZED?

There is no general agreement on what should be harmonized: the annual accounts, the consolidated accounts, the accounts of all entities, the accounts of all companies, the accounts of listed companies, the accounts of large companies, etc. In the UN and the OECD, there is an understanding that the discussions deal only with multinational companies. In the IASC, things are less clear. Some Board members believe that the IAS apply to both annual accounts and consolidated accounts and that they are valid for all types of companies, small and large, listed and non-listed. There is, however, no agreement, although the main focus seems to be on listed companies given the pressure by IOSCO.

In the EC, the directives apply principally to limited liability companies. There is no distinction between listed and non-listed companies. For SMEs, Member States may introduce accounting exemptions. These concern the amount of information which must be disclosed and the audit requirement. The harmonization deals with both annual accounts and consolidated accounts. Small groups may be exempted from the obligation to prepare consolidated accounts.

EXPERIENCES IN THE EC WITH HARMONIZATION OF ACCOUNTING STANDARDS

I think that most people would agree with me that the quality of financial reporting in the EC has considerably improved with the implementation of the accounting directives. This was one of the conclusions of the surveys on the annual accounts published on the basis of the Fourth Directive, produced by the European Federation of Accountants (FEE). It would be difficult to imagine an internal market in which companies would compete on unequal terms. A minimum of financial transparency seems necessary. This presupposes that financial information on the main actors in the economy (i.e. limited liability companies) is readily available. This was the first objective of the harmonization programme. All limited liability companies in the EC (some 3 million) must disclose annual accounts. Although this principle was already embodied in the First Company Law Directive of 1968 and subsequently confirmed in the Fourth Directive of 1978, it is still not standing practice.

Indeed, more than 90 per cent of German limited liability companies refuse to publish their accounts. This is a major political issue which is the subject of an infringement procedure introduced by the Commission against Germany. We hope that this matter can be settled in the very near future. Disclosure is one thing, but the content of the disclosure is another thing. People tend to forget that most Member States of the EC did not have any detailed accounting rules prior to the adoption of the Fourth Directive. It is therefore not difficult to say that things have changed profoundly since the implementation of the Fourth Directive. Accounting has become something serious in all Member States of the EC.

If one leaves out the adoption of the Seventh Directive on consolidated accounts and the sectoral directives on banks and insurance companies, one must admit that nothing has happened since 1978. This is all the more strange because most Member States have used the implementation of the Fourth Directive as an opportunity to set up an accounting standards setting-body in order to ensure that the accounting rules could be adapted at regular intervals to changing economic circumstances. The lack of dynamism at EC level could prove very dangerous. Indeed, as long as the directives are not amended, Member States must comply with them. New standards at national level can therefore be issued only within the limits set by the EC accounting directives. The absence of new common rules for subjects not dealt with in the accounting directives and the development of standards at national level on these matters could also result in disharmonization. Of course, this lack of progress at EC level is not limited to the accounting field. It seems to be our fate that we make real progress in European integration only when we are faced with a threat from outside. I would tend to argue that this threat is already there.

Based upon our experience, we have developed a harmonization model which allows for mutual recognition on the basis of minimum rules combined with options. This permits our Member States to take account of local particularities. International harmonization, notably through IASC, is less respectful of local particularities. In that context, options are bad, methods are categorized as good or as bad and costly reconciliations are imposed. Another 'threat' comes from the US, where very detailed rules determine the financial reporting behaviour of companies. This is very different from the less regulatory approach which some of the EC Member States would prefer. The lack of progress at national or at EC level has already led several major EC companies to turn to US GAAP. Some companies go as far as to state that their accounts are prepared in conformity with US GAAP without any further reference to the respect of their own national law. Other companies include a reconciliation to US GAAP in their annual report. And still other companies will prepare their own mix of accounting rules, inspired by US GAAP or by IAS. In Switzerland this is sometimes referred to as 'IAS light'. It is certainly true that some of these companies are listed in New York and must therefore conform to US GAAP. It is also a fact that the FASB and the SEC are very active in the accounting field and that the quality of the standards which they develop is impressive. But, could it be the hidden agenda of our Member States that the largest companies in the EC apply US GAAP in the absence of equivalent national or EC standards?

There is not only a lack of progress at EC level, there are also many problems with the transposition of the accounting directives into national law. On many points there are doubts whether the directives have been correctly implemented. Some of the problems have been settled informally. Others remain.

Some examples: the non-transposition of the true and fair view override, the possibility of revaluing intangible assets (such as brands), the non-depreciation of certain fixed assets, the deduction of goodwill from reserves in the annual accounts, the amortization of goodwill through reserves in the consolidated accounts, the deduction of acquired own shares from reserves, the treatment of prior year adjustments and changes in accounting policies (transit through reserves instead of through the profit and loss account), the non-respect of the group definition in the Seventh Directive, the incorrect exclusion of certain subsidiaries from full consolidation, etc. This is only a short list of some important infringements. The list is however much longer, unfortunately. As the internal market project is almost finished now, there is more time to examine the implementing legislation more closely. A systematic analysis of national legislation should help us to obtain a clearer picture on the problem areas. This is of course a delicate matter. Not everybody will be prepared to help the Commission carrying out this task, as this examination will inevitably force the experts to put their finger on the sore points of their national accounting legislation.

However, we cannot escape this responsibility. It is a question of credibility and of fairness towards other Member States. We cannot exclude the possibility that the European Court of Justice will have to deal with some of these infringements on the occasion of a preliminary ruling on a question put to the Court by a national court.

In this respect, I can only regret that the practice which existed before, whereby national officials who are responsible for the drafting of the implementing legislation would contact their colleagues in the Commission in order to discuss the draft prior to the adoption of the legislation, no longer exists as systematically as it used to. We therefore welcome wholeheartedly the initiative by many of the new applicant Member States to discuss their draft legislation with us. This is even more important for them because they have not been involved in the negotiation of the directives.

Lack of dynamism at EC level, problems of incorrect implementation, the bleak picture is not yet complete. More and more people complain about the deterioration of the quality of financial information in Europe. The most incredible things happen. I will give the example of the true and fair view override. Some companies in the UK interpret this override in a rather personal manner. I quote from the accounting policies in the annual report 1992 of George Wimpey (construction company):

> Investments held as current assets are stated at market value at the balance sheet date and the difference between cost and market value is taken to the profit and loss account.

This treatment is a departure from UK accounting rules which stipulate that unrealized profits be credited to a revaluation reserve. In the opinion of the directors, the treatment adopted is necessary to present a 'true and fair view'.

Or let us take an example from France. I quote from the notes to the 1991 consolidated financial statements in the annual report of Cap Gemini Sogeti:

> When the acquisition of companies allows the group to obtain significant positions in specific markets, the excess of purchase cost over the fair value of assets acquired is allocated to the market share acquired. Such market share is valued at the date of acquisition in relation to objective economic data with reference to activity and profitability indicators.

This solves the problem of goodwill, doesn't it? And valuation at market value solves the problem of depreciation.

Let there be no misunderstanding. Although my examples come from the UK and from France, I could certainly give you other examples from other Member States. The common thrust of these examples is that companies no longer stick to the accounting conventions and that, apparently, nobody calls them to order. This is not likely to increase confidence in investors.

EC companies which are listed in New York sometimes also refuse to give in Europe the information which they disclose in the US. This is certainly not acceptable. We have dealt with this problem in the EC context where all shareholders must be treated equally, but we do not yet have a similar requirement for companies which are listed outside the EC.

PERSPECTIVES

What are we going to do about this? What are our options?

a *We could stop all further harmonization efforts in the EC.* We have now achieved a certain level of harmonization. We can leave further developments in the hands of Member States or others.

   I think that this would be unfortunate. We would quickly lose the harmony which came out of the accounting directives. And let us not forget, unless the directives are amended, Member States and national standard-setting bodies will still have to comply with them.

b *We could leave everything to IASC.* After all, they have the experts. Unfortunately, things are not that easy. We have already experienced in the EC that IAS are not directly transposable in most of our Member States, because of the linkage between accounting and taxation which is totally overlooked by IASC. In addition, some Member States would argue that IASC does not sufficiently respect the prudence principle. Although the Commission is only an observer on the Board of IASC, we already face criticism from certain Member States because 'we act without a mandate'. It is true that the positions which are taken by representatives of the accounting profession of the EC Member States which are members of the Board of IASC are not the same as the official positions taken by the government representatives of these Member States around the Brussels negotiation table. This is unfortunate, but it is due to the fact that the accounting profession does not officially represent the Member States concerned.

c *We could also leave the work to the Americans.* So many companies in the EC are attracted by US GAAP. Why make their lives difficult? Give them what they want. Well, there may be some disagreement about this. Some of our Member States would certainly argue that they could do a better job than the Americans. But, after all, Europe cannot always leave the initiative to the Americans. From an accounting point of view, it is, however, interesting to see that German accounting practice is closer to US GAAP than to UK GAAP. And there is mutual recognition of accounts between the UK and Germany and not between the US and Germany.

d *We could also become a more active player in the harmonization debate.* This was the view of Member States, national accounting standard-setting bodies and users and preparers at the Commission's 1990 conference on the future of accounting harmonization in the EC. Most people present at that conference were of the view that EC harmonization should continue, although not necessarily with new directives. As a result of this conference, the Commission has set up the Accounting Advisory Forum which should advise the Commission on further steps to be taken in order to improve the existing level of harmonization. Members of the Forum are the national accounting standard-setting bodies, the European organizations representing the main users and preparers (including the accounting profession) and last but not least the EAA. One of the problems with the Forum is that so many organizations want to participate that we have already reached the number of about sixty people who attend the meetings. This makes a real debate difficult. Some interesting things have come out of the work of the Forum:

- there is large preference for a *pragmatic approach* rather than an

approach based upon a conceptual framework (although some members of the Forum would love to discuss the fundamentals of accounting);
- there *does not* seem to be a majority in favour of a *distinction* between *annual and consolidated accounts;*
- there is great *reluctance* to embark upon the road towards *reconciliation*: limited comparability is preferred over absolute comparability.

The Forum is still young. There are problems. The Commission will have to show that the efforts of the Forum are not bound to disappear into the drawers of professional harmonizers.

It is in this context that academics can help. Although there has already been a lot of research on harmonization in the EC, many questions still remain unanswered:

- Is harmonization of accounting standards in the EC really necessary or is it a mere luxury or pastime for government and other experts?
- What are the benefits of harmonization? Are the accounts published in other Member States consulted on a regular basis? Are they comparable?
- To what extent is harmonization necessary? For all companies? For large companies? For listed companies?
- What does comparability mean? Is absolute comparability possible or desirable?
- Does reconciliation make sense?
- On a broader international level: is it true that capital markets need harmonization of accounting standards?
- Are options so bad? Is it necessary to rule out accounting methods just for the sake of uniformity?
- Is it logical to stigmatize an accounting method as 'not the preferred one' but still to allow the method?
- What are the common features of European accounting? So far, there still is no book on European accounting. Most research concentrates on the differences.
- Can there be progress in harmonization by distinguishing between individual accounts and consolidated accounts? How far can such a distinction sensibly go?
- Are multinational companies prepared to reconcile with IAS and to accept the IASC as the standard setter of the world?
- Is it at all possible to make progress in the EC without a European accounting standards-setting body or a European watchdog for the financial markets such as the SEC?
- What are the prerequisites (objective and not political) for mutual

recognition of accounts between the EC and the US and between the EC and Japan?

These are a few suggestions for further research on harmonization. When I have all the answers to these questions, I will be better equipped to advise on whether harmonization in the EC is finished or should continue. Meanwhile, I would suggest that we adopt a pragmatic approach. Unless the EC invests more time and effort in the harmonization of accounting standards, Europe will continue to be absent from the international accounting debate. As long as some Member States continue to quarrel about whether the harmonization is completed or whether the EC has any role to play in this debate, the initiative will come from outside and rather than contribute in shaping the rules, our role will be limited to reacting to things which have already been decided. It is unfortunate that we spend so much effort and money in defending our national achievements and developing standards by ourselves rather than sitting together and combining our efforts.

For the moment, there is no alternative to the Accounting Advisory Forum. Its functioning can be improved. A more active participation from national accounting standards-setting bodies would be desirable. The Commission is not equipped nor does it have the ambition to take over the role of an active standard setter in the accounting field.

The objective is not to develop European standards for the sake of doing so. But, if we believe that we have a role to play, we must combine our scarce resources so as to be able to influence the international debate. Harmonization is so difficult because it requires modesty and respect the achievements of the others. We are fortunate in Europe to be different as we are. This is our common heritage. Why don't we use it?

This is a slightly amended version of the paper presented at the 16th Annual Conference of the European Accounting Association in Turku (29 April 1993)

QUESTIONS

1 Given the expanding role of IASC discussed in Chandler's article above, how can the development of an extra layer of international accounting regulation at the European level be justified?
2 What enforcement problems does Van Hulle identify?

3

COMPETITION SPURS WORLDWIDE HARMONIZATION

Gary Meek

Accounting is environmentally sensitive; accounting principles and financial reporting practices develop in response to a complex interaction of economic, political, and social variables. We know, for example, that there are fundamental differences in the way accounting rules are developed in 'code laws' versus 'common law' countries. We know, too, that the way that businesses secure capital affects financial reporting practices.

Generally, for example, less disclosure and more 'conservatism' accompany environments where banks are the primary source of funds. On the other hand, more disclosure and a greater 'investor usefulness' orientation are found where companies rely on a developed securities market for their financing needs. Given that there is a variety of business environments around the world, it is therefore hardly surprising that there are also numerous differences in accounting principles.[1]

None of these differences would matter very much were it not for the significant amount of transnational financing and investment that is occurring today. Corporations increasingly are securing capital beyond the boundaries of their respective countries of domicile, and more and more investors are diversifying their portfolios internationally. Emerging from this twin phenomena of global financing strategies by corporations and transnational portfolio investment by investors is the problem of 'transnational financial reporting' (TFR). These corporations are faced with a responsibility for reporting financial data to various national audiences-of-interest, while investors and financial analysts are finding that such data are not always what they are accustomed to seeing from their domestic companies.

From Management Accounting (August 1984) pp 47–49.
Reprinted with permission from Management Accounting.

As Mueller and Walker state:

> The problem unique to transnational financial reporting, as opposed to financial reporting within a country, is that those interested in the financial reports 'read' these reports with eyes and minds accustomed to reading reports which are apparently similar but which are in fact different in their foundations owing to different customs, different cultural heritages, different 'accounting principles' and different legal requirements. It is not just that the reports crossing national lines need to be stated in different languages and different currencies to be meaningful but, rather, that they must be 'translated' in such a way that the underlying events and their consequences will be communicated to audiences whose experiences and education in financial reporting differ from those of the reporters. In other words, the problem is to convey to a 'foreign' reader the same message as would be received by a native reader.[2]

HOW FIRMS HANDLE REPORTING

A number of studies have documented how corporations handle their side of the transnational financial reporting problem. Essentially, the approaches take one or more of the following forms:

1 *No Accommodation to Foreign Readers*. Financial statements, prepared according to local accounting principles, retain the native language and currency. This approach assumes a general applicability and usefulness in other countries, and leaves it to the reader to interpret the report. This is the prevalent practice of companies domiciled in the United States and in France.
2 *Convenience Translations*. Financial statements are still prepared using local accounting principles, but the text portions are translated into another language. Monetary units are not translated. In a sense, this approach assumes that to 'read' something familiar is better than nothing at all, but it still does little to accommodate the foreign reader. German and Swiss companies often adopt this approach.
3 *Convenience Statements*. These are convenience translations taken one step further. Here, the monetary amounts are translated as well (usually by applying the year-end foreign exchange rate to all amounts in the financial statements), so that both the text and monetary amounts are familiar to the audience-of-interest. Convenience statements are issued by some European and some Japanese companies.
4 *Disclosure of Impacts of Differences in Accounting Principles*. For the particular audience-of-interest, the financial statements include a special footnote or supplementary schedule reconciling net income (and sometimes asset and liability accounts) on the basis of the generally accepted

accounting principles of the home country to a net income amount based on the accounting principles of the country of the audience-of-interest. This is the minimum requirement for reporting to the U.S. Securities & Exchange Commission by non-U.S. companies in their 20-F reports. Also, the Dutch Philips Company routinely includes this disclosure in its annual report to U.S. shareholders.

5 *Multiple Reporting*. 'Primary' financial statements are prepared for local audiences in the native language and using local accounting principles. 'Secondary' financial statements also are prepared for audiences in other countries, the characteristics of which include:

   - The text material is in the language of the 'other country.'
   - The generally accepted accounting principles and disclosure criteria used are those of the 'other country.'
   - The monetary amounts are expressed in the currency of the 'other country' (as in convenience statements).

Essentially, this approach requires a company to keep more than one 'set of books.' It is typical for today's large Japanese multinationals.

6 *World Standards*. Here the company attempts to transcend national reporting differences by synthesizing the practices around the world. The financial statements, however, may or may not be consistent with the recommendations of the International Accounting Standards Committee. Each company selects what in its own management's opinion represents the 'best' of the practices in the world. Sometimes these financial statements will be appended to the local set, but they may actually be the primary financial statements. The statements of the Swiss CIBA-GEIGY Ltd. illustrate the former, while those of the Dutch/U.K. Royal Dutch/Shell illustrate the latter.

TFR LARGELY VOLUNTARY

At the present time, corporate responses to TFR are largely voluntary, and the lack of comparability in the way firms measure income and report financial results has bothered a number of observers for a long time. The International Accounting Standards Committee (IASC), founded in 1973, has endeavored to harmonize accounting principles, primarily by proscribing 'undesirable' practices and 'unnecessary' differences. Comparability is also an implicit goal of the reports of the several United Nations' 'Groups of Experts.' The IASC and UN are but two of a number of global and regional organizations currently involved (in varying degrees) with standard setting at the transnational level.[3]

Most of these organizations are concerned principally with the investor as the object of their efforts. The argument is that noncomparability is a 'friction' in the allocation of resources. Enhanced comparability is seen as a way to improve investors' decision making, thereby enhancing the efficient allocation of resources worldwide. The argument is a familiar one, yet no one has documented that it is indeed true. In fact, research by this author[4] gives some evidence that comparability may not be as important to users as many people contend.

A few of the organizations, the UN for example, desire harmonization of financial reporting practices as a way for nation-states to better control the activities of business. It is believed that comparable accounting information will help these countries judge on a relative basis whether corporations are behaving in a 'socially responsible' manner. Thus, governments are the object of the efforts of this group of organizations.

For the most part, compliance with the rules promulgated by the international organizations is voluntary. The lack of an enforcement mechanism is considered by many as a debilitating factor in the progress toward harmonization.[5] As far as investors are concerned, however, the argument ignores the power of the marketplace. It stands to reason that investors would demand a premium in their rate-of-return requirements if corporations were not providing them with the kinds of accounting information desired. Thus, the competition for investment funds should propel the harmonization movement. This development, indeed, appears to be occurring as multinational corporations increasingly adopt a variant of multiple reporting. One set of financial statements meets local, statutory requirements while another set is prepared for the worldwide user group, based on accounting principles compatible with a 'decision usefulness' orientation[6] (and consistent with IASC standards as well). With global strategies for production, marketing, and financing, the world's largest multinationals are literally transcending the environment of their home countries. In the process, some of the most significant differences in accounting principles and financial reporting practices are disappearing.

Whether harmonization is desirable as a tool for political control is, of course, a value choice. One should not forget, however, that governments are not powerless to control the information flow coming to them. A powerful supra-national enforcement agency, perhaps under the auspices of the United Nations, is probably not feasible anyway. It is doubtful that national policy-making bodies such as the Financial Accounting Standards Board would relinquish their sovereignty over such matters.

Differences in accounting principles exist worldwide. But they appear to be narrowing through the efforts of the IASC in describing desirable alternatives and through the force of a competitive, worldwide market for funds. In the future, the problems associated with transnational financial reporting will likely become less serious for both preparers and users of statements.

NOTES

1 A number of variables that influence financial accounting are discussed in Frederick D. S. Choi and Gerhard G. Mueller, *International Accounting*, Prentice-Hall, Inc., Englewood Cliffs, N.J., 1984, pp. 41–44. Important accounting principles differences among ten major industrial countries are highlighted in Frederick D. S. Choi and Vinod B. Bavishi, 'Diversity in Multinational Accounting,' *Financial Executive*, August 1982, pp. 45–49.

2 Gerhard G. Mueller and Lauren M. Walker, 'The Coming Age of Transnational Financial Reporting,' *Journal of Accountancy*, July 1976, pp. 67–74.

3 The interested reader can consult Lane A. Daley and Gerhard G. Mueller, 'Accounting in the Arena of World Politics,' *Journal of Accountancy*, February 1982, pp. 40–46, 48, 50. A short, though informative, description of the IASC is contained in J. A. Burggraaff, 'IASC Developments: An Update,' *Journal of Accountancy*. September 1982, pp. 104–107. Finally, a good description of the U.N.'s activities is contained in James Carty, 'Accounting Standards and the United Nations,' *World Accounting Report*, September 1982, pp. 9–15.

4 Gary K. Meek, 'U.S. Securities Market Responses to Alternate Earnings Disclosures of Non-U.S. Multinational Corporations,' *The Accounting Review*, April 1983, pp. 394–402.

5 See, for example, John N. Turner, 'International Harmonization: A Professional Goal,' *Journal of Accountancy*, January 1983, pp. 58–60, 62–64, 66.

6 The financial reporting practices of the U.S., UK, and Netherlands all have this orientation and more or less set the standard of quality in financial reporting.

QUESTIONS

1 Comparing the points made by Chandler, Van Hulle and Meek in the articles above, discuss the relevance of market forces as a spur for accounting harmonisation compared with other enforcement mechanisms.

4

INTERNATIONAL ACCOUNTING HARMONIZATION

The impossible (and unnecessary?) dream

Richard Karl Goeltz

If financial measurement standards are to be made more meaningful, one of the first issues to be confronted is the need for harmonization across national boundaries. While it may appear obvious that such a step is desirable, I believe that there are serious questions as to whether much money or effort should be expended to achieve a unified set of accounting principles across borders.

To be sure, a common denominator would be beneficial. To argue by analogy, most historians would agree that the nearly universal use of the English language and a single currency contributed greatly to the economic development of the United States. One language and one monetary unit reduce costs and friction, leading to greater economic efficiency. These benefits are still believed to be valid as is evidenced by the European Community's objective of ultimately creating one currency for that region.

It might seem that an equally strong case can be made for the harmonization of accounting standards. Clearly, advantages would be obtained from this step. Adjustments, often arbitrary and perhaps based on faulty assumptions, would no longer be needed in order to place the financial reports of companies in different domiciles on the same basis. Accuracy would be enhanced and effort saved. Investors, security analysts, academicians and other users would take comfort in a Global GAAP. Some have even asserted that international accounting standards are requisite for the

From Accounting Horizons (March 1991) pp 85–88.
Reprinted by permission of the American Accounting Association.

development of a global securities market. I would not only challenge that contention, but go further. Full harmonization of international accounting standards is probably neither practical nor truly valuable.

Consider first the matter of practicality. The record of domestic standard setting bodies in the United States where they have been well funded and supported by government regulators does not offer much hope that the infinitely more difficult task of gaining international agreement can be achieved in any reasonable time period.

An examination of the limited progress of the FASB in recent years leads quickly to the conclusion that consistent worldwide accounting standards are virtually certain to remain an elusive goal. In the last three years, for example, the FASB has promulgated only one completely new standard – FAS 105. It requires the disclosure of information about financial instruments. All the other standards during this period merely have modified in some way previous pronouncements. To illustrate, FAS 101 provides that when a regulated company becomes deregulated, regulatory accounting is no longer appropriate. This standard is certainly not contentious, nor does it seem to push forward the frontiers of accounting theory.

The recent decision to require a super majority at the FASB rather than a simple one seems likely to result in even more plodding, piecemeal efforts. I fear that this will lead to the Board addressing arcane but simple issues, while more important one will be avoided or deferred. As an example, there is speculation that the FASB may postpone yet again the implementation of FAS 96 to field test its position on the recognition of deferred tax assets. If an adopted standard cannot be implemented in three years, how long might we expect it to take for a standard covering an important but difficult and politically contentious topic such as accounting for inventories to reach fruition?

My purpose is not to attack the FASB. Rather, I cite the lack of significant output in recent years to support my contention that harmonization of international accounting principles is unlikely to come about. Too many different national groups have vested interests in maintaining their own standards and practices which have developed from widely different perspectives and histories. There is not a single, powerful champion of the proposal for harmonization. There is no authoritative body with the ability to mandate the adoption of Global GAAP. The situation is not analogous to that of the single currency unit (ECU) in the European Community. Even Canada and the United States, linked by many common business and accounting traditions and now by a common market as well, have been unable to agree on an entire corpus of sound accounting principles and financial statement presentation. We have been coming closer, but the melding is not complete.

An issue as potentially important as harmonization of international accounting standards should not be dismissed solely because numerous impediments to its adoption exist. If the value of the objective were substantial enough, a means would be found to achieve it. But it is not clear whether significant benefits would be derived in fact. A well developed global capital market exists already. It has evolved without uniform accounting standards.

Deregulation, the elimination of capital controls, improved communications, dis-intermediation and greater sophistication on the part of issuers and their advisors have expanded the sources of funds available to corporations. Absent a massive shock such as a worldwide depression, I am confident that the global capital market will continue to expand both in size and scope. Funds can flow to areas and activities which promise the highest returns or reduce risks with diversification.

Statistics from the IMF illustrate the robustness of the global capital market. Equities are more likely than debt instruments to be adversely affected by different accounting principles and therefore provide the more rigorous test. Equity securities sold to investors outside the issuer's home country jumped from $300 million in 1984 to $15 billion in 1989, a fiftyfold increase. Equity linked bonds placed internationally increased from $11 billion to $88 billion in the same period. While straight bonds grew less proportionately during these years, in absolute terms their growth was even greater, from $110 billion to $250 billion. It is not hyperbole to describe the recent growth of the international capital market as explosive, and it took place despite the absence of Global GAAP.

Focusing exclusively on new international equity and debt instruments does not, however, provide a comprehensive understanding of the extent of global integration of capital markets. The increasing importance of swap transactions must be recognized as well. Interest rate and currency swaps were virtually non-existent ten years ago, while today their total value probably exceeds $2 trillion. These derivative products are a substitute in many ways for the direct issuance of a debt security in a foreign market. A corporation can use swaps effectively to borrow fixed rate sterling or floating rate Swiss francs without ever leaving North America. Any discussion of the global capital market must recognize the economic substance of swaps. The lack of accounting harmonization has not hampered the growth of the swap market.

If issuers of securities have been well accommodated by international capital markets, it is reasonable to hypothesize that investors have also been cared for. This proposition is supported by empirical evidence. Transactions in domestic stocks involving non-residents have grown rapidly in the past decade. Such transactions now account for roughly 12 percent of the total world stock exchange trading value. One out of every nine equity trades involves a non-resident. It is worth noting in this connection that foreigners have been particularly enthusiastic investors on the Tokyo Stock Exchange, notwithstanding prodigious price/earnings multiples, numerous insider trading scandals and inscrutable Japanese accounting principles.

In addition to the increase in international transactions, there has been an equivalent increase in the cross border holding of investment assets. The percentage of pension plan assets held in foreign securities has risen steadily for every major industrial country. In the U.K. at the present time, 20 percent of private pension funds are dedicated to overseas investments. Even U.S. pension fund investors have broadened their view. From almost zero in 1980, over 5 percent of U.S. pension fund assets is not committed overseas.

There has also been a blossoming of closed-end country investment funds. As recently as five years ago these virtually did not exist in the United States. In the period from 1985 to the present, 41 closed-end country funds were launched in the U.S. raising a total of almost $5 billion for foreign investment.

These data suggest that investors as well as issuers seem able to make investment decisions without the convenience of international accounting standards. There seems no reason to expect that our integrated global capital markets are likely to shrink in the future as a result of this lack. Indeed, it seems much more plausible to expect these markets to continue to grow.

One related development which may help to expand international capital markets is the recent adoption of Rule 144A by the SEC. This rule provides an exemption from SEC registration and reporting requirements in connection with sales of securities to large institutional investors. This should result in a broader, deeper, more liquid market in the United States for instruments of foreign companies, since they will be able to issue debt and equity in the U.S. without complying with SEC registration requirements which include U.S. GAAP financial statements. Investors will, of course, demand financial information but the issuer's accounts prepared on the basis of its home country standards are likely to suffice. To the extent more data are necessary, the determination will be made by the market, not by accounting standard setters or regulators. This rule is still in its embryonic stage, and its effects cannot be forecast with confidence, but my assessment is that both foreign issuers and U.S. institutional investors are likely to embrace the opportunity enthusiastically. The fact that this is a step away from accounting standardization is not likely to weigh heavily in their thinking.

I have argued that Global GAAP is unlikely to be achieved due to the institutional impediments in the standard setting process, and because there is no demonstrated need in order to fuel the growth of robust international capital markets. My final argument is that evidence also seems to suggest that rational investors are able to pierce the accounting veil and focus on real economic results. This ability to use accounting and other data to predict future cash flows which are the ultimate source of investment value seems to rest on the effective use of data rather than its uniformity. Academic researchers in the U.S. have generally concluded that the market does not respond to changes in earnings caused by cosmetic changes in accounting policies. Accounting alternatives which have been tested for market impact include FIFO/LIFO, flow through vs. deferral of investment tax credits, full cost vs. successful efforts methods for oil exploration, and the effect of volatility in net income resulting from various foreign currency translation methodologies. The conclusions from this research suggest that the market does not simply accept reported earnings. Security analysts, portfolio managers and investors examine footnotes and other textual disclosures for differences in accounting when comparing the performance of and prospects for companies. The evidence for the U.S. stock market is that all publicly available information is included in market price; in other words, the market is information efficient.

While the evidence developed to date refers largely to the U.S. stock market, and I cannot conclude from it that fully efficient markets exist outside the U.S., I do believe that analysts around the world are able to adjust published financial statements sufficiently to determine the relative attractiveness of an investment vehicle, at least to the point where the crucial investment decision making variables are not based on accounting differences. Investors are rational and will expend the necessary time and money to analyze investment opportunities correctly.

QUESTIONS

1 Taking the title of this article, explain the grounds on which Goeltz sees international accounting harmonisation as:
   a Impossible.
   b Unnecessary.
2 Compare and contrast the arguments put forward by Van Hulle and by Goeltz.

5

SHOULD ACCOUNTING PRACTICES BE UNIVERSAL?

Different needs for different creeds

Gilles Chevalier

Until recently, the controversy over uniformity versus flexibility of accounting principles was almost exclusively confined to a national level.[1] But, with the increase in capital flow and trade between nations over the last decade, the controversy is now of international relevance. As with most controversies, the literature on the subject soon polarized into two points of view. One holds that international accounting practices should be standardized, arguing that accounting principles and practices are universal, as are the needs of the users of financial information. Wilkinson, a proponent of uniformity, was very emphatic about this point: 'We need uniformity but it must be uniformity of the right kind – meaningful uniformity – uniformity of principles and procedures for financial statements that are prepared for the same purpose . . . If the statements are to inform investors, principles and practices should not differ from country to country, *for information requirements of investors are the same in all countries*.'[2] (Author's emphasis).

Opponents of uniformity, on the other hand, feel that since accounting is affected by the various countries' social, economic and legal environments, it would be very difficult to standardize international accounting practices.[3] To evaluate these opposing viewpoints, we recently undertook a research project to determine whether different culture groups really do require the same type of information in financial statements (information is used here in a general sense and includes both accounting and non-accounting information). Before proceeding with the research, however, we first had to develop a theoretical model.[4]

From CA Magazine (July 1977) pp 47–50.

INFLUENCE OF CULTURE ON PERCEPTION

Our model to evaluate user needs was developed from the field of psychology. Developed primarily by Jerome Bruner and his associate Leo Postman, the model suggests that people will tend to perceive things or objects according to their need and values.[5] This may have interesting implications for accounting. Perhaps different accounting users perceive the same accounting information differently because they have different needs and values.

Studies on culture and perception show that culture definitely affects an individual's needs. Many authors on the subject of perception insist that culture is also a prime determinant of personality.

> '. . . Each one of us perceives (our social) environment in terms of his own personal habits of perceiving; and that culture groups may differ from one another in behaviour, because of fundamental differences in their ways of perceiving social situations.'[6]

Culture, then, exerts a dual impact on perception: a direct impact on the formulation of one's needs and an indirect impact through the influence it exerts on the development of personality.

If we agree that culture is a primary determinant in defining our needs and that we perceive objects according to our needs, then obviously persons of different cultural backgrounds may perceive the same thing differently. Transposed to an accounting application, the model suggests that the same accounting information may be perceived differently by different cultural groups.

Based on this discussion, the main research hypothesis was formulated as:

> 'There is no difference between the way one cultural group, French Canadians, and another cultural group, English Canadians, perceive the same accounting information.'

These two cultural groups were chosen as subjects for the study mainly because information for them was readily accessible.

DEFINITION OF IMPORTANT TERMS

Difference in perception

The problem here was one of operational definition. How do we measure perception and, in particular, differences in perception? A seven-point Likert-type scale,[7] which measures attitude, was used to map the subjects' perception of financial information. Along with the scale, subjects were given the following instructions:

> 'You are asked to evaluate on a seven-point scale the relative importance

which the following information had on the reasoning that led to your investment decision. Each item must be evaluated using a scale from 1 to 7, 7 representing a very important item in arriving at your decision process, and 1 an item which was not important.'

The following is an example of the scale:

	1	2	3	4	5	6	7
Amount of total assets							

Accounting information

Accounting information was interpreted in a broad sense; as well as referring to what is presently done in practice, it also covered what could be done. Professor Bedford, for example, proposed that accounting information should also include disclosure of:

1 Social costs.
2 Human resources.
3 Budgets and equipment status.[8]

Part of our study included many of Bedford's suggested disclosures.

RESEARCH DESIGN

Our next task was to come up with a research design to test empirically the theoretical model we had developed.

The participants

The participants were graduate students taking a coaching course preparatory to the CICA Uniform Final Examinations. Four universities were visited within a three-month period: two francophone universities – Laval and Sherbrooke – and two anglophone universities – McGill and Simon Fraser. As shown in Table 1, 70 French Canadians and 54 English Canadians took the test.

Table 1 Classification of participants

Ethnical group	*Universities*				
	Laval	*Sherbrooke*	*McGill*	*Simon Fraser*	*Total*
French Canadian	19	48	2	1	70
English Canadian	0	0	34	20	54
	19	48	36	21	124

Administration and content of the test[9]

We personally administered a questionnaire at each location taking special care to give each identical verbal instructions, in English at McGill and Simon Fraser, and in French at Laval and Sherbrooke. After an initial five minute introduction, we asked students to volunteer for the test, stressing that they were under no obligation to take it.

A business game was used to simulate a real world situation. The questionnaire contained two distinctive sections. In Section I the participants were asked to invest $10,000 in either Alpha Inc. or Beta Inc. (pseudonyms for Harcourt, Brace, Janovich and Prentice-Hall Inc., respectively). To prevent possible identification by the students, the real names of these two companies were not disclosed.

As a basis for their decision making, students were given information from the published financial statements of the two companies (see Appendix A) as well as a description of the general nature of each business and of its capital structure. This type of information was suggestion by R. K. Mautz in his study, *Financial Reporting by Diversified Companies.*[10]

In Section II, the students were given information based on Bedford's suggestions, i.e., information not presently available in published financial statements. They were asked to reconsider their investment decision in the light of new information, which included data on human resources (position, degree held, number of years with the company), earnings forecasts and management philosophy (see Appendix B) and to evaluate that additional information.

In the original research the information provided in Section I was called 'published financial information' and the information in Section II, 'unpublished financial information.' Such a classification gave rise to the following two hypotheses:

> 'There is no difference between French Canadians and English Canadians in their perception of published financial information'.

> 'There is no difference between French Canadians and English Canadians in their perception of unpublished financial information'

The first hypothesis was accepted for all thirty information items but two. These two isolated significant differences did not allow much useful inference. Various reasons may be offered to explain the test results. French Canadians as a cultural group live in an English business environment. It may well be that such a climate influences how French Canadians perceive published financial information. The fact that American business textbooks are used in French Canadian universities may suggest that participants perceived more readily information they were taught rather than information they needed. For the sake of brevity, only the testing of the second hypothesis is reported in this article.

Statistical methods used

A simple T-test was used to figure out the significant differences between the two cultural groups for each information item. This involved a pairwise comparison of the mean of the ratings of the information items by the subjects in each cultural group.[11]

Determination of the level of significance

In any empirical sampling involving group comparisons there will almost always be differences between the groups due to sampling errors. The question is, are the differences large enough to be able to infer that they are not likely to be caused by sampling errors? In this study we use a 5% significance level ($\alpha = .05$) which means that when the difference in perception between the groups is so large that it would only occur by chance less than 5% of the time, then we would reject our hypothesis of 'no difference.'

Table 2 provides the mean and standard deviation values for both ethnic groups on each of the ten information items given in Section II, the T-value and the test results of the hypothesis.

Table 2 shows that the two groups differed significantly on their perception of (and hence the hypothesis was rejected for) five information items:

Table 2 Scores of both ethnic groups on their perception of unpublished financial information

Information items	*Variable No.*	*French N = 69* Mean*	*std dev.*	*English N = 54 Mean*	*std dev.*	*Difference between means (F-E)*	*T-value*
Age of management	1	5.64	1.44	5.06	1.34	.58	2.32***
Degree held	2	3.96	1.81	4.09	1.46	–.13	.46
Number of years with the company	3	4.01	1.69	4.26	1.47	–.25	.86
Personnel development policy	4	5.54	1.18	5.26	1.49	.28	1.12
Style of management	5	6.16	1.16	5.57	1.27	.59	2.64**
Capital investment budget	6	5.43	1.38	4.56	1.52	.87	3.31**
Budgeted earnings per share	7	5.28	1.58	4.65	1.62	.63	3.35***
Budgeted revenues	8	4.75	1.40	4.48	1.32	.27	1.10
Financing policy	9	6.07	1.16	5.44	1.38	.63	2.67**
Information on expansion policy	10	5.75	1.39	5.48	1.48	.27	1.04

* One French candidate did not complete Section II of the test.
** Difference significant at = .01.
*** Difference significant at = .05.

Information items	*Difference found significant at x*
Age of management	.022
Style of management	.010
Capital investment budget	.001
Budgeted earnings per share	.033
Financing policy	.009

A closer look at Table 2 indicates that, for these items, the French group shows higher mean scores than the English group, thus implying a greater need for this type of information. Participants in general scored higher on what we classified as unpublished financial information indicating that the unpublished financial information was accorded higher importance in making their investment decision.

Both groups gave much weight in their decision to budgeted information, as shown by their mean scores on variables 6, 7 and 8. While generalization might be difficult because of the research design, these results do appear to favour the inclusion of budgeted figures in financial statements.

We observed that both groups differed on their perception of other information such as: age of management, style of management, financing policy. We had described the management style and financing policy of Alpha Inc. as liberal and of Beta Inc. as conservative. Both groups perceived this description as important information. The results clearly demonstrate the need for new and additional financial statement disclosure, with the needs of French Canadian investors appearing more urgent than those of English Canadian investors.[12] In addition, while the results do not provide conclusive evidence against the proposition that financial information users have universal needs, they nevertheless indicate the need for further research.

RESEARCH LIMITATIONS

Like most research projects of this nature, ours was not without some limitations.

Test design

To control as many extraneous variables as possible, the research was carried out in a laboratory setting. A limitation of such a setting has been referred to as 'lack of external validity.' In our research, we cannot generalize about the results to all French Canadian and English Canadian investors, even though some geographical representativeness has been obtained by including Simon Fraser University in British Columbia.

Use of business game

A business game was used to see how candidates perceived financial information. One pitfall of the simulation approach is that one does not really know whether subjects behave in the same way they would in the real world. There might be a difference between actually investing $10,000 and merely playing the role.

Students as surrogates for investors

The debate about whether it is wise to use students as surrogates for business executives is far from being settled, but there is empirical research that suggests they do not behave like business executives. About half of the participants in our study did have prior investment experience, thus providing some assurance about their behaviour as investors.

SUGGESTIONS FOR FURTHER STUDY

The study used members of the French culture (French Canadians) and members of the English culture (English Canadians). The possible impact of the fact that French Canadians live in an English-speaking environment has already been noted. Replication of the study using French subjects from France and English subjects from England, for example, may provide more definite results about the universality of needs of users of financial information.

Another topic which might be worth studying is the meaning of words in financial statements to various ethnic groups. It may well be that the word 'liability' does not have the same connotation to an English investor as to a French investor. The semantic differential technique might be a useful tool to such kinds of research.[13]

TO EACH, ACCORDING TO NEED

The importance of applying behavioural research to the perception of accounting information has been recognized in recent years[14] and the question to which this research is most often directed is: How do various individuals and groups perceive accounting processes and reports? Our research indicates that different users do have different needs for information. If this is so, instead of working towards universal accounting principles and practices, we should, in our opinion, be concentrating on evaluating the user needs we do perceive and extending our present information disclosures to satisfy them.

NOTES

1 For a good summary of the issues involved see 'Uniformity in Financial Accounting,' *Law and Contemporary Problems* (Autumn 1965), pp. 621–931.

2 Theodore L. Wilkinson, 'Can Accounting Be An International Language?' in *Readings in Accounting Theory*, ed. by Paul Garner and Kenneth B. Berg (Boston: Houghton Mifflin Company, 1966), p. 488.

3 This article uses the term 'accounting practice' as defined in *Professional Accounting in 25 countries* (New York: American Institute of Certified Public Accountants, 1964), p. 22. 'No attempt is made here to distinguish between principles, practices and methods. The "practices" is generally used to include all three. It is also used with regard to presentation, classification, and disclosure of items in financial statements.'

4 For a complete description of the model see: Gilles Chevalier, *Universality of Accounting Principles and Practices and Evaluation of the Universality of the Needs of Users of Accounting Information*. Unpublished PhD dissertation, University of Illinois at Urbana – Champaign, 1975).

5 Jerome S. Bruner, 'Symbolic Value as an Organizing Factor in Perception,' *Journal of Social Psychology* (May 1948), pp. 203–08. Leo Postman, 'The Experimental Analysis of Motivational Factors in perception,' *Current Theory and Research in Motivation*. Edited by J. S. Brown et al. (Lincoln, Nebraska: University of Nebraska Press, 1953), pp. 59–108.

6 Muzafer Sherif, 'A Study of Some Social Factors in Perception,' *Archives of Psychology*, No. 187 (July 1935), p. 5. See also Ralph Linton, *The Cultural Background of Personality*, 1945, quoted in John H. Chilcott, Norman C. Greenberg and Herbert B. Wilson *Readings in the Socio-Cultural Foundations of Education* (Belmont, California: Wadsworth Publishing Company, Inc., 1968), p. 89.

7 Rensis Likert, 'A Technique for the Measurement of Attitudes,' *Archives of Psychology*, No. 140 (1932), pp. 55–56.

8 Norton M. Bedford, *Extensions in Accounting Disclosure* (Englewood Cliffs: Prentice Hall, Inc. 1973), pp. 25–44.

9 A copy of the test is available on request.

10 R. K. Mautz, *Financial Reporting by Diversified Companies* (New York: Financial Executive Research Foundation, 1968).

11 Any basic text on statistics gives an explanation of this test. For example see: William L. Hays, *Statistics* (New York: Holt, Rinehart and Winston Inc., 1963), Chapter 10.

12 Highly correlated scores on certain variable may result in a distorted picture of the group differences when the T-Test is used. A more refined technique not discussed in the article, called discriminant analysis, takes into account correlations among variables. This technique, used in the original research, provided results compatible with those of the T-Test.

13 Charles E. Osgood, George J. Souci and Percy H. Tannenbaum, *The Measurement of Meaning* (Urbana: University of Illinois Press), 1967.

14 For examples: Edwin L. Caplan, *Management Accounting and Behavioral Science* (Reading, Mass.: Addison-Wesley Publishing Company, 1971), Chapter 5; and 'Report of the committee on Behavioral Science Content of the Accounting Curriculum,' *The Accounting Review* Supplement to Vol. XIVL, 1971, pp. 274–86.

APPENDIX A

Information given in section I	*Referred to as variable*
Growth potential	
Growth in earnings per share	1
Growth in net income	2
Growth in total assets	3
Managerial ability	
Return on common equity	4
Ratio of net income before interest on invested capital	5
Net income	6
Profitability	
Return on common equity	7
Net income on sales	8
Return on total assets	9
Amount of operating profit	10
Ratio of sales to total assets	11
Amount of net income	12
Increase in book value per share	13
Increase in market value per share	14
Stability	
Product line diversification	15
Nature of product	16
Net income on sales	17
Size as indicated by total assets	18
Size as indicated by total sales	19
Times interest charges are earned	20
Extent of geographical dispersion	21
Financial policy	
Dividend pay-out rate	22
Working capital ratio	23
Ratio of debt to shareholders' equity	24
Regularity of dividend payments	25
Financial condition	
Cash flow	26
Current ratio	27
Ratio of liquid test	28
Ratio of debt to shareholders' equity	29
Times interest earned	30

APPENDIX B

Information given in section II	*Referred to as variable*
Age of management	1
Degree held	2
Number of years with the company	3
Personnel development policy	4
Style of management	5
Capital investment budget	6
Budgeted earnings per share	7
Budgeted revenues	8
Financing policy	9
Information on expansion policy	10

QUESTIONS

1 Chevalier finds that different cultural groups have different information needs. What do you see as the advantages and disadvantages of this research having been conducted on two cultural groups in one single country, as opposed to using two different countries.
2 To what extent does this article reduce the case for international accounting harmonisation?

6

DISPELLING ARGUMENTS AGAINST INTERNATIONAL ACCOUNTING STANDARDS

*M. J. Aitken and M. A. Islam**

Most writers agree that differences in environments and institutional arrangements among countries constitute significant deterrents to the development of international accounting standards.[1] The same writers seem divided, however, as to whether such differences completely preclude the development of a set of uniform and effective standards which will transgress national boundaries. While alluding to environmental differences to indicate the obstacles posed by their existence, some believe that these obstacles should, and in fact can, be overcome. Hall, for example, refers to the difficulty which differences in legal, political, and cultural barriers have on the establishment of international accounting standards but concludes that '. . . pressures for achieving international financial standards are so great, and will become even greater, that they will ultimately overcome the problems in achieving them.'[2]

By way of contrast, however, others feel that because environmental conditions are so varied (among countries), there is doubt as to whether the development of a set of effective international accounting standards is possible. Mueller, for example, states:

> If we accept that (1) economic and business environments are not the same in all countries and (2) a close relationship exists between economic and business environments and accounting, it follows that a set of generally accepted accounting principles cannot be useful in all countries.[3]

The impetus for this paper comes from this latter view. If this view is found to be correct, it suggests that all efforts to establish international accounting

From International Journal of Accounting (Spring 1984) pp 35–46.

standards should end and, similarly, any hope for internationally relevant and comparable financial data on companies should be abandoned. Our study could develop in one of two possible directions. Either we must seek to explain why international accounting committees persist in trying to attain the impossible, or we must show why those, like Mueller, who maintain that this task is impossible, are wrong. The latter is our chosen direction.

To the best of our knowledge, Mueller was the first to propose this hypothesis. He articulately argues for international diversity of practice referring to twelve environmental and institutional 'variables' among countries. These included discussion of (1) relative stability of the currency account; (2) degree of legislative interference in business; (3) nature of business ownership; (4) level of sophistication of business management; (5) differences in size and complexity of business firms; (6) speed of business innovation; (7) presence of specific accounting legislation; (8) stage of economic development; (9) type of economy involved; (10) growing pattern of an economy; (11) status of professional education and organization; and (12) general level of education and tool processes facilitating accounting.[4]

That Mueller's work has become a common and accepted source of reference is evidenced by the inclusion of many of his 'variables' in the works of subsequent writers, notably Previts and Frank.[5]

We examine these twelve variables to ascertain whether differences in any of them call for different accounting standards in different countries. For the purpose of this examination, these twelve factors are grouped into three broad categories: (A) factors associated with the broader economic environment (factors 1, 8, 9, and 10); (B) features of business organizations (factors 3, 4, 5, and 6); and (C) institutional factors (factors 2, 7, 11, and 12). This taxonomy has been used for two reasons. First, we believe that there are three basic conclusions which may be attached to the twelve stated objections to the development of international accounting standards. Secondly, while there has been and will be other specific objections raised, as far as each objection can be classified under one or another of these categories, the objection is subject to one or another of the three general conclusions which we provide.

(A) BROADER ECONOMIC ENVIRONMENT

Relative Stability of the Currency of Account

Mueller argues that 'significant currency instability calls for some form of price index adjustment, *with the form of adjustment depending largely on the type of indexes available and reliable*' (emphasis added). However, given no indication as to how the availability and reliability of indices preclude the development of internationally appropriate standards, one is uncertain how differences in the availability and reliability of statistics can have a bearing on a general rule of action (standard). If a uniformly constructed statistic, such as the Consumer Price Index, is not available, this may indeed point to differences in standards underlying the gathering of statistics. It does not constitute an impediment, however, to general rules of action (standards) in accounting, such as the five fundamental rules of continuously contemporary accounting.[6] This is so because statistics only help achieve the job dictated by accounting and auditing standards. At best, Mueller's comments refer to the problem of numerical approximation, which is a different question.

Stage of Economic Development

Mueller argues that the accounting standards appropriate to a particular country depend on the stage of economic development reached in that country. This argument seems confused. By focusing on the relative economic achievements of nations, it overlooks the similarities in business entities in various countries, developed or underdeveloped. These similarities include the facts that businesses everywhere buy and sell in markets, own assets, borrow and lend money, buy and sell for cash and on credit, employ people, and pay taxes. Universally, their survival and prosperity depends on two factors: maintaining solvency and earning profits.

No reason is apparent as to why accounting standards cannot be developed to measure the financial performance and position of companies without reference to the stage of economic development reached by a country. The economies of India and Indonesia are much less developed than that of the United States. But this, in itself, does not suggest that the rules of measurement for assets, liabilities, or any other element of financial statements applicable for an Indian or Indonesian company should be different from those of an American company.

Type of Economy Involved

Mueller asserts that accounting standards should vary among countries in accordance with the extent to which a particular country relies on agriculture, mining, manufacturing, trade, or financial institutions. Once again, he provides no specific reason in support of his position. Our position is that heavy reliance on one or two sectors should not necessarily result in varying standards among countries. For example, the economies of the United States and United Kingdom are well diversified: almost all of the sectors are developed. If they can have, within their countries, generally applicable standards, such standards should also be applicable to countries with emphasis on one or two sectors. On the other hand, if the diversified economies have differing standards for specific sectors, some industry-specific standards would be applicable to the country which has only one or two sectors developed.

Growing Pattern of an Economy

Mueller argues that some accounting standards should vary, depending on whether an economy is a growing, stable, or declining one: 'If growth and expansion are typical, the capitalization of certain deferred charges is more feasible than under stable and declining conditions.'[7] In addition to not defining 'more feasible,' his argument seems to overlook an important point. While we are not concerned here with the case for or against capitalization of deferred charges, the oversight in the argument is indicated by noting that in a growing economy, firms may be both growing and declining. Therefore, the growing, stagnating, or declining trend in an economy is generally irrelevant to the determination of accounting standards directed to the measurement of performance and position of individual entities.

(B) FEATURES OF BUSINESS ORGANIZATIONS

Nature of Business Ownership

Mueller argues that accounting standards in a country with widespread ownership of company shares need to differ from those of another where shares are predominantly family owned. The argument does not seem to withstand criticism. Shareholders are by no means the only group for which financial statements are prepared; there are other groups, such as creditors, government, employees, and customers. Since solvency, profitability, and gearing are aspects of the company in which all these parties are interested, it follows that the information needs of these parties are essentially similar.[8] Even if a difference, in terms of how widely their respective shares are held, exists between companies, information needs of other parties common to both types of enterprises would require information of a comparable quality and quantity to be supplied in the financial statements. This may be one of the reasons why separate accounting standards have not been developed for the family-owned companies.

Level of Sophistication of Business Management

Mueller argues that when the sophistication of management personnel varies among countries, accounting standards would also necessarily vary, that is, become more sophisticated or complex. While management sophistication may be important for the companies managed, however, it can be argued that company financial statements are not the proper place for a reflection of management's cognitive and analytical capabilities, although some might indeed be so used under present conditions.

Accounting standards, as we have portrayed them, are applicable to the measurement of profit, the valuation of assets, and the representation of companies' financial performance and position, in a form understandable and usable by non-experts. What is important is the factual quality of the data, not the complexity of the standard; complexity gives no guarantee of the serviceability of information. From a national point of view, companies may also vary in terms of management sophistication; this does not prohibit the applicability of common accounting standards.

Differences in Size and Complexity of Firms

Mueller argues that large and complex organizations require accounting standards different from those of small and less complex organizations. Although no indications are given as to what constitutes a big and complex organization compared to a small and less complex one, he states by way of example that heavy advertising and research and development outlays by big and complex firms require 'recognition' (which presumably means capitalization), while smaller programs in similar firms may need to be expensed. It is not stated why there should be this difference in treatment, but such a situation has some interesting implications. While in the past it has been accepted that the size of a firm could be determined with reference to its asset holdings, Mueller seems to imply now that an asset is to be determined with reference to the size of a firm, placing us in something of a 'catch 22' situation.

Notwithstanding the unnecessary complications Mueller introduces with this point, that an answer to the apparent problem of size and complexity closely parallels that discussed under the heading 'Stage of Economic Development' should be noted. To reiterate briefly, he states that business entities everywhere make similar decisions to buy and sell goods, own assets, and the like. While there is no implication that every element in a decision will be similar, a number of the elements will be. To the degree they are, we regard the information needed for those decisions as within the domain of accounting information. Insofar as they are not, they are outside the domain of accounting. Thus, we establish accounting information as a necessary but by no means total factor in a decision process for all firms, large and small.

Speed of Business Innovations

Mueller further argues that practices such as engaging in business combinations, stock distributions, and leasing of assets are found in some countries and not in others. Therefore, countries in which such practices exist require accounting standards not needed in countries in which they do not. However, this argument does not really state anything against uniformity. After all, uniformity involves similar treatment of common accounting items only. International uniformity regarding items such as those previously mentioned would require similar treatment by the countries where a particular problem exists; there is no need to be concerned with the countries which do not have the problem. In any case, the phenomenon is not peculiar to the international context. In a national situation also, not all companies lease assets, form combinations, or distribute stock dividends, and this in no way implies that national accounting standards are unattainable.

(C) INSTITUTIONAL FACTORS

Degree of Legislative Interference

Mueller proposes that taxation statutes in some countries provide that taxation allowances regarding certain items can be claimed only if they are treated similarly in the company's financial statements. He further argues that even though the accounting methods implied by these requirements may not be adequate in terms of factual representation of the company's performance and position (since adoption or non-adoption of a method in financial statements makes a difference in cash outflow), managements of some companies tend to select the method which minimizes the tax liability without regard to its accounting propriety. Mueller cites as examples (1) the LIFO inventory method in the United States, which, in an inflationary period, results in undervaluation of inventory in the balance sheet, and (2) the Swedish inventory valuation procedures, which are unduly conservative, distorting both the income and inventory figures in the financial statements. In the latter case, a deliberate understatement of inventory from the lower of cost or market basis by 60 percent ordinarily and 70 percent in special cases is permissible.[9] These types of statutory requirements are said to be a part of the accounting environment, and accounting standards should properly vary between countries to accommodate such peculiarities in legislation. Two aspects of these types of legislative interferences should be considered: first, whether the methods induced by them are desirable methods in view of the common information needs of the parties at interest; and, second, how far international standardization is possible given statutes of this nature.

It has been argued that the desirability (soundness) of an accounting method must be determined with reference to the quality of information it yields, that is, whether it satisfies the quality of serviceable information. If it does, it is no hindrance to the development of international accounting standards since the method itself will deserve consideration for international application. But some legislative interferences may lead, or have already led, to the creation of undesirable accounting practice. For example, LIFO valuation of inventory does not satisfy the standard of relevance. Since the balance sheet valuation of inventory will be in terms of outdated prices in inflationary periods, this practice fails to comply with the standard of comparability (intercompany) as inventory may be represented in prices of different years. In this instance, the standard of neutrality will also be impaired since the method is selected to serve the interest of some parties and as such yields potentially misleading information to all parties in general. It is obvious that a method such as that for inventory valuation in Sweden meets none of those criteria. Thus, our conclusion is that the mere fact that an accounting practice was induced by a piece of legislation does not make it a valid practice.

When unsound accounting practices are encouraged by some statutory requirements, accountants have an obvious responsibility to report to the authorities concerning the probable undesirable consequences of, and inequities in, such legislation and, thus, attempt to amend the legislation. As long as the laws remain operative and management (and possibly shareholders and creditors) wish to enjoy the financial benefits of such a law, something must be done to supply reliable and relevant information in the financial statements. A practical remedy could be to compute amounts for items affected, following sound methods of accounting (in terms of the previously mentioned cornerstone concepts of solvency and profitability) and to supply such amounts in parentheses or in the notes to the accounts.

The establishment of international accounting standards can also exert pressure to help free accounting practice from the constraints of tax legislation. For example, Sweden, with other Scandinavian countries, is considering bringing its accounting practices more into harmony with those of the European Economic Community.[10] If that happens, the requirements of 'true and fair' by the Fourth Directive have the potential of freeing Swedish practice from constraining tax legislation. Therefore, Sweden's membership on the International Accounting Standards Committee will directly discourage the practice in that country of creating secret reserves and writing off inventory in an arbitrary manner.[11]

Presence of Specific Accounting Legislation

On this point Mueller argues that because the Companies Act or equivalent statutes are binding, and since those laws are not the same among countries, the accounting standards appropriate for one country may not be so for another. But as far as accounting standards are concerned, the law, in the majority of countries, does not prescribe in detail. Instead, the broad quality of financial statements, such as 'fair' or 'true and fair' representation, is emphasized. This leaves considerable latitude to develop and select accounting standards by referring to the user's needs and uses of accounting information.

In a small number of countries, the forms and contents of financial statements are prescribed by the relevant laws, such as in France and Germany. But in these countries, the provisions of the laws are also changeable. In Germany, company law was revised in 1965 to bring it much closer to the U.K. and U.S. requirements, and the French Plan Comptable was similarly revised in 1976.[12] Again, these laws are under revision to make them be consistent with the EEC Fourth Directive. It would seem that the institutional differences cannot act as a permanent deterrent to the acceptance of common accounting practices. The aim of any legislation in the commercial arena should be to promote and safeguard the public. This must also be the objective of proper accounting standards.

General Levels of Education and Tool Processes Facilitating Accounting

Under this heading, Mueller argues that 'statistical methods in accounting and auditing cannot be used successfully where little or no knowledge of statistics and mathematics exists. . . .'[13] This returns us, however, to the argument used to counter Mueller's first proposition regarding currency instability. Without considering whether the degree of skill required by Mueller (but nowhere specified) actually exists, it cannot be too strongly emphasized that statistical methods should only help to perform the jobs dictated by accounting and auditing standards. They are aids, determined independently of the standards. Any discussion of differences in statistical ability and/or the availability of relevant data in various countries does not impinge upon the development of accounting standards. In fact, the reverse holds. Without some aim, here defined as a set of 'ideal' international accounting standards, the differences in statistical ability and availability of relevant data will never be reconciled. On this interpretation, Mueller's suggestion only makes the development of international accounting standards more urgent.

Status of Professional Education and Organization

Under this heading, Mueller provides no specific argument to explain why different accounting standards depend on the development of accounting professionalism or the level of general education as he contends. Rather, he asserts that when adopting an accounting standard of foreign origin, the recipient country should modify that standard to suit the local conditions. But in view of the arguments presented here, the necessity for doing so is not apparent.

CONCLUSION

We have examined the environmental and institutional impediments suggested by Mueller under three broad classifications. This examination questioned Mueller's claims disputing the possibility and usefulness of international accounting standards. In the case of the first classification, namely 'The Broader Economic Environment,' the variation in these factors was shown generally to be irrelevant in the selection of an accounting method.

Further, the importance which Mueller ascribes to these factors is based on a misunderstanding of the relationship between accounting and the business environment. Mueller's arguments appear to be based on the premise that this relationship between accounting and the business environment is a direct one. Consider, as evidence of this, Mueller's comment:

> Let us postulate for a moment that accounting principles generally accepted in the United States were enforced in all countries of the world. This would create international uniformity which would have some intellectual appeal and would ease many problems in international practice and financial reporting. At the same time such uniformity would lack meaning. We would have to assume that business conditions are the same in all parts of the free world, and that the same stage of professional, social and economic development has reached everywhere.[14]

Although we cannot find fault with Mueller's observations that business conditions are not identical in all countries; that the same stage of professional, social, and economic development has not been reached everywhere; and that a relationship between accounting and the broader environment exists; we question his specification of this relationship as a direct one. This view ignores the only link between accounting and the broader environment, namely, the business entity. The function of accounting (the object of financial statements) is to measure and communicate the financial performance and position of specific business entities to shareholders, creditors, and other interested parties. Since the environmental conditions in a particular nation influence the financial affairs of a firm, measures of financial performance and position will automatically reflect the relevant environmental influences on the business firm. Thus, the focus for accounting is the entity, not its environment, and many of Mueller's arguments which fail to account for this relationship are invalid.

Concerning the second classification, 'Features of Business Organizations,' discussion of the various factors (size, complexity, ownership, management caliber) was couched in the context of a market economy. It was concluded that both national and international companies have a common interest in solvency and profitability (and these are the cornerstone concepts of an accounting system which provides necessary but by no means sufficient information for economic decisions). Therefore, a report to interested parties (shareholders, managers, creditors, employees, government) may be designed to include the same elements in financial statements (assets, liabilities, ownership, equity, profit) of all companies. This applies regardless of the individual idiosyncrasies mentioned by Mueller. Therefore, these statements do not require different accounting standards. We qualify our conclusion, however, to recognize that there may be some difference in the *extent* but not the *nature* of public disclosure of information for companies which are privately as opposed to publicly owned. Regardless of this qualification, there is no reason why the measurement methods applied should differ within or among countries.

On the third classification, factors pertaining to institutional differences, institutional and legal requirements were observed to be insignificant when judging the soundness of accounting methods, especially where common user needs are at variance with such practices.[15] Logically, they may, of course, place obstacles in the way of implementing internationally appropriate methods of accounting. In view of the trend toward uniformity of regulation, apparent in the case of member countries of the European Economic Community, however, these barriers can be expected to be progressively weakened. In the meantime, there is nothing to prevent the presentation of information (in parenthetical form), thereby enabling accurate assessments of solvency and profitability. The very act will tend to indicate to regulators the importance of such information.

NOTES

1 See, for example, Gerhard G. Mueller, *International Accounting* (New York: Macmillan, 1967), and 'Accounting Practices Generally Accepted in the United States versus Those Generally Accepted Elsewhere,' *International Journal of Accounting* (Spring 1968): 91–103: Edward Stamp, 'Uniformity in International Accounting Standards – A Myth or a Possibility,' *The Jerusalem Conference of Accountancy* (Israel: The Institute of Certified Public Accountants, 1971), 157–66: A. J. Enthoven, 'Standardized Accounting and Economic Development,' *CA Magazine* (December 1973): 57–60: M. K. Oldham, *Accounting Systems and Practices in Europe* (Epping, England: Gower Press, 1975): Irving L. Fantl, 'Frustrations Facing Accounting Uniformity,' *Accounting Forum* (May 1976): 27–31: W. D. Hall, 'Establishing Standards for International Financial Reporting' in *Accounting Research Convocation* (University of Alabama, 1978), 95–106: A. K. Mason, *The Development of International Financial Reporting Standards*, Occasional Paper No. 17 (Lancaster, England: University of Lancaster International Centre for Research in Accounting, 1978): and Werner G. Frank, 'An Empirical Analysis of International Accounting Principles,' *Journal of Accounting Research* (Autumn 1979): 593–605.

2 Hall, 'Establishing Standards,' 106.

3 Mueller, 'Accounting Practices,' 96–97. See also Mason, *Financial Reporting Standards*, 23.

4 Mueller, 'Accounting Practices.'

5 Gary J. Previts, 'On the Subject of Methodology and Models for International

Accounting,' *International Journal of Accounting* (Spring 1976), 1–12: and Frank, 'International Accounting.'

6 R. J. Chambers, 'Inflation Accounting in New Zealand,' *Occasional Paper 24* (Faculty of Business, Massey University, 1977), 20.

7 Mueller, 'Accounting Practices,' 99.

8 For empirical confirmation of this, refer to R. J. Chambers, *The Design of Accounting Standards*, Monograph No. 1 (University of Sydney Accounting Research Center, 1980).

9 A. P. Amiess, 'Developing Nations and Tax Oriented Accounting Principles – The Swedish Model,' *International Journal of Accounting* (Spring 1971), 94; and Oldham, *Accounting Systems*, 161.

10 Oldham, *Accounting Systems*, 163.

11 See paragraph 17 of IAS No. 2. *Valuation and Presentation of Inventories in the Context of Historical Costs* (1973).

12 See Oldham, *Accounting Systems*, 103–4.

13 Mueller, *International Accounting*, 150.

14 Mueller, 'Accounting Practices,' 97.

15 For empirical support of the proposition that there is a common set of user needs, see Chambers, *Design of Accounting Standards*.

QUESTIONS

1 Analyse the arguments of Aitken and Islam distinguishing between those which argue that international accounting harmonisation is *desirable* and those which argue that it is *achievable*.

2 Compare and contrast the articles by Goeltz and by Aitken and Islam.

7

WIDER STILL AND WIDER

The international expansion of the accounting profession

Richard Briston

In April a working paper entitled 'The Internationalisation of Professional Services', by Evan Davis and Carol Smales, was published by the Centre for Business Strategy at LBS, and on 19 June an article by John Kay, Professor of Industrial Policy at LBS, appeared in the *Daily Telegraph* under the headline 'Accountants get to grips with economies of scale'.

It is argued by the LBS authors that the trend towards internationalisation has been encouraged by three main factors. The first of these is the need for a firm to grow as its clients grow in order to be able to provide the increasing range of services that clients demand and to provide them in the locations they are needed. The growth of multinational companies during this century has been a major factor in the internationalisation of their auditors. This factor initially had a defensive aspect, in that auditors felt the need to establish offices around the world, at first on a correspondent basis but more recently by merger, in order to obtain greater control over the standard of services offered and to avoid the loss of the group audit to a firm which could offer more services worldwide. More recently this factor has had a less defensive impact in that parent company auditors appear to be much more aggressive in their attempts to persuade clients to transfer to them the audits of all subsidiaries in the group.

A second major influence has been economies of scale and of scope. As far as economies of scale are concerned, while there are undoubtedly several specialist areas which only a large firm can afford to service in the domestic market, it is doubted whether these specialist areas exist to the same extent at the international level, and the lack of international integra-

From The Accountant's Magazine, August 1989, 16–17.
Reprinted by permission of the the Institute of Chartered Accountants of Scotland.

tion in many of the large accounting firms provides evidence of this. Economies of scope are based on the argument that it is more efficient to have one firm providing all of the audit services for a multinational than to have a number of different auditors around the world. Both economies of scale, resulting in a full range of specialist services available worldwide, and economies of scope, resulting in a reduction of costs because of the auditor's familiarity worldwide with the client, have been adduced by larger accounting firms as arguments for taking over the audit of all group subsidiaries.

The third influence is reputation, which gives large accounting firms an enormous competitive advantage over smaller, local firms. When selecting an auditor, multinationals, government agencies or international agencies such as the World Bank have all been persuaded that the name of one of the Big Eight firms is a guarantee of quality. The work which this reputation has attracted has enormously facilitated their international expansion.

Acting against the internationalisation trend are various factors such as language, cultural and legal differences and the possibility that conflicts of interest might arise as the client base is extended. It is suggested by the LBS authors that these factors have prevented the internationalisation of law firms and advertising agencies. Even Saatchi & Saatchi, for example, has suffered from the loss of clients who do not wish to be represented by the agency which also acts for a competitor, and this factor may well have contributed to the poor performance of Saatchi's management consultancy division.

The accounting profession, however, has not suffered from these adverse factors to the same extent. Although legal differences have been important, the movement towards harmonisation in financial reporting is removing many of the local differences, particularly where listed companies are concerned. Certainly many of these differences remain, as was pointed out so forcefully by Andy Simmonds in the January issue of TAM, but if IAS E32 on the Comparability of Financial Statements is implemented, then the areas of difference will be significantly reduced.

Furthermore, the problem of conflict of interest is much less important in the field of auditing. A client is less likely to be alarmed if his auditor also audits a competitor; he may even prefer an auditor who has experience of that industry, and there have in the past been cases where an individual firm has been regarded as an audit specialist in a particular field.

However, it is quite possible that these adverse factors will be more important in the future in their effects upon the accounting profession. As far as harmonisation is concerned, it must be appreciated that there are considerable doubts about its feasibility or even value. Its feasibility may be questioned on the grounds that there is no recognised conceptual framework for financial reporting on an international basis, that the standards are fragmented and uncoordinated and, most damaging of all, they are based on the historical cost system. The treatment of goodwill and brand names is an obvious area in which there is little agreement – it is ironic that this particular area will have major implications for accounting firms when they are allowed to incorporate! The value of harmonisation is doubted because of the vast differences which exist between various countries in company law, financing of industry, economic systems, political systems, extent of public ownership, etc. Indeed, it has often been argued that countries should be encouraged to develop a reporting system designed to meet their own particular needs rather than adopt international standards, which may well be irrelevant or inappropriate.

With regard to conflicts of interest, accounting firms may discover, as they expand into new fields such as advising on take-overs, reporting on profit forecasts, advising trade unions in negotiations, etc, that they will much more often find themselves in conflict with the interests of other clients in ways which never occurred with their more traditional activities. This factor may well operate in the future to limit what has so far been a relentless expansion of accounting firms.

So far, the growth of the Big Eight seems mainly attributable to their success in creating a reputation and image based not only upon the quality of their work but also upon the public esteem which the audit function seems to enjoy. This reputation has been skilfully exploited to secure expansion by increasing their client base, both by attracting new clients and by obtaining clients through mergers with other accounting firms, at the national and the international level. The same audit-based reputation has been further exploited by using the image of high ethical standards generated by audit activity to enter new fields such as management consultancy and financial services. These new fields, however, are likely to give rise to more conflicts of interest, and firms must be very careful when accepting new work which might give rise to such conflicts to ensure that they do not lose more than they gain.

All in all, the internationalisation of accounting firms has been a very mixed blessing. It has undoubtedly helped to increase the quality of accounting services in many countries. On the other hand, that improvement may have been achieved at the price of distorting the local accounting system by moulding it to the UK/US model rather than allowing the evolution of a model based on local needs. The result is that accounting practices in more and more countries around the world are based upon a system which is supposedly designed to provide shareholders with useful information about the performance of listed companies. The irrelevance of such a system to the majority of nations around the world is surely self evident.

QUESTIONS

1. Analyse the factors leading to the growth of the major international accounting firms.
2. Compare Briston's concern at the problems of international accounting harmonisation with those of Goeltz.

8

AN INTERNATIONAL COMPARISON OF CONCEPTUAL FRAMEWORKS OF ACCOUNTING

Surendra P. Agrawal, Paul H. Jensen, Anna Lee Meador, and Keith Sellers

The accounting profession internationally is aware of the need for a conceptual framework that would guide the development of accounting standards and practices on a consistent and theoretically sound basis. This paper presents a status report on these developments, primarily in the United States, United Kingdom, Canada, and Australia, as well as on the framework of the International Accounting Standards Committee (IASC), with a brief comparative analysis. A select bibliography may help readers interested in further research in this area.

A HISTORICAL PERSPECTIVE

Although a number of attempts of this nature have been made over the past several decades, the most significant progress has been achieved during the 1970s and 1980s. In the United States, the Trueblood Committee presented its report on *Objectives of Financial Statements* in 1973. To follow up this report, the Financial Accounting Standards Board (FASB) started its conceptual framework project. Because of the extent of resources committed to this project, its development was not hampered by other major issues before the Board, such as accounting for the effects of changing prices,

From International Journal of Accounting (No 24 1989) pp 237–249.
Reprinted by permission of the University of Illinois.

foreign currency translation, and pension accounting. The project ultimately led to the issuance of six *Statements of Financial Accounting Concepts* between 1978 and 1985. Although not fully comprehensive, these Statements represent the most complete set of such concepts developed anywhere so far.

In the United Kingdom, *The Corporate Report* was published in 1975. Although far-reaching in nature, it was overshadowed by the report of the Sandiland's Committee on *Inflation Accounting* issued the same year. Several years later, the Accounting Standards Committee appointed Professor Richard Macve to study the problems involved in the development of a conceptual framework. In his report presented in 1981, Macve concluded, among other things, that an agreed conceptual framework was unlikely to be achieved and that accounting standards would have to be developed on an *ad hoc* basis. These developments seem to have effectively curtailed any further progress in the United Kingdom in this direction, even though some of the recommendations of the *Corporate Report* have been adopted by many companies.

The Canadian Institute of Chartered Accountants (CICA) issued a research study, *Corporate Reporting: Its Future Evolution*, in 1980. This represents the last serious attempt by the CICA towards the development of a conceptual framework. However, the newly organized Accounting Standards Authority of Canada (ASAC), which is not affiliated with the CICA, has revived interest in this direction and issued a statement, *Conceptual Framework for Financial Reporting*, in 1987. Further work in this area is expected in the near future both by the CICA and the ASAC.

The Australian Accountancy Research Foundation (AARF) published a research study by Kenley and Staubus, *Objectives and Concepts of Financial Statements*, in 1972. However, further developments in this area were severely hampered by the preoccupation of the Australian profession with the issues related to current cost accounting, and with the integration of the two professional bodies, the Institute of Chartered Accountants in Australia and the Australian Society of Accountants. The development of a conceptual framework has received renewed attention with the establishment of two new bodies in 1983: the Public Sector Accounting Standards Board (PSASB) and the Accounting Standards Review Board (ASRB). The PSASB has undertaken several projects related to a conceptual framework concerning public sector enterprises and has issued a statement in this regard. One of the first tasks of the ASRB was to sponsor or encourage the development of a conceptual framework for accounting standards in Australia. It has issued several discussion papers in this area and expects to issue final standards in the near future.

The need for a conceptual framework has also been recognized at the international level. The IASC has moved in this direction very quickly. After issuing an exposure draft in 1988, it published *Framework for the Preparation and Presentation of Financial Statements* in 1989. The framework has many similarities to its American counterpart and appears to be a more precise and refined version of the latter.

DEVELOPMENTS IN THE UNITED STATES

The Concepts Statements promulgated by the FASB specify the objectives of financial reporting and the qualitative characteristics of accounting information, define the elements of financial statements, and consider certain recognition and measurement issues. The FASB starts with a normative/deductive model but later seems to have adopted an inductive/positive approach. The framework achieves a great deal of technical precision and yet leaves a considerable amount of flexibility.

The objectives begin as broad statements, such as: to provide information that is useful to present and potential investors and creditors and other users in making rational investment, credit, and similar decisions; and to provide information to help in assessing the amounts, timing, and uncertainty of prospective cash receipts. These statements are followed by more detailed and narrower objectives, such as: to provide information on the economic resources, claims to those resources, and the effects of transactions, events, and circumstances that change them. Subsequent objectives place primary importance on the information relating to the earnings as a measure of performance. It is obvious that the FASB is moving away from the old concept of the objective of accounting as being a fair presentation (or presentation of a true and fair view) of an entity's financial position and results, and towards the decision usefulness of information provided by accounting. This is further reinforced by the specification of qualitative characteristics of accounting information, the first of which is relevance, defined as the capacity of information to influence a decision. However, the second primary qualitative characteristic, reliability, has been described as comprising representational faithfulness, verifiability and neutrality, which seems to be an attempt to retain the idea of true and fair view. Definitions of the elements of financial statements focus on assets, which are probable future economic benefits obtained or controlled by a particular entity as a result of past transactions or events affecting the enterprise. Such a scheme seems to detract from the primacy given to earnings in the objectives. Furthermore, the definitions provide a considerable amount of flexibility, such as in describing revenues as arising from delivering or producing goods. As a result of such flexibility, the FASB has not been able to specify a complete accounting model in its conceptual framework and fails to take a definitive stand on significant measurement and communication issues. What has been done in this regard is merely a listing of various options based on current practice with no indication of the criteria to be used in their selection.

DEVELOPMENTS IN THE UNITED KINGDOM

Although generally taking a normative/deductive approach, the *Corporate Report* seems to be guided more by pragmatism than technical precision. It makes an attempt to widen the scope of financial reporting considerably, and takes a definitive stand on many issues including a complete accounting model. It indicates a single fundamental objective: to communicate economic measurements and information concerning resources and performance of the reporting entity to those who have reasonable rights to such information. The concept of a reasonable right is an idea that is conspicuous by its absence in the FASB's thinking. The *Corporate Report* recognizes a number of user groups (equity investor, loan creditor, analyst-advisor, business contact, government, and the public), and a reasonable right is said to exist where the activities of an organization impinge or may impinge on the interests of a user group. User decisions and information needs, which have been discussed in some detail in the *Corporate Report*, reflect this concern. Among various other matters, the report refers to such things as voting decisions and social impact, and attempts to identify specific needs that may be fulfilled by corporate reports, with considerable emphasis on social/national aspects. A trend to the acceptance by business enterprises of multiple responsibilities is recognized, and it is stated that distributable profit is no longer the sole or premier indicator of performance.

The study discusses issues related to the communication of information, and seeks to expand the scope and content of corporate reports considerably. It recommends the addition of the following statements to those presented currently:

1 A statement of value added, which would, at a minimum, include turnover, purchased materials and services, employees' wages and benefits, dividends and interest payable, tax payable, and amounts held for investment. This statement is believed to help evaluate performance and activity.
2 An employment report, which would present details of the workforce in terms of such items as age, sex, functions, numbers employed, hours worked, reasons for any changes, costs, benefits, training, and safety and health information. This report is believed to help judge efficiency and productivity and show the role of the company as a life support system of its employees.
3 A statement of money exchanges between the entity and governments at home and abroad. This report shows the interdependence between the enterprise and governments.
4 A statement of transactions in foreign currency, to aid users in assessing overseas operations and investment.
5 A statement of future prospects showing likely levels of profits, invest-

ments, and any other possible future developments. These projections may have probability levels attached and would serve as a basis of judging managerial performance.

6 A statement of corporate objectives showing management philosophy or policy, and information on strategic targets in the areas of sales, added value, profitability, investment and finance, dividends, employment, consumer issues, environmental issues, environmental matters, and other social issues. These should be quantified when possible.

The *Corporate Report* recommends further study into methods of social accounting, with emphasis on the development of verifiable measurement techniques. Disaggregated information is also recommended with respect to turnover, value added, profits and losses before tax, capital employed, and employees. Descriptive reports by chairmen and five-year summaries of income and expenditure, financial position, and flow of funds are also encouraged.

After discussing the current practice and alternative accounting models, the *Corporate Report* recommends, pending further study of other models, the use of current purchasing power accounting. Sandiland's report studied the various models, and recommended the use of current costs based on the value to the business. This recommendation was converted into a required practice but has now been made optional.

DEVELOPMENTS IN CANADA

In Canada, the CICA Handbook has been effectively given the force of law by the Canada Business Corporations Act and by other practices and requirements of the various regulatory agencies. This Handbook is merely a compilation of the current accounting standards promulgated by the CICA. Thus, the CICA has found itself in a position of making *de facto* laws upon official adoption of a particular position. This quality of legal enforcement is quite useful in the setting of standards but carries with it a great deal of responsibility. It may be difficult for the CICA to endorse a conceptual framework that contains any degree of controversy without possibly affecting its status as a law setter. This may be one of the reasons why the CICA has shown such little interest in the development of a conceptual framework since the issuance of the research study, *Corporate Reporting: Its Future Evolution*, in 1980.

The objectives of the CICA study differ from those of the FASB, primarily in the matter of relative importance. The CICA places greater emphasis on accountability, minimization of uncertainty, recognition of cost/benefit factors, and reporting of economic reality. The first objective of the CICA study is to provide an accounting by management both to equity and debt investors, not only of management's exercise of its stewardship function but also of its success in achieving the goal of producing a satisfactory economic performance by the enterprise and maintaining it in a strong and healthy financial position. Another objective states that reports should disclose financial information that is relevant to the needs of users, and to provide it in such a form as to minimize uncertainty and enable the user to make his/her own assessment of the risks associated with the enterprise.

The CICA study identifies 15 user groups, together with 13 categories of their needs. Criteria are defined to judge whether the objectives and user needs are being met. Some of these criteria may be in conflict, such as, relevance, comparability, timeliness, clarity and completeness on the one hand, and objectivity, verifiability and precision on the other. But isomorphism, freedom from bias, rationality, non-arbitrariness, and uniformity are compatible with all other criteria. It is also stated that the most important criterion is relevance to user needs, that is, the information should be useful to users in their decision making. Several constraints (substance over from, materiality, cost/benefit effectiveness, flexibility, data availability, consistency, and conservatism) are also recognized.

The study does not attempt to define elements of financial statements on the ground that it would be far too difficult a task. It recommends several alternative measurements of the same items, though none of them might be considered to represent the economic reality in any absolute sense.

The CICA study seems to move away from the concept of true and fair view and toward decision usefulness but not to the same extent as the FASB. It also seems to move toward social accounting but again not to the same extent as the *Corporate Report* of the United Kingdom.

The ASAC relies heavily on the FASB's work in the development of its *Conceptual Framework for Financial Reporting*. However, several substantive differences between the two frameworks are apparent. For example, the ASAC adopts a normative position on measurement attributes and scales, stating that current prices and purchasing power units are preferable to historical prices and nominal dollars. However, the ASAC readily admits that the use of these attributes and scales may involve trade-offs with information qualities such as understandability and reliability. No attempt is made to reconcile these conflicts.

DEVELOPMENTS IN AUSTRALIA

As a comprehensive framework has not been developed in Australia as yet, the discussion here is limited to the related monographs recently issued by the AARF. The monograph *Objectives and Basic Concepts of Accounting*, prepared by Alan Barton, takes a standard analytical approach and covers various aspects of a conceptual framework: objectives, user information needs, qualitative characteristics, fundamentals of accounting and reporting, and internal and external financial reports. Barton's objectives are similar to the FASB's, but more comprehensive, as he includes not only decision making, but also control and accountability. He identifies a number of user groups and several areas of informational needs: cash flow, rate of return on investment, and financial risk (which, according to Barton, can be determined with the help of the former, with nothing additional needed). His qualitative characteristics are similar to those of the FASB, but his list includes understandability, which the FASB treats as user-specific. Barton takes an events approach, and introduces considerable flexibility by defining an event as any happening of consequence to the firm's financial position. Unlike the FASB, Barton is very emphatic on the system of measuring income and wealth. He favors current value accounting, based either on entry or exit values, and states that the only concepts of income, financial position, and earning power which can satisfy the information requirements of users are those based on current market values of assets.

In their monograph, *The Definition and Recognition of Revenue,* Coombes and Martin provide a very clear presentation of revenue recognition issues but only under the historical cost system. They discuss the underlying criteria of realization, external transaction, and critical event, and reject them all. They conclude that the resolution of uncertainty is the most fundamental test underlying the concept of revenue recognition in the historical cost system.

In *The Definition and Recognition of Liabilities,* Jean St. Kerr defines a liability as the future sacrifice of economic benefits that an entity may be required to make in satisfaction of a present obligation to transfer assets or provide services to other entities as a result of past transactions or events. The principal difference with the FASB here is that Kerr thinks that the uncertainty involved in the probability of future sacrifice should be a consideration only in the decision whether to recognize a liability and not in its definition.

From the various monographs and other publications in this area, Australia seems to be taking a more inductive approach than the United States devoting considerable effort to document the present practices. However, the concept of the true and fair view appears to be giving way to decision usefulness. The Australian framework may be expected to have a broad application and probably present a complete accounting model.

INTERNATIONAL DEVELOPMENTS

The IASC's framework seems to be a more precise and refined version of the US framework and avoids many of the logical deficiencies and other pitfalls of the latter. (For a discussion of such deficiencies and pitfalls, see, for example, Kripke (1989) and Agrawal (1987).) After identifying users and their needs, the framework deals with the objective of financial statements, the qualitative characteristics that determine the usefulness of information in financial statements, the definitions, recognition and measurement of the elements from which financial statements are constructed, and concepts of capital and capital maintenance.

The IASC identifies several groups of users and their informational needs, but emphasizes those that are common to all users. However, it further indicates that financial statements that meet the needs of investors (providers of risk capital) will also meet most of the needs of other users. Only one objective of financial statements is specified which, however, seems to capture the essence of the numerous objectives in the FASB's framework. The objective of financial statements is to provide information on the financial position, performance and changes in financial position of an enterprise that is useful to a wide range of users in making economic decisions. It is indicated that some users may use information to assess the stewardship or accountability of management; but this is also done to make certain economic decisions. To meet their objective, financial statements are prepared on the accrual basis and with a going concern assumption.

The principal qualitative characteristics of financial statements are similar to those specified by the FASB and other bodies. Their definitions also capture the essence of more detailed discussions found elsewhere.

1 *Understandability*: Users are assumed to have reasonable knowledge of business and economic activities and accounting and a willingness to study the information with reasonable diligence. Even so, relevant but complex matters should not be excluded.
2 *Relevance*: Information has the quality of relevance when it influences the economic decisions of users by helping them evaluate past, present, or future events, or confirm or correct their past evaluations. The relevance of information is affected by its nature and materiality. It is material if its omission or misstatement could influence the economic decisions of users.
3 *Reliability*: Information has the quality of reliability when it is free from material error and bias and can be depended upon by users to represent faithfully that which it either purports to represent or could reasonably be expected to represent. Faithful representation requires that transactions and events are presented in accordance with their substance and economic reality and not merely their legal form. Uncertainty surrounding events and circumstances is recognized by the disclosure of their nature and extent, and by the exercise of prudence in the preparation of financial statements. Prudence in this context is the inclusion of a degree of caution in the exercise of the judgements needed in making the estimates, such that assets or income are not overstated and liabilities or expenses are not understated. To be reliable, information must be complete within the bounds of materiality and cost.
4 *Comparability*: Users must be able to compare the financial statements of

an enterprise through time, and those of different enterprises. Thus, the measurement and display of the financial effect of similar transactions and other events must be performed in a consistent way. However, the need for comparability should not be confused with mere uniformity and should not be allowed to become an impediment to the introduction of improved accounting standards.

The achievement of relevance and reliability of information is subject to several constraints: timeliness, balance between benefit and cost, and trade-off between qualitative characteristics. Although the framework does not directly consider the concepts of true and fair view or fair presentation, it is stated that the application of the principal qualitative characteristics and of appropriate accounting standards normally results in financial statements that convey what is generally understood as a true and fair view of, or as presenting fairly, such information.

The framework lists only five elements: three for the balance-sheet and two for income statement. An asset is defined as a resource controlled by the enterprise as a result of past events and from which future economic benefits are expected to flow to the enterprise. A liability is defined as a present obligation arising from past events, the settlement of which is expected to result in an outflow from the enterprise of resources embodying economic benefits. Equity is the residual interest in the assets of the enterprise after deducting all its liabilities. In assessing whether an item meets any of these definitions, attention needs to be given to the underlying substance and economic reality and not merely the legal form.

Profit is frequently used as a measure of performance or as the basis for other measures, such as return on investment or earnings per share. Elements directly related to the measurement of profit are income and expenses. Income is defined as increases in economic benefits during the accounting period in the form of inflows or enhancements of assets or decreases of liabilities that result in increases in equity other than those relating to contributions from equity participants. The definition of income encompasses both revenue and gains. Revenue arises in the course of the ordinary activities of an enterprise, and gains represent other items. Expenses are decreases in economic benefits during the accounting period in the form of outflows or depletions of assets or incurrences of liabilities that result in decreases in equity, other than those relating to distributions to equity participants. This definition encompasses both expenses that arise in the course of the ordinary activities of the enterprise and other items referred to as losses.

The international framework does not use a concept similar to the comprehensive income found in the FASB's framework. This distinction acquires more importance when considered in the context of the concept of capital maintenance.

The international framework differs from the FASB's framework in regard to recognition. Two criteria must be met for recognition of an element in the financial statements: (1) it is probable that any future economic benefit associated with the item will flow to or from the enterprise; and (2) the item has a cost or value that can be measured with reliability. An item that possesses the essential characteristics of an element but fails to meet these criteria may none the less warrant disclosure in the notes, explanatory material or in supplementary schedules.

On measurement of elements, the IASC does not take a definitive stand. It lists several measurement bases: historical cost, current cost, realizable value, and present value. The framework states that the basis most commonly adopted is historical cost, usually combined with other bases. It also states that some enterprises use the current cost basis as a response to the inability of the historical cost accounting model to deal with the effects of changing prices of non-monetary assets. The framework addresses the question of the stability of the unit of measurement only in the context of capital maintenance and not as a measurement issue.

The framework discusses two concepts of capital maintenance: financial (measured in either nominal monetary units or units of constant purchasing power) and physical. The selection of the appropriate concept of capital by an enterprise should be based on the needs of the users of its financial statements. The concept chosen indicates the goal to be attained in determining profit. However, a financial concept of capital is adopted by most enterprises in preparing their financial statements.

The physical capital maintenance concept requires the adoption of the current cost basis of measurement. All price changes affecting the assets and liabilities of the enterprise are viewed as changes in the measurement of the physical productive capacity of the enterprise: thus, they are treated as capital maintenance adjustments that are part of equity and not as profit. Profit represents only the increase in physical productive capacity over the period.

The financial capital maintenance concept does not require the use of a particular basis of measurement. If capital is defined in terms of nominal monetary units, profit represents the increase in nominal money capital. Thus, increases in the prices of assets (holding gains) are, conceptually, profits, although they may not be recognized as such until the assets are disposed of. When the concept of capital is defined in terms of constant purchasing power units, profit represents the increase in invested purchasing power. Thus, only the increase in the prices of assets that exceeds the increase in the general level of prices is regarded as profit. The rest of the increase is treated as a capital maintenance adjustment, and, hence as part of equity.

The selection of the measurement basis and concept of capital maintenance will determine the accounting model used in the preparation of the financial statements. This framework is applicable to a range of accounting models and provides guidance on preparing and presenting the financial statements constructed under the chosen model. At present, it is not the intention of the Board of the IASC to prescribe a particular model other than in exceptional circumstances, such as for those enterprises reporting in the currency of a hyperinflationary economy.

CONCLUSIONS

The following conclusions may be drawn from the foregoing discussion:

1 A strong need is perceived for a conceptual framework to guide accounting standards and principles. However, there is no consensus on some of the basic issues, particularly on a complete model of accounting, either within a country or at the international level. As a result, issues relating to the recognition and measurement of various elements of financial statements and to the concept of capital maintenance remain unresolved.
2 There is considerable uncertainty as to the users of accounting information and their informational needs. Although exhaustive lists of potential users and of examples of decisions they might make are often given, there is no unanimity on which particular user group(s) or information needs are expected to be addressed by financial statements. Mere assertions that information useful for a particular group or for a particular purpose would also be useful for all the other groups or for all the other purposes are not an adequate basis for developing the theory of accounting.
3 There is a definite shift from the concept of the true and fair view (or fair presentation) to decision usefulness of information. This is a significant change in the paradigm of accounting based on theoretical considerations. The full implications of this change for accounting practice are not yet clear. A whole-hearted adoption of this concept might obviate the need of a single accounting model and might necessitate reporting of multiple measures of different elements and various combinations and permutations of the same.
4 Greater emphasis seems to be placed on earnings and other measures of performance of enterprises in contrast to a passive reporting of their financial position. Furthermore, a need is perceived for the measurement of uncertainty surrounding various events and circumstances.

The issues raised above need to be resolved by further theoretical and empirical research. Research questions should relate to the identification of users of accounting, decisions these users make, decision models they use, and the information that is relevant for such models. After conclusions are reached on these issues, further research will be needed to identify information that should be the subject matter of accounting which will have an adequate degree of reliability and certainty and can be provided on a timely basis.

BIBLIOGRAPHY

Accounting Standards Authority of Canada (1987) *Conceptual Framework for Financial Reporting*, Vancouver, BC, ASAC.

Accounting Standards Review Board (1985) 'Criteria for the Evaluation of Accounting Standards.' Melbourne, *ASRB Release 100*, ASRB.

Accounting Standards Review Board (1985) 'Procedures for the Approval of Accounting Standards.' Melbourne, *ASRB Release 200*, ASRB.

Accounting Standards Steering Committee (1975) *The Corporate Report*, London, ASSC.

Agrawal, S. P. (1987) 'On The Conceptual Framework of Accounting.' *Journal of Accounting Literature*, 165–178.

American Accounting Association Committee to Prepare A Statement of Basic Accounting Theory (1966) *A Statement of Basic Accounting Theory* (ASOBAT) Sarasota, Fl, AAA.

American Accounting Association (1974) 'Report of the 1972/3 Committee on Concepts and Standards, External Reporting.' *The Accounting Review (Suppl)*, 203–222.

American Institute of Certified Public Accountants, Accounting Principles Board (1970) *Statement No. 4*, 'Basic Concepts and Accounting Principles Underlying Financial Statements of Business Enterprises.' New York: AICPA.

American Institute of Certified Public Accountants (1972) *Objectives of Financial Statements* Chairman R. M. Trueblood, New York, AICPA.

Australian Accountancy Research Foundation (1962) Accounting and Taxation Concepts of Business Income, *Technical Bulletin No. 9*, August.

Australian Accountancy Research Foundation (1968) 'An Enquiry into the Purposes of Published Financial Statements' *The Australian Accountant*, Also in *The Chartered Accountant in Australia*, July 1968.

Barton, Allan D. (1982) *Objectives and Basic Concepts of Accounting* Monograph No. 2 Melbourne, Australian Accountancy Research Foundation.

Bedford, Norton M. (1976) 'The Corporate Report: A Discussion' *Accounting Organizations and Society*, No. 1, 111–116.

Beresford, Dennis R. (1981) 'A Practitioner's View of the FASB's Conceptual Framework' *The Ohio CPA*, Spring, 65–67.

Beresford, Dennis, R. (1983) 'The Challenges of Employing the Conceptual Framework: Examples from Contemporary Standards' *The Ohio CPA*, Autumn, 169–172.

Canadian Institute of Chartered Accountants (1980) *Corporate Reporting: Its Future Evolution*, Toronto: CICA.

Cason, Roger, (1981) 'Conceptual Framework Begins to Affect Current Standards' *Journal of Accounting, Auditing and Finance*, Summer, 369–373.

Coombes, Robert, J. and Martin, Carrick A. (1982) *The Definition and Recognition of Revenue* Monograph No. 3, Melbourne, Australian Accountancy Research Foundation.

Dopuch, Nicholas and Sunder, Shyam (1980) 'FASB's Statements on Objectives and Elements of Financial Accounting: A Review.' *The Accounting Review*, January, 1–21.

Financial Accounting Standards Board (1974) *Conceptual Framework for Accounting and Reporting: Consideration of the Report of the Study Group on the Objectives of Financial Statements*. Discussion Memorandum, Stamford, CI: FASB.

Financial Accounting Standards Board *Statements of Accounting Concepts*, Stamford, CT: FASB
(1978) *No. 1*, 'Objectives of Financial Reporting by Business Enterprises.'
(1980) *No. 2*, 'Qualitative Characteristics of Accounting Information.'
(1980) *No. 3*, 'Elements of Financial Statements of Business Enterprises.'
(1980) *No. 4*, 'Objectives of Financial Reporting by Nonbusiness Organizations'
(1981) *No. 5*, 'Recognition and Measurement in Financial Statements of Business Enterprises.'
(1985) *No. 6*, 'Elements of Financial Statements.'

Gole, V. I. (1983) 'The First Thirty Years.' *The Australian Accountant*, January/February, 20–30.

Graham, A. W. (1972) 'The Profession in Australia – Problems and Developments.' *The Chartered Accountant in Australia*, May, 4–14.

Harrison, R. B. (1976) 'Corporate Report: A Critique.' *CA Magazine*, January, 26–33.

Holder, William, W. and Eudy, Kimberley, Ham (1982) 'A Framework for Building an Accounting Constitution.' *Journal of Accounting, Auditing and Finance*, Winter, 110–125.

Hutchison, I. A. M. (1964) *Reliance on Other Auditors. A Research Study*, Toronto: The Canadian Institute of Chartered Accountants.

International Accounting Standards Committee (1989) *Framework for the Preparation and Presentation of Financial Statements*, London, IASC.

Ipri, Y. (1975) *Theory of Accounting Measurement. Studies in Accounting Research No. 10*, Sarasota, Fl., American Accounting Association.

Kenley, W. J. (1970) *A Statement of Australian Accounting Principles, Accounting Research Study No. 1*, Melbourne, Australian Accountancy Research Foundation.

Kenley, W. J. and Staubus, George, I. (1972) *Objectives and Concepts of Financial Statements, Accounting Research Study No. 3*, Melbourne, Australian Accountancy Research Foundation.

Kenley, W. J. (1972) 'The Accountancy Research Foundation.' *The Chartered Accountant in Australia*, October, 10–11.

Kerr, Jean, St. G. (1984) *The Definition and Recognition of Liabilities. Monograph No. 4* Melbourne, Australian Accountancy Research Foundation.

Kripke, H. (1989) 'Reflections on the FASB's and on Auditing.' *Journal of Accounting, Auditing and Finance*, Winter, 3–65.

Macve, Richard (1981) *A Conceptual Framework for Financial Accounting and Reporting*, London: The Institute of Chartered Accountants in England and Wales.

McCaslin, Thomas, L. and Stanga, Keith, G. (1983) 'Related Qualities of Useful Accounting Information.' *Accounting and Business Research*, Winter, 35–41.

McMonnies, P. N. (1976) 'Corporate Reporting in the Future.' *Accounting and Business Research*, Spring, 95–106.

Miller, Malcolm (1985) 'A Conceptual Framework for Australian Accounting Standards: Is It Worth the Effort?' *The Chartered Accountant in Australia*, August, 48–52.

Miller, Paul, B. W. (1985) 'The Conceptual Framework: Myths and Realities.' *Journal of Accountancy*, March, 12–71.

Moonitz, Maurice (1961) *Accounting Research Study No. 1. The Basic Postulates of Accounting*, New York: American Institute of Certified Public Accountants.

Myers, J. H. (1959) 'The Critical Event and Recognition of Net Profit.' *The Accounting Review*, October, 528–532.

Renshall, J. M. (1976) 'Changing Perceptions Behind the Corporate Report.' *Accounting Organizations and Society*, No. 1, 105–110.

Solomons, David (1986) 'The FASB's Conceptual Framework: An Evaluation.' *Journal of Accountancy*, June, 114–124.

Solomons, David (1983) 'The Political Implications of Accounting and Accounting Standard Setting.' *Accounting and Business Research*, Spring, 107–118.

Sprouse, Robert, I. and Moonitz, Maurice (1962) *Accounting Research Study No. 1.* 'A Tentative Set of Broad Accounting Principles for Business Enterprises.' New York: American Institute of Certified Public Accountants.

Stamp, Edward (1980) 'Accounting Standard Setting: A New Beginning.' *CA Magazine*, September, 38–44.

Stamp, Edward, (1982) 'First Steps Towards a British Conceptual Framework.' *Accountancy*, March, 125–130.

Standish, Peter, F. M. (1972) *Australian Financial Reporting: Accounting Research Study No. 2*, Melbourne, The Australian Accountancy Research Foundation.

Stanga, Keith, G. (1980) 'The Relationship Between Relevance and Reliability: Some Empirical Results.' *Accounting and Business Research*, Winter, 29–39.

Sterling, Robert, R. (1982) 'The Conceptual Framework: An Assessment.' *Journal of Accountancy*, November, 103–108.

Sutcliffe, P. (1984) Financial Reporting in the Public Sector: A Framework for Analysis and Identification of Issues, *Monograph No. 5*, Melbourne, Australian Accountancy Research Foundation.

Taylor, D. W. (1977) 'Financial Accounting Objectives and Standards Setting: Part I.' *The Chartered Accountant in Australia*, September, 19–22.

Taylor, D. W. (1977) 'Financial Accounting Objectives and Standards Setting: Part II.' *The Chartered Accountant in Australia*, October, 17–20.

Walton, Peter (1984) 'One Step Forward, Two Steps Back.' *Accountancy*, June, 126–7.

Zeff, Stephen A. (1973) *Forging Accounting Principles in Australia*, Melbourne, Australian Society of Accountants.

Zeff, Stephen, A. (1972) *Forging Accounting Principles in Five Countries*, Champaign, Il: Stipes.

QUESTIONS

1 Discuss the variations in the view of users to be served by accounts identified in the different conceptual frameworks outlined in this article, and compare this with the position in any other country with which you are familiar.

9

THE INTERACTION BETWEEN NATIONAL AND ORGANIZATIONAL CULTURES IN ACCOUNTING FIRMS

Joseph Soeters and Hein Schreuder

One way to look at the problem of organization is to view it as a manifestation of the general problem of social order (e.g. Smircich, 1983). From that perspective, culture is an indispensable element of organizational analysis, since it is the pivotal concept in the study of social order. Through culture, individuals are integrated into social units, such as families, clubs and associations, firms, regions, or nations. They internalize the values and norms of these social units in their personalities and thus, generally, tend to exhibit more stable and predictable behavior. In this way they render possible the existence of a social order and, consequently, of organizations.

There are nearly as many definitions of culture as there are authors writing about this subject (e.g. Ansari & Bell, 1985; Frost *et al.*, 1985). For the purposes of this study culture refers to 'a collective programming of the mind which distinguishes one group from another' (Hofstede, 1980, p. 25). Cultures can be observed through myths, rituals, habits, beliefs and taken-for-granted assumptions about reality. But especially important are the values espoused by the individuals of a group (Goode, 1984; Schein, 1985).

The concept of culture can be studied at different levels of analysis. In the organizational literature two levels have attracted most attention:

Reprinted with permission from Accounting Organisations and Society, Vol 13, No 1, pp 75–85, 1988, 'The interaction between national and organizational cultures in accounting firms', J Soeters and H Schreuder.
Elsevier Science Ltd, Pergamon imprint, Oxford, England.

1 the influence of *national cultures* upon organizations (Hofstede, 1980, 1983; Lammers & Hickson, 1979, p. 403)
2 the concept of *organizational culture* itself (Pettigrew, 1979; Smircich, 1983; Frost *et al.*, 1985; Schein, 1985).

However, the *interaction* between national and organizational cultures has not yet received very much attention. Such interaction may occur in mergers across national boundaries or in the creation of foreign subsidiaries by multinational companies. In these cases one may observe the development of cultures which are hybrids between the international organizational culture and the local national cultures (Hofstede, 1985; Negandhi, 1987).

Like many other industries, the accounting profession shows a trend toward increasing internationalization. This trend is manifested in international mergers of accounting firms and in the establishment of international associations of local accounting firms. The most recent example is the merger between KMG and PMM into KPMG. In such cases the compatibility of the organizational cultures is a major area of concern, particularly with regard to human resource management. It is highly likely that organizational cultures vary with national cultures. It is, therefore, surprising that very little is known about the interaction between national and organizational cultures.

One of the few studies addressing this issue examined Japanese firms in the United States (Lincoln *et al.*, 1978). It was found that the number of Japanese or Japanese-American employees varied inversely with the degree to which narrowly defined occupational roles (functional specialization) were found within these firms. However, no significant effects could be demonstrated with respect to centralization, formalization or vertical differentiation (Lincoln *et al.*, 1978, p. 845). This supports the idea that Japanese management styles, if embedded in a Western environment, may converge with those of the West. Note, however, that all these measures concern the *formal* structure, the official design, of the organization. It may well be that 'the actual interaction structures, which develop in the course of day-to-day activities', do show effects of the national culture of the mother organization (Lincoln *et al.*, 1978: 845; see also Meyer & Rowan, 1977). Lincoln *et al.* (1978) refer to such actual interaction structures in terms of organizational culture. Following such an interpretation, the influence of the national culture of the mother organization on subsidiaries overseas may be particularly noticeable in their organizational cultures, and not in their formal structures. However, until now, there is no evidence to support this hypothesis. This finding provides the point of departure for the present research.

RESEARCH PROBLEM

This study forms part of a larger research project which was directed towards the examination of cross-national differences between accounting firms.[1] As such, the original design of this research allowed the investigation of national cultural effects upon similar firms. In this paper we address a different research problem. Broadly defined our research problem is what are the cultural differences between local[2] and international (U.S.-oriented 'Big Eight'[3]) accounting firms, operating in the same national (Dutch) culture?

In brief, a comparative examination of local and international accounting firms offers an opportunity to assess to what extent national and organizational cultures interact, as reflected by the work-related values of their Dutch employees. Thus, the research problem may be defined in terms of two questions:

1 Is it possible to detect the influence of the U.S. culture upon the Big Eight international firms to explain any differences between measurements of work-related values for employees in these firms and in the Dutch firms?
2 If so, is it possible to identify which cultural influence is dominant, the national or the organizational?

As compared with the Dutch firms, the Big Eight accounting firms have only recently entered the Dutch market. By consequence, they are much smaller in both personnel and average fee income (International Accounting Bulletin, 1985). On average there are roughly 1000 professional staff members in the three Dutch firms and some 100 in the three international firms. However, the growth rates of the fee income are much more impressive for the Big Eight firms. Whereas the Dutch firms show yearly growth rates of fee income varying from 0 to 10%, the corresponding figures for the Big Eight firms range from 15 to 25% (IAB, 1985).

In preliminary interviews with key informants of the six firms which provided the focus for the study, organizational policies were observed to differ quite markedly between the types of firms. The international firms have adopted a number of policies elaborated at the group level and are, as such, heavily influenced by U.S. practice. A particular case in point are the personnel policies with respect to career development. The Big Eight firms tend to operate an 'up or out' policy, whereas in the Dutch firms many more employees are traditionally maintained in sub-partner level ranks without prospects of further promotion and without any 'pressure' to leave the organization. All six firms work virtually entirely with Dutch employees.

RESEARCH DESIGN AND METHOD

To operationalize the concept of culture for the sample of six accounting firms, we used Hofstede's (1980) method and instrument. Strictly speaking, Hofstede's approach was developed to quantify the effects of national cultures upon organizations. There are several reasons, however, why this method also appears to be appropriate for this research.

Hofstede collected measurements in 40 countries, but the measurements pertained to 40 different offices of only one multinational company. One must conclude, therefore, that his results reflect both national and organizational characteristics. While he presents his results as indicators of differences in national cultures, they also incorporate features of organizational culture. Moreover, his instrument was developed at the organizational level, and that is where we wish to apply it. In addition, the method has been replicated and validated in subsequent research (Bosland, 1984). Finally, the use of this method provides comparative data for both The Netherlands and the U.S.

Three Dutch and three international Big Eight firms were requested to participate in this study; all agreed to participate. A mail-back questionnaire was sent to the home addresses of all the employees of these firms who:

a were active in the accounting and auditing practice (thus excluding the tax and consulting practice as well as administrative and other supporting staff);
b had been evaluated on their performance at least once; and,
c had not yet reached the partner level.

These criteria produced a population of 986 potential respondents of whom 818 (83%) were employed by the Dutch firms. The response rate exceeded 65% (643 respondents) with firm response rates ranging from 60% to 81%.[4]

The distribution of respondents illustrates that our research design could not preclude the potential occurrence of confounding effects. In The Netherlands the international Big Eight firms are smaller and have been established more recently than their comparable Dutch counterparts. Of course, we could have approached smaller and younger Dutch firms, but then we would have potentially introduced other confounding effects, since those firms work primarily on a regional basis, have very different client portfolios than the Big Eight firms, and thus operate in different task environments. Subsequent research should try to separate the effects of age, size and origin.

Measures and Procedures of Data Analysis

Hofstede's method involves the measurement of values and perceptions of individual members of the organization. These individual measurements are then aggregated to form organizational scores. For each organization a score on each of four cultural dimensions was obtained:

1 the degree of (perceived) *power distance;*
2 the degree of *uncertainty avoidance;*

3 the degree of *individualism*; and
4 the degree of *masculinity*.

The degree of *power distance* may be interpreted as the subjective counterpart of the well-known centralization/decentralization dimension. The dimension is measured on the basis of responses to three items: (1) the percentage of non-supervising respondents indicating (with examples) that they have an authoritarian or paternalistic superior; (2) the opinion of the same respondents about desirable styles of supervision; and, (3) the number of instances in which subordinates do not dare to express their disagreement with superiors.

The degree of *uncertainty avoidance* represents an indicator of the formalization or rule-orientation in the organization and is again measured on the basis of responses to three questions. The first asks for (dis)agreement with the statement that 'an organization's rule should not be broken, even when the employee thinks it is in the organization's best interest'. The second ascertains the number of employees who do not expect to work another five years for this organization. The third measures the (perceived) stress at work. In organizations where stress is perceived, it is hypothesized that members would tend to avoid uncertainty-generating situations.

The *individualism index* is based on responses to four questions which deal with physical working conditions, personal relations, the sufficiency of leisure time, and the quality of the living environment. If importance is attached to good physical working conditions and good personal relations, a collective orientation is indicated. If, on the other hand, importance is attached to leisure time and a pleasant living environment, this is taken to reflect an individual orientation.

The *masculinity index* reflects the Western achievement-orientation. Respondents who value income and promotion opportunities higher than job security and good personal relations score highly on this index. Computational formulas for the four dimensions are presented in Appendix 1.

A few technical remarks are necessary concerning the analysis of the data. When making comparisons of organizations on one characteristic, such as organizational culture, it is necessary to control for other properties (Galtung, 1967). In our study, this implies that the basic characteristics of the respondents in the two categories of offices have to be the same. Examining these basic characteristics, it was found that the employees of the Big Eight offices were on average somewhat younger ($F = 21.2$; $p < 0.001$). Furthermore, they had fewer years of formal education ($F = 12.4$; $p < 0.001$) and occupied lower positions than their counterparts in the Dutch firms ($F = 30.0$; $p < 0.001$). As might be expected, position and years of formal education were significantly correlated ($R = 0.25$; $p \leq 0.001$). This implies that the standardization of culture scores can be restricted to the characteristics position and age. As the standard model we have chosen the position/age distribution of the three Dutch offices. In this standardization we have excluded from the computations those position/age combinations based on less than four respondents. This was done in order to reduce the influence of individual fluctuations. The standardized culture scores are weighted averages.

Finally, it should be noted that our results refer to the concept of culture at the organizational level. Hence, we have only six observations. Fisher's Exact Probability Test is an appropriate means for significance testing in this case (Siegel, 1956). The results of this test are presented in Appendix 2. In addition, one way analyses of variance have been performed on the 13 items comprising the four cultural dimensions. The results are also presented in Appendix 2. Although, strictly speaking, such an item-by-item analysis does not directly refer to organizational culture, the results do give a more detailed view of the underlying structure of our data.

RESULTS

The results for the six offices with respect to Hofstede's four culture dimensions, are presented in Tables 2 and 3. Table 1, on the other hand, presents comparative results for the national cultures of the U.S. and The Netherlands, as observed by Hofstede (1980).

The differences between the two nations are not very pronounced with respect to power distance (relatively modest in both countries, slightly larger in the U.S.). The culture dimension of uncertainty avoidance is relatively weak in both countries, but slightly stronger in The Netherlands.

Further, one can see a somewhat higher degree of individualism and a very high degree of masculinity in the North American culture. On the latter dimension, the strong achievement-motivation of (parts of) the North American society is apparent. This characteristic of the United States has been previously documented (e.g. R. & H. Lynd, 1937). From Hofstede's (1980) study it could be hypothesized that, if any differences exist between the Big Eight offices and the Dutch firms, they would be especially pronounced on the dimension of masculinity. Table 2 presents data on this hypothesis.

Table 1 The four culture dimensions in the locations in The Netherlands and the United States (Hofstede, 1980)5

	U.S.A.	*The Netherlands*	*(U.S.-Neth.)/ Range)* 100*	*Range*
1. Power distance*	40	38	2	11–94
2. Uncertainty avoidance*	46	53	−7	8–112
3. Individualism*	91	80	11	12–91
4. Masculinity*	62	14	48	5–95

* A high value indicates a high score on the dimension measured.

Table 2 The four culture dimensions in the six offices; standardized weighted averages*

	Netherlands 1 (1)	*Netherlands 2 (2)*	*Netherlands 3 (3)*	*Netherlands total (4)*	*Big Eight 1 (5)*	*Big Eight 2 (6)*	*Big Eight 3 (7)*	*Big Eight total (8)*
1. Power distance	45 (59)	45 (211)	43 (42)	45 (312)	25 (18)	35 (42)	50 (28)	38 (88)
2. Uncertainty avoidance	5 (170)	20 (253)	–13 (95)	9 (518)	–33 (23)	–43 (47)	–34 (36)	–38 (106)
3. Individualism	62 (170)	44 (253)	64 (95)	53 (518)	62 (23)	71 (47)	53 (36)	63 (106)
4. Masculinity	16 (170)	10 (253)	38 (95)	17 (518)	45 (23)	58 (47)	81 (36)	63 (106)

* A higher value in the table indicates a higher degree of the dimension measured. Between parentheses we have added the number of respondents in each cell. For tests of significance see Appendix 2.

Table 3 Partial correlations between length of employment and the most discriminating items of the four cultural dimensions (controlled for age)

	The Netherlands (N = 523)	*Big Eight (N = 116)*
1. Subordinates are afraid to express disagreement with their superiors (low = very frequently)	0.12*	−0.08
2. Duration of period one thinks one is likely to continue working for this company (low = short period)	0.24†	−0.02
3. Importance attached to good physical working conditions (low = little importance)	−0.04	−0.14
4. Importance attached to having an opportunity for high earnings (low = little importance)	0.01	−0.06

* $0.001 < p \leq 0.01$ † $0.000 < p \leq 0.001$

With regard to power distance, the Dutch offices do not differ among themselves; the Big Eight offices, however, do. Both the office with the smallest and the office with the largest power distance is a Big Eight office. As a whole, the Big Eight offices show a somewhat smaller power distance than the Dutch offices. This difference, however, is not significant. This deviates from Hofstede's findings which showed a slightly larger degree of power distance in the United States. Given the divergent scores for the Big Eight firms, it appears that the national North American culture had no influence on the Big Eight offices in The Netherlands regarding this cultural dimension. The varying results may be best explained by other dimensions or by differences in organizational cultures.

National cultural influences, however, are apparent with respect to the dimension of uncertainty avoidance. All three Big Eight offices have significantly lower scores in this regard than their Dutch counterparts (see also Appendix 2). Furthermore, the standard deviations are uniformly small. This finding is consistent with Hofstede's results and implies that the employees in the Dutch firms offices are more concerned about avoiding uncertainty-generating situations than their colleagues in the Big Eight offices. In particular, the employees in the Dutch firms are far less inclined to seek another job in the short term.

In one respect, however, there is an important deviation from Hofstede's (1980) findings. Five of the scores for uncertainty avoidance that were obtained in this study are much lower than even the lowest scoring country in the Hofstede study. In fact, four negative scores were observed which do not occur in Hofstede's study at all (although they are possible by definition). The most likely explanation for this deviation is thought to be as follows. In the uncertainty avoidance index the intention of the employee to seek another job plays an important discriminating role, and since Hofstede's results pertain to locations of one multinational enterprise, which is characterized by a system of long-term (or even lifetime) employment, this item plays a much less prominent role in his study than in ours. The promise of lifetime employment is not given by accounting firms and certainly not by the Big Eight firms with their philosophy of 'up or out'. This means that labor mobility in accounting firms in general, and especially in the Big Eight firms, is an important element both of these organizations' personnel policies and of the individual's career planning. To the extent that the 'up or out'- philosophy is more prominent in the Big Eight firms than in the Dutch offices, this circumstance can also explain the difference in uncertainty avoidance between these two categories of firms.

With respect to the cultural dimension of uncertainty avoidance, we have thus found a certain influence of the North American national culture on the Big Eight firms in The Netherlands. Secondly, we have demonstrated an industry-specific cultural influence. Our accounting firms as a group appear to be different from Hofstede's multinational company in this respect.

With respect to the index of individualism we find no significant difference between the Dutch and the Big Eight firms (see Appendix 2A). Table 2 shows that the aggregate score for the Big Eight firms signifies a somewhat more individualistic culture, which corresponds to Hofstede's findings. Further analysis reveals that this is due to the relative weight assigned to a particular item of the index. This item (the importance attached to good working conditions, see Appendix 1) points toward the Big Eight firms having a more individualistic culture, although the difference with the Dutch firms is not significant (see Appendix 2B). The other three items show mixed results. As a whole, therefore, no conclusive findings emerge from our data on this dimension.

The Hofstede (1980) findings are completely confirmed with respect to the last cultural dimension, the index of masculinity. In the Big Eight offices it is possible to distinguish a strong national cultural influence from the U.S., particularly with respect to a strong orientation towards high income and good career perspectives. Tenure and good relations with colleagues are considered less important. This huge difference in achievement-orientation is probably the most salient and significant distinction between the cultures of The Netherlands and the United States.

(Self-)Selection Versus Socialization

From our results it appears that there are significant effects of the U.S. culture upon the organizational cultures of the Big Eight firms operating in The Netherlands. These are surprising if one takes into account that these firms employ very few U.S. citizens. In our sample only four of the respondents in these firms were not Dutch by birth. Thus, the Big Eight firms do not differ significantly from the Dutch firms in the composition of their work force. At the same time, the values and norms of the Dutch employees in these Big Eight firms form the building-blocks of an organizational culture which is strongly U.S.-oriented in several respects.

Two hypotheses can be postulated to explain this phenomenon (see also Schneider & Reichers, 1983). The first is the (self-)selection hypothesis which would indicate that employment in a Big-Eight firm is attractive to those Dutch accountants who already conform to certain aspects of the U.S. culture. Alternatively, such a selection process could be carried out by the Big Eight firms themselves. Of course, the two mechanisms of self-selection and selection by the firm may be mutually reinforcing. The second is the socialization hypothesis which would indicate that employees internalize aspects of the U.S. culture through organizational processes of socialization. Salaman (1979), as well as Peters & Waterman (1982), has identified such processes. New employees follow certain rites of passage. To a certain extent they may be indoctrinated as to what is considered to be important in the organization, what standards of conduct are upheld, what kind of humor is acceptable, and so on. Possibly such processes are more pronounced in multinational organizations since a certain degree of bi-cultural integration has to be achieved.

The validity of these hypotheses was investigated in two different ways. First, we examined whether the employees of the Big Eight firms explicitly demonstrated an earlier interest in the U.S. culture before entering the firm. However, our evidence shows that these employees do not differ from their colleagues in the Dutch firms in the following respects:

a they received their primary, secondary as well as tertiary education in The Netherlands;
b they obtained their accounting degree in The Netherlands; and,
c their work experience was primarily in The Netherlands.

Hence, we can find no explicit indications in our data of an earlier interest in the U.S. culture. However, it is possible that the Big Eight firms receive applications and select from a sample of Dutch citizens whose work values resemble those of the U.S. labor supply.

To further test for the possibility of (self)-selection vs socialization, we computed partial correlations between the length of employment at the firm and four items from the questionnaire; the four items were selected because they were found to discriminate best (for each dimension of culture) between the Dutch firms and the Big Eight firms. If the socialization hypothesis is valid one would expect the typical features of U.S. culture to become more prominent over the years. However, if the (self-)selection hypothesis is valid, one would expect the employees to already exhibit their U.S. orientation upon entry to the firm (leading to low correlations over time).

Of the eight correlations presented in Table 3, two are significant. These correlations point towards mechanisms operative in the Dutch firms. Their employees expect to stay longer with the firm as their employment time increases. This simply points towards the existence of older employees at the sub-partner level in these firms. That these employees dare to contradict their superior more often over time is understandable. It is, however, not an aspect prominent in the Dutch culture, but one found more commonly in the U.S. culture. In fact, the absence of any correlation significantly different from zero for the international firms, lends support to the (self-)selection hypothesis. All in all, we can hardly find any indications that the cultural differences between the Dutch and the Big Eight firms are to be explained by socialization processes, which figure so prominently in the literature on organizational cultures (e.g. Peters & Waterman, 1982). The differences in work-related values of the employees of these firms do not increase over time, but appear to exist from the onset.[6]

If anything, our data can be interpreted as pointing towards the (self-)selection hypothesis.[7] This result conforms to some earlier findings in the literature. Lammers (1963), for instance, studied the recruitment of Dutch Navy officers and found that self-selection is the most important mechanism in this regard. Socialization after entry into the Navy only provided the 'finishing touch' (see also Hines, 1973). Waller & Chow (1985) also detected the importance of the self-selection mechanism. They found that workers select among alternative employment contracts based on their performance capability. Thus, it may be concluded that self-selection of the workers of the Big Eight firms, in combination with the selection policies of these firms themselves, is probably the best explanation for the U.S.-oriented culture in these organizations.

SUMMARY AND DISCUSSION

Using Hofstede's Value Survey Module we have empirically studied the cultures of six accounting firms in The Netherlands. We found rather pronounced effects of the U.S. national culture upon the organizational cultures of the Big Eight firms in our study. On the dimensions of Uncertainty Avoidance and Masculinity there were significant differences from the three Dutch firms. On the dimensions of Individualism, mixed results were obtained, whereas no significant differences were established with respect to Power Distance. In addition, an industry-specific component of organizational culture was demonstrated with respect to the dimension of Uncertainty Avoidance. As a group, our six accounting firms differed from Hofstede's (1980) multinational firm on this dimension.

Our second research question was whether national or organizational culture is dominant. We found no general answer to this question. For the Power Distance and Individualism dimensions no systematic differences emerged. For the Uncertainty Avoidance and Masculinity dimensions the differences were significant and systematic. Thus, a clear influence of the external (U.S.-)culture could be detected. For these latter dimensions our results are in line with the hypotheses derived from Hofstede's (1980) earlier work.

A further analysis of our data revealed that these results were probably best explained by a mechanism of self-selection best explained by the employees and/or selection by the firms. We found little support for the hypothesis that a socialization process is operative in which the Dutch employees gradually internalize U.S.-oriented work values.

In interpreting our results one caveat should be repeated. Given the composition of international Big Eight firms and their local counterparts in The Netherlands, our research design could not preclude potentially confounding effects of age and size. The Big Eight firms are younger and smaller than the comparable Dutch firms. Future research in other countries should try to control for such factors. In addition, it would be interesting to explore the relationships between organizational culture on the one hand and strategy, structure and performance on the other (cf. Lincoln *et al.*, 1978; Pennings & Gresov, 1986).

For the accounting firms in our study our results may have several potential implications. The Dutch firms may, for instance, want to evaluate their recruitment and training policies in the light of the increasing internationalization of the accounting profession (see also Negandhi, 1987). Given the substantial differences which already exist on several dimensions with the Big Eight firms in The Netherlands, it may be expected that similar or greater differences exist with some of the foreign partners in the international associations of which these Dutch firms have become a member. For the Big Eight firms our results provide insights into the type of Dutch employees they attract. Our findings suggest that the work values of these employees are already mainly oriented toward U.S. culture upon entry. Thus, the recruitment policies of these firms may be more important than their training (or socialization) policies in this respect. Finally, our results may be indicative of the points at which tensions may arise if attempts are made to set up joint ventures between Dutch and Big Eight firms, or to merge such firms. Further work in this area may provide empirical content to the observed phenomenon of 'culture clashes' on such occasions (Walter, 1985).

APPENDIX

Appendix 1

The four cultural dimensions are computed on the basis of the following formulas:

*Power distance index** = 135–25 (mean score 'employees are afraid to disagree') + (% perceiving the superior to take decisions in an autocratic or persuasive/paternalistic way) – (% preferring the superior to act in a consultative style).

*Uncertainty avoidance index** = 300 – 30 (mean score 'rule orientation') – (% intending to stay less than 5 years) – 40 (mean stress score).

Individualism index† = 76 (mean score 'importance good physical working conditions') – 43 (mean score 'importance of having sufficient time left for personal or family life') + 30 (mean score 'importance to work with people, who cooperate well with another') – 27 (mean score 'importance living in an desirable area') – 29.

Masculinity index† = 60 (mean score 'importance of working with people, who cooperate well with another') – 66 (mean score 'importance of having an opportunity for high earnings') + 30 (mean score 'importance of having security of employment') – 39 (mean score 'importance of having an opportunity for advancement to higher level jobs') + 76.

* Hofstede (1980)

† Hofstede (1982). The weights of these items are based on the factor loadings of the original study.

Appendix 2. Significance Tests

(A) A first test has been computed using the mean cultural scores of the six accounting firms. Since there are very few observations ($N = 6$), only Fisher's Exact Probability Test is appropriate (see Siegel, 1956, pp. 96–104). For each cultural dimension the six scores have been dichotomized into high and low scores, using the median as the cut-off point. In this way Table 2 could be reorganized in four 2 × 2 contingency tables, as follows:

	Cultural dimension							
Type of company	*PDI*		*UAI*		*IND*		*MAS*	
	H	*L*	*H*	*L*	*H*	*L*	*H*	*L*
Dutch	2	1	3	0	2	1	0	3
International	1	2	0	3	1	2	3	0

Using Fisher's test, respectively the p-values for PDI and IND are 0.45 and 0.05 for UAI and MAS. Using the table of critical values in the Fisher Test (Siegel, pp. 256–257) it can be concluded that the UAI and the MAS-index show significant differences between the Dutch and International firms at the 5% level.

(B.) A further test of significance included one way analyses of variance with regard to the 13 work related values (Dutch firms: $N = 526$; Big Eight firms: $N = 117$).

These are as follows:

	Dutch firms	*International firms*	*F-value*	*Significance*
Power distance				
Employees afraid to disagree (low = very infrequently)	3.3	3.8	31.4	†
Perceived superior (low = paternalistic)	2.6	2.3	3.4	N.S.
Preferred superior (low = paternalistic)	2.8	2.7	3.3	N.S.
Uncertainty avoidance				
Rule orientation (low = strong)	3.8	4.0	3.7	*
Intention to stay with the company (low = short period)	2.7	1.8	69.3	†
Perceived stress (low = always)	3.3	3.2	0.5	N.S.
Individualism				
Imp. good working conditions (low = high importance)	2.0	2.2	3.5	N.S.
Imp. time for family life (low = high importance)	1.7	1.9	7.7	†
Imp. of good cooperation (low = high importance)	1.5	1.6	2.2	N.S.
Imp. of living in a desirable area1.5 (low = high importance)	1.7	8.4	†	
Masculinity				
Imp. of good cooperation (low = high importance)	1.5	1.6	2.2	N.S.
Imp. of high salary (low = high importance)	2.3	1.9	18.4	†
Imp. of job security (low = high importance)	2.2	2.6	14.5	†
Imp. of career prospects (low = high importance)	1.8	1.5	14.1	†

* $0.01 < cp \leq 0.05$. † $0 < cp \leq 0.01$.

NOTES

1 This larger project is coordinated at the University of Washington, Seattle, U.S.A. by Jamie Pratt. This international project will yield results about the cross-national differences in cultures of accounting firms. In our study we have focussed on national and organizational cultures of accounting firms *within* a particular country.

2 Our local Dutch firms have relatively recently become part of international associations of accounting firms. This has, however, not (yet) had a significant impact on their local philosophies and policies.

3 While most of the Big Eight firms have historical roots in the U.K., they have been rather strongly Americanized over time. The firms in our sample have their

headquarters and general management in the U.S. Moreover, their organizational and personnel policies have a strong U.S. orientation, as confirmed by the local partners in these Big Eight firms in pilot and exit interviews with us.

4 Both the highest and the lowest response rate were obtained for an international firm. The three firms which included their own introductory letter to our questionnaire attained the highest response rates.

5 Two of the four culture-dimensions (i.e. Individualism and Masculinity) do not fully identify with Hofstede's original instruments. This is due to some changes, proposed by himself. As a consequence, for these two dimensions, both studies are only comparable in terms of central tendencies.

7 The texts of the advertisements for new personnel of the two types of organizations underline this (self-)selection mechanism. The Big Eight firms want to have employees, who 'hardly have time for a girlfriend, but know everything about foreign daughters'. The new employees of these firms will 'probably lack leisure time, but will certainly have enough career-opportunities' (text from an advertisement for the recruitment of new employees, April 1985). Dutch firms advertise with more sober slogans.

8 One caveat must be mentioned here. In our variable 'length of employment' the lowest value is 'six months to one year'. Thus, on the basis of our analysis it cannot be excluded, that socialization effects occur within the *first* (half) year of employment (Ouchi, 1982).

REFERENCES

Ansari, S., & Bell, J., (1985) *Symbolism, Collectivism and Rationality in Management Control*, Working paper, San Francisco.

Bosland, N. (1984) Some Studies on the Value Survey Module, M.A. thesis, Catholic University, Tilburg.

Frost, P. J., Moore, L. F., Louis, M. R., Lundberg, C. C. & Martin, J. (1985) (eds), *Organizational Culture* (Beverly Hills: Sage).

Galtung, J. (1967) *Theory and Methods of Social Research* (London: George Allen & Unwin).

Goode, E. (1984) *Sociology* (Englewood Cliffs, NJ: Prentice-Hall).

Hines, G. K. (1973) The Persistence of Greek Achievement Motivation across Time and Culture, *International Journal of Psychology* p. 347–357.

Hofstede, G. H. (1980) *Culture's Consequences, International Differences in Work-Related Values* (London: Sage).

Hofstede, G. (1982) *Scoring Guide for Values Survey Model* (Arnhem: IRIC).

Hofstede, G. H. (1983) The Cultural Relativity of Organizational Practices and Theories, *Journal of International Business Studies* pp. 75–89.

Hofstede, G. H. (1985) The Interaction between National and Organizational Value Systems, *Journal of Management Studies* pp. 347–357.

International Accounting Bulletin, (May 1985) Dutch Firms Venture out from Audit Base, pp. 8–11, also: Dutch Firms Fight for Growth in a Flat Market (April 1985) pp. 12–15.

Lammers, C. J. (1963) *Het Koninklijke Instituut voor de Marine. Een Sociologische Studie van de Inlijving van Groepen Adspirant-Officieren in de Zeemacht* (van Gorcum: Assen).

Lammers, C. J., Hickson, D. J. (1979) *Organizations, Alike and Unlike; International and Inter-Institutional Studies in the Sociology of Organizations* (London: Routledge & Kegan Paul).

Lincoln, J. R., Olson, J., & Hanada, M. (1978) Cultural Effects on Organizational

Structure: the Case of Japanese Firms in the United States, *American Sociological Review* pp. 829–847.

Lynd, R. S. & Lynd, H. (1980) *Middleton in Transition* (New York: Harcourt Brace Jovanovich, 1937) partly reprinted in Coser, L. A., (ed.) *The Pleasures of Sociology* pp. 48–645 (New York: Mentor).

Meyer, J. W. & Rowan, B. (1977) Institutionalized Organizations, Formal Structure as Myth and Ceremony *American Journal of Sociology* pp. 340–363.

Negandhi, A. R. (1987) *International Management* (Boston: Allan & Bacon).

Ouchi, W. G. (1982) Theory Z, an Elaboration of Methodology and Findings, *Journal of Contemporary Business* pp. 27–41.

Pennings, J. M. & Gresov, C. G. (1986) Technoeconomic and Structural Correlates of Organizational Culture: an Integrative Framework, *Organization Studies* pp. 317–334.

Peters, Th.J., & Waterman, R. H., Jr, (1982)*In Search of Excellence; Lessons from America's Best Run Companies* (New York: Harper & Row).

Pettigrew, A. M. (1979) On Studying Organizational Cultures, *Administrative Science Quarterly* pp. 570–581.

Salaman, G. (1979) *Work Organizations, Resistance and Control* (London/New York: Longman).

Schein, E. (1985) *Organizational Culture and Leadership* (New York: Harcourt Brace Jovanovich).

Schneider, B. & Reichers, A. E. (1983) On the Etiology of Climates, *Personnel Psychology* pp. 19–29.

Smircich, L. (1983) Concepts of Culture and Organizational Analysis, *Administrative Science Quarterly* pp. 339–358.

Siegel, S. (1956) *Non-Parametric Statistics for the Behavioral Sciences* (New York: McGraw-Hill).

Waller, W. S. & Chow, C. W. (1985) The Self-Selection and Effort Effects of Standard-Based Employment Contracts: a Framework and some Empirical Evidence, *The Accounting Review* pp. 458–476.

Walter, G. A. (1985) Culture Collisions in Mergers and Acquisitions, in Frost, P. J. *et al.* (eds), *Organizational Culture* (Beverly Hills: Sage).

ACKNOWLEDGEMENTS

We wish to acknowledge the assistance of Patrick Jaspers and Jenny Sutton, and the constructive comments of Geert Hofstede (IRIC and University of Limburg), Cor Lammers (University of Leiden), the anonymous reviewers and the participants in the workshop on 'Accounting and Culture' organized by the European Institute for Advanced Studies in Management, Amsterdam, June 1985. This paper forms part of an international project coordinated by Jamie Pratt, University of Washington, U.S.A.

QUESTIONS

1 The article by Soeters and Schreuder demonstrates that the international accounting firms differ in their organisational culture from national accounting firms. Compare this with Briston's views outlined in the previous article.

10

ACCOUNTING PRACTICES IN DEVELOPING COUNTRIES

Colonialism's legacy of inappropriate technologies

Mfandaidza R. Hove

For some time, many issues related to the transfer of technology from developed to developing countries have been considered, particularly in the literature regarding the economic development.[1] These issues primarily include the nature of the technology transferred, the process of the transfer, the major effects on the economies of the less developed countries (LDCs), and the resultant dependency of the LDCs on the developed countries.[2] Most, if not all, of such research studies focus, however, on manufacturing and scientific technology. The few that have mentioned the transfer of accounting technology to the LDCs have done so only briefly; their concern tended to be with the topical issue of the harmonization of international accounting practice.[3]

This paper discusses the transfer of accounting technology in relation to the following issues:

- The process by which the accounting technology of the developed country was transferred to the LDC (i.e., the channels of transfer)
- The problems created by such methods of technology transfer
- The role of such accounting technology in the economies of LDCs
- The appropriateness (or the lack of it) of existing accounting practice in the LDCs and solutions to the problem.

From the International Journal of Accounting (Fall 1986) pp 81–100.
Reprinted by permission of the University of Illinois.

MECHANISMS FOR THE TRANSFER OF DEVELOPED COUNTRY ACCOUNTING PRACTICE

This paper submits that existing accounting practice in almost all developing countries was imposed by developed countries initially through colonialism and then through the operations of transnational corporations, professional accounting institutes, and the special conditions in economic aid agreements, rather than in response to the societal needs of those countries.

Colonialism

This is perhaps the most effective way by which accounting technologies of developed countries were imposed on LDCs. As Fantl notes, '. . . just as the Roman Legions carried the language and culture of Rome Northward and Westward through Europe, Western capital is carrying its business practices into the third world.'[4] Briston supported this view when he argued,

> In a number of countries, of course, the British influence is very long standing, and almost all of the colonial territories in which any substantial degree of industrial development took place under British rule will have had imposed upon them a British Companies Act with the usual reporting and auditing requirements.[5]

In Zimbabwe, and quite possibly in the rest of Anglophone Africa, the British Companies Act of 1948 is the basis of corporate legislation, including financial disclosure requirements. Although the United Kingdom has had several amendments to that act (including those in 1967, 1876, and 1981), obviously to respond to changing requirements in the corporate environment, the act has largely remained the same in the former colonies. The consequences, particularly in regard to some business practices of transnational corporations in LDCs, can be disastrous.

That accounting technology was not only exported through colonialism, but that it was also imposed on LDCs without any consideration of the needs of these countries should be noted. Wilkinson argues this point.

> The accounting principles of one country have never been 'sold' to another country on the basis of convincing arguments in support of those principles . . . accounting principles of one country have moved to another country when two conditions have existed:
>
> 1 the second country had no organized body of accounting principles in the first place, and
> 2 large amounts of capital from the first country were invested in business in the second country, with the consequent ability on the

part of those investors to impose their own accounting requirements on the business.[6]

TRANSNATIONAL CORPORATIONS

The opening of new territories enabled international business to establish itself in those areas. Large amounts of capital were invested in enterprises in the 'new world' and, naturally, the owners in the developed countries required explanations as to the use to which these funds were put. As Seidler explains:

> . . . the strongest vehicle for the current international dissemination of accounting information is the Multinational Corporation and its associated activities. The vast majority of such enterprises have their most significant ties to the United States or the United Kingdom. The investors in these two countries, where the shares of these corporations are generally traded, have for many decades required audited financial statements, with the result that US- and UK-based independent accountants have developed worldwide practices.[7]

The transnational corporation has been the main channel of transfer of accounting and other types of technology, and this has in many ways benefited the LDCs; the fact this transfer was made to serve the interests of international business has not necessarily benefited the developing countries. No attempt was made to ascertain the information requirements of governments in LDCs for the operation of enterprises in their economies in general, and the operations of the transferring transnational corporations in particular. The motives of the transnational corporations were – and one could argue with some justification that they still are – to expand the frontiers of international business with the hope of maximizing the wealth of shareholders in the developed country. The literature on the harmonization of accounting notes that the international business community sees harmonization as a means to facilitate international trade and business, especially in the areas of capital flows[8] and reliability of information as a basis for foreign investment decision making.[9]

This does not imply that LDCs have not or will not benefit from increased international trade; the point is that if harmonization of accounting practice is to be achieved in the same way that accounting technology was transferred (i.e., no consideration for the needs of the LDCs), perhaps these countries should not participate in any harmonization arrangements. Stated differently, if harmonization efforts are not based on an explicit acceptance that the accounting needs of developing nations differ vastly from the services required of accountancy in advanced economies, accounting policy makers in LDCs must reject these efforts. As transnational corporations established subsidiaries in the LDCs, their accounting and auditing firms in the home countries also established offices in the developing countries. These firms not only practiced accounting and auditing in accordance with practices in the developed countries, but they also trained local people in those practices and, in certain cases, sent local people to the home country for training. Seidler summarizes the role of professional accounting firms in imposing the developed country's accounting technology.

> Slowly, but increasingly, the international offices of international firms have found a market for 'American Style' accounting services with local businesses. Some of this local practice development has been a result of the semicoercive efforts of international development organizations such as the World Bank, which typically require local loan applicants to provide American-style audited financial statements.[10]

Perera attempted to explain the complex link between the various channels used to transfer accounting technology.

> The entire accounting education and training in Sri Lanka is based on the British system. For example, the whole gamut of business activity was directed towards the plantation sector which was introduced to the economy by the British. Initially almost all the joint stock companies were owned by British investors and the required personnel for their management, including accountants, came from the UK. Therefore even though these firms were actually located in Sri Lanka, they were managed as if they were in Britain, and no attempt was made to develop an accounting system suitable for local conditions.[11]

Whether the links between all the transferring channels (colonialism, transnational corporations, professional accountancy institutes, and economic aid) can be adequately explained is perhaps not important; the significance must surely be that each of these channels assisted the transfer and, therefore, complemented one another in that process.

PROFESSIONAL ACCOUNTANCY INSTITUTES

In most, if not all, Anglophone developing countries, the following British accountancy bodies that are members of the Consultative Committee of Accountancy Bodies (CCAB) are represented in one form or another: the Institute of Chartered Accountants in England and Wales, the Institute of Chartered Accountants in Scotland, the Institute of Chartered Accountants in Northern Ireland, the Chartered Association of Certified Accountants, the Institute of Cost and Management Accountants, and the Chartered Institute of Public Finance and Accountancy. In this writer's own country, Zimbabwe, all of the bodies are represented, although the Institute of Cost and Management Accountants and the Chartered Association have only branches.

As colonialism expanded and facilitated the establishment of transnational corporation subsidiaries in the LDCs, a need developed for the necessary organizational infrastructure; accounting was one of several invaluable links required. Accordingly, British accountants immigrated to the colonies and formed the nucleus of the establishment of these bodies in the LDCs. Table 1, which is based on the work of Johnson and Caygill,[12] reports the growth in membership of British professional accountancy bodies throughout the empire and the commonwealth. These immigrant members subsequently formed the local branches indicated in Table 2; these in turn formed the foundation of autonomous professional bodies. South Africa, Zimbabwe, Nigeria, Ghana, Sri Lanka, and many other former U.K. colonies have a local Institute of Chartered Accountants. Before full autonomy was granted, however, the 'mother-country' body remained responsible for administering all of the examinations. Eventually, the branches were allowed to conduct examinations locally, under very strict control; for example, the three Chartered Institutes (England and Wales, Scotland, and Ireland) established an Overseas Accountancy Examinations Advisory Board, which

> . . . required evidence that the body requesting help in running examinations had a proper constitution and by-laws and could provide local organizers and examiners. The local body was asked to provide syllabuses and these were approved by the Board and its British examiners.[13]

Tables 3 and 4 indicate the growth in examination centers approved by U.K. bodies.[14]

As previously mentioned, most of these former branches now operate as autonomous bodies; however, British accountancy bodies continue to exert considerable influence in both the general administration of professional bodies in LDCs and in the style of the examining process. Gbenedio notes that in the first six years that it was administered, only eight people passed the Nigerian examinations for the Institute of Chartered Accountants.[15] He stated his belief that the high failure rate was due to the fact that the content of the examination relied heavily on its British counterpart, which presupposed comparable instruction. Whether or not such continued influence by British accounting bodies on organizations in LDCs is in the interests of these organizations will be discussed in a subsequent section. One of the major aims of those who argue for the perpetuation of this influence may well be the establishment of a commonwealth association of accountants which may, in turn, perpetuate the use of British accounting practices in the LDCs. As Johnson and Caygill observe:

> One of the dangers of these commonwealth organizations is that they will lead to attempts to establish standards and procedures which are essentially derived from British experience and have little relevance for

Table 1 Empire, Commonwealth, and Total Membership of British Professional Accountancy Bodies 1900, 1920, 1930, 1960

	Regional distribution				*Membership*		
					1	*2*	
	Africa	*Asia*	*Aus-tralia*	*Others*	*Empire and common wealth*	*Total*	*1 as % of 2*
1900s							
ICA Scot (1900)	11	6	5	3	25	710	4
ICAEW (1902)	19	25	14	5	63	2,813	2
SIAA (1904/5)	176	21	85	5	287	2,047	14
IMTA (1905/6)	2	—	1	—	3	328	1
LAA (ACCA) (1910)	—	17	—	4	21	1,110	2
	208	69	105	17	399	7,008	6
1920s							
ICA Scot (1920)	23	65	11	76	175	1,580	11
ICAEW (1921)	46	134	25	54	259	5,343	5
SIAA (1927)	162	97	93	30	382	4,629	8
IMTA (1920)	6	5	-	10	21	458	5
LAA (ACCA) (1929)	83	41	27	34	185	2,875	6
ICWA (1922)	-	-	-	-	(est) 16	422	4
	320	342	156	204	1,038	15,307	7
1930s							
ICA Scot (1940)	126	215	27	125	493	4,435	11
ICAEW (1939)	193	323	31	94	641	13,068	5
SIAA (1939)	453	229	39	37	758	7,509	10
IMTA (1938)	2	9	-	1	12	1,466	1
ACCA (1939)	144	139	23	69	375	6,075	6
ICWA (1938)	13	22	7	8	50	1,223	4
AIA (1937)	163	68	3	17	251	1,301	21
	1,094	1,005	130	351	2,580	35,077	7
1960s							
ICA Scot (1968)	266	140	86	378	870	8,006	11
ICAEW (1969)	1,438	617	170	668	2,893	45,500	6
IMTA (1969)	133	5	8	30	176	5,024	3
ACCA (1969)	698	199	113	366	1,376	12,140	11
ICWA (1969)	622	505	106	204	1,437	10,841	13
AIA (1969)	130	288	10	106	534	1,564	34
SCA (1967)	296	157	172	52	677	3,500	19
	3,583	1,911	665	1,804	7,963	86,575	9

ICS Scot – Institute of Chartered Accountants of Scotland
ICAEW – Institute of Chartered Accountants in England and Wales
SIAA – Society of Incorporated Accountants and Auditors
IMTA – Institute of Municipal Treasurers and Accountants
LAA – London Association of Accountants (later Association of Certified and Corporate Accountants, ACCA)
ICWA – Institute of Cost and Works Accountants
AIA – Association of International Accountants
SCA – Society of Commercial Accountants
Source: Johnson and Caygill

Table 2 Year of Establishment of Branches and Affiliated Societies of British Accountancy Bodies

Year	SIAA*	ICA	ACCA	ICWA	IMTA
1886	Victoria				
1894	S. Africa, W				
1902	S. Africa, N				
1903	N. South Wales	S. Africa			
1905	Montreal				
1910		Straits Settlement			
1913			Jo'burg, SA		
1923			India		
1928	S. Africa, F.				
1931	Bombay				
1932		India Burma Egypt			
1933	Bengal				
1936		Malay States	Malaya		
1941		N. Borneo			
1948			Kingston, Jamaica Trinidad		
1950			Hong Kong		
1952			Salisbury		
1954	Central Africa, Salisbury			S. Africa	
1955			Cyprus		
1956			Br. Guiana		
1957					N. Rhodesia (Zambia)
1960			Lagos		E. Africa
1961			Bahamas		S. Rhodesia
1967			Toronto Dar-es-Salaam		

Source: Johnson and Caygill.
*See Table 1 for an explanation of abbreviations.

developing countries. The genuine belief that 'high standards' are the greatest need should not, as is sometimes the case, be confused with a view that uniform standards are necessary throughout the commonwealth.[16]

THE ROLE OF ECONOMIC AID

The economic aid given to LDCs by international development organizations, such as the World Bank and the International Monetary Fund

Table 3 The Expansion of Examination Centers Operated by the Society and Association in the Empire and Commonwealth: 1900–35

Year	*Center*	*Year*	*Center*	*Year*	*Center*
1900	Melbourne	1920	Hyderabad	1935	Singapore
1905	Johannesburg		Ottawa		Kuala Lumpur
	Transvaal		Br. Columbia		Antigua
1910	Bombay	1925			
1915	Natal		Gwalior		
	Bihar		Gorakhpur		
	Calcutta		Tanganyika		
	Madras	1930	Nairobi		
	Lahore		Simla		
	Jamaica		Gibraltar		
	British		Nyasaland		
	Guiana		Selangor		
1920	Accra		Bulawayo		
	Lagos		Salisbury		
	Hong Kong		Trinidad		
	Queensland				
	Colombo				

Source: Johnson and Caygill.

(IMF), perhaps best illustrates how accounting practices in developed countries have been imposed on the Third World. The funds utilized for aid by these organizations are the private-sector funds of investors in developed countries. As a result, two important considerations apply to the manner in which these funds will be managed: (1) the accountability and stewardship

Table 4 Commonwealth Accountancy Examination Centers for British Qualifications, 1969

	Number of centers				
	ACCA	*Association of International Accountants*	*ICWA*	*IMTA*	*Society of Commercial Accountants*
Africa					
S. Africa & Rhodesia	3	2	12	—	—
Other	25	19	14	4	12
Asia					
India	—	2	5	—	1
Other	19	11	11	—	7
Australia	—	1	6	—	1
Europe & Near East	3	2	3	—	2
W. Hemisphere					
Canada	2	2	4	—	1
Other	14	6	4	—	2
Total	80	45	59	4	26

Source: Johnson and Caygill

concepts as understood during the emergence of the joint stock company apply because managers of the World Bank and the IMF must account for the use of the funds to the owners (investors in the developed country), and (2) these managers will seek to maximize shareholders' wealth. To comply with the accountability and stewardship concepts, managers must prepare periodic financial statements that are useful to their users (in this case, primarily the investors in the developed country); many factors determine what is 'useful' in this context. One critical factor is the need for such financial statements to be prepared according to the generally accepted accounting practices of the developed countries. Indeed, as noted previously, Seidler sees this as the '... semicoercive efforts ... which typically require local loan applicants to provide American-style audited financial statements.'[17] The author sees no justification for describing this and other conditions as the basis for granting a loan as 'semicoercive'; these conditions are in fact coercive and a definite channel for the imposition of the accounting practices of developed countries on LDCs.

Although the expectation of investors in the developed countries that the financial statements related to their investments be in a familiar language is not unreasonable, the value of such financial statements to authorities in the developing country in appraising the benefit of such aid to economic development is questionable. Developing countries may well be wise to insist on additional disclosure if this would improve the usefulness and relevance of the statements. Such methods of reporting have been recommended in some official pronouncements,[18] which, however, failed to receive widespread support.[19]

EXISTING ACCOUNTING PRACTICE IN LDCs

It is vitally important that those concerned with accounting practice not assume that what might be good accounting for the developed countries 'will automatically be economically relevant and good for the emerging nations and the process of development.'[20] Accounting is fundamentally a social institution; it provides both a basis of measurement and a method of controlling activities within an enterprise. As a result, '... in each country accounting should develop in a manner relevant to the society in which it exists.'[21] It must respond to the ever-changing needs of society and must reflect the social, political, legal, and economic conditions within which it operates. 'Its meaningfulness depends upon its ability to mirror these conditions.'[22] Although these points should not be difficult to understand and accept, they have not been implemented. Accounting practices in LDCs have largely remained those of the developed countries which imposed them initially. No evidence of any meaningful adaptation of practices in developed countries exists to suit local conditions, despite claims by some researchers.[23]

In Zimbabwe, the Companies Act is still based on the British Act of 1948, and the profession applies all international accounting standards (IAS) without modification. Similar practices have been adopted by other countries in the region.[24] It is important to recognize that IAS are issued by the International Accounting Standards Committee (IASC), a body created by developed countries. The extent to which developing countries with professional bodies that are members of the IASC are willing and able to ensure that local conditions are considered before they accept an international standard is not clear.[25] Such a situation is unlikely to prevail, as Samuels and Oliga argue:

> The International Accounting Standards Committee is a political body; its standards are those appropriate for industrial countries with a large private sector and a well-developed capital market. The main users of accounting reports in such countries are the shareholders, analysts, bankers and other businesses. Accounting reporting practices and standards are quite rightly designed to provide these users with the information they require.[26]

To the extent that no sophisticated capital markets exist in LDCs and that both local and national governments tend to be larger than the private sector, it is unlikely that these groups would also be the main users of financial statements in LDCs. The accounting problems in LDCs, therefore, include those related to the fact that accounting practice was imposed on them with no concern for their needs, as well as those that emanate from the fact that the developed countries themselves have still not properly defined the objectives of accounting. Thus, a technology has not only been arbitrarily imposed, but the imposed technology is inappropriate. The consequences for LDCs are serious.

Some Effects of the Imposition of Accounting Technology on LDCs

As with any other method developed by people to assist their efforts to make their environment a better place, accounting should develop in response to the needs of particular environments; accounting has not evolved in the industrialized world as an absolute science, however, but as a response to the economic and social factors prevailing in those parts of the world. This is the form of accounting that was imposed on LDCs. Information produced on the basis of such practice is not likely to give the correct signals to the governments of LDCs, nor is it likely to be relevant for their decision models or to the overall problem of economic development. How can it be when it was developed in accordance with the environmental needs of a different part of the world, as well as a society with different socioeconomic needs? If such differences are not recognized and accommodated in any development efforts, '. . . there is a serious danger that accountants will continue to propound techniques which evolved under circumstances which no longer exist and which are irrelevant or even positively harmful.'[27]

One such possible negative result of the continued imposition of inappropriate accounting practices of developed countries on LDCs is the inability of such practices to disclose information related to some of the potentially harmful practices of transnational corporations operating in LDCs. These unacceptable practices include transfer pricing techniques and technology transfer practices. Accounting, as presently practiced in the LDCs, is incapable of disclosing information that may enable the governments of LDCs to detect the use of unfair transfer pricing techniques, especially for taxation purposes.[28] Those who own the transnational corporations and export them to the Third World cannot realistically be expected to develop accounting practices to detect practices which are harmful to host LDC nations, although they are consistent with the global objective of maximization of profits. The developing countries themselves must ensure that their accounting practices mirror their societal needs.

Other areas that are of special interest to LDCs and that are not disclosed under current accounting practice include the effects of the activities of enterprises, particularly of transnational corporations, on environmental protection (e.g., water and air pollution), employment generation, and the effects of some of the products of the transnational corporations on the well-being of society; examples of the latter include the dangers inherent in using powdered infant formula in bottles. This practice is inappropriate technology in LDCs in view of the paucity of hygienic facilities essential for proper sterilization of the bottles used with the formula. Value-added reports suggested by the Corporate Report[29] may, as has been argued,[30] contain information more useful to LDC governments than the current information being published. These views are also well supported by the efforts of the United Nations[31] in attempting to solve the problem of the inadequacy of the disclosure practices of transnational corporations. It is very disturbing, however, that the United Nations Commission on Transnational Corporations is considering the international standardization of corporate reporting.[32] Although this paper does not present the arguments for and against the international standardization of corporate reporting, it must, however, note that any efforts to standardize corporate reporting are likely to fail because they cannot possibly consider all of the different social, political, legal, and economic environments (and therefore the reporting needs) of all countries.

The inability of existing accounting practice in the LDCs to report vital information, particularly on the activities of transnational corporations, is not the only detrimental effect of the imposed technology. Other affected areas include, inter alia, the accounting education and training procedures currently followed by LDCs, and the extent to which such procedures help to perpetuate the continued use of such inappropriate accounting technologies.

ACCOUNTING EDUCATION AND TRAINING POLICIES OF LDCs

This paper argued earlier that the role of British professional accountancy institutes in imposing their accounting practices on LDCs is significant. That same influence was exerted on accounting education and training methods in LDCs. The result, as we see today, is overemphasis on the technical aspects of accounting to an extent that almost always produces technicians incapable of understanding the debiting and crediting procedures, whether a better way exists, what the purpose of accounting is for their societies, and whether this purpose is being accomplished. Perera describes LDC accounting training policies as follows:

> . . . the approach to accounting has always been one that emphasizes the technical or mechanical aspects of accounting. Practically trained accountants tend to eliminate from serious consideration all abstracts and abstruse concepts of accounting possible because such complexities are not well received or understood by them.[33]

The source of such training policies was clearly the United Kingdom, as Scott observes: 'British accounting emphasizes practical aspects of accounting, as is especially evident in the requirement of extensive on-the-job training and lengthy, part-time self-study programs for public accounting asperants.'[34] No doubt, considerable changes in training methods have occurred since Scott's article was published, because institutes in the United Kingdom now prefer graduates as articulated clerks; this practice shortens the period of training from five to three years. The point, however, remains valid, especially in regard to the influence of British professional firms on the education and training methods adopted by LDCs. In his pioneering article, Scott suggests that an inter-disciplinary approach to the education and training of accountants may be better for LDCs; he described this 'liberal' approach as follows:

> The link between a liberal education for accountants and their ability to adapt accounting to a changing environment suggests the possibility that the most important requirements of the accounting of developing nations may not be to acquire more technical expertise in accounting. Perhaps more important is the education of accountants to be amendable to changing environments.[35]

Gbenedio comments on the extent to which British training methods have been adopted by most LDCs in his discussion of the Nigerian Institute of Chartered Accountants.[36] More examples are undoubtedly available, including the situation in Zimbabwe.[37] A matter that has further aggravated this situation is the existence of a multiplicity of professional accountancy bodies in LDCs. The observations of Johnson and Caygill concerning the imposition by all of the major British professional accountancy institutes of U.K. accounting practices on LDCs were mentioned earlier.[38] A fragmented profession can only make the task of solving Third World accounting problems more difficult. Levievre and Levievre argue that '. . . Cooperation among the groups [various professional institutes] is imperative since a young and developing nation can ill afford the folly of a divided accounting profession.'[39] As is the case in the United Kingdom where efforts to integrate the British profession have tended to be 'vetoed' by members of the ICAEW, in some developing nations,[40] the same groups have maintained a similar professional intransigence and extreme levels of parochialism regarding some LDCs.

POSSIBLE SOLUTIONS TO THE PROBLEM

The nature and extent of the problems discussed here indicate the need for action by LDCs. Such action must begin with a complete overhaul of the accounting profession in these countries. The precise action must be determined by the particular circumstances of the specific country concerning the level to which the profession has been developed; in some countries, no organized professional accountancy institute may exist.

In Zimbabwe, which has an organized profession represented by more than one professional accountancy body, immediate steps toward integration must be taken. A fragmented profession will achieve nothing unless it takes action that is guided by national interest. Talks on integration should focus on how this integration can best be achieved. Should one or two professional institutes continue to be intransigent and fail to recognize the issues, the government must, as the custodian of the national interest, intervene. Governments in the LDCs cannot continue to assume that because economic actions are taken to speed economic development, accounting development will somehow automatically follow. Indeed, it has been argued that 'formal assessment of the role of accounting in the developing country does not exist despite its importance in the evaluation of aggregate economic performance, development programming, private enterprise development and the establishment of capital market.'[41] One explanation for this situation could be the extent to which the British belief in the need for the profession to regulate itself has affected accountants and governments in the LDCs.

Involvement of the governments in LDCs is crucial in those nations where the profession has not yet been formally organized. The governments must take the initiative and assist financially in establishing an indigenous professional accountancy institute.

After ensuring that an organized accountancy body (achieved either by the integration of various institutes or the establishment of a new body) exists, the next step must be to determine what the accounting objectives in the individual LDCs should be. Unlike other suggestions,[42] this author recommends that the accounting objectives of *each* developing nation, not those of *all* developing nations, should be determined. In addition, these objectives should not be determined by the International Accounting Standards Committee, the American Accounting Association, or the United Nations, for example; they should be determined by the natives of those developing countries on the basis of the legal, economic, and social conditions there in accordance with the understanding within each country of the basic economic facts underlying business transactions. The usual problems inherent in the process of determining objectives for any organization, not least of which is the significant influence of value judgments, will undoubtedly apply, but at least these are not cross-cultural value judgments. The determination of accounting objectives should lead, among other aspects, to the specification of enterprise information requirements that are consistent with the development needs of the LDC. This is likely to increase disclosure requirements, particularly for transnational corporations.

With respect to the education and training of accountants, broad-based degree programs with the objective to produce 'thinking' people rather than 'number crunchers' are needed. In addition, steps should be taken to develop lower level accounting programs (technician level courses); these are not only in great demand in most LDCs due to the small size of most enterprises there, but are also relatively inexpensive to administer. In Zimbabwe, accounting technicians trained by the Zimbabwe Association of Accounting Technicians are filling critical positions in both the private and public sectors of the economy.

CONCLUSION

This paper has argued that an examination of the sources of existing accounting systems in developing countries reveals that those systems were primarily imposed by powerful foreign investors or extended from the home to the host countries through the influence of transnational corporations, foreign aid, and professional accountancy institutes of developed countries. Accounting information produced on the basis of such systems is not relevant and useful for the decision models of governments of LDCs. In some cases, such as the system's failure to report some practices of transnational corporations, the consequences can be disastrous. The accounting education and training policies of LDCs have also been based on those of developed countries which, in the case of Anglophone developing nations, have remained largely technique oriented. Those who advocate the standardization of accounting practice internationally will not solve the problem; only the nationals of the LDCs themselves can and should find ways to correct the situation. Developed countries can, however, assist in providing consultancy services and financial assistance for whatever accounting research projects must be conducted as part of the process of adapting existing accounting practice to suit the needs of developing countries.

NOTES

1 For a list of research studies on technology transfer, see Farock J. Contractor and Tagi Sagafi-nejad, 'International Technology Transfer: Major Issues and Policy Responses,' *Journal of International Business Studies* (Fall 1981), 113–35.
2 See, for example, United Nations Conference on Trade and Development (UNCTAD), 'Major Issues in the Transfer of Technology to Developing Countries: A Case Study of Chile' (New York: United Nations, 1974); H. W. Wallender 'Technology Transfer and Management in the Developing Countries' (Cambridge, Mass.: Ballinger, 1977); J. S. Hill and R. R. Stil, 'Cultural Effects of Technology Transfer by Multinational Corporations in Less Developed Countries,' *Columbia Journal of World Business* (Summer 1980), 40–51.
3 These include T. L. Wilkinson, 'United States Accounting as Viewed by Accountants of Other Countries,' *International Journal of Accounting* (Fall 1965), 3–14; Lee J. Seidler, 'Nationalism and International Transfer of Accounting Skills,' *International Journal of Accounting* (Fall 1969), 35–45; Gerhard G. Mueller, 'Accounting Principles Generally Accepted in the United States versus Those Generally Accepted Elsewhere,' *International Journal of Accounting* (Spring 1968), 91–103; Irving L. Fantl, 'The Case against International Uniformity,' *Management Accounting* (May 1971), 13–16; and J. M. Samuels and J. C. Oliga, 'Accounting Standards in Developing Countries,' *International Journal of Accounting* (Fall 1978), 105–20.
4 Fantl, 'International Uniformity,' 13–16.
5 R. J. Briston, 'The Evolution of Accounting in Developing Countries,' *International Journal of Accounting* (Fall 1978), 105–20.
6 Wilkinson, 'United States Accounting,' 3–14.
7 Seidler, 'Nationalism and the International Transfer of Accounting Skills,' 35–45.
8 Shawki M. Farag, 'The Problem of Performance Evaluation in International Accounting,' *International Journal of Accounting* (Fall 1974), 45–53.
9 Belverd E. Needles, Jr., 'Implementing a Framework for the International Transfer of Accounting Technology,' *International Journal of Accounting* (Fall 1976), 44–62.
10 Seidler, 'Nationalism and the International Transfer of Accounting Skills,' 35–45.
11 H. B. Perera, 'Accounting and Its Environment in Sri Lanka,' *Abacus* (June 1975), 86–96.
12 T. J. Johnson and M. Caygill, 'The Development of Accountancy Links in the Commonwealth,' *Accounting & Business Research* (Spring 1971), 155–73.
13 Ibid.
14 Ibid.
15 P. O. Gbenedio, 'The Challenge to the Accounting Profession in a Developing Country: The Nigerian Case' (Ph.D. dissertation, University of Cincinnati, August 1977).

16 Johnson and Caygill, 'The Development of Accountancy Links,' 155–73.
17 Seidler, 'Nationalism and the International Transfer of Accounting Skills,' 35–45.
18 See, for example, the recommendations of the Accountants International Study Group in Its International Financial Reporting Study Number 11 (Toronto, Canada: AISG, 1975).
19 See criticisms of these recommendations by Frederick D. S. Choi, 'Primary-Secondary Reporting: A Cross-Cultural Analysis,' *International Journal of Accounting* (Fall 1980), 83–104.
20 Adolf J. H. Enthoven, *Accountancy and Economic Development Policy* (Amsterdam: North Holland, 1973).
21 Michael N. Chetkovich, 'An Appeal for Unity in Establishing Financial Accounting Standards,' *International Journal of Accounting* (Fall 1972), 99–107.
22 Mueller, 'Accounting Principles,' 91–103.
23 See, for example, claims regarding the state of accounting in Singapore by Roger Y. W. Tang and Esther Tse, 'Accounting Technology Transfer to Less Developed Countries and the Singapore Experience,' *Columbia Journal of World Business* (Summer 1986), 85–95.
24 The writer is familiar with practices in Botswana, Lesotho, Swaziland, Malawi, and Zambia. In the case of Zambia, the writer has acted as External Examiner for the University of Zambia at Ndola for two years.
25 In the case of Zimbabwe, the Institute of Chartered Accountants of Zimbabwe is a member of the International Accounting Standards Committee. The writer is in touch with this body, as well as with some of its committees, including the Accounting Practices and Education Committees, in his capacity as chairman of the Department of Accountancy at the University of Zimbabwe. The writer is not aware of any changes made to any of the international accounting standards – all of which have been adopted – other than those of cosmetic nature that relate to differences in terminology used.
26 Samuels and Oliga, 'Accounting Standards in Developing Countries,' 69–88.
27 Briston, 'The Evolution of Accounting in Developing Countries,' 105–20.
28 Between February 1984 and April 1986, the writer served as a member of a Commission of Inquiry into Taxation appointed by the President of the Republic of Zimbabwe on the recommendation of the prime minister, chaired by Professor R. J. Chelliah, an internationally known taxation expert then director of the Indian Institute of Public Finance. In giving his evidence before the Commission and in response to a question by the writer concerning mechanisms available to the Department Tax to detect any unfair transfer pricing practices of transnational corporations, the Commissioner of Tax said that it was impossible for his department to detect this given current reporting practices.
29 *The Corporate Report* (London: Accounting Standards Committee, 1975).
30 See, for example, Dhia D. AlHashim, 'International Dimensions in Accounting and Implications for Developing Nations,' *Management International Review*, vol. **22**, (1982).
31 United Nations Economic and Social Council, *Some Aspects of Corporate Accounting and Reporting of Special Interest to Developing Countries* (New York: United Nations, 1976); and *International Standards of Accounting and Reporting for Transnational Corporations* (New York: United Nations, 1977).
32 United Nations Commission on Transnational Corporation, *Towards International Standardization of Corporate Accounting and Reporting* (New York: United Nations, 1982).
33 M. H. B. Perera, 'Accounting and Its Environment in Sri Lanka,' *Abacus* (June 1975), 86–96.

34 George M. Scott, 'Price Enterprise Accounting in Developing Nations,' *International Journal of Accounting* (Fall 1968), 52–65.
35 Ibid.
36 Gbenedio, 'The Challenge to the Accounting Profession.'
37 In Zimbabwe, entry into the profession is mainly on the basis of a Bachelor of Accounting qualification offered by the Department of Accountancy at the University of Zimbabwe. On graduation, holders of this degree need serve only three years of articles with a firm of chartered accountants and have only one professional section of the Institute's examinations (i.e., the Final Qualifying Examination) to take. This means that the Bachelor of Accountancy degree program must be structured in a manner to fit the Institute's program; indeed, this has been the case since the degree was first offered in the early seventies. This means that the more technical aspects of accounting have been emphasized almost to the total exclusion of the more intellectual aspects of the subject. The structure has always stressed the traditional auditing and financial reporting aspects of accounting. Beginning with the academic year in March 1986, however, the writer has been instrumental in introducing major structural changes to the program. These changes move from the traditional approach and emphasize the importance of adopting an interdisciplinary approach and of introducing more courses in management accounting (a vital course for LDCs), public-sector accountancy, and general management.
38 Johnson and Caygill, 'The Development of Accountancy Links,' 155–73.
39 T. Levievre and C. Levievre, 'Accounting in the Third World,' *Journal of Accountancy* (January 1978), 72–75.
40 In Zimbabwe, for the least three years, the writer, in the capacity as chairman of the Zimbabwe branch of the Chartered Association of Certified Accountants, pioneered and participated in discussions with all of the other professional accountancy bodies with a view to integrating the profession. Members of the Institute of Chartered Accountants of Zimbabwe, as in the United Kingdom, voted against integration.
41 Needles, 'International Transfer of Accounting Technology,' 44–62.
42 See, for example, Financial Accounting Standards Board, *Statement of Financial Accounting Concepts No. 1*, 'Objectives of Financial Reporting by Business Enterprises' (Stamford, Conn.: FASB, 1978).

QUESTIONS

1 Explain the processes by which the accounting approaches of the developed countries have come to be applied, in Hove's view inappropriately, in the developing world.

Part II

SOME SPECIFIC NATIONAL EXAMPLES

FOREWORD

In the study of international accounting consideration of specific countries illustrates the rich variety in national practices. The papers selected here do not claim to offer a comprehensive overview of any one country's accounting system. Our objective is to offer illustrations of a range of aspects of distinctive national accounting practices across a range of types of country.

Adams (1992) compares the US and the UK in the light of the IASC's standards and proposals. This paper is of particular interest in comparing two countries which are traditionally considered to be similar in accounting practices and particularly close to the formulation of international standards.

An interesting perspective on accounting in the USA is revealed by Slepian (1985). This paper explains how, in response to a perceived 'economic consequences' threat implicit in a proposed change in accounting regulation, a vigorous process of lobbying successfully resisted the proposal. The article is of particular significance because:

(a) It shows how tax factors can affects US accounting regulation.
(b) It addresses the effects of accounting regulation over a range of sizes of business, as opposed to the focus on public listed companies normally found in the literature on accounting in the USA.

Haller (1992) offers a full discussion of the link between tax regulation and accounting regulation in Germany. It is particularly interesting to note in this paper:

(i) that the German authorities have contrived to implement the EC fourth directive without any departure from their traditional approach.
(ii) The justification for the tax-accounting link in the context of the general use of German accounts.

In Eastern Europe new accounting regulations have to be drafted rapidly in response to the needs of a market economy. Jaruga (1992) reports on the range of influences affecting accounting developments in Poland.

Outside North America and Europe different economic environments create other distinct accounting issues:

(a) Jagetia & Nwadike (1983) discuss Nigeria's distinctive accounting needs.
(b) Small developing countries have to chose which set of accounting standards to adopt, since it is unduly costly to develop their own. Mwesigye (1988) considers this problem in the context of Papua New Guinea.
(c) Gao (1992) looks at how the Chinese accounting profession is responding to the challenge of a rapidly developing economy.

11

THE IASC'S COMPARABILITY PROJECT

Will it bridge the divide between UK and US GAAP?

Carol Adams

The prime objective of the IASC's comparability and improvements project is to reduce the number of alternative treatments allowed in the International Accounting Standards (IAS) issued to date.

E32 was issued in January 1989, and as paragraph 3 states: 'This Exposure Draft is the first stage in the improvements process. Its purpose is to set out proposals for the removal of free choices of accounting treatments presently permitted in International Accounting Standards. Such free choices were necessary in the past to gain acceptance of certain Standards.'

Most International Accounting Standards currently have two acceptable alternative treatments. According to Arthur Wyatt, chairman of the IASC, this situation arose because of the necessity to ensure that the required 75 per cent of the 14 voting members of the board voted in favour.

According to Wyatt, the project also aims to:

- Provide additional guidance beyond that in the standard
- Look at disclosure requirements to see if they include all necessary rules and eliminate those that are unnecessary.

The main impetus for these changes is the increase in cross-border financing. Both the IASC and The International Organisation of Securities Commissions (IOSCO) are aware of the need to tighten financial reporting regulations for companies wishing to raise capital in (initially) the countries that are members of both IOSCO and the IASC.

From Certified Accountant (July 1992) pp 39–41.
Reprinted by permission of the Chartered Association of Certified Accountants.

Table 1 Comparison of US and UK GAAP with the proposed I-GAAP (See end for meaning of abbreviations)

Issue	*E32 (or IAS)*	*US GAAP*	*UK GAAP*
Inventory			
AP	E32	ARB 43	SSAP 9, CA 85
PT	FIFO & WAC	FIFO, WAC & LIFO	FIFO & WAC
AAT			LIFO & base stock (Note 1)
NA	Base stock formula and LIFO (Note 1)		
Correction of fundamental errors resulting from accounting policy changes			
AP	E32	APB 20, FAS 32	SSAP 6
PT	Adjust opening retained earnings and amend comparative information	Cumulative effect of change to be shown as a separate item in profit and loss account	Adjust opening retained earnings and amend comparative information
AAT	Include in income of the current period and present amended pro forma comparative information	In certain circumstances restatement of prior year figures is allowed	SSAPs 22 & 24 give alternative treatments for goodwill and pension costs
NA		Restatement of prior year figures except in certain circumstances	
Research and Development costs			
AP	E32 (as amended by Statement of Intent, July 1990)	FAS 2, 68 & 86	SSAP 13, CA 85
PT	Recognise as assets when they meet specified criteria and as expenses when they do not	Write off immediately	
AAT		Recognise as assets when specified criteria are met. (US criteria are most restrictive)	
Recognition of profit and revenue on long-term contracts			
AP	E32	ARB 45	SSAP 9
PT	Percentage of completion	Percentage of completion and completed contract method	Percentage of completion

NA	Completed contract method		Completed contract method
Valuation of property, plant and equipment			
AP	E32	APB 6 & ARB 43	SSAP 12, CA 85
PT	Cost	Cost	Cost
AAT	Valuation		Valuation
NA		Valuation	
Foreign currency translation			
AP	E32	FAS 52	SSAP 20, CA 85
Exchange rate for translating profit and loss account			
PT	At date of transaction or average rate	At time of recognition or weighted average rate	Average rate of closing rate (Note 2)
NA	Closing rate		
Subsidiaries operating in hyper inflationary economies			
PT	Restate financial statements before translation	Temporal method	Restate financial statements before translation
NA	Translate financial statements without prior restatement		
Business combinations			
AP	E32	APB 16	SSAP 14 & 23, CA 85
PT	Purchase method for acquisitions, pooling of interests method for uniting of interests (Note 3)		Acquisition and merger accounting are not necessarily mutually exclusive (Note 4)
NA	Purchase method for uniting of interest		
Goodwill			
AP	E32	APB 17 only	SSAP 22
PT	Capitalise and amortise over a maximum period of 20 years	Capitalise and amortise over a maximum period of 40 years	Immediate write-off against reserves
AAT			Amortise over useful economic life
NA	Immediate write-off	Immediate write-off	

Table 1 Comparison of US and UK GAAP with the proposed I-GAAP (contd.)

Issue	*E32 (or IAS)*	*US GAAP*	*UK GAAP*
Borrowing costs			
AP	E32 (as amended by Statement of Intent, July 1990)	FAS 34 as amended by FAS 42, 58 & 62	CA 85
PT	Write off immediately *OR* Capitalise if it takes a substantial period to get the asset ready for use	Capitalisation compulsory for certain assets	Capitalise or write off immediately
Dividends			
AP	IAS 10	Reg. S-X	SSAP 17, CA 85
PT	Provide for or disclose proposed dividends	No provision for dividends undeclared at the year end	Provision must be made for dividends relating to the financial year although not declared until after it ends
Extraordinary items			
AP	IAS 8	APB 30 & 16	SSAP 6, CA 85
PT	Refers to 'unusual' items only – no definition of exceptional or extraordinary items	US and UK definitions are similar, but the US definition is less liberally applied with regard to the treatment of gains and losses on disposals of businesses, ie, in the US they are treated as exceptional items	

Notes to Table

AP – Authoritative pronouncements: PT – Preferred treatment: AAT – Allowed alternative treatment: NA – Not allowed

Notes:

1 Although LIFO and base stock are allowed by CA 86 in the UK, they are not allowed by SSAP 9 or the Inland Revenue and so are rarely used. In the US LIFO is allowed by the Internal Revenue Service and is in widespread use. LIFO was an allowed alternative treatment in the original E32, but was eliminated in the IASC's Statement of Intent July 1990.

2 Most UK companies use the closing date.

3 The IASC and US restrictions on the use of the pooling of interests (merger accounting in UK terminology) method differ.

4 ED 48 seeks to make merger and acquisition accounting mutually exclusive although there are still significant differences from the conditions that have to be satisfied for the use of pooling accounting in the US.

Wyatt claims that the AICPA, along with other accounting bodies, has agreed in writing to put pressure on the standard-setting bodies in their countries to move toward international standards.

Not only has IOSCO given the IASC its backing in this project, but, says Wyatt, if it is happy with the quality of the IASC changes (and the degree of adherence they command), IOSCO will also consider making its own changes. These will oblige securities regulators in countries to require that the financial statements of companies engaged in raising capital in IOSCO member countries comply with International Accounting Standards.

BARRIERS TO CHANGE

However, the IASC faces a problem. There is likely to be considerable opposition to its comparability project, particularly in areas where countries now find that they are not in compliance.

The table compares UK and US GAAP with E32 (as updated by the Statement of Intent, July 1990), or existing IAS where no amendment has been proposed. The US is not in compliance with IASC recommendations in respect of the following:

- The cumulative effect of changes resulting from the correction of fundamental errors that occurred because of accounting policy changes are shown as a separate item in the profit and loss account
- The completed contract method is used for the recognition of profit and revenue on long-term contracts
- The temporal method is used for the translation of the profit and loss accounts of subsidiaries operating in hyper inflationary economies
- The LIFO method of stock valuation is allowed.

The UK is not in compliance in that:

- Most UK companies use the closing rate method for translating the profit and loss account of foreign subsidiaries
- Acquisition and merger accounting are not mutually exclusive (see table, Note 4)
- The preferred treatment of goodwill is immediate write-off against reserves.

Dennis Beresford, chairperson of FASB in the US, argues that to get full comparability between US GAAP and IAS, the following differences would have to be eliminated (see 'Internationalisation of Accounting Standards', *Accounting Horizons*, March 1991):

- US pronouncements cover more topics
- US pronouncements cover topics in greater depth
- US pronouncements are accompanied by a large body of common

practice, which is an integral part of US GAAP, although not covered by formal pronouncements.

He is concerned about the disadvantage to domestic registrants on US stock exchanges if they were to be forced to comply with US GAAP, while foreign registrants had to comply only with IAS. Noting some of the specific differences between E32 and US GAAP, he does not say what FASB's response will be, but says that it will be seeking advice from its Advisory Council and all its constituents as it proceeds.

UK REACTION

The technical director of the Accounting Standards Board, Allan Cook, has said the ASB is watching the progress of the comparability project with great interest. He argues that the project will not be successful if it is expected to carry as much detail as the national standard setting process, but considers that the greater level of generality does not mean that International Accounting Standards are not useful.

International Accounting Standards figure in the discussions of national standard setting bodies when evolving their own standards and in the discussions of international bodies, such as the OECD and the EC, and as such, they should reflect best practice.

The major areas of difference between UK GAAP and E32 are under review. Cook does not rule out the possibility of differences remaining, but argues that in such a case, the ASB would enter into further discussions with the IASC.

TOO WIDE A GAAP?

The comparability project will not achieve its objective of reducing the number of allowed alternatives unless it gets a high degree of support from the US and UK accounting bodies. If it does not successfully reduce the number of allowed alternatives, it will not get the support of the major stock exchanges.

One of the strongest criticisms of the IASC has been the over-representation of the interests of developed nations with a resulting tendency to address only those issues relating to advanced economic environments.

The relevance of International Accounting Standards to less developed countries has been questioned by many and the comparability project will do nothing to allay their fears.

QUESTIONS

1 Given the common use of the term 'Anglo-American' to describe an

accounting approach, how significant are the contrasts that Adams identifies between US and UK accounting rules.

12

HOW A PROPOSED ACCOUNTING CHANGE THREATENED AN INDUSTRY

Differences in accounting theory almost soured Hawaii's sugar and pineapple industry.

Steven L. Slepian

Issues of accounting principle can and do affect our personal lives. The pineapple and sugarcane growers of Hawaii can testify to that.

Industry practice had long ago accepted the use of an accounting method in which the costs associated with growing crops are expensed as incurred rather than being inventoried. Proposed changes by the Auditing Standards Division of the American Institute of CPAs would have disallowed this method, thereby threatening a special tax exemption previously negotiated by the industry with the IRS. Loss of this special exemption would have been disastrous for the growers, residents, and state of Hawaii.

Responding to the threat of this proposed change in accounting methods, industry accountants prepared a persuasive issues paper that documented the industry position and refuted those arguments developed by the Agribusiness Special Committee of the Auditing Standards Division in support of the change. Although these events represented, potentially, the most important news story in the state, they went unreported by the general media.

From Management Accounting (November 1985) pp 47–51.
Reprinted from Management Accounting.

ACCOUNTING PRACTICES VARY

Concerned because of the lack of guidance from professional pronouncements, and the many different accounting methods in use, the Agribusiness Special Committee (the Committee) of the Auditing Standards Division of the AICPA published in July 1981 an Issues paper titled 'Accounting by Agricultural Producers and Agricultural Cooperatives.' One of the five issues discussed in the paper was accounting for inventories by agricultural producers including the issue of accounting for growing crops.

In preparing its report, the Committee surveyed published financial reports and found that there were many different methods of accounting for growing and harvested crops. Some of the methods involved: 'charging costs to operations when incurred, including crop development costs in deferred charges until amortized, stating costs in balance sheet at unchanging amounts substantially less than costs incurred and charging all current costs to operations when incurred, or deferring all costs and writing them off at harvest or, for perennial crops, over the estimated productive life of the planting.'[1]

In addition, the Committee found that there was nothing authoritative or recorded in accounting literature that specifically addressed the problem of accounting for growing crops although accounting for inventories in general had been previously examined by Accounting Research Bulletin 43, 'Restatement and Revision of Accounting Research Bulletins,' Accounting Principles Board Statement 4, 'Basic Concepts and Accounting Principles Underlying Financial Statements of Business Enterprises,' and Accounting Research Study 13, 'The Accounting Basis of Inventories.' The Committee reviewed these pronouncements focusing on permissible exceptions to the lower of cost or market rule.

- *Accounting Research Bulletin 43, Chapter 4, Statement 9.* . . . any other exceptions (other than precious metals) must be justified by inability to determine appropriate approximate costs, immediate marketability at quoted market price, and the characteristic of unit interchangeability.
- *Accounting Principles Board Statement 4, Chapter, 6, Paragraph 152.* . . . Sometimes revenue is recognized at the completion of production and before a sale is made. Examples include certain precious metals and farm products with assured sales prices. The assured price, the difficulty in some situations of determining costs of products on hand, and the characteristic of unit interchangeability, are reasons given to support this exception.
- *Accounting Research Study 13, Chapter 9.* . . . A value market basis is acceptable (for inventory valuation) if the products have immediate marketability at quoted market prices that cannot be influenced by the producer, have characteristics of unit interchangeability, and have relatively insignificant costs of disposal. The accounting basis of those

kinds of inventories should be their realizable value, calculated on the basis of quoted market prices less estimated direct costs of disposal.

TROUBLE IN PARADISE

Surveying accountants in the agribusiness industry, the Committee learned that respondents generally favored accounting for harvested crops at market value rather than at cost. The reasons most often cited were: many producers cannot determine a meaningful cost figure; users of the financial statements of agricultural producers were most often lenders concerned with the value of collateral pledged or to be pledged against loans (and thus would best be served if inventories were stated at market); management needed to identify separately the gains and losses attributable to the growing cycle as opposed to the marketing function, information not represented when inventories are valued at cost; and the use of market value was long established in practice.

In determining its position on the issue of accounting for inventories of *harvested* crops, the Committee examined the conditions necessary for an exception to the lower-of-cost or market rule as detailed by the authoritative sources. Members found, in contradiction with the requirements, that 'costs are either available or can be determined with acceptable accuracy,' and that 'restrictions exist that affect the ultimate realization of quoted market prices of agricultural products including variations in grade and quantity, distance from central markets, and hazards of shipment.' The third necessary condition of unit interchangeability was not addressed.

In a compromise between practice and theory, however, the paper concluded that although the lower-of-cost or market was the general rule, 'an agricultural producer should be permitted to account for harvested crops and livestock held for sale at market, less estimated costs of disposal, when all the following conditions exist:

- The product has a reliable market price that is readily available.
- The product has relatively insignificant and predictable costs of disposal.
- The product is available for immediate delivery.'

Regarding the issue of accounting for *growing* crops, the Committee did not specifically refute the various methods currently in practice and reported on as a result of their survey of published financial statements. Nor were arguments offered in support of a preferred method. However, the theoretical support for charging costs to operations when incurred, the method used by the Hawaiian plantations, was judged to be nonpersuasive.

Without further discussion, both the Committee and AcSEC concluded decisively that growing crops *should be inventoried* (at the lower-of-cost or market) by the vote of 13 YES, 1 NO, and 12 Yes, 1 ABSTAIN, respectively. This recommendation was repeated in paragraph 38 of the subsequent exposure draft, Proposed Statement of Position, Accounting by Agricultural Producers and Agricultural Cooperatives, issued on September 10, 1982. To the community of Hawaiian agribusiness accountants this seemingly innocuous conclusion threatened the demise of their industry and the fiscal soundness of the state of Hawaii.

HISTORY OF PLANTATION ACCOUNTING

Pineapple and sugarcane are Hawaii's dominant agricultural products. Both are strongly tied to the folklore as well as the economic development of the state. Many local families are descendents of plantation laborers who contracted to work the fields during the 19th century. Plantations covering thousands of acres have existed on all of the major islands, and because of the special nature of their unique geography the Hawaiian plantations are unlike those found anywhere else in the United States.

Defined by the interplay of mountains and sea, the fields range in size from a few acres to many hundreds of acres and in elevation from sea level to over 2,500 feet. Rainfall varies from 20 to 120 inches per year depending upon field location. Unlike the U.S. mainland freezing never occurs, making possible the cultivation of superior strains requiring two-years' growth to maturity. Operations are thus continuous throughout the year, permitting greater use of plantation assets. These unique conditions result in the production of two to three times the tonnage of sugar per acre than for other domestic sugar producing states.

The history of plantation accounting in Hawaii includes the use of two distinct methods, known in the local industry as the 'deferred crop' method and the 'annual accrual' method. Under the former method all plantation costs, both direct and indirect, are deferred (inventoried at the lower of cost or market) until crops are harvested. Under the latter, these costs are charged to operations in the year incurred. The deferred crop method was the prevalent method until the turn of the century.

Conversion to the annual accrual method for financial statement purposes began around 1913 and for tax purposes in 1937. A three-year study of the relative merits of the two systems prepared by the New York consulting firm of Booz, Allen and Hamilton in 1953 recommended the adoption of the annual accrual method and all but extinguished the use of the deferred crop method from use in Hawaii.

In 1954, several of the plantations sought and subsequently received tentative approval from the IRS to change to the annual accrual method for tax purposes. Final approval was delayed, however, because of questions posed by the Joint Committee and the IRS concerning the appropriateness of this method for financial statement purposes.

To provide a third party opinion, another study was undertaken in 1957, this time authored by Weldon Powell, first director of the Accounting Principles Board. The study concluded that, in the case of the Hawaiian plantations, the annual accrual method was the more appropriate method for financial statement purposes. This position was subsequently embraced by the chief accountant of the SEC, and, shortly thereafter, the IRS issued its blanket approval for Hawaiian plantations.

In 1975, Congress proposed significant changes to the tax code that would have required corporations engaged in farming to use the deferred crop method. By the summer of 1976, however, it appeared likely that the Senate Finance Committee would delete this restriction from the bill, soon to become the Tax Reform Act of 1976. The IRS responded immediately to this threat of deletion by issuing its own similar ruling requiring the use of the deferred crop method. Additionally, it rescinded all previously issued rulings, some dating back to 1921, which had allowed the use of the annual accrual method. Included in this call-back were those favorable rulings previously issued to Hawaiian producers.

In an act of self-preservation, the plantations negotiated an arrangement with the IRS whereby, in return for supporting Congress' general capitalization rule for others, the industry would be granted a special exemption from the deferred crop restriction. This special exemption is now embodied in the Code as Section 447 (g). The allowance of this exemption was predicated on the recognition of the annual accrual method by generally accepted accounting principles as an acceptable method for financial statement purposes. The conclusion reached by the Proposed Statement of Position reversed this acceptance. Professional endorsement of the annual accrual method would thus vanish, leaving no basis for the special exemption.

DEPRESSION PREDICTED

To evaluate the effect that the proposed change in accounting treatment would have on the sugarcane industry, a computer simulation model was developed by Mr. Joe H. McDonald, controller of C. Brewer and Co., Limited, and chairman of the Hawaiian Sugar Planters Association Accounting Committee. The model used actual industry production, market realization and cost data for the period 1970 through 1981 and, as such, 'the results (were) not strictly theoretical but rather a retrospective demonstration of the disastrous consequences that would have resulted if the industry had been forced to adopt a (deferred) crop method in 1970.'[2]

Among the key assumptions underlying the model were that approximately 35% of each year's plantation costs were related to planting and cultivation, i.e., the amount to be inventoried (rather than expensed) under the deferred crop method, and that the IRS would allow for a deferred tax basis representing the initial inventory to be established with the tax bite spread over 10 years. The financial impact of such a change, according to the model, was a devastating $170 million cash outflow, comprehending tax payments, higher dividends due to increased reported earnings, and financing costs associated with replacing the loss of funds.

The study concluded that if such a change were to be enacted in 1985, the total cost to the industry might reach $400 million because of inflation over the 10-year period. According to Mr. McDonald, 'no agency would elect to continue employing its lands in sugar if the alternative were to make additional investment to accommodate an accounting change. In short, the perceived value of sugar's future in Hawaii is insufficient to support a growing crop inventory on the industry's balance sheet. Should this change go through, it would almost certainly trigger swift and sudden death to the state's 150-year-old cash cow.'

Two years prior to the development of this model, in December of 1981, the First Hawaiian Bank released a study prepared by its Senior Vice President and Chief Economist Dr. Thomas K. Hitch titled *How the Collapse of the Sugar Industry Would Impact on Hawaii's Economy*. The not-so-surprising conclusion reached by Dr. Hitch was that a sudden closing of the sugar industry would be devastating to the state's economy and would result in the almost complete collapse of the neighbor island economies.[3] The statistics developed in this study were subsequently updated in a short presentation prepared by Peat, Marwick, Mitchell & Co. to include the pineapple industry as well, and are summarized below:

Jobs employed by these industries	14,400
Nonindustry jobs dependent upon these industries	32,926
Total	47,326

Personal income attributable to these industries	$733,000K
Drop in employment if industries perish	13%
Percentage of state income	14%
Decline in general fund tax revenues	17%
State unemployment rate if industries perish	18%

The above analysis grossly underestimates the all encompassing effect that such a collapse would have had on the people of Hawaii. Additional welfare-related costs alone would strain the state's decreased resources to the limit. An increase in the crime rate, virtually unavoidable under such conditions of economic duress would hurt Hawaii's tourist business and thus further erode cash in-flows. Psychologically, its residents would be in shock. A statewide depression similar to what happened in the 1930s would not be an unrealistic scenario.

Needless to say, the group of accounting professionals representing the pineapple and sugarcane growers were concerned with the requirements of the Proposed Statement of Position. There was more at stake here than differences in accounting theory; the economic well being of an entire state was threatened. It was decided that the Committee should be made aware of the far-reaching consequences of its proposal and persuaded to limit the applicability of its pronouncement on growing crop inventories to nontropical growers.

As these events were unfolding, the Honolulu news media made no reference to Proposed Statements of Position, deferrals, accruals, or even the Committee. The most significant news story of the year remained untold, a secret to everyone but a few. Hawaiian residents would continue to dream throughout the night, undisturbed, oblivious to the consequences that the impending change in accounting methods might bring.

FIGHTING BACK

The industry's reaction was strong and swift. An informational packet containing position papers prepared by the two principal industry groups as well as substantial supporting documentation was sent to Donald F. Linsteadt, chairman, AICPA Agribusiness Special Committee. Persuasive arguments were developed to support the conclusion that both theory and practice would best be served by acceptance of the annual accrual method for the specific conditions present in the Hawaiian plantations.

Here is a summary of the arguments developed by plantation accountants and their advisors.

The basic intent of the Proposed Statement of Position is a more proper matching of revenue and expense. By requiring that the costs associated with planting and cultivation be inventoried (at the lower-of-cost or market) the Statement is treating these costs as if they were similar to the work-in-process of a manufacturing enterprise. While work-in-process inventories of a manufacturing enterprise do contribute to a proper matching of revenue and expense, the analogy with farming operations has little merit because:

- Manufacturing and the growing of crops are unrelated activities in a most basic sense, and accounting systems should not be transferred from one activity to the other without due consideration. Manufacturing occurs through the application of labor to materials. Crops grow as a result of a natural process. In most manufacturing operations a cessation of costs would result in a cessation of production. On a Hawaiian plantation a cessation of costs might result in a reduction of crop yield but the crop would continue to grow and possibly reproduce in self-perpetuation.
- The nature of human involvement in the two processes is altogether

different. In a manufacturing operation, management has direct control over product quality and quantity. In a farming operation this is just not so. Weather, pests, and disease are but a few of the many natural forces that can affect the outcome of a planting. For Hawaiian plantations with two-year crop cycles, the quality and quantity of future harvests is open to great uncertainty.

- A more meaningful matching of revenues and expenses would not occur through use of the deferred crop method. For a manufacturing operation, amounts are inventoried as work-in-process because they are indicative of future expected cash inflows and will be matched against such upon the sale of the completed product. Write-downs of inventory from cost to market rarely occur as future sales price is most often determined by those work-in-process costs of production. For a farming operation such as pineapple or sugarcane, the future sales price is determined by fluctuating world market conditions and not by costs of production. Amounts so inventoried could be misleading if interpreted as being representative of future cash in-flows. Frequent writedowns of inventoried amounts to market would occur as market conditions change, accentuating fluctuations in the reported income of future periods. In any event, such a matching of revenue and expense would have no intrinsic meaning as particular costs so inventoried would not affect the future sales price against which they were being matched.
- Information provided by such an accounting method would not be useful for decision making. In a manufacturing operation per-unit costs for identical units produced are generally constant per production run. This per-unit information is useful to management for planning and control purposes when there is a direct relationship between costs of production and ultimate sales price. For plantations such as those found in Hawaii with significant variations in field size, elevation, rainfall, and soil characteristics, the per-field (unit) costs – if they were possible to develop in a meaningful way – would vary considerably. Such information however is useless to management because, again, ultimate sales price has no relation to those per-unit costs. Only costs of the plantation as a whole are relevant.
- Other accounting methods designed for manufacturing firms with a product development cycle of greater than one year (notably the percentage-of-completion method for long-term construction contracts) are equally unsuited to the environment of the Hawaiian plantation where the future sales price of growing crops, the contract price in the analogy, cannot be determined in advance, and progress billings on work-in-progress (growing crops) is an impossibility. Moreover, while an uncompleted construction project may have a significant scrap or salvage value, the market value of unripened sugarcane or

pineapple is, for all practical purposes, nil. The pineapple industry purposefully plants its crops so that there is no ripe fruit in the fields at the balance sheet date. The ripening of crops is scheduled for the summer months when the weather is most favorable for harvest and labor is cheap. Surely amounts inventoried as growing crops would be misleading if the market value of these crops is arguably nil, except for the two-week period within their two-year life cycle when the crops are ready for harvest.

- Practice has shown that the annual accrual method provides information that is useful in decision making. As the ultimate future sales price of growing crops cannot be affected by management decision, control over overall plantation costs must be its primary concern. Under the annual accrual method, writedowns of inventoried amounts to a lower market value would not, by definition, occur. Unlike the results reported under the deferred crop method, then, plantation costs, which are more or less constant from year to year, would be so represented by the annual accrual method. As current costs are constantly expensed as incurred, the annual accrual method approaches a perfect LIFO, a method solidly endorsed by generally accepted accounting principles. The annual accrual method is simple in concept and inexpensive to apply. Uniform use by companies within the industry makes comparisons between entities meaningful.

The Agribusiness Special Committee reviewed this material in preparation of the then soon-to-be-released final draft of the Proposed Statement of Position. For the pineapple and sugarcane growers of Hawaii a moment of historic importance had arrived.

On January 4, 1984, the AICPA issued its final draft of 'Accounting by Agricultural Producers and Agricultural Cooperatives.' Paragraph one states in part:

> 'This statement also does not apply to growers of timber, *pineapple and sugarcane grown in tropical regions*, raisers of animals for competitive sports . . .'

NOTES

1 Agribusiness Special Committee, Auditing Standards Division, AICPA, Issues, Paper, 'Accounting by Agricultural Producers and Agricultural Cooperatives,' July 31, 1981.

2 'Impact Analysis of Proposed Change in Accounting Method,' letter to Senior Sugar Executives Committee of the Hawaiian Sugar Planters Assn. from Joe H. McDonald, chairman, Hawaiian Sugar Planters Association Accounting Committee, dated May 3, 1983, and contained in the informational packet sent to the Committee on behalf of the pineapple and sugarcane growers.

3 Hitch, Dr. Thomas K., *How the Collapse of the Sugar Industry Would Impact on Hawaii's Economy*. First Hawaiian Bank, Honolulu, Hawaii, December 4, 1981.

QUESTIONS

1 'Economic consequences' issues have been identified as a key factor explaining the lobbying processes to which accounting regulators are subject. Explain how the various interested parties in this case responded to the 'economic consequences' issue raised.

2 If you were asked by the US tax authorities to argue the case *for* this proposed accounting charge, how would you reply to the arguments against the proposal laid out in this article?

13

THE RELATIONSHIP OF FINANCIAL AND TAX ACCOUNTING IN GERMANY

A major reason for accounting disharmony in Europe

Axel Haller

Research in international accounting has shown that the reason for the lack of international comparability of financial statements is not primarily the specific accounting regulations of the countries but the different basic conceptions and functions of accounting. A typical example of this is the close relationship between financial accounting and accounting for tax purposes in Germany. This relationship, the so-called 'Massgeblichkeitsprinzip' – here translated as the principle of congruency[1] – is one of the main accounting principles in Germany and has a strong influence on its accounting regulations and accounting practice. Although there is interaction between tax and financial accounting in other countries also (for example, France, Italy and Belgium), the German situation is, with regard to the intensity, the role, and the closeness of interdependence, a special one.[2]

During recent years, the principle of congruency has been strongly criticized by academics. Nevertheless it is more important and has a stronger impact on accounting today than ever before. The German legislature did not want to take the chance of separating the two accounting schemes by the transformation of the 4th Directive of the European Eco-

From International Journal of Accounting (1992 Vol 27) pp 310–323.
Reprinted by permission of the University of Illinois.

nomic Community (EEC) into German commercial law, which would have increased harmonization in accounting in Europe. On the contrary, after the transformation of the Directive into German law and the most recent German tax law reform in 1990, the interaction of financial commercial accounting and tax accounting in Germany has become very close.

The 'Massgeblichkeitsprinzip' has a long tradition. It was in 1874 in Bremen and Sachsen – in those days the states ('Länder') had the authority to impose taxes – when the first tax law of a state referred to the income of the commercial accounts as a tax computation base. In 1920 this concept of income taxation became part of the Income Tax Code of the German Reich. In 1934 the 'Massgeblichkeitsprinzip' was already expressed in the German Tax Code, the Einkommensteuergesetz (EStG), in nearly the same manner as it is today.

DEFINITION AND STRUCTURE OF THE 'MASSGEBLICHKEITSPRINZIP'

The German tax law requires the determination of taxable income by comparing the net assets of a firm at the beginning and the end of the fiscal year. For this reason companies (except very small ones) must prepare a special balance sheet for tax purposes (Steuerbilanz) to compute taxable income. In calculating a company's profit, German tax authorities are more concerned with the balance sheet than with the income statement. This special balance sheet must be prepared in accordance with the tax regulations. The basic section which deals with the computation of taxable income of a firm and which is the source of the principle of congruency is Sec. 5 EStG. It states that for asset comparison and income computation in the tax accounts the generally accepted commercial accounting principles are binding. This Section is usually interpreted to mean that the recognition and the valuation of the assets and liabilities in the tax balance sheet must be in accordance not only with the regulations of German commercial law but also with the concrete reporting in the commercial accounts of a specific firm. In other words, the recognition and valuation of the commercial accounts of a specific firm. In other words, the recognition and valuation of the commercial accounts must, in general, be incorporated into the tax balance sheet. Thus the substantive basis to prepare a tax balance sheet is the published financial balance sheet (Handelsbilanz) of the company.

Only for some specific items and circumstances does the tax law require specific accounting treatment which differs from commercial accounting regulations. The reason for this is to attain an acceptable degree of objectivity for the taxable income computation, and in this way to guarantee the equity of income taxation. These exceptions to the 'Massgeblichkeitsprinzip' apply to some recognition and valuation options in German commercial accounting which allow the company to choose alternative accounting treatments for one specific circumstance in its financial balance sheet. Most of these exceptions are the result of decisions of the highest tax court (Bundesfinanzhof). The main departures from commercial accounting are in the areas of recognition options and depreciation. In general, all commercial recognition options which refer to assets are recognition requirements in the tax balance sheet and all commercial recognition options which refer to liabilities are not allowed for tax purposes.[5] There is only one main exception to this general rule, namely the commercial recognition option of the 'organizational start up and business expansion expenses' (Sec. 269 Handelsgesetzbuch[6]). As a so-called 'Bilanzierungshilfe' (these are special accruals which are not regarded as 'assets' in the German sense), their recognition is not allowed in the tax accounts. In summary it can be stated that there are no recognition options in the tax balance sheet.

In addition to the recognition differences, German tax law differs from commercial law in that it contains a number of strict depreciation requirements. For example the depreciation period of goodwill acquired in an asset transaction must be 15 years and the maximum percentage of the declining depreciation method is 30 percent. All these stricter requirements of the tax law have as their objective the reduction of the possibility of accounting policy and income manipulation in the tax accounts. In all areas where there are strict and specific tax requirements, the principle of congruency has no effect and, therefore, the financial accounts can differ from the tax accounts.

Nevertheless, these special tax requirements are only exceptions to the 'Massgeblichkeitsprinzip.' As a result of the wide range of accounting options, there are many possibilities for the company intentionally to influence taxable income.

The 'Massgeblichkeitsprinzip' embodies not only the influence of commercial law and financial accounting practice on income tax computation but also a converse effect, so that special tax accounting rules have a specific impact on commercial accounting. There are a variety of tax benefits in the form of higher write-downs, special tax depreciation allowances ('steuerliche Sonderabschreibungen'), and tax-free reserves ('steuerfreie Rücklagen') which can be adopted by the German taxpayer to reduce the taxable income of a period. These are all instruments of the economic and financial policy of the government with the objective to support specific regions or branches (for example, tax benefits for companies in the former GDR). In Sec. 5 Para. 1S. 2 EStG the Tax Code states that these special income-reducing tax valuations must be applied equally in the commercial accounts to be allowed for tax computation. Thus every tax-allowed special depreciation also affects the published commercial balance sheet. Because these valuations do not refer to the 'real' economic value (whatever this

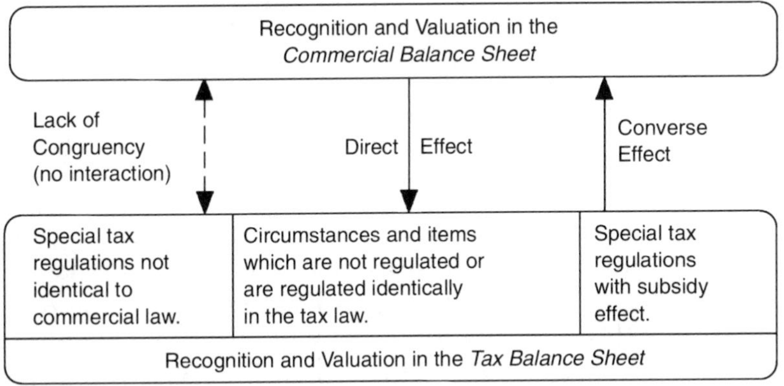

Figure 1 Scope and effect of the principle of congruency

might be specifically) of the assets, which should be included in the commercial accounts, there are special provisions in German commercial law which allow these – economically spoken – 'false' values to be included in the commercial accounts (Secs. 254, 279 Para. 2. 280 Para. 2 HGB). This direct impact of the tax law on financial accounting is called the 'umgekehrtes Massgeblichkeitsprinzip' (principle of converse congruency). It is a logical consequence of the aim of the tax authorities to achieve a consistent and close relationship between tax and commercial income computation.

In summary, the 'Massgeblichkeitsprinzip' states that balance sheet items and their valuation must be identical in the financial statements and the tax statements, except for those special recognitions and valuations which are excluded by special tax regulations. All of the valuation options in the tax law are dependent on their use in the published accounts. For this reason, the 'Massgeblichkeitsprinzip' is called the 'cornerstone' of tax accounting in Germany.[7] Consequently, the profit reported in the published accounts of a German company usually do not differ significantly from those in the tax accounts.

Finally it can be stated that the principle of congruency in Germany has three characteristics:

1 Basically, the recognition and the valuation of assets and liabilities in the commercial financial statement is also legally required for the taxable income computation.
2 For some items, specific and strict tax regulations require a special treatment in the tax accounts.
3 Tax benefits in the form of special depreciation allowances and tax-free reserves are only allowed if they are also exercised in the commercial financial accounts (principle of converse congruency).

THE REASONING OF THE 'MASSGEBLICHKEITSPRINZIP'

The substantive reason for this very close interaction between the commercial and the tax income computation is the historical evolution of the concept and the functions of accounting in Germany. The determination and the presentation of the assets of a company, the function of which is to protect the claims of the creditors, are traditionally the central objectives of financial accounting in Germany. The commercial asset presentation recognizes that the company must fulfill its obligations (liabilities) on the one hand and should remain a going concern on the other. This view has a very strong influence (even after the implementation of the 4th EEC Directive) on the recognition and valuation of balance sheet items and is manifested in the dominant principle of prudence ('conservatism'), the so-called 'Vorsichtsprinzip.' Related to this, the commercial balance sheet is seen as an instrument to compute prudently the income of the company, which can be given to the owners (as dividends) without deteriorating or harming the position of the creditors. Thus the main function of the balance sheet in Germany is the computation of the distributable income of a company in determining the prudently valued increase of net assets to prevent the overstatement of net assets and income. The objective of providing relevant information and the accrual convention are subordinated to this function of the prudent determination of net assets. This fact must be viewed as one of the basic differences between the Anglo American and the German accounting concept.[8]

This interpretation of financial accounting is similar to the income computation for tax purposes. The measure of income taxation is the full economic capacity of a corporation. In the opinion of the German tax authorities, as already mentioned, the income computed by the comparison of net assets at the beginning and the end of a period is an adequate indicator of this taxable measure. In addition the taxation should be reliable and equal, thus the income computation must be based on objective and generally accepted principles. Traditionally the principles of proper bookkeeping and accounting, the norms of financial accounting, have been regarded by the German tax authorities as adequate for this goal of reliable income computation. This attitude should first and foremost be seen as a legislatory simplification which allowed the legislator not to create a complete set of tax accounting rules and a tax-specific definition of income. Additionally, as a result, this is to the advantage of the companies, as the taxation (because of the principle of conservatism) is based on a moderately computed income, which reduces the tax payments)[9]

The reason why the German tax authorities have required the reverse impact of undervaluing tax rules on the published accounts is the reduction of distributable commercial income. Because of the special tax valuation (low), the tax authorities receive less of the companies' income in the form of income taxes. Because of this disclaimer on the part of the tax authorities, in a sense of fairness, the owners also should disclaim a part of their income. Thus the distributable income must be reduced in the commercial accounts.

The major argument mentioned to justify the 'Massgeblichkeitsprinzip' is the fact that the firms have the opportunity to prepare only one set of financial statements for both purposes (commercial and tax), which is more practical and economical. This argument is supported by observed accounting practice. Statistics prove that most of the enterprises (for example, more than 90 percent of the limited liability companies), prepare only one set of financial statements, which is called the 'unified balance sheet' (Einheitsbilanz).[10] Only the listed companies generally prepare two sets of statements. Their reason for this is to take advantage of commercial accounting options concerning items which are regulated by specific and strict tax norms and therefore have no tax effect when they are exercised in the commercial accounts. These companies try to achieve different accounting policies in the different accounting systems and to publish commercial accounts which are, as far as possible according to the tax law, not totally 'falsified' by tax-motivated values.

In summary, the basic objective of the principle of congruency and its converse effect is to represent economic items identically in both balance sheets as far as possible. The main reason for this has been simplification for the tax legislator and the practical and economical advantage for the companies to have the possibility of preparing only one set of accounts.

EFFECTS OF THE 'MASSGEBLICHKEITSPRINZIP'

The illustration in Fig. 2 shows that there are direct and indirect effects of the close interaction between the accounts for tax and for commercial purposes.

Direct Effects of the 'Massgeblichkeitsprinzip'

The close interdependence of financial and tax accounting influences to a large extent the concepts of the balance sheet in Germany. It is one reason why the German balance sheet has been and still is seen as an instrument to determine prudently the income distributable to the owners. The balance sheet therefore is the basic and main financial statement in comparing the net assets. Financial accounting in Germany is based on the presentation of assets measured by their historical costs. That is the reason why it is called a static concept of financial accounting. In addition to its influence on the concepts of financial accounting the principle of congruency had

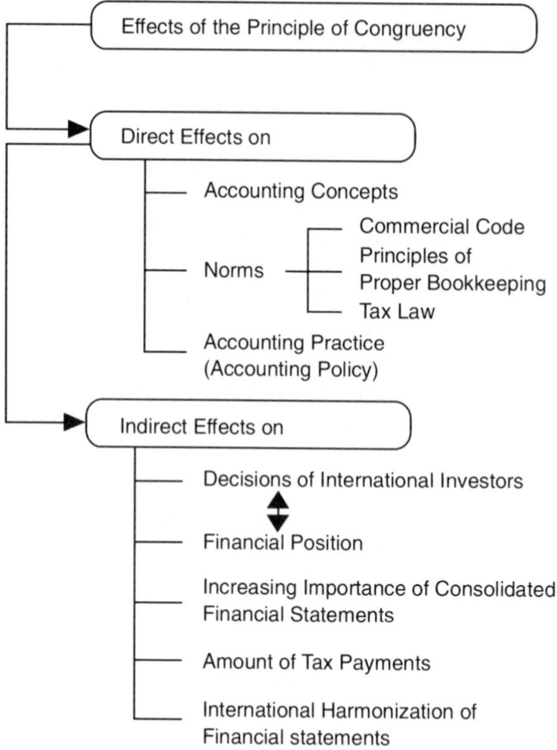

Figure 2 Effects of the principle of congruency

and still has a strong impact on commercial and tax accounting principles, rules, and regulations.

Impact on Tax Law

Because of the general reference in Sec. 5 EStG to the principles and rules of commercial accounting, the Tax Code does not embody many accounting regulations. The major areas of special tax accounting regulations are depreciation and write offs. But these are only exceptions to the general rule of tax accounting being tied to commercial accounts.

This general reference causes judicial rulings to play a very important role in establishing tax accounting principles because the tax courts must interpret commercial accounting principles in deciding doubtful cases. The main decisions are the basis for the Einkommensteuerrichtlinien (EStR), the income tax directives which are binding for the tax authorities and agents in judging specific income computation problems. The main exception to the principle of congruency is based on a decision of the Great Senat of the 'Bundesfinanzhof' in 1969, when it ruled that assets with the option of recognition in commercial law must be capitalized in the tax balance sheet and accruals with the option of recognition in commercial law are not allowed to be recognized in the tax balance sheet. This general tax accounting rule still has legal force.[11]

As a result of this decision, two items (in contrast to the commercial law) must be capitalized in the tax balance sheet:

The difference between the amount to be repaid on a debt and its value when issued ('Disagio') (Sec. 250 Para. 3 HGB):
The goodwill acquired by an asset merger ('derivativer Firmenwert') (Sec. 255 Para 4 HGB).

An option exists in the commercial code to recognize some accruals ('Aufwandsrückstellungen') which are not based on liabilities to other persons, these are:

Accruals for repairs and maintenance expenses, if the repairs and maintenance are performed after the first three months of the following year but within the following financial year (Sec. 249 Para. 1 HGB) ('Rückstellungen für Instandhaltung'):
Precisely determined accruals (Sec. 249 Para 2. HGB) ('spezielle Aufwandsrückstellungen').

These accruals are not allowed to be included in the tax balance sheet.

Not covered by this general rule are the so-called 'Bilanzierungshilfen', items which are not regarded as assets but can nevertheless be capitalized in the commercial balance sheet. These are, as already mentioned, 'organizational start-up and business expansion expenses' (Sec. 269 HGB) and 'deferred tax assets' (Sec. 274 HGB). They are not allowed to be capitalized in the tax balance sheet. All of these stricter rulings in tax accounting are aimed at avoiding accounting options, to restrict tax accounting policy, and to cause the income computation to be more objective.

Impact on Commercial Law

Codified Regulations.

In Germany all groups concerned, the political parties and the Government, have agreed that in implementing the EEC Directive,[12] an increase in the tax burden on the firms must be avoided in all circumstances. This attitude of a taxation-neutral implementation of the EEC accounting rules had a very substantial impact on the transformation of the Directives into German law because of the existence of the 'Massgeblichkeitprinzip,' which (as a sacred cow) has not been changed or even restricted by the legislator. Consequently, there was the strong intention to change the accounting principles as little as possible in implementing the Directives, because nearly all changes would have had an influence on the tax computation.

Thus the principle of congruency was the main reason for the very conservative transformation of the 4th Directive in Germany. This effect becomes very clear especially with regard to the 'true and fair view' principle which has been interpreted in Germany in a quite different and much weaker manner than, for example, in Great Britain.[13] The basic codified objective of commercial accounting is not (as it should be according to the 4th Directive) the presentation of the 'true and fair view' but, as it was before the transformation of the Directives, conformity with the regulations and the principles of proper bookkeeping, the so-called 'Grundsätze ordnungsmäßiger Buchführung' (GoB). The German Commercial Code requires that financial statements must be prepared comprehensively and clearly within required recognition and valuation principles and must give a clear and 'legally' correct view of the financial position and the earnings of the company. According to the German legislator and the general opinion of accountants, the 'true and fair view' does not influence the income computation but the information given in the notes to the financial statements. The notes should comply with the principles of a true and fair view in giving information in excess of the balance sheet and profit and loss account. Having no direct impact on the items and the valuation in the commercial balance sheet, the 'true and fair view' has no influence on the taxable income computation.[14]

This very restrictive interpretation of the true and fair view principle was necessary to comply with the objective of the tax-neutral transformation of the EEC Directives. According to the legislator, it has the advantage of reliability and objectivity in commercial accounting (and due to the principle of congruency also in tax accounting) because the presentation of an item in the balance sheet does not depend on individual specific case decisions. Additionally a consequent transformation of the principle of a true and fair view in the British sense into German law would have meant the end of the strict principle of congruency because the two principles are in a conflicting relationship.

The conflict arises because the congruency principle values enter into the commercial accounts, which are only motivated by tax considerations and do not comply with the 'fair' presentation of the economic situation of a firm. For example the tax-motivated charge of accelerated depreciation allowances against the profit is not 'fair,' but it is certainly 'correct' or 'legal.'[15]

The following points are examples of the lack of compliance with the true and fair view concept in German financial accounting caused mainly by the 'Massgeblichkeitsprinzip:'

Prohibition of the valuation with present values (a valuation which would be possible according to Art. 33 of the 4th Directive).

Prohibition of the valuation of investments at equity amounts in the corporate financial statements (a valuation which would be possible according to Art. 59 of the 4th Directive).

Prohibition of the capitalization of research and development costs (which would be possible according to Art. 37 and Art. 34 of the 4th Directive).

Application of tax-allowed depreciation: According to Sec. 254, 279 Para. 2 HGB, undervaluing the assets in the commercial accounts to take advantage of depreciation options of the tax law is allowed.

Nullification of the write-up requirement of the 4th Directive: According to Sec. 280 Para. 2 HGB, asset values need not be written up, if the write-up in the commercial balance sheet causes a write-up in the tax balance sheet which leads to a higher taxable income. Because of the principle of congruency, this inter-relationship always exists. Thus the write-up requirement of the Directive is effectively turned into a write-up option in German financial accounting.

Special item with an equity portion: It is allowable to create a special item, 'Sonderposten mit Rücklageanteil.' in the German commercial balance sheet, between the owner's equity and the liabilities sections, to benefit from tax-free reserves. This type of reserve is permitted in German tax accounting to transfer hidden reserves of assets leaving the company to new assets which will be purchased in the near future. These special items are necessary because of the required 'umgekehrtes Massgeblichkeistprinzip' (converse congruency principle) in tax law. Their recognition leads to a reduction of commercial income which is not in compliance with the 4th Directive.

Little importance of deferred taxes: The close connection between taxable and commercial income has as a result that companies do not show a large difference in the profit disclosed in the published accounts as compared with those prepared for tax purposes. Thus in German companies the amount of deferred taxes is quite small compared, for example, to those in Great Britain. There are usually deferred tax assets which according to Sec. 274 HGB need not be recognized. Companies that prepare only one set of financial statements (unified balance sheet) logically do not show any deferred taxes in their balance sheets.

In accordance with the provisions of the 4th Directive (Art. 35 Para. 1d: Art. 39 Para. 1e: Art. 43 Para. 1 No. 10), the German legislator has tried to reduce the impairment of the information content of the commercial balance sheet and profit and loss account caused by the principle of congruency. Thus if a company has adopted higher depreciation allowed by the tax code in its financial statements, there is an option to show a special item with an equity portion on the capital side of the commercial balance sheet ('Sonderposten mit Rücklageanteil') in the amount of the difference between the valuation deemed admissible for tax purposes and the correct commercial valuation (thus the so-called 'special item with an equity portion' in a German balance sheet can comprise tax-free reserves and portions of tax-motivated higher depreciation allowances). In this way the depreciated asset is represented with its 'real commercial book value' in the balance sheet. As for the true and fair view principle and the information content of the balance sheet, it is a pity that companies are not obliged by the legislator to report higher tax depreciation in this way. Statistics show that less than one quarter of the German companies choose this specific representation of tax-motivated depreciation in the special financial balance sheet position.[16]

As already mentioned, the notes to the financial statements have the function to give adequate information to help to present a true and fair view of the situation of the firm and to comply with the requirements of the 4th Directive. Therefore, the amount of write-ups not made in the financial year for tax reasons shall be mentioned in the notes and appropriately justified (Sec. 280 Para. 3 HGB). The same must be done with the amount of depreciation charged in the financial year based solely on tax provisions, separately for fixed and current assets. Furthermore, income from the reversal of special items with an equity portion or transfers to those items shall be noted separately in the profit and loss account or mentioned in the notes. (Sec. 281 Para. 2 HGB). Additionally there shall further be disclosed in the notes the extent to which the results of the year were influenced by depreciation or write-ups of assets not made in the financial year or in earlier years, which were based on tax regulations (Sec. 285 No. 5 HGB).

These disclosures in the notes cannot totally cure the information distortion caused by the 'Massgeblichkeitsprinzip,' on the one hand, because of the fact that the information in the notes has no material influence on the result of the balance sheet, the commercial income; on the other hand, the experience gained in recent years shows clearly that the companies only interpret these disclosure rules in their minimal sense. The information usually given on the influence of the principle of congruency on the commercial accounts is very short and often incomprehensible for interested parties, especially those with no profound knowledge of German tax law.

Principles of Proper Bookkeeping.

The impact of the 'Massgeblichkeitsprinzip' on the principles of proper bookkeeping, GoB, is dual. First, there is the impact of the tax courts on the interpretation of the GoB because there are many more tax lawsuits than commercial ones. It is mainly the tax courts that must interpret these commercial accounting principles and decide whether an accounting method is in conformity with the GoB and can be accepted as proper accounting. This results in a strong influence of tax accounting assumptions on the German concepts of commercial accounting.

On the other hand, many tax accounting principles, primarily to simplify accounting problems and to increase the practicability of accounting, are meanwhile practiced to such an extent that they can be called generally accepted in financial accounting. Examples of these simplifications are the computation of the depreciation of an asset in the year of purchase (a purchase date in the first half of the financial year leads to a full depreciation allowance: a purchase date in the second half of the financial year leads to a half depreciation allowance) or the full depreciation for assets under 800 DM in the purchase year (Art. 44 Para. 2 EStR. Sec. 6 Para. 2 EStG).

Impact on Accounting Practice (Accounting Policy)

Because of the 'Massgeblichkeitsprinzip' the two balance sheets (tax and commercial) are very closely linked. This has a strong impact on accounting policy decisions of a firm. In most cases, the decision reported in the commercial balance sheet is binding for the tax balance sheet and vice versa. This results in a very characteristic situation for German accounting with companies often having to deal with conflicting aims. A desired high income in the commercial accounts leads to higher tax payments, and the realization of the aim to minimize taxable income, on the other hand, decreases commercial income. Usually the minimization of tax payments is the primary goal and the more compelling argument in accounting-policy decision making in German companies. It can generally be said that tax accounting dominates commercial accounting. Taxpayers who want to take advantage of a low valuation of assets in the tax balance sheet must chose the same low-valuation accounting methods for the commercial accounts. In addition, companies which prepare only a unified balance sheet, one balance sheet for both purposes, must disclaim the recognition and valuation options given in the Commercial Code (HGB) which are not covered by tax law. The principle of congruency stimulates a desire to create hidden reserves. The undervaluation of assets for tax reasons tends to lead to a more pessimistic presentation of the financial position and economic situation of a company than the very strong principle of prudence already does.[17]

INDIRECT EFFECTS OF THE 'MASSGEBLICHKEITSPRINZIP'

Decisions of International Investors

As demonstrated, the 'Massgeblichkeitsprinzip' is one of the major reasons for undervaluation practices in German financial accounting. The actual value of the assets, the financial position, and the profitability of a company are represented in a very conservative way. Investors can not easily interpret the correct financial and economic situation of a company. Furthermore, the distributable income of a company is smaller, which means that the owners tend to receive less cash in the form of dividends than in countries without this particular interaction of tax and financial accounting. This can be seen as one main reason why international investors are restrained in their equity investments in German companies. The result is the relatively small portion of owners' equity of German stock corporations and limited liability companies, which is on average less than 20 percent of the total capital. Generally speaking, the principle of congruency is a disadvantage for German companies competing in the international capital markets.

Increasing Importance of Consolidated Financial Statements

In Germany the consolidated accounts only have the function of giving relevant information to interested parties. Neither dividends nor tax payments are dependent on the results of the consolidated statements. Therefore the influence of the principle of congruency on the consolidated accounts is much less because the Commercial Code gives the opportunity to represent the consolidated financial statements without consideration to the tax accounts. That is why during the last few years there has been a tendency in Germany to rely more and more on the financial information given in the consolidated statements to judge the economic power of a parent company. Consolidated financial statements are becoming more important for financial analysis in Germany.

Amount of Tax Payments

That the mode of computing taxable income influences the amount of taxes and the reliability of tax payments received by the state is very understandable.

International Harmonization of Accounting

At the beginning of the preparation of the 4th Directive, the EEC Commission was against the influence of tax accounting rules on financial accounting because this would be in conflict with the true and fair view concept. However, Germany was reluctant to and resisted this initiative carried mainly by Great Britain, Ireland, and the Netherlands and succeeded to have some regulations included in the 4th Directive which refer to the existence of the interaction between these two accounting systems. This firm position was the result of the goal of the German government that the implementation of the 4th Directive should, as far as possible, be tax-neutral.[18]

A strong impact of tax accounting on financial accounting is generally a substantial point of hindrance to the international harmonization of accounting. Tax reforms and political intentions which can vary substantially from country to country influence the representation of the financial position of a company differently in each country. As has been shown, the strong principle of congruency in Germany leads to a violation of the rules incorporated in the 4th EEC Directive. One of the main facts that hinder the comparison of German financial statements with others in Europe is the very weak interpretation and the lack of acceptance of the true and fair view principle in a British sense in Germany. This basic difference in accounting conception, caused substantially by the 'Massgeblichkeits-prinzip,' is the major reason for accounting disharmony in Europe.

SUMMARY

The very close interaction of financial accounting and tax accounting in Germany, called the 'Massgeblichkeitsprinzip,' is a significant characteristic of German accounting. This principle of congruency has a number of direct and indirect effects on accounting regulation and practice. As a result German financial accounting is dominated by tax rules and tax-motivated accounting decisions of the companies. This results in a pessimistic presentation of the net worth, the financial position, and the results of a company. The few rules that require incremental information in the notes and the balance sheet of financial statements are unable to compensate for these negative effects of the 'Massgeblichkeitsprinzip,' namely the impaired information content of the published commercial accounts. German commercial financial statements can hardly be correctly interpreted, even by a person with a sound and comprehensive knowledge of the German tax law. The principle of congruency leads to a deformation of the financial statements and is in conflict with the central principle of the 4th EEC Directive, the true and fair view. It even leads to specific violations of the rules of the 4th EEC Directive. In short, the true and fair view concept is not applicable to German balance sheets. This fact results in a disharmony in European accounting, not only in regard to the specific rules but particularly in regard to the general interpretation and the concepts of accounting.

The problem of the relationship between financial income and taxable income computation has become a very current one that the EEC Commission must consider in creating a EEC Directive to harmonize the taxable income computation in Europe. A first step has already been taken with the issue of an exposure draft in 1988. A consensus on this point will be the basis for income tax harmonization in Europe, which is schedule to be achieved in the mid-1990s.

NOTES

1 The term 'Massgeblichkeitsprinzip' is extremely difficult to translate into English. In some English literature it is translated as the 'principle of bindingness:' Christopher Nobes, *Interpreting European Financial Statements: Towards 1992* (London: Butterworths 1989), 8–9. The meaning and the scope of the term 'Massgeblichkeitsprinzip' should become clear by reading the paper.

2 Winfried Gail, Michael Greth and Roland Schumann, 'Die Massgeblichkeit der Handelsbilanz für die Steuerbilanz in den Mitgliedstaaten der Europäischen Gemeinschaft.' *Der Betrich* (No. 27/28, 1991). 1389–1400.

3 Joachim Schulze-Osterloh, 'Handelsbilanz und Steuerbilanz.'*Steuer und Wirtschaft*. (August 1991), 284–296; Arndt Raupach 'Von der Massgeblichkeit der Handelsbilanz für die steuerliche Gewinnermittlung zur Prädominanz des Steuerrechts in der Handelsbilanz.' *Betriebswirtschaftliche Forschung und Praxis* (No. 6, 1990), 515–526; Wolfgang Ballwieser 'Ist das Massgeblichkeitsprinzip überholt?' *Betriebswirtschaftliche Forschung und Praxis* (No. 6, 1990), 477–498.

4 Walter Mathiak, 'Massgeblichkeit der tatsächlichen Handelsbilanzansätze für die Steuerbilanz und ungekehrte Maßgeblichkeit,' *Steuerberaterjahrbuch 1986/7* (München: Beck, 1987), 79–107; Klaus Pohl, *Die Entwicklung des ertragsteuerlichen Massgeblichkeitsprinzips* (Köln, 1983).

5 Decision of the Bundesfinanzhof of February 3rd, 1969, Bundessteuerblatt II 1969, 291.

6 The Handelsgesetzbuch (HGB) is the German Commercial Code.

7 Karlheinz Kütting, 'Auswirkungen der umgekehrien Massgeblichkeit auf die handelsrechtliche Rechnungslegung.' *Betriebswirtschaftliche Forschung und Praxis* (No. 2, 1989), 109–122.

8 Fouad K. AlNajjar and William H. Volz, 'The Status of Accounting and its Environment in West Germany: An Overview.' *International Journal of Accounting* (1991), 104–117.

9 Franz W. Wagner, 'Tax Balance Sheet,' in Erwin Grochla et al., eds., *Handbook of German Business Management* (Stuttgart C.E. Poeschel, 1990) 2334–2340.

10 Hans G. Rautenberg, 'Externe Rechnungslegung, Massgeblichkeitsprinzip und Finanzierung,' in Dieter Ahlert et al., eds. *Finanz und Rechungswesen als Führungsinstrument* (Wiesbaden: Gabler, 1990) 253–268.

11 Decision of the Bundesfinanzhof of February 3rd, 1969, Bundessteuerblatt II (1969), 291.

12 There are three EEC Directives which are relevant for accounting. These are the 4th Directive (Directive 78/660/EWG), the 7th Directive (Directive 83/349/EWG), and the 8th Directive (84/253/EWG).

13 Art. 2 Para. 3 of the 4th Directive claims: 'The annual accounts shall give a true and fair view of the company's assets, liabilities, financial position and profit or loss.'

14 Christopher Nobes, *Interpreting European Financial Statements: Toward 1992* (London: Butterworths, 1989). 8–9; Heinrich Beisse, 'Die Generalnorm des neuen Bilanzrechts und ihre steuerrechtliche Redeutung,' *Handelshilanz und Steuerbilanz* in Winfried Mellwig et al., eds., (Wiesbaden: Gabler, 1989), 15–32.

15 Christopher Nobes, *Interpreting European Financial Statements Toward 1992* (London: Butterworths, 1989), 8–9.

16 Treuarbeit *Jahresabschlüsse* '87 (Düsseldorf: IDW-Verlag, 1989), 110.

17 Walter Mathiak, 'Massgeblichkeit der tatsächlichen Handelsbilanzansätze für die Steuerbilanz und umgekehrte Maßgeblichkeit.' *steuerberaterjahrbuch 86/87* (München: Beck, 1987). Thomas Schildbach. 'Massgeblichkeit – Rechtslage und Perspektiven.' *Betriebs-Berater* (No. 21, 1989), 1443–1453.

18 Joachim Schulze-Osterloh, 'Handelshilanz und Steuerrechtliche Gewinnermittlung.' *Steuer und Wirtschaft* (No. 3, 1990) 284–296.

BIBLIOGRAPHY

AlNajjar, Fouad K., and Volz, William H. (1991) 'Status of Accounting and its Environment in West Germany: An Overview.' *International Journal of Accounting*. No. 26, 104–117.

Alsheimer, Herbert. (1974) 'Jahre Prinzip der Massgeblichkeit der Handelsbilanz für die Steuerbilanz' *Zeitschrift für Betriebswirtschaft*, 841–848.

Ballwieser, Wolfgang. (1990) 'Ist das Massgeblichkeitsprinzip überholt?' *Betriebswirtschaftliche Forschung und Praxis*, No. 6, 477–498.

Beisse, Heinrich. (1989) 'Die Generalnorm des neuen Bilanzrechts und ihre steuerrechtliche Bedeutung', Winfried Mellwig et al., eds., *Handelsbilanz und Steuerbilanz* Wiesbaden: Gabler, 15–32.

Coenenberg, Adolf G. (1992) *Jahresabschluß und Jahnesabschlußanalyse*, 13th edn. Landsberg al . . . mi Verlag.

Gail, Winfried, Greth, Michael, and Schumann, Roland. (1991) 'Die Massgeblichkeit der Handelsbilanz für die Steuerbilanz in den Mitgliedstaaten der Europäischen Gemeinschaft.' *Der Betrich*, 1389–1400.

Knobbe-Keuk, Brigitte. (1989) *Bilanz und Unternechmenssteuerrecht*, 7th edn. Köln: Verlag Dr. Otto Schmidt KG.

Küting, Karlheinz, (1989) 'Auswirkungen der umgekehten Massgeblichkeit auf die handelsrechtiche Rechnungslegung. *Betriebswirtschaftliche Forschung und Praxis*, 109–122.

Mathiak, Walter. (1987) 'Massgeblichkeit deh tatsachlichen Handelsbilanzansätze für die Steuerbilanz und umgekehrte Maßgeblichkeit.' *Steuerberaterjahrbuch 86/87*. München: Beck, 77–107.

Nobes, Christopher, (1989) *Interpreting European Financial Statements Towards 1992*, London: Butterworths.

Pohl, Klaus, (1983) *Die Entwicklung Hertrag des steuerlichen Massgeblichkeitsprinzips*. Köln: Diss.

Raupach, Arndt. (1990) 'Von der Massgeblichkeit der Handelsbilanz für die steuerliche Gewinnermittlung/ut Prädominanz des Steuerrechts in der Handelsbilanz.' *Betriebswirtschaftliche Forschung und Praxis*. No. 6. 515–526.

Rautenberg, Hans G. (1990) 'Externe Rechnungslegung, Massgeblichkeitsprinzip und Finanzierung.' in Dieter Ahlert et al., eds., *Finanz und Rechungswesen als Führungsinstrument*. Wiesbaden; Gabler, 253–268.

Schildbach, Thomas. (1990) 'Massgeblichkeit – Rechtslage und Perspektiven.' *Betriebs-Berater*, No. 21. 1443–1453.

Schulze-Osterloh, Joachim. (1991) 'Handelsbilanz und steuerrechtliche Gewinnermittlung.' *Steuer and Wirtschaft*, No. 3, 284–296.

Treuarbeit, (1989) *Jahresabschlüsse 87*, Düsseldorf: IDW-Verlag.

Wagner, Franz W. (1990) 'Tax Balance Sheet.' in Erwin Grochla et al. eds., Handbook of German Business Management. Stuttgart: Poeschel-Verlag, 2334–2340.

QUESTIONS

1 Discuss reasons why, and ways in which, Germany might move closer to international accounting harmonisation despite the tax and accounting relationship.

2 Compare the thinking behind the German approach to the tax – accounting link outlined by Haller with the example of a tax induced accounting rule in the USA discussed in the previous article by Slepian.

14

CHANGING RULES OF ACCOUNTING IN POLAND

Alicja Jaruga

INTRODUCTION

Changes taking place in Poland and other countries of Central and Eastern Europe have great social, political and economic importance. As far as the transition from planned to market economies is concerned, accounting is seen as a potentially active instrument of economic calculation as well as an internationally understood business language facilitating the role of markets in economic co-ordination and growth. The changes also constitute a challenge to the social sciences to formulate new theoretical frameworks to provide a basis for the new institutional and legal arrangements, on which, in turn, changes in concepts, norms and standards can rely. This challenge is particularly important for accounting as an applied science.

Accounting in centrally planned economies was treated as an administrative instrument employed to monitor the implementation of plans by state enterprises, and to reconcile the nominal profitability of state enterprises with the state budget (Jaruga, 1987, 1988; Bailey, 1988). Now, in the period of transition to a market economy, the opening up of the country to foreign capital and the influence of the EC, a change of accounting purpose, functions and therefore regulations is unavoidable. Pressure is also exerted by the International Bank for Reconstruction and Development and the International Monetary Fund. The representatives of these organizations want the enterprises to which they grant loans to prepare clear and understandable financial reports which comply with International Accounting Standards.

At the same time, owing to cultural connections with Western Europe, as well as closer co-operation with the EC, new accounting regulations are being considered in the context of the requirements of the Fourth Directive.

From European Accounting Review 1993, 1, 115–126. Reprinted by permission of European Accounting Review.

This paper attempts to identify issues concerning the restructuring of accounting in Poland in the wake of the transition to a market economy, and to discuss those issues which seem the most important, and those for which a consensus has yet to be found. Until recently academic circles interpreted (*de lege lata*) mainly the accounting principles and plans of accounts provided by the Ministry of Finance for implementation (Jaruga, 1992). We consider the current changes a unique opportunity to grasp the influence of the transition to a market system upon the regulation of accounting and reporting. Will the system have to be entirely changed or can elements be preserved from the previous system of accounting?

BUSINESS LAW AND ACCOUNTING REGULATIONS: THE SEQUENCE OF CHANGE

Owing to the transition of the economic system to a market mechanism, and the establishment of related institutions connected with, among other things, commercialization, privatization and development of a securities exchange, the legal infrastructure is being changed. The legislation process will stretch over a long period of time because the transition period calls for frequent changes and corrections, e.g. of the tax law by introducing the value added tax (VAT), as well as dealing with the problem of joint ventures promotion (Świerkocki and Jaruga, 1990). Recent legislation/regulation in this area which is relevant here is listed in Appendix 9.

Changes which have already been introduced in the legal environment call for the restructuring of accounting regulations. A question arises, then, whether the restructuring of accounting regulation:

(a) should be carried out simultaneously with legislative change;
(b) should be carried out by stages in accordance with the changes in legislation;
(c) should precede the legislative changes.

New regulations have been issued by the Ministry of Finance (Order on Accounting, Dziennik Ustaw 10, Jan. 15. 1991). As they precede the changes in the legal framework, they are thus, seen from a legal point of view, of a low order which improves the image neither of accounting nor of the accounting profession. Moreover, this can be treated only as a temporary solution. However, on the positive side, the changes reflect an attempt to comply with many of the requirements of the Fourth Directive of the EC, thus bringing Polish accounting closer to the accounting of the EC member countries.

THE SCOPE OF ACCOUNTING REGULATIONS

The hitherto existing regulations, or the so-called general accounting principles, were related exclusively to entities in the state and co-operative economy, as this was the predominant sector. Although in the past few years many companies and joint ventures have emerged, more than 60 per cent of the national income is still produced by the public sector. The structure of enterprises has changed in favour of small and medium-sized firms. A question arises, then, of whether accounting regulations should be uniform, or should they be differentiated according to the legal and ownership form of the company and the size of business. The former option, uniform regulations, was adopted in the new order of the Ministry of Finance; this refers to both legal and natural persons. It also covers all budgetary units (governmental, non-profit, etc.). Only banks and financial institutions are exempted.

It means, according to the Ministry, the equalization of economic entities irrespective of their legal form of ownership and property title. Slight simplifications were provided for small business. It is to be questioned if this unification is the optimum solution.

EC DIRECTIVES AND THE NEW 'ORDER ON ACCOUNTING'

The harmonization of accounting within the framework of the EC member countries must affect the system of accounting regulations in any country which wishes to integrate with the European Community. The issue is, then, when and to what extent the EC Directives should be taken into account and be incorporated in commercial law and other national accounting regulations.

An opinion prevails that the Fourth Directive should be fully taken into account in all types of accounting regulations.

The present regulations include:

(a) principles of accounting record keeping, and some general concepts;
(b) requirements for stock taking;
(c) assets and liabilities valuation principles;
(d) preparation of annual accounts, financial statements and other reports (their form and content).

Introducing a uniform basic chart of accounts is a basic aim. Publication of annual financial reports is not expected (except for joint stock companies) and disclosures are limited.

Amendments to the Commercial Code, in the section referring to accounts and audit, and changes in these parts of the Enterprise Act, are under debate. There is no National Accountancy Council of all users of financial statements in Poland, or even a council dealing with methodology and constituting a conceptual and technical base for setting accounting standards.

The new accounting regulation has incorporated many of the requirements of the Fourth Directive, but not all. It relates to general principles, provision of reserves and disclosures. It is quite understandable that not all of it has been implemented yet, considering the fact that France and Germany needed about six years for research, discussions and preparation of changes in their national legislation and guidelines when introducing the Directive.

The development of financial markets, and the Securities Commission legislation, has visibly increased international comparability.

The Seventh Directive requires even greater preliminary preparation, because consolidation has been neither applied in practice nor taught in theory.

INTERNATIONAL ACCOUNTING STANDARDS AND THEIR IMPORTANCE TO CHANGES IN ACCOUNTING REGULATIONS

We believe in Poland that international accounting standards have great educational value for us: not only to the accountants and their associates who are involved in developing national standards and rules, but also to economists and lawyers. These latter groups have little understanding of accountancy and the value measurements it involves. For these reasons IASs have already been translated into Polish by academics, and will be made widely accessible. It is one of the ways of building bridges to the global financial market. The use of a common professional language of concepts with identical meaning will increase mutual understanding.

In particular cases, e.g. leasing, joint ventures, the IAS Exposure Drafts have been used directly in amending Polish regulations. IASs should be taken into consideration in national accounting standards development as well. So far many of them have been kept under the umbrella of the so-called 'financial system'. It requires a change of a perception of accounting by the legislature to formalize their usage legally.

The accounting profession in Poland has a better understanding of the contents of the EC Fourth Directive than of IASs, due to the fact that the latter are structured according to the Anglo-American approach to accounting. The philosophy of 'the true and fair view' calls for switching to an entirely new way of explaining accounting 'regularities', even on the part of academics. In the legislation, there is still no clear resolution of this issue.

MAKING USE OF THE EXPERIENCE OF WEST EUROPEAN NATIONS

The Polish tradition has more in common with the codified approach to accounting regulations than with the common law one, and involves usage of a 'General Chart of Accounts'. Such a chart of accounts, compatible with the Fourth EC Directive, proved to be very useful as an aid. It accelerated the process of incorporating the new accounting regulations.

For these reasons an opinion prevails that Polish accounting regulation could benefit from the French experience, as well as from the German. Those who believe in greater flexibility point to Great Britain as a source of inspiration.

The French and German experiences and their approach to the incorporation of the EC Directives have been studied very carefully and recommendations have been given to the Ministry of Finance by researchers from universities, in particular Lodz and Gdańsk.

Since a capital market emerged in Poland only very recently, it is not easy to judge whether the accounting regulations should take into consideration mainly the information needs of shareholders, as in the US and UK, or those of financial institutions as in Germany and Switzerland. Besides, some of the Polish state-owned enterprises have not been fully commercialized, and thus require more uniform accounting rules.

Thus it is required that all enterprises must have their own plans of accounts. A target chart of accounts has been issued by the Ministry of Finance; it is based on the old traditional format. The choice of the cost accounting system has been left to enterprises, as it is in France.

Plans of accounts for budgetary units and local government have been treated separately. These are compulsory statements prepared in a uniform way according to the rules of the Ministry of Finance in compliance with the requirements of the 'Budget Law'. It is the Polish tradition to maintain full consistency between the general ledger and appropriate 'subsidiary ledgers' (analytical accounts). Because of this, accounting systems in practice have been very well developed, and are easy to audit. Accounting developments and traditions of this kind will be preserved.

ACCOUNTING REGULATION PROBLEMS CONCERNING THE NEWLY ESTABLISHED STOCK EXCHANGE IN WARSAW AND THE SECURITIES COMMISSION

Following the promulgated Law on Public Exchange of Securities, and Trustees' Funds (Act of Parliament 22.03.1991), the Order of the Board of Ministers (29 July 1991) was issued concerning requirements which should be met by the Prospectus for Sale of Ordinary Shares. The Order includes, among others, requirements in relation to 'Financial Data'.

The following are the most important:

- report from auditing financial statements, specifying the valuation methods;
- income determination, etc. by authorized auditors for the last three years;
- financial report consisting of: balance sheet, profit and loss statement,

funds flow and cash flow statement for (a) banks as issuers of shares, (b) issuers other than banks, insurance companies and local governments.

The format of these financial statements is different from that recommended in the afore-mentioned accounting regulations included in the Ministry of Finance Order. In addition, a funds flow and cash flow statement is required.

It is very clearly visible that shareholders, being investors, will be much better informed than other information users included in the Ministry of Finance Order. It seems that the Securities Commission takes care of the interests of capital investors, whereas the Ministry of Finance cares more for taxes and protection of the property of state enterprises. It may be expected that in future it will be the Commission that will be responsible for keeping a high standard of accounting regulations.

RECENTLY PROMULGATED ACT ON FINANCIAL STATEMENTS, AUDITING AND THE AUDITORS

On 19 October 1991 the Act on Auditing and Publication of Financial Statements and on Chartered Auditors and their Self-government was promulgated. The provisions of the EC Eighth Directive (from 10 April 1984) were taken into consideration while preparing the draft of this Act.

The Act imposes compulsory annual auditing of the financial reports of the majority of business and governmental entities (art. 2 section 1 and 2). Small businesses have, as usual, been excluded.

The purpose of auditing is to prepare a written statement on the correctness (true) and reliability (fair) of financial reports.

The auditing of financial reports is to be conducted by chartered auditors (*biegly rewident*), operating as sole practitioners, and/or chartered auditing firms. Thus, the Act creates a new 'office' of independent chartered auditor. The above article is similar to the provisions of the EC Eighth Directive.

Under the terms of the Act, commercial companies and co-operatives are obliged to make audited financial reports available to shareholders, business partners and members. In addition to this, all economic units (specified in art. 2 section 1 and 2) are obliged to submit their financial reports for publication within two weeks of their approval, along with a chartered auditor's opinion and a copy of the approving statement of the Supervisory Board.

By the terms of art. 13 the reporting unit should render accessible to the auditing unit the financial statements, ledgers and other documents, and give all information and explanations essential for making out the auditor's report.

The requirements which should be met by chartered auditors who are licensed to audit financial reports individually, or on behalf of the firms authorized to carry out auditing, are specified in the Act in art. 15 section

1. There are certain differences between the resolutions of the Eighth Directive and the provisions of this Act. The Act, unlike the Directive, allows only persons with a higher education to carry out audit. Persons with a long accounting practice, but with only secondary education, are not permitted to become auditors.

It is left to the National Council of Chartered Auditors to work out the details of the theoretical and practical qualifications necessary, the examination procedures and the programmes for training candidates to be chartered auditors. The testing of candidates aspiring to be chartered auditors will be conducted by a State Examination Committee, appointed for a three-year term by the Minister of Finance and the National Council of Chartered Auditors.

The Polish Law lacks a clear statement on whether it is possible or not for financial statements to be audited by chartered auditors from other countries. It allows registration of those chartered auditors from other countries whose 'qualifications guarantee proper execution of professional duties'. This is clearly not sufficiently precise. A more detailed statement by the National Council of Chartered Auditors of the requirements to be met by foreign chartered auditors, and the methods by which they are to be verified, has been issued recently. The provisions of the Eighth Directive in this respect refer only to chartered auditors from the EC member countries, whereas Polish law contains no restrictions regarding an auditor's country of origin. The US and Canadian CPAs have been included by the National Board.

Under the terms of the Eighth Directive, member countries should recommend that persons authorized to carry out compulsory auditing of financial reports are independent. In Poland a majority of members of Parliament were in favour of creating the conditions to ensure independence of chartered auditors. However, the resolutions made by Parliament do not guarantee auditors' independence; this is because it was considered that there was too great a possibility of interference on the part of the Minister of Finance with the activities of the National Council of Chartered Auditors (art. 34).

The Act on Auditing, like the Eighth Directive, introduces obligatory disclosure to the general public of information about persons and institutions entitled to conduct auditing. Such a list (including names and addresses of chartered auditors along with a list of information about names, locations, legal form, names and addresses of chartered auditors and partners or shareholders of institutions licensed to carry out audit or financial statements) is published by the National Council of Chartered Accountants. Currently (December 1992) over 8,000 chartered auditors are listed, and over 120 firms.

The Act also regulates legal questions relating to professional self-government of chartered accountants. It constitutes a National Chamber of

Chartered Auditors as the governing body of chartered auditors, gives it independent legal status, defines its duties and gives directions for the election of its executive committees. Membership of the Chamber is compulsory for chartered auditors. The Bodies of the Chamber are as follows (art. 22):

1 National Congress of Chartered Auditors[1]
2 National Council of Chartered Auditors
3 National Auditing Committee
4 National Disciplinary Court
5 National Disciplinary Attorney.

The National Council of Chartered Accountants has responsibility for audit standards setting and registration (chartered) of auditors and auditing firms.

The Act defines as amenable to the law (liable to prosecution) persons who:

1 include false data in financial statements or give false information to supervisory organs of the entity or to the auditor;
2 are responsible in a given entity for the failure to prepare financial reports, failure to submit them for auditing and failure to publish them;
3 make out false reports on the audited financial statements, ledgers, and on the financial position of the audited entity.

The Polish Act is more comprehensive than the Eighth Directive. It regulates the questions of auditing and publishing financial statements of firms, and institutes a new office of a chartered auditor and the self-government of chartered auditors. This is quite understandable. While in most EC countries an independent profession of chartered auditors has been operating over a long period of time, no such a profession carrying out this role in a market economy existed in Poland. The following issues were the most controversial of the ones discussed before this Act was passed:

- the scope of the act;
- the giving of the authority for the regulation of issues related to financial statements, audit, and the chartered auditors' profession to a ministry other than the Ministry of Finance, e.g. before 1939 these matters were subject to the Ministry of Industry and Trade.
- securing the self-administration and intellectual independence of the accounting profession in truly democratic organizational structures.

The Securities Commission has been entitled to enter the names of the first 200 former state authorized accountants on the list of chartered auditors. The first congress of chartered auditors, during which its executive committees were appointed, took place in June 1992.[1]

There is one question that has not been settled so far, namely the question of former chartered accountants who do not work as auditors, but as directors of enterprises, consultants, etc. There should be an appropriate amendment to the Act in the near future.

THE ROLE OF THE ACCOUNTING PROFESSION IN THE LEGISLATIVE PROCESS

During the last fifty years no mechanism for laying down rules, standards and procedures of accounting has existed in Poland. In the inter-war period, the legal basis for accountancy was regulated by the Commercial Code (1934). During the German occupation the rules of the uniform German General Plan of Accounts were in force. Since the 1950s the centrally planned economy has used a very detailed set of financial rules and a uniform plan of accounts initially patterned strictly after the former USSR models, but modified after 1956. These were usually Acts of a lower order promulgated by the Ministry of Finance (Jaruga, 1972, 1988).

Hence the new accounting regulations gave rise to a defensive reaction from accountants, to strong criticism from the Accountants Association in Poland and to many comments and recommendations from academics, in particular to the first exposure draft of the Order. This process of making recommendations to the legislation is the start of *'de lege ferenda'*. The production of a comprehensive act on accounting has been initiated, hence the Order on Accounting is being treated as a temporary one. It will have to be revised in the near future.

The restructuring of the Polish economy, as well as accounting, began only very recently, and this means there has only been a very short time for accountants to absorb the new approach.

One of the advantages of the regulations seems to be maintaining a well-developed, consistent accounting system in existing state-owned, mostly very large enterprises. At the other end of the scale, small firms, the number of which amounts to nearly 400,000, are often served by Polish accounting and consulting firms.

FINAL REMARKS

The return to the market economy, which involves starting from a situation where state ownership is dominant, and where there is no free market environment, creates very complicated conditions for legislative activities, among them the creation of new accounting regulations. Not only the lack of a financial market environment, but also insufficient knowledge and understanding of the logic of capital market relations are a major problem.

Considering the size of the public sector, we cannot expect that the transition period will be a very short one. Thus the process of restructuring accountancy will have to be gradual and firmly anchored in economic reality.

We cannot make use of any direct expert advice, for no country has had similar experiences in this respect. Fortunately, we have some basis for this work in the form of our old Commercial Code, which dates back to the inter-war period, a period where there was a market economy in Poland.

The new Act requires major amendments and supplements. New accounting regulations promulgated by the Minister of Finance can therefore only be seen as a form of temporary solution.

There is no National Accounting Standards Board to formulate accounting requirements and accounting standards development, to monitor practice, and so on. Instead, the Department of Accounting of the Ministry of Finance has taken sole responsibility for all these tasks without any institutional advisory body. Comments to various drafts have mainly been received from the Accountants Association in Poland, and from accounting academics. The users of accounting information have scarcely been involved in this process yet. The Central Statistical Office has issued its own rules for financial reports.

The recently published 'Order on Accounting Requirements' is based to a certain extent on the traditional structure, a structure well known to professional accountants. While the impact of the Fourth Directive can be clearly seen on the Regulations, as can some influence from the International Accounting Standards, the Order is nevertheless deficient in many respects, particularly on the issue of valuation rules.

Among academics an opinion prevails that a thorough reconstruction of accounting regulations should be incorporated into the commercial code. In that case, the legal framework of accounting has to be distinguished from the standards enforced by the Ministry of Finance. The former could benefit from the advice of foreign accounting experts, who have already incorporated the EC directives into national company law or into commercial codes. The latter requires a better understanding and recognition of accounting and financial reporting by economists and lawyers.

There is an urgent need to establish a mechanism for the setting of accounting regulations which involves all interested parties, like the National Council of Accounting in France, or the recently established institutionalized mechanism in UK. Unfortunately, until now there has been no proper understanding of this problem by managers, trade unions and other new users of accounting information. This is one reason why the dominant influence in the area comes from the financial and tax authorities.

APPENDIX

Governmental Acts Regulating Accounting in Poland

1. Order of the Minister of Finance of 15 January 1991 on the Principles of Accounting.	*Law Gazette* (1991), No. 10, item 35
2. Decree of the President of the Republic of Poland of 27 June 1934: The Commercial Code.	*Law Gazette* (1934), No. 57, item 502 with later changes
3. Act of 19 October 1991 on the Examination and Disclosure of Financial Reports, and Auditors and their Self-Government.	*Law Gazette* (1991) No. 111, item 480
4. Act of 15 February 1992 on the Taxation of Legal Entities	*Law Gazette* (1992) No. 21, item 85
5. Act of 13 July 1990 on Privatization of State Enterprises.	*Law Gazette* (1990) No. 51, item 298 with later changes
6. Act of 14 June 1991 on Companies with Foreign Shareholdings.	*Law Gazette* (1991), No. 60, item 253
7. Order of Minister of Finance of 27 March 1992 on the Matter of Assets to be Considered as Fixed Assets, Intangible and Legal Assets, Principles and Rates of Depreciation, and the Method and Time Limits for the Revaluation of Fixed Assets.	*Law Gazette* (1991), No. 30, item 130
8. Act of 1989 on National Statistics	*Law Gazette* (1989), No. 40, item 221
9. Decree of the Council of Ministers on Detailed Requirements for Listed Securities Projects	*Law Gazette* (1991) No. 71, item 308

NOTE

1 The first Congress took place on 20 June 1992. The author has been elected to the National Council, which consists of nine members.

REFERENCES

Bailey, D. T. (ed.) (1988) *Accounting in Socialist Countries*, London: Routledge, p. 184.

Jaruga, A. A. (1972) 'Problems of Uniform Accounting Principles in Poland', *The International Journal of Accounting*, 8(1): 25–42.

Jaruga, A. A. (1986) *Accounting Research*, International Exchange Programs, Guest Lecture Series, Tokyo: Meiji University Press.

Jaruga, A. A. (1987) 'Accounting Functions in Socialist Countries', *Proceedings of the Sixth International Conference on Accounting Education*, Kyoto.

Jaruga, A. A. (1988) 'Accounting in Poland', in Bailey, D. T. (ed.) *Accounting in Socialist Countries*, London: Routledge, pp. 122–33.

Jaruga, A. A. (1992) 'Eastern Europe: Poland', in Alexander, D. and Archer, S. (eds) *The European Accounting Guide*, London: Academic Press; New York: Harcourt Brace Jovanovich, pp. 975–90.

Swierkocki, J. and Jaruga, A. A. (1990) 'Joint Ventures and Accounting in Poland', in *European Accounting 1990*, EAA.

QUESTIONS

1 Poland offers an interesting case of a rapid change in the cultural and economic framework of a country being matched with a corresponding change in the accounting system. Identify the major problems arising in the implementation of this change.

15

ACCOUNTING SYSTEMS IN DEVELOPING NATIONS

The Nigerian experience

*Lal C. Jagetia and Evaristus C. Nwadike**

Although the basic principles of accounting may be quite similar in all nations, the accounting systems among nations often vary, as they do among different industries. Such diversity of accounting systems can be attributed to the differences in the level(s) of economic development, social climate, and, to a great extent, the degree of accounting sophistication of financial information users in the various countries and industries.[1] Furthermore, and equally significant, analyses of accounting systems among nations indicate that no two accounting and business environments are quite the same. Each national accounting and business environment is different and may require an accounting system with a different approach from that used in other countries.

Given this viewpoint and approach to analyzing the accounting systems of different countries and different business environments, an ideal goal for the accounting bodies of emerging nations would be to adopt those aspects of generally accepted accounting principles and techniques applicable to their particular environment. Ironically, most developing nations have chosen to engage in the erroneous and often regrettable practice of 'importing' accounting systems from developed nations.[2] Such imported accounting systems have been indiscriminately adopted in some developing nations, such as Nigeria, without proper modification to the needs of the nation's specific accounting and business environment, a practice which has sometimes led to rather chaotic practices.[3] This paper discusses the current accounting system in Nigeria and offers suggestions to improve it.

From International Journal of Accounting (Spring 1983) pp 69–81.

THE CURRENT ACCOUNTING SYSTEM AND PROCEDURES IN NIGERIA

The Nigerian accounting system closely parallels and follows the general philosophical approach of British (and to a very limited extent, U.S.) accounting and auditing practices. Such an accounting system, as adopted by the Nigerian body of professional accountants without determining modifications, relies heavily upon 'private sector' accounting practices and concepts. This accounting system includes the double-entry method of reporting the balance sheet, namely that all assets must equal all liabilities and owner's equity for the basic accounting equation to hold. It also includes another conventional business financial statement – the profit and loss account. The present Nigerian accounting system as adapted from the British is not limited to these two general-purpose statements. It also includes the following systems, to name a few: financial and operating statements, ledgers, journals, and other source documents, most of which are generated through sales and cash collecting; purchase and payment; timekeeping and payroll; and product and cost reports.

All companies affected by the Nigerian Companies Decree are required to keep proper books of account, showing receipts and expenditures, sales and purchases, and assets and liabilities.[4] This requirement is met by designing the accounting system from the source documents to the general journal entries and to postings in the general ledger of accounts, and from the ledger accounts to the special assignment, such as preparing the trial balance accounts and preparing the worksheets. The result of the various stages of such an accounting cycle includes the preparation and reporting of the various forms of financial statements: the balance sheet, the profit and loss account, and the statement of changes in financial position. The financial statements and reports are prepared on a monthly basis and serve as reports which management, as well as outside investors, can use to measure the performance of a particular firm and to determine its financial position. They also provide monthly and year-to-date figures. In addition, the consolidated statements of changes in financial position are reported in the event of a merger or acquisition between a parent company and its subsidiaries (Appendices 2A and 2B). Additionally, various forms of accounts are classified as listed in the general ledger and expense ledger accounts and are subsequently arranged in the balance sheet and the profit and loss statements and, in most cases, are numbered according to a formal numeric coding system.

Under the Debits and Credits section, the possible debits and credits are entered following general practice.

The journal section of the accounting cycle contains a complete set of journals. The profit and loss account of each individual firm follows the conventional pattern of Western countries.

These are the traditional reporting methods passed to the Nigerian accounting body by its colonial master, the British. The Nigerian accounting profession has substantially retained their original forms, format, wording, and item classification without total concern as to whether the practices meet the basic accounting requirement of usefulness in Nigeria's unique accounting environment. The Nigerian accounting professional body must often deal with the perennial question of whether these traditional statements, without necessary modification, are useful within the country's accounting environment, given the characteristics of its financial information users, most of whom are unsophisticated in interpreting accounting statements.[5]

Weaknesses in the Current Reporting Method

The problems of accounting in Nigeria and other developing countries have been well documented. Typical managerial problems include poor internal control; lack of management accounting concepts; incomplete, inaccurate and late records; closing; and unauditable systems.[6] The problems are primarily due to the critical shortage of qualified staff and the lack of good accounting systems.[7] And, as stated earlier, the Nigerian accounting profession has applied the accounting practices of the developed countries without modifying them to meet its needs. These imported accounting systems are geared to serve the needs of financial information users in advanced nations who are quite often far more advanced in accounting matters than their Nigerian counterparts.[8] For developing nations, the Nigerian experience re-emphasizes the need for more relevant and useful accounting systems which consider the environmental variables of operation and the level of accounting sophistication of financial information users. The conventional balance sheet, for example, has outlived its usefulness within the Nigerian context. It must be modified to meet the changing needs of the Nigerian accounting and business environment.

Following the Company Decree of 1968 which, to a very great extent, is a copy of the British Company Decree, the Nigerian accountant currently adheres to the reporting method with the conventional balance sheet, and profit and loss accounts previously mentioned. The Nigerian Company Decree of 1968 states: 'Every balance sheet of a company shall give a true and fair view of the state of affairs of the company as at the end of its financial year, and every profit and loss account of a company shall give a true and fair view of the profit and loss of the company, . . .'[9] This Decree insists on fairness in financial reporting and does not in any form or manner emphasize relevance and objectivity in the accounting system and procedures. This in itself is a major problem of the Nigerian Company Decree as adapted from the British and, thus, is a major shortcoming in Nigeria's current overall accounting practices. Professionals generally accept the view that any financial statement will serve its communication function best when it organizes accounting data in the format most understandable to users. Such financial statements often avoid giving the impression of 'conclusiveness,' especially when one realizes that the usual balance sheet and earnings statements are not final statements in themselves but are dynamic in nature. Another vital point that accounting experts often associate with an 'ideal' financial statement is that of making full disclosure of all important and material accounting information.

Given these facts, it becomes imperative to evaluate the entire concept of full disclosure in light of Nigeria's current accounting system in order to determine to what extent, if any, it has been successful in the Nigerian context. The study of the present Nigerian accounting system has shown major violations of some, if not all, of these acceptable standards of financial statement reporting. In no area are such pitfalls more noticeable than in the balance sheet, which is still prepared in the traditional format in Nigeria.

The major faults with this traditional method of preparing and reporting the balance sheet account are that it is not only foreign to the Nigerian accounting environment, but it is also too long and too complex to be comprehended by the various financial statement users in Nigeria. With respect to the accounting information generated from both the external and internal financial reporting needs, accounting systems in Nigerian industries are deficient. The information generated from external reporting formats provides little information relevant to investment decisions, and potential investors are uncertain as to the validity and reliability of that accounting information. Based on his observation, Mahon has also noted the lack of reliability of financial statements prepared in developing countries.[10] Seidler noted the inadequacy of financial information in Turkey.[11] The internal accounting system in Nigeria has also been noted to be deficient in these regards. It cannot be considered effective for top management's decision-making purposes because it is rudimentary and offers management little or no vital information. Seidler notes that:

> in a number of the less developed countries, information systems which provide reliable financial data are few in number . . . . each time a production, pricing or investment decision is made without adequate knowledge of its consequences, the probability of misdirected efforts, wasted resources and economic loss is increased.[12]

Suggestions for Improving Current Accounting Reporting

In his recent study, Skinner concluded the ultimate objective of accounting to be 'to convey information that is relevant to the needs of the user.'[13] Indisputably, this statement highlights 'usefulness' as the primary objective of accounting, and is indeed accurate in the context of the Nigerian accounting environment. The various accounting information users in Nigeria include investors, trade unions, the government and government agencies, various institutions, and businesses. They are primarily nontechnical people, often uninformed and unsophisticated in financial and accounting matters. Given this fact, it becomes imperative that the Nigerian Institute of Chartered Accountants adopt necessary steps to reduce the use of technical terms and simplify formats to increase the reader's grasp of the message without jeopardizing the Institute's professional standards. Too great a deviation from the necessary standard accounting vocabulary may partially distort the financial statement's message to the users. The concept of materiality will inevitably become a vital element in preparing a suggested financial statement for the Nigerian financial information user as illustrated in Appendices 1 and 2. Such financial statements are simple, comprehensive, and are also written in layman's language. Nigerian users' lack of sophistication in interpreting these financial statements has been mentioned. Readers of financial statements usually center their interests around activities rather than technical and statistical discourse; therefore, it is imperative that reports reveal the ebb and flow of activities during the normal cycle of an enterprise. Such systematic reporting would enable the unsophisticated reader to see the flow of 'costs' into factors of production, and to determine the success/failure rate achieved in converting products or services into liquid funds, and in using liquid assets in different productive factors, as in liquidation of debts. Another advantage to this systematic approach to financial statement reports is that it increases the 'beauty' of accounting as an art and a scientific discipline. For example, the relationship between assets and liabilities need not be completely lost; it should be a matter of secondary interest rather than a focal point of reporting.

Financial statements would better serve users in developing countries if they report profit information clearly, as well as reveal the nature of the business enterprise and the economic function of management instead of possibly distorting vital financial information. With every expansion of realization by the public that business provides Nigeria its primary source of consumption goods, and its wages (the primary means to buy what is produced), the Nigerian Institute of Chartered Accountants will be called to use accounting to make business understandable. Accurate and understandable reporting, as well as dependable auditing data, is very much in the public interest. The message in the financial statements should use fewer technical terms so that the users can understand the accounting information and thus become more adequately informed.

Varying from the traditional standardized balance sheet format may make presentation of financial data more informative, understandable, and clearer. As suggested previously, balance sheet data, as well as the profit and loss statement data, must be arranged to highlight the most significant aspect of the particular situation (Appendices 1 and 2). The heading need not always be that used in the British System. Whatever heading is used, many professional accountants in Nigeria contend that the balance sheet data need not be presented in the traditional format. Traditional arrangements should be modified whenever a useful purpose might be served without loss of information, the new balance sheet must substitute informative and descriptive phrases for technical terms, it must reduce complexities, and it must clearly separate the various parts of the message to meet the needs of unsophisticated users of financial information in Nigeria and in other developing countries.

Most of the published accounts of Nigerian companies are in the 'T' account format. A 'vertical' reporting format (Appendix 3), however, if properly arranged, should be appropriate within the Nigerian accounting environment. In this format, which is currently being suggested for universal application in Nigeria, current liabilities would be subtracted from current assets, thus directly disclosing working capital. To the amount of working capital thus reported, 'other assets' are added and 'other liabilities' deducted to determine the owner's equity (Appendix 3). This format, as opposed to the conventional format of reporting changes in a firm's financial position, has the advantage of highlighting working capital, an important reporting need, and also facilitates comparisons between years.

The current Nigerian accounting practice of using just one year's comparative figures for financial reporting purposes should be changed. Comparative figures for periods of no less than three years should be made compulsory for all businesses and institutions except in cases where the company has not been in operation for such a length of time. If these data cannot be reported in the body of the statement, they should be shown in subsidiary statements. This method of preparing the balance sheet and profit and loss statement has the advantage of disclosing important changes and gives an idea of the business' financial development over the years. In order not to mislead readers, the comparative figures should reflect the consistent application of generally accepted accounting principles from period to period. Any reason for noncomparability of the statements should be disclosed. It is strongly suggested that comparative figures for the same periods of earnings per share, if any, be shown immediately below the reported profit and loss statement. It is also vital that current market value per share and return on equity be shown immediately at the bottom of the reported balance sheet. This is primarily for Nigerian shareholders who are more interested in the profitability ratio than in the financial analysis ratio. Financial information that depicts profitability, and returns on equity and investments reported in the layman's language will be most useful in Nigeria.

Useful disclosures should be made in the body of the financial statement with a description of each item. Also, any additional useful information may be shown in footnotes or included in the firm's report to the directors.

Next, but most important of the recommendations, is the need for all statement items appearing to be described in clear, easily understandable language. Such simplified balance sheets, as compared with the present complex, traditional form adopted from the British, should be reworded to make them understandable to unsophisticated financial information users. Appendix 3 exhibits such a balance sheet.

The new series of accounting principles designed specifically to meet the needs of the Nigerian accounting and business environment would best serve Nigeria. Accounting principles, concepts, and practice will have meaning only if they are constantly tested and modified against the unique economic background of the nation involved. According to Professor Enthoven,

> . . . accounting must integrate with its socioeconomic environment. Since this environment differs from country to country, it follows that any profession that ignores its environment is heading for trouble or, at least, hampering its ability to render as full service to the country as possible. This does not mean, of course, that accounting professions must start from scratch, but rather that methods and procedures that have worked in one country cannot automatically be assumed to work in another.[14]

Since developing nations are often plagued with heavy inflation and the impact of rapid technological changes, the factors which determine what increases net assets may differ in such an environment from those in the developed nation. Professor Enthoven recommends current value accounting in the economies which are highly controlled by governments because there is considerable likelihood that current prices reflect current government policies which do not necessarily underlie economic reality.[15] Technical changes may occur faster in the developing countries than in the developed countries, and the need for accurate value measurement of such items as capital output for cost, profit, taxation, and replacement cost in developing countries may vary from that of developed nations.

In summary, what developing nations need are systematic and carefully planned accounting systems designed to meet the unique needs of the individual country's accounting and business environments. Variables to be considered are type of economy, political system, business ownership, social climate, sophistication of business management and financial community, pace of business innovations, and stages of economic development.[16] Such accounting systems can be patterned after the accounting systems of developed nations, such as the United States, but they must be modified to suit the unique need of the accounting and business environment of the specific country as Professor Enthoven suggests.

NOTES

1 Frederick D. S. Choi and Gerhard G. Mueller, *An Introduction to Multinational Accounting* (Englewood Cliffs, N.J.: Prentice-Hall, 1978), pp. 23–28.
2 Adolf J. H. Enthoven, *Accountancy and Economic Development Policy* (New York: North-Holland, 1973), pp. 276–86.
3 Ibid., p. 279.
4 Ernst & Whinney, *Nigeria* (1979), p. 4.
5 Merrill E. Cassell, 'Economic Development Accountancy,' *Management Accounting* (May 1979): 24. According to him, illiteracy in Nigeria may be a factor. Only 7.2 percent of school-age children in Nigeria attend school.
6 H. P. Holzer and J. S. Chandler, 'A Systems Approach to Accounting in Developing Countries,' *Management International Review*, vol. 21, no. 4 (1981): 23.
7 Ibid., p. 24.
8 Ibid., pp. 23–28.
9 The Federal Republic of Nigeria Official Gazette, Decree No. 51 – *Companies Decree of 1968*, vol. 55 (Lagos, 1968).
10 James J. Mahon, 'Some Observations on World Accounting,' *Journal of Accountancy* (January 1968): 34–35.
11 Lee J. Seidler, *The Function of Accounting in Economic Development – Turkey as a Case Study* (London: Frederick Praeger, 1967).
12 Robert E. Seiler, 'Accounting Information System and the Underdeveloped Nations,' *Accounting Review* (October 1966): 653.
13 R. M. Skinner, *Accounting Principles – A Canadian Viewpoint* (Toronto: Canadian Institute of Chartered Accountants, 1972), p. 304.
14 Frederick D. S. Choi and Gerhard G. Mueller, *Essentials of Multinational Accounting: An Anthology* (Ann Arbor, Mich.: University Microfilms International, 1979), p. 607.
15 Ibid., p. 407.
16 Choi and Mueller, *Introduction to Multinational Accounting*, pp. 23–28.

QUESTIONS

1. Analyse the specific problems in applying a developed country's accounting approach in a developing country that this article reveals.

APPENDIX

Appendix 1A. Conventional Method of Preparing the Balance Sheet Statement

Nwosu and Sons Co.
Consolidated Statement of Financial Position
(Amounts in Thousands Naira)*

	December 31	
ASSETS	198_	198_
Current assets		
Cash and cash equivalent	4,581	2,592
Accounts receivable	46,584	28,815
Inventories	82,100	43,662
Deferred income taxes	5,314	3,428
Total current assets	138,579	78,497
OTHER ASSETS		
Goodwill and other intangibles	18,635	4,739
Property, plant and equipment		
Land	4,058	1,939
Buildings	39,040	24,101
Machinery and Equipment	91,423	59,469
Less allowance for depreciation	(39,934)	(35,646)
	94,587	49,863
Unexpended construction funds	222	1,842
	94,809	51,705
Total assets	252,023	134,941
LIABILITIES AND OWNER'S EQUITY		
Notes payable	4,500	0
Accounts payable	18,489	8,100
Accrued expenses	24,782	11,318
Taxes and other income taxes	13,027	7,971
Current maturities of long-term debt	1,300	1,390
Total current liability	62,098	28,779
Long-term debt and others	92,414	35,708
Capitalized lease obligations	3,758	4,060
Deferred income taxes	6,860	4,549
STOCKHOLDER'S EQUITY		
Preferred stock	60,688	48,383
Common stock (10 million shares at $5 par)	26,205	13,462
Total Liabilities and Owner's Equity	252,023	134,941

* Naira (Nigerian currency) = $1.58 U.S.

Appendix 1B. Suggested Balance Sheet Statement for use in the Nigerian Accounting Environment

Nwasu Corporation
Simplified Report on Financial Position
December 31, 1980
(Amounts in Thousands Naira)*

	198	197
Our cash and other items readily convertible into cash are		
Money in form of cash held in safe	2,581	1,592
Money in form of cash held in bank	2,000	1,000
Amount owing to us by our customers	46,584	28,815
Materials and other stock of goods for sale or use	222	1,842
The total of the above items in terms of cash	51,387	33,249
Against this we owe the following:		
Amount due to our suppliers and others	22,989	8,100
Current expenses yet to be settled	26,082	12,708
Accrued taxes not yet paid	13,027	7,971
The total of what we owe currently	62,098	28,779
After settling what we owe currently, the net working capital left for business operations is	(10,711)	4,470
To this we add our plant, property and equipment	43,098	26,040
Machinery and plant (after deduction of allowance for wear and tear)	51,489	23,823
Investments and other property owned	106,049	51,829
Therefore, the total of what we have to work with is	189,925	106,162
Against this, if we deduct what we owe in terms of our long-term borrowing, deferred taxes, etc., totaling	103,032	44,317
We have the remaining balance	86,893	61,845
Represented by		
Investment preferred shareholders	60,668	48,383
Investment by common shareholders	26,205	13,462

* Naira (Nigerian currency) = $1.58 U.S.

Appendix 2A. Consolidated Statement of Changes in Financial Position

Nwosu Corporation and Subsidiaries
(Amounts in Thousands Naira)*

SOURCES OF FUND	198	197
Net earnings	7,009	4,975
Provisions for depreciation and amortization	4,440	4,975
Noncurrent deferred income tax	(1,358)	2,375
Total from operation	10,091	11,722
Decrease in assets + Other costs	4,498	0
Disposal of property, plant and equipment	1,496	781
Decrease in other assets	258	0
Increase in long-term debt	7,540	28,700
Increase in capital lease obligations	2,080	0
Increase in other long-term liabilities	509	0
Shares issued for acquisition	0	...
Shares issued – Stock option	153	242
	26,625	41,445
APPLICATION OF FUNDS		
Property + Other assets	0	...
Long-term depreciation, pension liability, others	0	...
Addition to property, plant and equipment	6,460	7,887
Unexpended construction fund	1,842	0
Cash dividends	2,420	2,135
Decrease in long-term debt	8,520	27,555
Decrease in capitalized liabilities	253	438
Decrease in other liabilities	518	861
Deferred realignment cost	...	2,197
Increase in notes receivable and other assets	...	174
Increase in working capital	6,612	154
Other, net	...	48
	26,625	41,445
INCREASE (DECREASE) IN WC		
Cash and cash equivalents	(1,954)	(1,869)
Accounts receivable and notes receivable	8,002	3,702
Inventories	7,139	2,072
Deferred income tax and prepaid expenses	(243)	(257)
Notes payable – Banks	0	...
Accounts payable	(261)	(4,099)
Accrued expenses + Other liabilities	(2,144)	806
Taxes, other than income tax	(63)	(396)
Income taxes	(3,917)	550
Current maturities – long-term debt	53	(355)
	6,612	154

* Naira (Nigerian currency) = $1.58 U.S.

Appendix 2B. Statement of Suggested Changes in Financial Position

Nwosu and Sons Company
(Amounts in Thousands of Naira)*

The source of our new working capital for running the business were made up of:	
Net profit and loss account'	13,779
Add: Expenses *not* involving spending funds	
Allowance for wear and tear of buildings	19,967
Allowance for wear and tear of machinery	19,967
Provisions for deferred income taxes	6,860
Funds provided from internal operations	60,573
Add: External sources through which we raise funds	
Sale of preferred shares	33,536
Sale of ordinary shares	53,357
Borrowing on long-term basis	103,553
Total of our new working capital (internal and external)	251,019
From this we *deduct* the following uses made of funds	
Addition to buildings	34,040
Purchase of new lands	4,058
Part payment of long-term borrowing	40,538
Payment of dividends	
Preferred shares	15,000
Ordinary shares	10,000
NET INCREASE (DECREASE IN WORKING CAPITAL)	147,383

* Naira (Nigerian currency) = $1.58 U.S.

Appendix 3. Suggested Balance Sheet Account in its Vertical Format for the Nigerian Accounting Environment

Nwosu and Sons Limited
Balance Sheet – Vertical Format
December 31, 198?
(Amount in Thousands Naira)*

Add ALL current assets	600
Less ALL current liabilities	(200)
Net working capital	400
Add 'Other assets'	250
Less 'Other liabilities'	10
OWNER'S EQUITY	640

* Naira (Nigerian currency) = $1.58 U.S.

16

ADOPTION OF INTERNATIONAL ACCOUNTING STANDARDS BY PAPUA NEW GUINEA

Is there an alternative?

Evarist B. Mwesigye,

INTRODUCTION

Accounting standards have as their main objective the harmonisation of accounting practice and reporting. They achieve this by narrowing down differences in practice and reporting. They ensure that as little harm as possible is done to the users of financial statements. Standards enhance the confidence that users of financial statements put in those statements. Accounting standards also help the accounting profession in making judgement on accounting transactions and how best effectively to measure and report those transactions.

Papua New Guinea, like most other developing countries, has until recently had no specific accounting standards to guide its accountants. The first step towards standardizing accounting practice and reporting was made in 1982 with the introduction of a single standard by the Papua New Guinea Association of Accountants (PNGAA). A year later several international accounting standards were adopted. Apart from the standard introduced in 1982 all subsequent standards have been international standards. The PNGAA had earlier (in 1980) indicated that it intended to base PNG accounting standards on the international accounting standards, supported where appropriate by standards issued by Australian accounting bodies.[1] Evidently, the PNGAA intends to adopt international accounting standards to guide accounting practice in the country.

From Papua New Guinea Journal of Accounting (September 1988) pp 41–44.
Reprinted by permission of the Papua New Guinea Journal of Accounting.

Is this trend by the PNGAA in the best interests of the profession? Should not some caution be exercised in adopting international accounting standards?

This paper addresses itself to the question above. It tries to trace the history of accounting standards in PNG, and the history of international accounting standards and how they have been received in other countries. The paper makes some suggestions on how the PNGAA could handle the difficult exercise of standardizing accounting practice and reporting in PNG.

PNG AND ACCOUNTING STANDARDS

The accounting profession in PNG is in its infancy. The PNGAA was set up, among other things, to register accountants and regulate their practices. Accounting standards are meant to assist in the latter objective. Because the profession is young, it has relatively few members and minimal financial and technical resources. The small number of members and the limited resources impede the ability of the PNGAA to draw up its own accounting standards. Recognising these limitations, the profession found it convenient to adopt ready-made accounting standards from Australia and later copied most of the existing international accounting standards.

The accounting standards adopted by the PNGAA consist of PNG AS1 'Profit and Loss Statement' which is a replica of AAS1 – an Australian accounting standard.

The international accounting standards adopted are: IAS1, IAS2, IAS3, IAS4, IAS5, IAS8, IAS10, IAS12, IAS16, IAS17, IAS18, IAS20, IAS21, IAS22, IAS23.[2]

Those which have not been adopted include IAS6, IAS7, IAS9, IAS11, IAS13, IAS14, IAS15, IAS19, IAS24, IAS25, and IAS26.

The list above indicates that not all existing international accounting standards have been adopted. It is curious that some of the standards have been rejected. Does it mean that they are inappropriate? Are those which have been adopted suitable for the PNG profession? The PNGAA does not answer these questions. A closer look at international accounting standards is perhaps warranted.

INTERNATIONAL ACCOUNTING STANDARDS

International accounting standards are published and issued by the International Accounting Standards Committee (IASC). The IASC was set up in 1973. It comprises of almost 100 accounting profession bodies operating in about 70 countries worldwide. The IASC aims at encouraging uniformity of accounting reporting throughout the world by publishing accounting standards and promoting their acceptance and observance. It is assumed that by adhering to international standards, accounting reporting worldwide will result in more reliable and comparable accounting information. This is very desirable because the world has become a smaller place with the growth and increase in numbers of multinational companies. It is now common for companies to have branches and subsidiaries in several countries. Investors and other users of financial statements wish to be assured that the reported results of companies operating in different countries are not clouded by differences in accounting practices and reporting prevalent from country to country.

The IASC has therefore set out to draw up international accounting standards that should harmonise accounting reporting across national borders. The IASC encourages its members to comply with international accounting standards. The committee does not prohibit its members from issuing their own national accounting standards but it hopes that when such standards are issued they do not conflict with international accounting standards.

The international accounting standards have no worldwide legal backing. Hence they are not mandatory. Nevertheless member bodies of the IASC are not expected to encourage their observance. Implicitly the IASC recognises the fact that international accounting standards have a secondary role to play to national accounting standards. Again this is understandable as financial statements must not only comply with accounting standards but also with other relevant regulatory requirements (e.g. companies acts, stock exchange rules etc) which may differ from country to country. Where the reporting requirements of these bodies are vague or incomplete, the national accounting standards help to fill in the gap. This role cannot be fully satisfied by international accounting standards.

OPTIONS AVAILABLE TO COUNTRIES WITH NO ACCOUNTING STANDARDS OF THEIR OWN

As mentioned earlier, developing countries do not have sufficient resources to draw up their own accounting standards. There are at least four options available to them:

1 have no accounting standards,
2 develop from scratch their own accounting standards,
3 adopt accounting standards drawn up by some other country and
4 adopt international accounting standards.

The first option is undesirable as it will leave the country with no accounting profession regulation of practice and reporting. The second option is unrealistic for most developing countries as they do not have sufficient human and material resources to put up competent standards of their own. The third option has limitations in that the business, legal and social environments (which are paramount in drawing up accounting standards) differ from country to country. The fourth option appears more palatable because international accounting standards by their nature, are supposed to have international applicability. They are drawn up in general terms and are not constrained by any particular statutes. To date no international companies act is in existence and none will become available in the foreseeable future. A closer examination of the fourth option is necessary to gauge its appropriateness for PNG.

The major shortcoming of the fourth option is that international accounting standards are not drawn up primarily to satisfy the needs of countries with no accounting standards of their own.[3] By their nature, international accounting standards are a summary of accepted accounting practices in the developed countries. The IASC tries as much as possible to avoid issuing accounting standards already issued in countries that finance and support the IASC.[4] The IASC encourages support for its standards and to achieve this it avoids contradicting accounting standards in the developed countries. All this results in international accounting standards reflecting accounting practices in the UK and US.[5]

PNG is a developing country and its business, legal and social environment differ greatly from those existing in developed countries. Therefore it would seem unwise for PNG to adopt wholly these international accounting standards.

AUSTRALIAN ACCOUNTING STANDARDS – SUITABILITY FOR PNG

It was pointed out at the beginning of this paper that accounting standards are meant to help both the preparers and users of financial statements. Before deciding on the standards to adopt, it may be useful to take a closer look at the two groups.

The preparers of financial statements are the members of the PNGAA. Most members of the PNGAA are also members of the two professional accounting bodies in Australia. Australian accountants are likely to continue influencing accounting reporting in this country for some years to come. This fact favours adoption of Australian accounting standards. Such a step would benefit the country by facilitating staff transfers between Australia and PNG (both in terms of training and practice). Time and money would also be saved because the majority of accounting practitioners would already be familiar with the accounting standards in use. Additionally, many of the multinational companies operating in PNG have their headquarters in Australia. Preparation, consolidation and comparability of their reports would be enhanced through the adoption of Australian accounting standards.

The users of financial statements would in the majority be PNG citizens. National identity and sovereignty might prompt arguments to break ties with the Australian profession. However, as pointed out earlier, international accounting standards are not drawn up to be used by countries with no accounting standards of their own but rather to foster harmonisation of accounting reporting worldwide. Some PNG citizens and bodies hold investments in Australian companies that have branches or subsidiaries in PNG. Uniformity in reporting would enhance the utility that such investors derive from the financial statements of those companies.

Lastly the historical and geographical closeness that exists between PNG and Australia scales down the environmental differences between the two countries. Environmental differences are the cause of disparities in accounting standards.

CONCLUSION

Examination of the needs of preparers and users of accounting standards and also of the nature and usefulness of international accounting standards all point towards the desirability of adopting Australian accounting standards. The PNG business and legal environments are more related to those of Australia than those which the international accounting standards purport to serve.

For those who may be worried about national identity, it is heartening to note that several developing countries have successfully adopted accounting standards of some of the developed countries.[6] It should also be remembered that accounting standards everywhere are being continuously withdrawn or revised as circumstances change. If the PNGAA decides to adopt Australian accounting standards, and circumstances change at some future date, it could always adopt some more suitable standards. Lastly and probably more importantly. Australian accounting standards conform with international accounting standards.[7] Adoption of Australian accounting standards could be a case of killing two birds with one stone: enjoying the benefits of similarities in business and legal environments of PNG and Australia and also retaining the good intentions shown so far by the PNGAA accounting standards committee.

This paper therefore suggests that the stance taken by the PNGAA to date of basing PNG accounting standards on international accounting standards supported by Australian standards be reversed. The PNGAA could serve the interests of users and preparers of financial statements better by basing PNG accounting standards on Australian accounting standards supported by international accounting standards.

NOTES

1 M. Pratley, 'Papua New Guinea Association of Accountants Inc, Statement of Accounting Standards – Materiality in Financial Statements', *Papua New Guinea Journal of Accounting*, Vol. 5, No. 4, Page 3.

2 PNGAA, 'What is the IASC?,' *Papua New Guinea Journal of Accounting*, Vol. 5 No. 4 Page 13.
3 F. E. Amenkhienan, *Accounting in Developing Countries – A Framework for Standard Setting*, UMI Research Press, Ann Arbor, Michigan, 1986, Page 24.
4 A. K. Mason, 'The Evolution of International Accounting Standards,' In D. S. Choi, *Multinational Accounting – A Research Framework for the Eighties*, UMI Research Press, Ann Arbor, Michigan, 1981, Page 160.
5 C. Nobes and R. Parker, *Comparative International Accounting*, Philip Allan/St Martins Press, 1975, Page 337.
6 Ibid Page 340.
7 P. J. Shrives, 'International Accounting and International Accounting Standards,' *Students' Newsletter*, The Chartered Association of Certified Accountants, August 1987, Page 6.

QUESTIONS

1 Why does Mwesigye feel that International Accounting Standards are an inadequate basis for accounting regulations in Papua New Guinea, and what is the basis for his alternative approach?

2 Compare and contrast Mwesigye's approach to the problems of accounting regulation in a developing country with the arguments put forward by Hove in an earlier article.

17

THE ACCOUNTING PROFESSION IN THE PEOPLE'S REPUBLIC OF CHINA

Shan Sheng Gao

1. INTRODUCTION

Recently, many western people are interested in Chinese accounting in both academic and practical aspects. A number of introductory papers concerning Chinese accounting have been published[1]. However, the detailed discussion of the accounting profession in China has not been seen in the literature. This article attempts to introduce the Chinese accounting profession. In China, the accounting profession generally cover all the occupations which are directly related to accounting practical work including bookkeepers, financial managers, CPAs, and senior accountants etc. Many accountants who are engaged in auditing work are also belong to the accounting profession. Those people are generally called Caikuai Zhuanye Renyuan in Chinese. Therefore, the next part of this article will introduce the accounting profession in China mainly focusing on the Chinese Certified Public Accountants (CPAs) and the Chinese CPA firms. The third part of the article will introduce the auditing profession in China with particular emphasis on the Chinese audit system including the state audit, social (public) audit, and internal audit. The final part will present a conclusion.

2. THE CHINESE ACCOUNTING PROFESSION

2.1 The Chinese Accounting System

The Chinese accounting system can essentially be separated into two broad principal categories: enterprise accounting and budgeting unit accounting

From Pacioli Journal (October 1992) pp 15–18.
Reprinted by permission from Pacioli Journal.

(e.g., administrative and nonprofit unit accounting)[2]. Further, the accounting system in China, which has been established on the concept of 'fund' and the theory of 'socialist economy', are characterized by a high degree of uniformity and detailed regulations. In fact, China has separate unified accounting systems for different industries or sectors of the economy. Although these systems differ in some aspects, all unified accounting systems usually have similar parts or sections, such as general rules, chart of accounts, types and formats of financial reports, and their submission and interpretation etc. For example, the financial statements for state industrial enterprises in China are comprised of 13 statements, including the balance sheet, income statement, and various other statements related to costs, fixed assets, special funds, special appropriations, current funds etc. which are unified within all the industries in the economy.

2.2 The Chinese Accounting Profession

According to Chinese, the accounting profession, in a wide sense, cover all the occupations which are directly related to accounting, auditing and corporate finance work; in a narrow sense, it means accountants, senior accountants, and Certified Public Accountants. We take the narrow sense in this section. As in other countries, accountants in China are staff members rather than line members. One of their primary responsibilities is to be good advisors to top managers. However, accountants in China not only contribute to better performance in their own enterprises, but may also have opportunities to contribute to others. In other words, the Chinese accountants in an enterprise usually serve in a dual position. On the one hand, they have to represent the nation or the central government authorities to strength financial supervision and to implement financial discipline to protect the interests of the national economy; on the other hand, they have to properly utilize the economic forces and information, such as prices, funds, costs and profits, to make the enterprise vital, to exploit its financial resources, to optimize its operational decisions, and to improve the effectiveness of its business management to increase its total operational economic benefits.

The Accounting Society of China, reorganised in 1980 after a brief suspension during the Cultural Revolution, have multiple goals associated with the development activities within the profession. More importantly, the Society was made responsible for coordinating relations with similar bodies in the Western world. The national system of recognizing and supervising certified public accountants (CPAs) ended in 1951 shortly after the founding of the People's republic of China. The new national policy of opening up to the outside world and of increasing foreign investments in China, as well as the establishment of shareholding companies and joint ventures with foreigners has greatly stimulated the resumption of the CPA system in China.

In January 1985, the National People's Congress passed the Accounting Law of the People's Republic of China. This Law specified the duties of accounting personnel and the operation of accounting offices. Further implementation of the Accounting Law came with the promulgation of 'the Regulation Concerning Certified Public Accountants of the People's Republic of China' (the Regulation, hereafter) by the State Council on 3 July 1986. The Regulation provided for the establishment of public accounting firms to independently undertake the work performed by CPAs. The Regulations also stipulated a CPA to be associated with an accounting firm. The CPAs were given the permission to form their professional institute. In China, the Ministry of Finance was administratively responsible for CPAs.

No CPA examinations and specified regulations are set in China prior to 3 July 1986. The majority of the CPAs were given the title through recommendation and selection according to their schooling, experience, and professional competence. Initially, those having university degrees and over twenty years of experience were certified. On 3 July 1986, the Regulation was issued to regulate the academic requirements at a consistent level across the country. According to Article 6 of the Regulation, each candidate sitting for the CPA examination must be a Chinese citizen and must be a college graduate or a person with an equivalent academic education and have worked in the accounting or auditing field for more than three years. The CPA examination is directed, organized, and supervised on a uniform basis by a national examination board approved by the Ministry of Finance. The examination may cover financial accounting, management (cost) accounting, financial management, auditing, economic laws, and relevant regulations. A division of the China Institute of Certified Public Accountants (CICPA) has been established to make general arrangements for the examination which is held either once a year or every two years. Accountants and staff of CPA firms and other accounting practitioners are encouraged to take the examination. Also, an applicant for registration as a CPA can waive the examination requirement and qualify through an evaluation process. The applicant must be either a senior accountant, an accounting professor and/or associate professor, a research fellow or an associate fellow with experience in accounting practice. Some individuals with a college or equivalent education and with 20 years of experience in the financial accounting field also may apply. However, no staff working in government agencies may be registered to practice as a CPA.

2.3 The China Institute of Certified Public Accountants (CICPA)

After the Regulation became effective on October 1 1986, the CICPA, was founded in November 1988, to be in charge of all affairs related to CPAs, such as CPA registration, registration of CPA firms, and CPA examinations. Generally speaking, the objectives of the CICPA are:

- to set rules and issue professional statements for CPAs covering auditing, insolvencies, ethics and scale fees;
- to organise and set annual or half yearly uniform examination for CPAs;
- to maintain contacts with professional accounting organizations outside China and with international accounting firms;
- to 'encourage, supervise and check' that public accounting firms abide by laws and regulations and practice in an appropriate way, maintaining professional standards;
- to act as a conduit for the suggestions, opinions and requirements from CPAs to government departments and to seek government support for the profession;
- to act as a forum for CPAs for exchanging of professional experience;
- to organize continuing professional education for CPAs.

Usually, CPAs registered in China are members of the CICPA, while outstanding accounting professors, academics, and practitioners may become members of the CICPA upon recommendation and approval by the Executive Board of the CICPA. Local CPA firms are also members of the CICPA, and local institutes of CPAs are considered as local organizations of the CICPA. One difference between the CICPA and its Western counterparts such as the CICA, AICPA, etc., is that the uniform examination and certification procedures still vest with the Ministry of Finance.

2.4 Chinese Accounting or CPA Firms

Currently, there are about 1,500 Chinese CPA firms established in major commercial and industrial cities, employing about 6,700 Chinese CPAs. Generally speaking, Chinese accounting or CPA firms are independent, self-financed, private business organisations. Many Chinese accounting or CPA firms have signed cooperative agreements with foreign accounting firms. Clients of Chinese CPA firms are not limited to enterprises with foreign participants. In addition to Chinese-foreign joint ventures and foreign enterprises, the clients also include Chinese domestic enterprises of various ownerships and non-profit institutions or organisations. Government organisations as clients, can also secure services from accounting or CPA firms. Most Chinese accounting or CPA firms render a wide scope of services including:

1 annual audits of financial statements;
2 business and financial management consultative services;
3 tax services;
4 feasibility studies for investment;

5 accounting system design and application assistance;
6 acting as agent for patent applications, business establishments, changes, dissolutions, and liquidations;
7 settlements of claims and debts;
8 participation in preparing articles of association, deeds, contracts, and agreements or other business document; and
9 conduct of training programs and operating part-time vocational schools open to the general public.

Although Chinese accounting or CPA firms contribute a wide scope of services, public auditing is generally a major part of the services. The annual audit of the financial statements of Chinese-foreign joint ventures by accounting firms registered with the government is legislatively mandated. Relevant stipulations can be found in the 'Rules for the Implementation of the Law of the People's Republic of China Concerning Chinese Foreign Joint Ventures' (Article 90) and 'The Accounting Regulations of the People's Republic of China for the Joint Ventures Using Chinese and Foreign Investment' (Article 73). However, the financial statements of Chinese state-owned enterprises are normally not audited by CPA firms but are reviewed by relevant, higher organisational units, and they are audited by state audit organisations. Since the Chinese CPA system was suspended for three decades, several generations of competent CPAs have been lost. Currently, the older generation, who had been CPAs before 1951 or those who had been well trained at that time, continue to play an important role. Although they are experienced, they have some difficulty in mastering new technology. Most young accountants without CPAs who are working in the CPA firms are recent college graduates. They have acquired current auditing knowledge, but it takes time for them to become certified.

Noticeably, China's CPA firms are in many respects different from audit firms. Audit firms are established with the approval of the Audit Administration of the People's Republic of China or the audit institutions, while CPA firms employ CPAs and are approved by the Ministry of Finance or Finance Bureaus at the provincial level. A CPA firm must have at least a Certified Public Accountant, whereas an audit firm may not have any CPA.

3. THE CHINESE AUDITING PROFESSION

3.1 The Chinese Auditing System

In September 1983, the Audit Administration of the People's Republic of China (AAPRC) was established. The establishment implies that the audit function was resumed in China after an absence of nearly 35 years. Following the creation of the AAPRC, the Auditing Society of China was established in 1984[3]. Broadly speaking, the auditing profession includes state auditors, internal auditors, independent CPA auditors, and their professional bodies. In China, state audit is the main part of the auditing profession and it is led by the AAPRC. The AAPRC is the highest audit institution in China, which comprises functional administrative departments, audit agencies stationed in key regions and government departments, and research and training institutions. Under the leadership of the Premier of the State Council, the AAPRC organises and directs the audit work of the whole country, and carries out audits that fail under its direct jurisdiction. Local audit bureaus at county, municipal and provincial levels organize and direct the audit work in their respective administrative areas. Also, internal auditing and social auditing are also guided by the AAPRC.

Generally speaking, the AAPRC and other audit agencies have the independence and authority to audit any administrative institution, any public organisation, or any individual. In China, there is also an extensive internal audit process which is an integral part of the overall state audit system. Presently, China has developed a system combining the AAPRC, local audit bureaus, audit firms and internal audit units, as a means of addressing its unique needs. Following the established of the AAPRC in 1983, more than 3,000 government departments at and above the county level, have successively set up audit institutions with over 74,000 employees. Also, about 45,000 government departments and state-owned enterprises established internal audit units with over 107,000 internal auditors. In addition, there are about 2300 public audit agencies or firms set all over the country, employing 18,000 professional people[4].

3.2 The State Audit

Under the control of the AAPRC, the state auditing system was set up and it included local audit bureaus at county, municipal and provincial levels. This system is supplemented by public audit firms which are separate business entities, subject to the administration and professional guidance of the AAPRC. The legal status of state audit is defined by the 1982 constitution. Further, the State Council in November 1988 promulgated the 'Regulation on Audit of the People's Republic of China', the first relatively comprehensive statute on state audit. In addition, state audit institutions also formulated a number of rules and regulations guiding audit practice.

State audit institutions undertake audits in a wide range of organisations such as government departments, banking institutions, state enterprises, joint ventures and various other enterprises. The audit scope defined in the regulations is wide-ranging and extends beyond traditional audit of financial areas. Generally, two types of audit are recognised in China: the financial audit and the economic effectiveness audit. Besides, reviews of the implementation of state budget allocations, credit plans, capital construction projects and the use of borrowed foreign funds and international aid are important areas of audit. The state audit institutions also review the implementation of the business contract system and undertake audit that protect state economic interests against embezzlement, serious losses and waste. According to the Regulation on Audit, state audit organisations should carry out supervision through audit of the authenticity, legitimacy and efficiency of the use of financial revenues and expenditures of the departments of the people's government at all levels. In a country like China state ownership dominating the economy, the audit coverage is wider than that of most of other countries in the world. Statistics for 1991 show that over 860,000 organisations were subject to state audit. However, with its limited resources, state audit often employs outside assistance to help meet the objectives of the audit regulations. Firstly, the state audit institutions can entrust audit firms and accounting firms to complete audits of some companies, government departments or organisations. Secondly, they can request internal audit organizations to finish part of the examination. When state audits believe that some audit findings in their work have universal implications, they may refer these findings to the local government bodies or internal audit organisations for their consideration.

Audit procedures recommended by the AAPRC are very similar to those adopted by CPA firms in West. These include planning the audit, writing the audit programme, conducting the fieldwork, reporting the findings, and developing audit conclusions and recommendations. However, the state auditors go further than the CPAs and do not finish their work with the audit report. They also make audit conclusions or decisions on fraudulent activities, and inform the audited unites and other relevant units for their attention. If an audited unit disagrees with the audit conclusions or decisions, it may apply to the next higher-level audit institution for re-examination. The audit result is expressed in two forms, namely, the audit report and the audit conclusion or decision. An audit report prepared by the state auditors is different from that prepared by CPAs. CPA auditors usually issue audit reports to express their opinions on the financial statements, and a separate management letter is prepared to suggest recommendations. The Chinese state audit reports combine these into one. The audit report is forwarded to the higher audit institution for approval.

3.3 Public Audit Firms

Social (public) audit organisations or audit firms are a new type of audit institution that have developed rapidly in recent years in China. They usually undertake an audit attestation and consultation service. Audit firms are economically independent, and they must register with the local administration bureau for industry and commerce, and obtain a business licence in accordance with the state regulations. On the one hand, they are independent of government in the sense that they are business entities established to serve the public and survive on their own income. On the other hand, audit firms are subject to the administration and professional guidance of the state audit institutions like the AAPRC. The audit engagement is commissioned by the state audit institution, the audit report prepared by the audit firm shall be submitted to the latter for review. The state audit institutions have great influence on the activities of public audit firms. Moreover, Chinese public audit firms in major cities are often empowered by the AAPRC to exercise audit supervision in a number of areas. For example, they may be responsible for the audit of financial receipts and expenditures of enterprises and undertakings under the jurisdiction of the central government, and also for the audit of major capital construction projects financed by the central government; they may join the audits organised by the AAPRC to audit the receipts and expenditures of provinces, autonomous regions and cities under direct jurisdiction of the central government; they may coordinate the local audit institutions in major public financial problem areas. These firms are generally small but are an entrepreneurial response to the burgeoning demand for audit and accounting services. The public firms normally provide a full range of auditing, accounting and consultancy services which include investigations of fraud and other irregularities on behalf of Government agencies.

As mentioned before, audit firms are in many aspects different from accounting firms. Audit firms are established with the approval of the AAPRC or the audit institutions, whereas accounting firms employ CPAs and are approved by the Ministry of Finance or Finance Bureaus at the provincial level. The qualifications of auditors practising in audit firms are not specifically defined. At present, there are not many CPAs in the audit firms. The regulation on social audit states that the audit firm must have a number of audit staff who are confident in explaining government policies, and have adequate auditing skills. They must be equivalent to an assistant accountant or assistant auditor in a county level audit firm, and equivalent to an accountant or auditor in the firms at the regional level or above. The terms used here are rather vague. In contrast, the qualifications of Certified Public Accountants in accounting firms are more clearly defined in a specific regulation. Audit firms are involved mainly in the audit of the public sector, while accounting firms are mainly involved in the audit of joint ventures with Chinese and foreign investment. However, recently, the Audit-general of China announced that thirty large Sino-foreign joint ventures will be audited for the first time by the state audit institutions and audit firms in 1992, in order to guard against the 'squandering' of capital.

3.4 Internal Audit

Internal audit in China is considered as an integral part of the Chinese audit system. Internal audits are classified into two categories: department internal audit and unit internal audit organisations. A department internal audit organisation is established in the supervisory department such as government department, administrative companies or bureaus. The unit internal audit department is established within a large or middle sized enterprise. By the end of 1991, more than 42,000 departmental and unit internal audit organisations had initiated in the country, with full time and part time staff members numbering over 100,000.

4. CONCLUSION

This article introduced the Chinese accounting profession including the auditing profession. According to Chinese, the accounting profession covers all the occupations which are directly related to accounting practical work including bookkeepers, financial managers, CPAs, and senior accountants etc. Many accountants who are engaged in auditing work are also belong to the accounting profession.

As far as the Chinese accounting profession is concerned, the majority of people in the profession are not titled CPAs. The Chinese CPA system was resumed in the middle of 1980s, and the China Institute of Certified Public Accountants was only established three years ago. Although a number of CPA firms have been set up in China to conduct independent business services, those firms are generally small and inexperienced. Particularly, those firms must be approved by the Ministry of Finance and guided by both the Ministry of Finance and the Audit Administration of the People's Republic of China in many aspects like public auditing. As far as the auditing system is concerned, China has generally developed a system which combine the AAPRC, local audit bureaus, public audit firms and internal audit unit, which have been discussed separately in this article.

Although in its infancy, the Chinese accounting profession is expanding rapidly. Generally, the accounting profession in China is closely regulated by government concerning admission to membership, examination, scope of duties, and fee income. However, the seeds have been sown for change, and with great emphasis on individual performance within a socialist environment, the Chinese accounting profession will play a role similar to that of its Western counterparts.

NOTES

1 For example, see Bai (1988); Zhong (1988); Fang and Tang (1991); Bromwich and Wang (1991).

2 For the details, see the joint research study by Shanghai University of Finance and Economics, and the University of Texas at Dallas: Accounting and Auditing in the People's Republic of China, 1987.

3 The Auditing Society of China is an academic association mainly formed by the

Chinese professors, academics, and some practitioners in the field of auditing and accounting.

4 According to Mr. Lu Pei Jian, the Audit-general of the People's Republic of China, see the People's Daily, overseas edition, March 13, 1992.

REFERENCES

Bromwich, M., and Wang, G. (1991) *'Management Accounting in China: A Current Evaluation'* The International Journal of Accounting, 26:51–66.

Bai, Z. L. (1988) *'Accounting in the People's Republic of China*, Contemporary Situations and Issues in Recent Accounting and Economic Developments in the Far East ed. by V. K. Zimmerman, the University of Illinois.

China: (1985) *'The Accounting Law of the People's Republic of China.'*

Fang, Z., and Tang, Y. (1991) *'Recent Accounting Developments in China: An Increasing Internationalization'*, The International Journal of Accounting, 26:85–103.

Zhong, H. Z. (1988) *'Chinese Accounting Systems and Practices'* Accounting, Organization and Society, Vol. 13, No. 2., pp. 207–224.

State Council, the People's Republic of China, (1986) *'Regulation of the People's Republic of China on Certified Public Accountants'*.

QUESTIONS

1 Identify the measures taken to develop an accounting profession in China equipped to cope with a major and rapid change of direction in the economic system.

2 Comparing this article with the Briston article above, what contribution do you think the major international accounting firms could make to China's needs?

Part III

INTERNATIONAL COMPARISONS OF SOME SPECIFIC ACCOUNTING ISSUES

In this section we consider some specific international accounting issues, including those which arise in the particular context of the multi national enterprise, those where there are marked contrasts in different national approaches, and examples of distinctive national internal accounting systems.

Blake (1993) discusses the issue of foreign currency translation, identifying the lead set by the USA in this field and pointing out that the US rules in this area appear to have been established in response to economic consequence issues specific to that country.

Nobes (1990) reviews the variations in group accounting practice that continue to arise across the European community despite the issues of the EC seventh directive.

A growing number of countries are moving from a funds flow to a cash flow statement. Dowds and Blake (1992) compare developments in this area in four countries.

The USA and the Netherlands both require capitalisation of finance leases. However Vergoossen (1992) identifies fundamental differences in the definition of a finance lease that underlies this requirement.

Freedman & Stagliano (1992) address the issue of the diversity of social accounting disclosure in Europe.

18

FOREIGN CURRENCY TRANSLATION

A challenge for Europe

John Blake

INTRODUCTION

Foreign currency translation poses a major challenge to European accountants. There are several reasons for this.

First, there is no guidance in the European Community's seventh directive on foreign currency translation. Therefore European practices in this field are even more diverse than in other areas of accounting.

Secondly, exchange rates between countries fluctuate substantially. For example, the Spanish peseta has moved against three other currencies over five years:

End of:	*UK*	*£US*	*$Brazil cruzeiro*
1986	195	132.40	8826
1987	204	109.00	1514
1988	205	113.45	148
1989	176	109.72	9.7
1990	187	96.91	0.55

Source: International Monetary Fund 1991

The fluctuations give rise to foreign currency transaction and translation gains or losses that are substantial in relation to profits.

Thirdly, Economists recognise a relationship between currency fluctuations, different national inflation rates, and different national interest rates. Thus any theoretical analysis of foreign currency translation issues is bound up with a consideration of the problems of inflation accounting.

From Journal of European Business Education (Vol 2 No 2 May 1993) pp 30–44. Reprinted by permission from the Journal of European Business Education.

Given that the Netherlands is the only European country where any form of inflation accounting is in common use, and even there only by a small number of companies, then European accountants have to tackle the foreign currency translation problem within the context of a historic cost accounting system. As we shall see below, this gives rise to major distortions of the underlying economic reality.

EXCHANGE DIFFERENCE EXPOSURE

Companies are 'exposed' to exchange differences in two ways:

- Transaction Exposure – Transaction exposure arises when there is a difference between the exchange rate at the time when a transaction is entered into and the time when it is completed. These realised gains or losses are quantified by the circumstances of the transaction, and there is general agreement that they should be taken through the profit and loss account.
- Translation Exposure – Translation exposure arises when there is a difference between the exchange rate at the time when an item is brought into the accounts and the exchange rate used to translate that item at the balance sheet date. Broadly speaking, various systems of translation apply either the historical exchange rate, being the rate of exchange ruling at the date when an item is first entered in the accounts, or the closing exchange rate, being the rate of exchange ruling at the balance sheet date. Therefore translation differences will only arise in relation to those items translated at the closing rate.

There are a number of translation methods and a number of ways of treating translation differences in the accounts.

ECONOMIC RELATIONSHIPS

Two economic relationships are particularly significant in understanding the arguments over foreign currency translation:

- The 'Fisher' effect, whereby it is argued that there is a link between interest rates and expectations as to future exchange rate movements, so that the weaker the currency the higher the interest rate. This relationship arises because lenders will expect to receive a high return in the form of interest to compensate for the loss which arises because when the foreign currency loan is repaid it will convert into fewer units of the home currency than when the loan was first made.
- The purchasing power parity effect, whereby it is argued that there is a link between the rate of inflation and the strength of currency, so that the higher the rate of inflation the weaker the currency and vice versa.

It is not claimed that either of these relationships is cast iron, but research has shown that over a number of years, both these effects tend to operate in practice. For example, Giddy (1977) looked at the correlation between exchange rate changes and relative inflation and interest rates. Over the short run (i.e. three month periods) correlation was poor, but over longer periods (e.g. 3 years) correlation was much closer.

ACCOUNTING APPROACHES

The Basic Problems

As we have seen when discussing translation exposure, there are two basic accounting problems in foreign currency translation:

- Deciding on the exchange rate to be applied in translation.
- Deciding where to show translation gains and losses in the accounts.

Translation Methods

We have already seen that the two rates of exchange most commonly used in translation are the historical rate and the closing rate. This leads to the possibility of using the closing rate throughout (the closing rate method) or using a mixture of historical and closing rates (the historical rate method). There are four major translation methods, the first three being based on a mixture of historical and closing rates.

- Current/Non-Current – With this method current items e.g. stock, debtors, bank overdrafts, would be translated at the closing rate while long term items e.g. plant, debentures, would be translated at the historical rate.
- Monetary/Non-Monetary – Monetary items, being assets and obligations fixed in monetary amount e.g. cash, loans, debtors, and creditors, are translated at the closing rate while non-monetary items e.g. plant, stock, are translated at the historical rate.
- The Temporal Method – This method is based on the view that items should be translated by reference to the exchange rate ruling at the date when their value has been established in the accounts. For monetary items this will be the closing rate, since the monetary amount expresses their value at the balance sheet date. In the case of unmodified historical cost accounts non-monetary items will be translated at the historical rate, so that the temporal method will operate in the same way as the monetary/non-monetary method. However, where asset revaluations have been introduced into the accounts the exchange rate at the date of valuation will be used. Revaluation in the context of historic cost accounts is common in respect of fixed assets in a number of

European countries. Inventories are also normally shown at a valuation where this is lower than cost. Where replacement cost accounting is used then all items are expressed at value at the balance sheet date, so that under the temporal method the closing rate will apply to all items.

Where historical rate methods are used, often the average rate for a year is accepted as an acceptable approximation to be applied to all transactions in that year. The average rate will not necessarily reflect a simple average of the exchange rates reported during a year, but may be weighted in line with the flow of transactions in the year.

- Closing Rate Method – applies the closing rate to all balance sheet items and either the average rate or the closing rate to all profit and loss items. Since all items in the balance sheet are subject to translation exposure it is the net investment in each foreign enterprise which is exposed and accordingly this is often referred to as the closing rate/net investment method.

THE U.S. LEAD

In the field of foreign currency translation, as in so many other aspects of accounting, the lead has been taken by the USA with the issue of FAS 52 in 1981. It is not surprising that the USA should lead on this issue, given the strength of the USA professional and academic community and the position of the USA as the home country of many of the world's multi-national enterprises. Nevertheless, the US approach is open to criticism both because of the way in which FAS 52 emerged as a response to some short term economic problems and because the theoretical approach that underpins the standard is inconsistent with other accounting principles. These criticisms are discussed below.

FAS 52 states that its basic objective is to achieve *compatibility with expected effects*. This means that if a change in the exchange rate is expected to have a beneficial effect on the parent company cash flows and equity then the translation should reflect that. Conversely, if a change is expected to have an adverse effect on the parent company, that should also be reflected.

Two other major objectives are stressed in FAS 52:

- Translation should produce results conforming with Generally Accepted Accounting Principles.
- The results and relationships in the foreign currency accounts should be retained on translation, so that the original accounting ratios are not distorted.

FAS 52 then identifies two different types of foreign operations:

- Self-contained and integrated foreign operations. It is argued that each such operation should be viewed as representing one net investment to which the closing rate should be applied. Changes in the exchange rate do not affect the cash flows of the parent company, because the foreign operation is regarded as self-contained, so that on consolidation gains or losses on translation of the net investment should not be taken through the income statement but should be taken direct to the equity.

- Components or extensions of parent company domestic operations. Where a foreign operation is an integral part or extension of the parent company's domestic operations, such as in the case of an import or export business, then it is argued that changes in the exchange rate directly affect individual assets and liabilities employed on behalf of the parent company. Accordingly the temporal method is used. Gains or losses on translation are reflected in the consolidated income statement because they have effects on the parent company's cash flows. Foreign currency balances in a company's own accounts are treated in the same way.

A full account of the rules of FAS 52 can be found in Rubin (1991).

EUROPEAN COMMUNITY PRACTICE

The European Community Directives do not specifically require any particular accounting treatment for foreign currency translations. Coopers and Lybrand (1991) offer an authoritative analysis of the accounting practices in nine of the E.C. states. Table 1 summarises the Coopers and Lybrand analysis of how foreign operations are translated for each of the nine countries. The majority of countries appear to follow the practice in the USA.

Table 2 shows how the same countries account for translation gains or losses. While the US approach again has a strong influence, in this case we can see that some countries resist taking translation gains as part of profit. Such gains are either deferred or excluded from the accounts. This is in line with the accounting principle of conservation.

'HEDGES'

There are various ways in which a company can 'hedge' against the risk of foreign currency fluctuations. As a simple example, suppose that a company has sold goods in a foreign currency on credit terms with payment receivable 3 months after the time of sale. The company can enter into a forward exchange contract to sell the equivalent amount of the foreign currency in exchange for the domestic currency in 3 months time. Thus the company has certainty about the amount of domestic currency that will be received as a result of the sale – in other words, the risk has been transferred from the trading company to the financial

Table 1 Translation of Foreign Operations

	Temporal or closing rate method	*Generally closing rate*	*Closing rate if self-sustaining Temporal method if integrated*	*No clear rule or practice*
BELGIUM	✔			
DENMARK		✔		
FRANCE			✔	
GERMANY				✔
IRELAND			✔	
ITALY				✔
NETHERLANDS			✔	
SPAIN			✔	
U.K.			✔	

markets. It is a relatively simple matter to account for a hedging transaction of this kind since the debtor should clearly be translated at the appropriate forward exchange rate that represents the amount that the company can confidently expect to receive.

In practice a wide range of hedging arrangements are possible, with varying degrees of certainty in their outcome. A company with a net investment in a foreign subsidiary can effectively hedge the translation exposure by borrowing in the same currency. An accounting problem then arises because the translation differences on consolidation of the net investment in the subsidiary do not appear on the income statement while the related translation difference on the loan in the holding company's own

Table 2 Treatment of Translation Differences

	FOREIGN CURRENCY TRANSACTIONS		*SELF SUSTAINING FOREIGN OPERATIONS*
	Short term monetary items	*Long term monetary items*	
BELGIUM	GD	GD	R
DENMARK	I	V	R
FRANCE	GD	V	R
GERMANY	GD	GD	V
IRELAND	I	I	R
ITALY	I	I	V
NETHERLANDS	I	I	R
SPAIN	I	GD	R
U.K.	I	I	R

D = Deferral of exchange differences permitted or required.
GD = Exchange gains deferred or not recorded; losses offset against previous gains and any excess recognised in income.
I = Exchange differences recognised in income.
V = Variety of treatments.
R = Exchange differences taken direct to reserves.

accounts, which would normally be in the opposite direction (i.e. a loss if there is a translation gain on the net investment and vice versa) does appear in the income statement. Therefore there is a case for allowing translation gains or losses on the loan to be taken direct to the equity rather than through the income statement.

As an example, such an accounting treatment is permitted in the UK.

INFLATION

We have seen above that there is an economic relationship between exchange rates, interest rates, and inflation rates. As a simple example, during 1989 Brazil experienced inflation of some 1300% compared with a rate of 6.8% in Spain. Thus the massive devaluation of the Brazilian cruzeiro from 148 pesetas to 9.7 pesetas during 1989 is not surprising.

Let us consider the example of a Spanish company that invested 1 million pesetas in Brazilian assets at the beginning of 1989. Such an investment would appear very differently in the books of the Spanish company depending on whether it was translated by the temporal or the closing rate method.

The investment in cruzeiros at the beginning of 1989 would be:-

$$1{,}000{,}000 \times \frac{1}{148} = 6756 \text{ cruzeiros}$$

Assuming an investment in non-monetary assets, this would translate back to 1,000,000 pesetas in future years under the temporal method. However, under the closing rate method at the end of 1989 the cruzeiro balance would translate as:-

$$6756 \times 9.7 = 65533 \text{ pesetas}$$

Thus a loss of 934467 pesetas would be recorded.

Assuming that the assets purchased in Brazil kept their value approximately in line with inflation then their real value at the end of 1989 would be:-

$$\text{cruzeiro } 6756 \times 1300\% = 87828 \text{ cruzeiro}$$

This would translate as:-

$$87828 \times 9.7 = 851932 \text{ pesetas}$$

This shows a much less significant loss on the investment of 148068 pesetas – some 15% rather than 93%, of the original investment.

The example illustrates why the translation of the historic cost accounts of a company in an environment of hyperinflation give distorted results under the closing rate method. There are two broad approaches that can be taken in response to this problem:-

- Require use of the temporal method in such situations. The USA adopts this approach.
- Require inflation adjustments to the subsidiary's accounts before applying the closing rate. This is the UK approach.

CHOICE OF REPORTING CURRENCY

Normally a parent company will report in the currency of the country in which it is incorporated. However there are alternative approaches:-

- Where the major part of a company's transactions are conducted in another country's currency then the relevant foreign currency may be used. A survey of 300 Canadian companies found that 9 reported in US dollars for this reason (CICA 1989 p. 51).
- Jacobi (1984) suggested the use of Special Drawing Rights (SDR's) as the unit for reporting by multi-nationals. There are interesting implications here for European multi-nationals that might wish to account in ECU.

Relative Merits

Nobes (1980) reviews the history of the various translation methods. He finds that:

- The closing rate was used by British accountants in the nineteenth century.
- The current/non current method was advocated in the USA by Dicksee in 1911 and officially recommended by the Certified Public Accountants in 1931.
- The monetary/non monetary method is traced back to 1956.
- The temporal method was first recommended by Lorenson (1972).

The current/non current method was common in the inter-war years when exchange rates tended to fluctuate reasonably gently. The underlying logic is that current items, by definition, turn into cash in the short term so should be translated at the closing rate. By contrast non current items take some time to create related cash flows, by which time the exchange rate may have moved back towards the historic rate; in view of the unpredictability of this process, departure from a simple historic cost basis cannot be justified.

This process lost its attraction with freely floating exchange rates. It is interesting to reflect, however, that similar arguments might still be justified when translating between currencies within a stabilisation system such as the European Monetary System.

The monetary/non monetary method is again based on a view as to whether an asset or liability will lead to cash flows. Since monetary assets or liabilities will be received or paid in cash eventually they are translated by the closing rate, which is the most recent piece of available evidence as to the likely equivalent of the prospective related cash flows. Non monetary assets are not, by definition, expected to be converted into cash. Application of the historic rate therefore preserves the historic cost principle.

The temporal method has the same effect as the monetary / non monetary method in pure historic cost accounts. It has three major advantages over the monetary non monetary method:

- It offers a considered approach to items that are revalued within the historic cost accounts.
- It offers a consistent and coherent approach that is equally applicable to historic cost, replacement cost, and constant purchasing power accounts.
- It offers a conceptual basis for applying the closing rate to monetary assets based on their valuation basis rather than on expectations as to cash flows.

In practice the temporal method has generally come to be considered as the best method of those which involve some use of historic rates. Recent accounting debate has focussed, therefore, on the relative merits of the temporal method and the closing rate method.

Benefits of the temporal method include:

- As we have seen above, it is consistent with the historic cost convention. At the same time, it is also consistent with alternative conventions.
- The closing rate method treats a foreign subsidiary as one 'net investment'. This is not consistent with the normal 'line by line' basis of consolidation. By contrast the temporal method does address the accounts on an item basis.

Benefits claimed for the closing rate method are:

- It is said to be more economically realistic. This claim is discussed below in considering experience in the USA, and is open to question.
- The accounting ratios of a subsidiary are not distorted on consolidation. The validity of this position depends on whether, from the point of view of a parent company, such results are meaningful.
- The method is simple to operate and understand. While simplicity helps achieve economy in accounting, on a major issue it should not be a major factor.

On balance, the theoretical arguments have generally been regarded as favouring the temporal method. In a rigorous analysis, Beaver & Wolfson (1982) concluded that:

- Historic cost accounts translated by the temporal method were theoretically consistent but not economically meaningful. Historic cost accounts translated by the closing rate method were also not economically meaningful and were also inconsistent.

- Current value based accounts translate in the same way for both methods and were both consistent and economically meaningful.

The U.S. Experience

We have seen that the balance of arguments based on accounting theory tend to support the temporal method rather that the closing rate method. In practice, however, accountants in the USA moved from the temporal method, prescribed in FAS 8 in 1975, to the closing rate method for most subsidiaries, prescribed by FAS 52 in 1981. The change came about because of vigorous lobbying by US multi-nationals. One reason for this was that the inclusion of foreign currency translation gains and losses in the income statement had a major, and fluctuating impact on reported profits.

Consider, for example, the experience of ITT in 1981:

> 'In the first quarter, the company, whose annual sales revenue exceeded $23 billion, reported a reduction in earnings from the previous year of 45 per cent. However, excluding translation effects, ITT's earnings were actually unchanged from the previous year. In the following quarter, ITT reported an earnings improvement of 109 per cent, but if translation gains were excluded, its earnings had actually declined by 29 per cent.' (Choi & Mueller 1984 p142).

It is not surprising that, as Alleman (1982) reports, ITT were pleased with the change to FAS 52.

The second problem arose from the conflict between translation exposure and what was seen as economic exposure. For most foreign subsidiaries there will tend to be net assets but net monetary liabilities, because investment in plant and stock will be partially financed by borrowing. In this situation translation by different methods will tend to show dramatically different results. We can illustrate this with the simple example of a Spanish company that invests 50,000,000 pesetas in a new subsidiary in Ruritania when 1 peseta = 0.2 crowns. At the same time the subsidiary borrows 10,000,000 crowns and buys a building for 20,000,000. One year later there is no profit or loss in the books of the subsidiary and 1 peseta = 0.25 crowns. Table 3 shows how the closing balance sheet will translate under each method.

When the foreign currency gets weaker (as in our example) the temporal method shows a gain, because the liability can be repaid with a smaller cash outflow in terms of the parent currency. The closing rate method shows a loss because the net investment in the subsidiary is an asset. The converse applies when the foreign currency gets stronger. Table 4 summarises these translation effects.

Table 3 Closing Balance Sheet

	m. crowns	Temporal Method Translation Rate	Temporal Method m. pesetas	Closing Rate Method Translation Rate	Closing Rate Method m. pesetas
Building	20	$\frac{1}{0.2}$	100	$\frac{1}{0.25}$	80
Loan	10	$\frac{1}{0.25}$	40	$\frac{1}{0.25}$	40
	10		60		40
Equity (opening)	10	$\frac{1}{0.2}$	50		50
Translation gain/(loss)	—		10		(10)
	10		60		40

During the late 1970's the dollar weakened against many major currencies, so that application of the temporal method tended to result in translation losses for the major US multi-nationals. This caused two objections from US companies:

- The impact of the temporal method seemed perverse, since an investment in a foreign subsidiary can be expected to produce net cash inflows to the parent, and if the related foreign currency is getting stronger then the value of these inflows will increase.
- To avoid translation exposure to losses US multi-nationals were tending to 'hedge' their foreign investments. At a time of a weakening dollar this was economically inefficient. This effect was identified in studies by Burns (1976), Evans & Folks (1979), Shank, Dillar & Murdock (1979), and Evans, Folks & Jilling (1978).

'Economic exposure' can be defined as the possibility that the benefit to the parent company of the foreign subsidiary's cash flows will be affected by exchange rate movements. In the late 1970's in the USA the steady depreciation of the US dollar against major trading partners' currencies meant that to some extent 'accounting exposure' under the closing rate method coincided with 'economic exposure'. However, 'economic exposure' arises

Table 4

	Temporal Method	Closing Rate Method
Strong foreign currency	LOSS	GAIN
Weak foreign currency	GAIN	LOSS

Impact on profit of translation by different methods when net investment in subsidiary is an asset and the subsidiary has net monetary liabilities.

for a wide range of reasons and varies according to the subsidiary's trading pattern.

To give one example:

A company which exports most of its products in an internationally competitive market will suffer from a stronger domestic currency because its prices in foreign currency terms will increase. Either the company will lose business as a result of less competitive pricing or it will have to cut prices, and therefore profit margins, in order to preserve market share. In either case, the cash flows for the company, and therefore its power to remit funds to any holding company will decrease. Thus in this particular case a strong foreign currency leads to a loss in the value of the foreign subsidiary to its parent i.e. the economic exposure is in the same direction as the accounting exposure under the temporal method and in the opposite direction to the accounting exposure under the closing rate method.

This example is only one of many ways in which currency fluctuation can affect a company's cash flows. Walker (1991) offers an extensive discussion on economic exposure. In practice the range of reasons for economic exposure is so wide and varied that it is impossible to devise a set of accounting rules whereby accounting exposure will coincide with economic exposure.

The position taken by the FASB in prescribing the closing rate did not, therefore, achieve the declared objective of matching accounting and economic exposure. It represented a response to the concern of companies on how accounting rules would reflect the economic environment of the USA at a particular point in time, the late 1970's. FAS 52 represents an example of the way in which companies will lobby for preferred accounting treatments, because of the 'economic consequences' they wish to promote in their published accounts rather than on grounds of accounting theory. Some writers see it as inevitable that such pressures will exist, to the point where accounting regulation becomes a political rather than a technical process (See Gerboth 1972, 1973, Horngren 1972, 1973, 1976, and Rappaport 1977). Some writers see 'economic consequences' as a threat to the integrity and credibility of the accountancy profession. They argue that only by a strictly 'neutral' approach, which does not respond to the biased lobbying of special interest groups, can accountants perform a useful role. (See Solomons 1978, 1979, and Stamp 1980). Perhaps the most balanced view is that accounting regulation must be dominated by technical considerations, but, in order to be effective, cannot ignore economic consequences. (See Zeff 1978).

What is clear is that the US accounting rules in FAS 52 represented a response to intense lobbying by US companies rather than the considered technical judgement of the accounting profession. The lobbying arose from a particular set of circumstances affecting US business at a particular point in time, so cannot be said to be of general international relevance. However, as we have seen, the US example has dominated accountants across the world, leading to very similar accounting rules from Canada, the UK, and the International Accounting Standards Committee.

CONCLUSION

Apart from a requirement in the Seventh Directive to disclose the basis of foreign currency translation, there is no European Community guidance on foreign currency translation. European accountants have tended, in practice, to follow the US approach.

While this is convenient as a basis for international harmonisation, US practice is open to some criticism. It has emerged as a result of political lobbying rather than technical judgement, and may not prove suitable in future economic circumstances.

European accountants should, therefore, be prepared to consider alternative approaches in the future if economic circumstances make the dominance of the closing rate method inappropriate.

REFERENCES

Alleman, R. H. (1982) 'Why ITT Likes FAS 52', Management Accounting, July pp. 23–29.

Beaver, W. H. & Wolfson, M. A. (1982) 'Foreign Currency Translation and Changing Prices in Perfect and Complete Markets', Journal of Accounting Research, Autumn.

Burns, J. M. (1976) 'Accounting Standards and International Finance', American Enterprise Institute for Public Policy Research.

Choi, F. D. S. & Mueller, G. G. (1984) 'International Accounting', Prentice-Hall.

CICA (1989) 'Financial Reporting in Canada 1989', Canadian Institute of Chartered Accountants.

Evans, T. G., Folks, W. R. & Jilling, M. (1978) 'Impact of Statement of Financial Accounting Standards No. 8 on the Foreign Exchange Risk Management Practices of American Multi-nationals: An Economic Impact Study', FASB Research Report, Stamford. Financial Accounting Standards Board.

Evans, T. G. & Folks, W. R. (1979), 'SFAS No. 8: Conforming, Coping, Complaining & Correcting', International Journal of Accounting, Fall.

Gerboth, D. (1972) 'Muddling Through with the APB', Journal of Accountancy, May pp. 42–49.

Gerboth, D. (1973) 'Research Intuition & Politics in Accounting Inquiry', Accounting Review, July pp. 475–482.

Giddy, I. H. (1977) 'Exchange Risk: Whose View?' Financial Management, Summer pp. 23–33.

Horngren, C. T. (1972) 'Accounting Principles: Private or Public Sector?', Journal of Accountancy, May pp. 37–41.

Horngren, C. T. (1973) 'The Marketing of Accountancy Standards', Journal of Accountancy, October pp. 61–66.

Horngren, C. T. (1976) 'Will the FASB be Here in the 1980's?', Journal of Accountancy, November pp. 90–96.

International Monetary Fund (1991) 'International Financial Statistics', March.

Jacobi, M. (1984) 'The Unit of Account in Consolidated Financial Statements of Multi-national Enterprise', In Holzer H. P. 'International Accounting', Harper & Row, pp. 105–121.

Lorenson, L. (1972) Accounting Research Study No. 12: Reporting Foreign Operations of US Companies in US Dollars, AICPA, New York.

Nobes, C. W. (1980) 'A Review of the Translation Debate', Accounting & Business Research, Autumn, pp. 421–430.

Rappaport, A. (1977) 'Economic Impact of Accounting Standards – implications for the FASB', Journal of Accounting, May, pp. 89–98.

Rubin, S. (1991) 'Consolidation, Translation and the Equity Method', In Carmichael, D. R., Lilien, S. B. & Mellman, M., Accountants' Handbook, CH 7, Wiley.

Shank, J. K., Diller, J. F. & Murdock, R. J. (1979) 'Assessing the Economic Impact of FASB No. 8', New York, Financial Executives Research Foundation.

Solomons, D. (1978) 'The Politicisation of Accounting', Journal of Accountancy, November, pp. 65–72.

Solomons, D. (1989) 'Guidelines for Financial Reporting Standards', Institute of Chartered Accountants in England and Wales.

Stamp, E. (1980) 'Corporate Reporting: Its Future Evolution', Canadian Institute of Chartered Accountants.

Walker, D. (1991) 'Foreign Exchange Risk Management', In Nobes C. & Parker R. 'Comparative International Accounting', Prentice-Hall, pp. 454–475.

Zeff, S. A. (1978) 'The Rise of Economic Consequences', Journal of Accountancy, December, pp. 56–63.

QUESTIONS

1 Why has the lead given on this topic by the USA been so influential?

19

EC GROUP ACCOUNTING

Two zillion ways to do it

*Christopher Nobes**

The Seventh Directive is the European Community's instrument for harmonising the very varied European group accounting practices. Consolidation was unknown in some EC countries, even in the 1980s. In Germany a 1965 Act required a partial form of consolidation for public companies, while in France consolidation for listed companies gradually became the norm from the early 1970s.

As a result of this lack of development in much of continental Europe, the Seventh Directive, which was first published in draft in 1976, was based largely on the developed practices of the UK, Ireland and the Netherlands, which in turn owed much to US precedents.

Directives are, of course, the result of political compromises between member states. Consequently some items, such as currency translation rules in the case of the Seventh Directive, have to be left out because they are too controversial. In other areas, there have to be options, and as will be seen, these can be numerous. Nevertheless, the Directive takes several major steps to remove the worst European differences.

For example:

- Consolidation becomes compulsory for all groups above medium-sized (criteria as in the UK's 1985 Companies Act, eg above 250 employees). Previously, consolidation was rare in Spain, Portugal and Greece. It was not compulsory in most other countries. In Germany it applied only to public companies.
- Consolidation must include subsidiaries, whether domestic or foreign, incorporated or unincorporated. In Germany, it had not been necessary to include foreign subsidiaries. In the UK, the law had not covered unincorporated entities.

From Accountancy (December 1990) pp. 84–85.
Reprinted by permission of Professor Christopher Nobes.

- Goodwill must be calculated once (at the date of acquisition) and by reference to fair values. In much of continental Europe, goodwill had been calculated by reference to book values. In Germany there was a recalculation at each year end of the 'difference arising on consolidation'.
- The equity method (as in SSAP 1) must be used for associated companies. This was normal practice in the UK, Ireland, the Netherlands, Denmark and France, but not in some countries and it was illegal in Germany.

In addition, the Directive makes several other demands, and these are being implemented throughout the EC. The main compulsory items are shown in Table 1. As can be seen, most of these fit with prior UK practice, so little change is required here.

The implementation dates are shown in Table 1, although the laws come into force somewhat after their enactment. For example, although the UK law was enacted after the German, Greek or Spanish laws, it comes into effect marginally before the German law, and well before the Greek and Spanish laws. Most of the laws will have taken effect by the end of 1991.

The Directive also covers less fundamental areas of practice, but many of these contain options. There are 51 obvious options, as outlined in a survey of EC implementation conducted earlier this year by the Fédération des Experts Comptables Européens. If they are all assumed to be yes/no options, that means 2^{51} ways of implementing the Directive, that is, approximately 2×10^{15} or 2 zillion.

In fact, several of the options are complex, allowing that 'member states may require or permit'. So the number of ways for implementation is much larger. On the other hand, a number of options have not been taken up by any member state, so these represent merely a potential lack of standardisation.

Table 2 lists some of the Directive's options. These have been implemented in the 10 member states with laws or draft law (see Table 1) as follows:

Table 1 Implementation

France	1985
Germany	1985
Greece	1987
Luxembourg	1988
Netherlands	1988
Spain	1989
UK	1989
Belgium	1990
Denmark	1990
Italy	Draft published
Ireland	No draft
Portugal	No draft

Table 2 Main options in the seventh directive

	Option	*Source countries*
Art 1.2	Group companies to include those managed on a unified basis or dominantly influenced	Netherlands
Art 4	Requirement to consolidate may be restricted to parents that are companies	UK, Ireland, Netherlands
Art 5	Financial holding companies may be exempted	Luxembourg
Art 6	Consolidation may be restricted to 'large' groups	Approx France, Germany
Art 11	Groups exempted if owned by non-EC parents that prepare equivalent accounts	Netherlands
Art 20	Merger accounting allowed	UK
Art 30	Goodwill may be written off immediately to reserves	UK, Ireland, Netherlands
Art 32	Proportional consolidation allowed	France, Netherlands

1 The definitions of a subsidiary may include those based on dominant influence or unified management as well as those based on ownership of majority voting rights and power to control the votes on the board. Of the 10 member states covered, all but Italy and Luxembourg would treat an undertaking as a subsidiary if there was a participating interest, combined with dominant influence or unified management. A participating interest is one intended for the long term and for the benefit of the investor. In the case of the UK, the adoption of this option was seen as part of the fight against off balance sheet finance.
2 The requirement to consolidate may be restricted to those parents that are limited companies. In Belgium, France and Greece, no such exemption is allowed. In Spain, the exemption relates only to people. In the other six member states, more extensive exemptions are allowed; for example, in the UK only limited company parents must consolidate.
3 Financial holding companies may be exempted from the need to prepare consolidated accounts. This is only allowed in Greece and Luxembourg.
4 Small and medium-sized groups can be exempted from preparing group accounts. This is so for eight member states. However, Denmark and the Netherlands have only exempted small groups (eg below 50 employees). Germany, Greece, Luxembourg and the UK take advantage of the Directive's option to use larger size criteria and figures before consolidation adjustments. Six member states (Belgium, France, Germany, Greece, Italy and Luxembourg) have taken advantage of the Directive's option to increase the size criteria for a transitional period of up to 10 years (eg below 500 employees).
5 Under certain conditions, the Directive allows the exemption from consolidation for intermediate parents to be extended to cases where the ultimate parent is outside the EC. A majority of countries grant this exemption, but not Denmark, Germany, Italy or Ireland.

6 Merger accounting may be required or allowed under certain conditions. So far, the law does not require this in any country, although it would be required in the UK under the draft standard ED 48. It is allowed in Belgium, France, Germany, Luxembourg and the UK.
7 Goodwill may be allowed to be immediately written off to reserves. This is allowed in all member states except for Belgium and Spain.
8 Proportional consolidation may be required or permitted for joint ventures. It is required in France, recommended in Belgium and allowed for all joint ventures in most member states. However, in the UK it is only allowed for unincorporated joint ventures and, in Greece, it is not allowed at all.

The above are just some of the Directive's major options. It can be seen from this that great variety can, and does, exist. However, the differences that existed before the Directive were so great that the state of affairs in the 1990s does represent substantial harmonisation.

In the UK, some of the flexibility allowed by the Directive and in the Companies Act 1989 will be reduced when ED 50 is implemented as a replacement for SSAPs 1 and 14. For example, 'dominant influence' is defined; the 'dissimilarity' exemption is controlled (see Table 3); the location of minority interests in the balance sheet is specified; and the

Table 3 Main provisions of the seventh directive

	Requirement	*Source countries*
Art 1	Subsidiaries are defined largely in terms of *de jure* criteria	UK, Ireland
Art 3	Consolidation to include foreign subsidiaries	UK, Ireland, Netherlands, France
Art 4	Consolidation irrespective of legal form of subsidiary	Germany
Art 4	Consolidation by all types of companies	UK, Ireland, Netherlands
Art 7	Exemptions from preparation of group accounts by wholly owned subsidiaries	UK, Ireland, Netherlands, France
Art 14	Exclusion on basis of dissimilarity	UK, Ireland, Netherlands, France
Art 16	True and fair view	UK, Ireland, Netherlands
Art 17	Uniform formats to be used	Germany, France
Art 18	Goodwill to be calculated once-for-all	UK, Ireland, Netherlands
Art 19	Goodwill to be based on fair values	UK, Ireland, Netherlands
Art 29	Tax-based valuations to be 'corrected' or at least disclosed	UK, Ireland, Netherlands
Art 33	Equity method for associated companies	UK, Ireland, Netherlands, France

method of inter-company eliminations is set down. In most other EC countries there is no such mechanism for the narrowing down of legally-permitted practices.

No more EC Directives on accounting are planned, so the differences discussed here will remain in 1992, and probably in 2002. Thus there is still scope for confusion and still a need for care and expertise when making European accounting comparisons.

QUESTIONS

1 Summarise what this article illustrates about the European Union's procedures, achievements, and limitations, in relation to accounting harmonisation.

20

SOME REFLECTIONS ON THE USES OF THE CASH FLOW STATEMENT IN AUSTRALIA, NEW ZEALAND, THE UK, AND THE USA

J. Dowds and J. Blake

In recent years accounting standards on cash flow reporting have been issued in a number of countries including Australia (AASB 1026 in 1992), New Zealand (SSAP-10 in 1987 revised to FRS-10 in 1992), the USA (FAS-95 in 1987) and the UK (FRS-1 in 1991). In this article are considered:

- Some evidence on the need for, and how to use, the cash flow statement.
- A review of the major differences in approaches to presentation in each country's accounting standard.
- A consideration of the objectivity of cash flow analysis.

The topics are approached in this order because it is felt necessary, in the first instance, to discuss the use of the Statement of Cash Flows to emphasise its significance as a financial statement. Then presentation of the statement in different countries is considered in order to draw attention to the different approaches. The problems associated with these approaches tend to be in the nature of classification and comparability which lead to the question of objectivity and the fact that some exercise of judgement is necessary in the preparation of a cash flow statement.

From Accounting Forum (September 1992) pp 53–74.
Reprinted by permission of Accounting Forum.

USING THE CASH FLOW STATEMENT

An extensive literature exists which examines the usefulness of cash flow numbers. Neill, Schaefer, Bahnson and Bradbury (1992) in a useful review and synthesis of this literature state that:

> early studies that employed crude cash flow measures consistently failed to detect incremental information content. Subsequent research has employed increasingly sophisticated cash flow definitions and empirical methodologies, but has resulted in mixed evidence (emphasis added).

Charitou and Ketz (1991) suggest that 'support for cash flow reporting has been provided by several researchers, among those, Hawkins (1977); Heath (1978); Ijiri (1978); Largey and Stickney (1980); Gombola and Ketz (1983); Rayburn (1986); Wilson (1986/1987) and Charitou and Venieris (1990)'. These and significant studies in USA by Bowen, Burghstahler and Daley (1986, 1987), provide evidence, weak in nature, that disclosure of cash flows provides information which is incremental to that contained in the earnings statements. An Australian study by Percy and Stokes (1992) examines the external validity of the results obtained by Bowen et al and concludes among other things that: '. . . Traditional cash flow measures better predict future cash flows than models based on earnings or a more refined cash flow measure'. Baydoun and Papasyriopoulos (1992) examined the incremental information of accruals and cash flows as disclosed by New Zealand firms and concluded that 'cash flows, particularly CFAI have significant incremental information content only in 1987'. Further results suggest that: 'accruals possess incremental information content beyond cash flows in 1989 and 1990'. The authors' argue that the 1987 result was directly related to the stock market crash and that 'users seem to have lost confidence in the earnings figures and became more concerned with cash flows. Since 1989 things have improved and accruals seem to have gained credibility'.

Board, Day and Walker (1989) and Board and Day (1989) in studies conducted in the UK suggest however that cash flow disclosures provide no useful information over and above that in the earnings statements. Green and Stark (1989) argue that: '. . . overall, there is no clear-cut consensus on the valuation-relevance of cash flow numbers'.

Nevertheless, although studies on the usefulness of cash flows have tended to produce evidence which is at best inconclusive, there can be no doubt that among accounting standard-setters and users of financial statements there has been an increasing demand for such information during recent years.

Assertions that a Statement of Cash Flows (SCF) is a useful part of the financial statements tend to focus on its usefulness for assessing liquidity and solvency. For example, Edmonds, Rogow and Rezaee (1990) argue that

When used with other financial statements, the SCF will help appraisers, investors, creditors and others evaluate:

- a firm's ability to generate positive future cash flows;
- differences between net income and associated cash receipts and payments;
- the extent to which a firm's cash flow is impacted by the purchase and sale of fixed assets;
- a firm's ability to pay obligations, including dividends and interest;
- a firm's need and use of external sources of financing.

The move towards cash flow statements can be seen as a response to the 'inadequacy of the statement of changes in financial position as a means for extracting information about cash flows. Indeed, the stated purpose of the 17-year-old funds statement is simply to explain all significant changes in financial position, regardless of whether the changes directly affected cash or working capital' (Emmanuel 1988, p. 17).

Edmonds et al (1990, p. 15) also see the provision of an SCF as providing '. . . an excellent source of data. Because the data is more accessible and reliable than old sources, it will make the (investment) appraisal process easier and more exact'.

In New Zealand SSAP-10, Statement of Cash Flows, replaced the older SSAP-10, Statement of Changes in Financial Position, in 1987. Paragraph 4.1 of SSAP-10 states that: 'The objective of a Statement of Cash Flows is to provide information about the . . . activities of an entity and the effect of those activities on cash resources.' The information '. . . *should help investors, creditors, and others* . . .' Whiteman and Newby (1989) suggest that the *overriding* intention of SSAP-10 is to provide *users* with *useful information*. The additional usefulness of cash flow figures is described in paragraph 4.2, which emphasises the point that '. . . users of financial statements are better informed as to liquidity and financial flexibility', paragraph 4.3 which argues that 'actual cash flow information . . . enables users to assess better the cash performance of the entity . . . and hence be in a position to make projections of future cash flows'; and paragraph 4.4 which states that 'inflows and outflows of cash are not influenced by the subjective cost allocations which affect reported income. Thus cash flow information should improve comparability between financial statements of different entities'. It is this subjectivity of the accruals process which has caused users of financial statements to express dissatisfaction of their use as transmitters of decision useful information and in this regard the previous 'funds flow statements' did not contribute to an increase in user confidence since it was, in effect, 'little more than an extraction exercise for the elements contained in the balance sheet' (Carslaw and McNally, 1990, p. 28). Indeed, in practice the funds flow statement was not adequate for skilled analysts to extract full cash flow data (Drtina and Largay, 1985).

The stock market crash in 1987 coincided with the introduction of a cash flow statement requirement in New Zealand and helped to focus attention on the need to fully understand the concepts of cash flow as a component in the prevention of company collapses. Warren Head, publisher of the New Zealand Company Register, Volume 28, 1989–90 expressed a view felt by others when he stated that, 'Nil or limited understanding of cash-flow has been behind the failure of most businesses'.

A number of studies have tested the predictive quality of cash flow based data, including the following:

1 Largay and Stickney (1980) explored the value of cash flow analysis for indicating prospective corporate bankruptcy in an analysis of one particular case, the collapse of the then largest retailer in the USA, WT Grant and Co., in 1975. While a range of traditional accounting ratios failed to indicate the company's weakness, at least until 1973, the fact that operating cash flows were negative in eight out of the ten years up to the company's collapse should have provided investors with an early signal of problems (p. 54). Similarly Lee (1982) analysed five year's of cash flow data for Laker Airways, a UK company that collapsed in February 1982, and argued that a fall in operating cash flows as a percentage of total cash inflows in 1979 and 1980 gave advance warning of the company's problems. Currie (1987) offers a similar analysis for an unnamed Australian Company where four years of operating cash outflows led up to corporate failure.

2 Dambolena and Shulman (1988) in the USA looked at two multivariate ratios for the prediction of corporate bankruptcy, one being the Z-score model developed by Altman (see Altman 1968, 1983), the other being presented by Gentry et al 1985. In each case the predictive ability of the models was improved by including a measure of the change in net liquid balances as one component in the ratio. They conclude:

> We have found that the inclusion of a net liquid component, derived either from a funds flow or cash flow statement, significantly improves established accrual based, funds based and cash based bankruptcy models (p. 74).

The study indicates the value of combining analysis of the cash flow statement with other parts of the financial statements.

3 Gentry et al (1990) in the USA analysed the cash flow profiles of 333 sample companies and found that key cash flow ratios varied across company size and across industry groups. Not surprisingly, as with other forms of ratio analysis, cash flow analysis comparisons are only meaningful with other enterprises in a similar line of business of a similar size.

4 Gahlon and Vigeland (1988) in the USA examined a range of cash flow

ratios for 60 bankrupt companies and compared these with the ratios for 204 non bankrupt companies. They found that a number of ratios, most of them linked to operating cash flows, demonstrated significant differences between the two categories up to five years before bankruptcy. Cash operating income as a proportion of total assets was a particularly useful indicator.

5 Livnat and Zarowin (1990) in the USA considered the extent to which the information content of components of cash flows, as required by the US standard on cash flow reporting, helps explain share price movements. They tested the significance of various measures of cash flow and found that 'individual components of operating cash flows (excluding tax payments) have strong associations with security returns' (p. 42). The study is relevant both as a demonstration of the importance of operating cash flows in an analysis of the cash flow statements and as an indicator of the usefulness of the breakdown of operating cash flows given by the 'direct' method.

6 Lawson (1980) in the UK applied cash flow analysis to nine major UK companies during the 1960s and 1970s. He computed tax cash flows in relation to equity earnings cash flows and concluded that 'the UK corporate tax system virtually confiscated equity earnings'. This paper is of interest both in demonstrating the usefulness of cash flow analysis in place of the inflation-distorted accruals based accounts, and in using cash flow data to provide insights into issues of public policy.

The main factors identified as important in these studies are linked to operating cash flows. They support the view of Hovey (1986) that 'A firm's operating cash flows are its essence'. Authors who suggest a range of ratios for cash flow statement include cash flow from operations or elements thereof as a key component in many of them; seven out of fourteen in the case of Giacomino and Mielke (1988), eleven out of thirteen in the case of Carslaw and McNally (1990), nine out of sixteen in the case of Gahlon and Vigeland (1988).

While there is not yet a consensus on the most useful ratios to be computed from a cash flow statement, one which is frequently cited is the ratio of operating cash flow to operating profit, sometimes referred to as 'quality of earnings'. Emmanual (1988) argues:

> The cash flow statement can and should be used to measure the quality of earnings. The analysis of earnings quality facilitates an understanding of the income statement by linking income and expense data to cash flows. By measuring the gap between accrual income and net cash flow from operations, the true operating strength of the entity can be ascertained. (p. 24).

In the UK the ASB, in FRS-1, referring to 'the quality of the profit earned', appears to support this view. Indeed, on issuing FRS-1 the ASB drew attention to the fact that the UK company Polly Peck had collapsed recently and that 'The company's difficulties . . . would have been quite apparent in a cash flow statement' (reported in *Accountancy*, November 1991, p. 10). However, an analysis of the Polly Peck collapse by Gwilliam and Russell (1991) identifies the major accounting issues as the treatment of foreign currency translation losses and the problem that substantial free cash balances in Northern Cyprus could not be remitted to the UK. Singleton-Green (1991) reports a review of UK companies operating cash flows in relation to operating profits. He points out that while the Polly Peck accounts indicated negative operating cash flows the other major corporate collapse in the UK at that time, Brent Walker, showed an operating cash inflow of £171 million compared with operating profit of £118 million, ie. an apparently high 'quality of earnings'. He further points out:

> To take the extreme cases, a fixed capital intensive company in decline might be flattered by its cash flow figures, a non-fixed capital intensive and rapidly expanding company might present an unduly gloomy picture.

Murphy (1991) argues that if analysts use simple criteria for assessing cash flow statements, 'looking for companies with not only positive, but increasingly positive cash flows', then there is a danger of promoting a short termist approach by management. 'Short term positive cash flow management can very often be inconsistent with long-term economic management.'

The problem of the misleading indications given by a single period measure of operating cash flow data is addressed by an experienced advocate of cash flow when Lee (1992) asserts that 'operating and other cash flows are inevitably lumpy due to the cyclical nature of business activity'. He argues the need to judge cash flow data on a longer term basis than a single period. On this basis the ratio of operational cash flow to operating profit then becomes significant as an indicator of 'the extent to which the reporting entity has been successful at converting earnings into hard cash'.

Broadly speaking, useful cash flow based ratios can be computed in two ways:

1 The ratios used to relate the components of accruals based accounts can be adapted to relate the equivalent components of cash flow. For example, the relationship between operating cash flows and financing cash flows gives an insight into gearing.
2 Ratios can be computed relating cash flows to accruals based data. For example, the ratio of cash inflows from customers to accruals based turnover gives insight into the control of trade credit, and avoids the problem of using balance sheet debtor figures that might be distorted by the year end date. Similarly the ratio of operating cash flow to total assets gives a picture of the liquidity generated from asset utilisation.

ISSUES OF PRESENTATION

Most countries, including New Zealand, the USA, and Australia, provide for three major headings in the cash flow statement being 'operating activities', 'investing activities', and 'financing'. The UK standard FRS-1 has two additional headings *'returns on investments and servicing of finance'*, which embraces interest received and paid and dividends received and paid, and *'taxation'*. The Australian standard is more flexible than other countries, requiring only that 'operating activities and other activities' be identified. Table 1 shows the requirements for presentation of the main components of the cash flow statement in the USA (FAS-95), the UK (FRS-1), the original New Zealand statement issued in 1987 (SSAP-10), and the revised New Zealand statement issued in 1992 (FRS-10), together with the suggested presentation illustrated in the Australian standard (AASB 1026). Although the variety of treatments can easily be identified on the face of the cash flow statement, these will require adjustment by analysts working on transnational comparisons. These variations are unlikely to be reduced by IASC harmonisation since the international exposure draft, ED-36, provides 'interest and dividends received and paid should be classified in a consistent manner from period to period and each separately disclosed as one of operating, investing, or financing activities.'

There are two ways of showing the cash flow from operating activities:

- The **direct** method shows the operating cash flows that make up the net cash flow from operations, eg. cash receipts from customers, cash payments to suppliers, cash payments to or on behalf of employees.
- The **indirect** method shows the operating profit and adjusts it for non cash charges and credits to reconcile it to the net cash flow from operations.

In the UK FRS-1 requires that a reconciliation between operating profit and cash flow from operations be shown as a note to the cash flow statement. It should **not** be shown on the face of the statement because the operating profit figure is not a cash flow. Operating cash flow as shown on the face of the funds flow statement may then be shown either 'gross', itemising operating cash flows (ie. the direct method), or 'net', as computed by the indirect method. The effect is that the information required by the 'indirect' method **must** be shown and that required by the 'direct' method **may** be shown. In the USA a choice is permitted between the two methods in FAS-95, the standard on cash flow reporting. This has resulted in a majority of companies opting for the indirect method (Sondhi et al, 1988), although analysts see the permitted choice as leading to a lack of comparability (Zega, 1988, p. 67). By contrast, in New Zealand and Australia only the 'direct' method is permitted.

Table 1 Main components of cash flow statement

	UK *FRS-1*	*Australia* *AASB 1026*	*New Zealand SSAP-10*	*New Zealand FRS-10*
OPERATING ACTIVITIES (includes taxation, dividends received, interest received and paid)	OPERATING ACTIVITIES	OPERATING ACTIVITIES (illustration includes taxation, returns on investments, and interest paid)	OPERATING ACTIVITIES (includes taxation)	OPERATING ACTIVITIES (includes taxation, dividends received, interest received and paid)
	RETURNS ON INVEST-MENTS AND SERVICING FINANCE			
	TAXATION			
INVESTING ACTIVITIES	INVESTING ACTIVITIES	INVESTING ACTIVITIES	INVESTING ACTIVITIES (includes returns on investments)	INVESTING ACTIVITIES
FINANCING (includes dividends paid)	FINANCING	FINANCING (includes dividends paid)	FINANCING (includes servicing of finance)	FINANCING (includes dividends paid)

In 1991 the New Zealand Society of Accountants (NZSA) reviewed their accounting standard on cash flow reporting, SSAP-10. They found that 47 respondents favoured a continued requirement to use the direct method, compared with 6 respondents against. Thus experience seems to support such a requirement. The two major arguments against appear to be:

1 *Cost*. Deloitte Ross Tomahatsu report (letter to the NZSA dated 15 May 1991) that a number of their clients refuse to incur the costs involved in analysing operating cash flows under the direct method, to the point where:

> Fully 20% of all qualifications and disclaimers of opinion issued by the practice in the year prior to 28 February 1991, were for non compliance with SSAP-10.

2 Lack of international support. Given that most countries do not prescribe the direct method, multinationals find it inconvenient to prepare the accounts of a New Zealand subsidiary on that basis. Thus Shell New Zealand Holding Co. comments, in a letter to the NZSA dated 15 May 1991:

> The Shell Group worldwide presents its cash flows from operating activities using the indirect method in compliance with FAS-95. This method of presentation would be Shell New Zealand's preference as the information is readily accessible from data already prepared. The extra work incurred in complying with the current SSAP, in our opinion, gives no material advantages.

THE 'OBJECTIVITY' OF CASH FLOW

One argument put forward in support of the cash flow statement is that it avoids the elements of judgement and subjectivity inherent in accrual accounting. As Lee (1992) summarises the case, the cash flow statement:

> is devoid of the effects of periodic accounting accruals and cost allocations. It represents the observable effects of economic transactions, and can therefore be said to be a statement entirely of economic substance and free of legal form.

Similarly to Edmonds et al (1990) one of the two major reasons for current interest in cash flow reporting is: 'lack of confidence in the accounting procedures now being used to derive earnings'.

Neill et al (1991), p. 118) cite a number of authorities who have identified significant manipulation by management of accrual based accounting as grounds for preferring cash flow based information.

The problems associated with the funds flow type of statement which preceded cash flow statements were described by Broadbent, Webb and Hassall in the following terms:

> They derive from statements employing accrual accounting which it could be argued, provided no additional information for users and contained all the **measurement** problems associated with income determination (emphasis added).

The problem can, however, be one of the disclosure as well as measurement and an example of this has been illustrated in a New Zealand study by Sharma and Robb 1991 – see later.

In the UK the cash flow statement is seen as particularly significant in promoting comparability because it is more detailed, and therefore promotes greater uniformity than SSAP-10 on funds flow (Ghosh, 1991).

However, the preparation of the cash flow statement also involves the exercise of judgement in the analysis between operating, investing, and financing cash flows. In New Zealand, Sharma and Robb (1991), review six cash flow statements from companies in the finance industry, and identify a number of problems in the allocation of cash flows.

To take just two examples:

- Dividends paid to shareholders were treated as an operating item in one case, as a financing item in four cases, and do not arise in one case.
- Increases or decreases in government securities were treated as an operating item in one case, as an investing item in two cases, as a financing item in one case, and as a change in the form in which cash balances were held in two cases.

In some instances companies showing different accounting treatment had the same auditors.

CONCLUSION

The requirements to produce a cash flow statement responds to a range of evidence that cash flow data is important for the evaluation of the financial position of an enterprise. However, with respect to the use of the statements the following points need to be considered:

1 There is still much work to be done in developing ratio analysis approaches that use cash flow data.
2 There are possibilities of variations in presentation, particularly between different countries.
3 While avoiding some of the areas of judgement inherent in accruals accounting, cash flow reporting still involves some exercise of judgement and some conflict of 'substance versus form'.

Accordingly a number of relevant research areas develop from this analysis. In particular work on the predictive ability of data drawn from various parts and forms of the cash flow statement may help us understand the most useful forms of presentation and analysis.

REFERENCES

Altman, E. I. (September 1968) 'Financial Ratios, Discriminant Analysis, and the Prediction of Corporate Bankruptcy', *Journal of Finance*, 589–609.

Altman, E. I. (1983) *Corporate Financial Distress*, New York: John Wiley and Sons.

Baydoun, N. and Papsyriopoulos, N. (1992) 'The Incremental Information Content of Cash Flows: Additional Evidence', *British Accounting Association Conference*, University of Warwick.

Board, J. L. G. and Day, J. F. S. (Winter 1989) 'The Information Content of Cash Flow Figures', *Accounting and Business Research*, 3–12.

Board, J. L. G., Day, J. F. S. and Walker, M. (1989) 'The Information Content of Unexpected Accounting Income, Funds and Cash Flow', *Institute of Chartered Accountants in England Wales.*

Broadbent, J. M., Webb, B. W. and Hassall, T. (January–February 1992) 'Making the Cash Flow', *Certified Accountant*, 20–22.

Bowen, R. M., Burgstahler, D. and Daley, L. A. (October 1986) 'Evidence on the Relationships Between Earnings and Various Measures of Cash Flow', *The Accounting Review*, 713–725.

Bowen, R. M., Burgstahler, D. and Daley, L. A. (October 1987) 'The Incremental Information Content of Accrual versus Cash Flows', *The Accounting Review*, 723–747.

Carslaw, C. and McNally, Q. (August 1990) 'Statement of Cash Flows – Opportunities for Reappraisal', *Accountants Journal*, 28–31.

Charitou, A. and Ketz, E. (1991) 'An Empirical Examination of Cash Flow Measures', *Abacus*, Vol. 27, No. 1, 51–64.

Charitou, A. and Venieris 'The Need for Cash Flow Reporting: Greek Evidence', *The British Accounting Review*, Vol. 22, 107–117.

Currie, C. (March 1987) 'Should Cash Statements Replace Funds Statements?', *Chartered Accountant in Australia*, 61–64.

Dambolena, I. G. and Shulman, J. M. (September–October 1988) 'A Primary Rule for Detecting Bankruptcy: Watch the Cash', *Financial Analysts Journal*, 74–78.

Drtina, R. E. and Largay, J. A. (April 1985) 'Pitfalls in Calculating Cash Flow from Operations', *Accounting Review*, 314–326.

Edmonds, C. P., Rogow, R. B. and Rezaee, Z. (Fall 1990) 'Statement of Cash Flow: A Benefit to Appraisers', *Real Estate Appraiser and Analyst*, 9–15.

Emmanuel, C. B. (June 1988) 'Cash Flow Reporting, Part 2: Importance of Cash Flow Data in Credit Analysis', *Journal of Commercial Bank Lending*, 16–27.

Gahlon, J. M. and Vigeland, R. L. (December 1988) 'Early Warning Signs of Bankruptcy Using Cash Flow Analysis', *Journal of Commercial Bank Lending*, 4–15.

Gentry, J. A., Newbold, P. and Whitford, D. T. (September–October 1985) 'Predicting Bankruptcy: If Cash Flow is not the Answer, What Is?', *Financial Analysts Journal*, 47–56.

Gentry, J. A., Newbold, P. and Whitford, D. T. (July–August 1990) 'Profiles of Cash Flow Components', *Financial Analysts Journal*, 41–48.

Ghosh, J. (November 1991) 'Implementation Hints on a Maiden Standard', *Accountancy*, 32.

Giacomino, D. E. and Mielke, D. E. (1988) 'Using the Statement of Cash Flows to Analyse Corporate Performance', *Management Accounting (US)*, 54–57.

Gombola, M. J. and Ketz, J. E. (January 1983) 'A Note on Cash Flows and Classification Patterns of Financial Ratios', *The Accounting Review*, 105–114.

Green, P. and Stark, A. W. (1989) 'A Comparison of Profit and Cash Flow Performance for Irish Companies', *Irish Accounting Association Conference*, Cork.

Gwilliam, D. and Russell, T. (January 1991) 'Polly Peck: Where were the Analysts?', *Accountancy*, 25–26.

Hawkins, D. F. (November–December 1977) 'Toward an Old Theory of Equity Valuation', *Financial Analysts Journal*, 48–53.

Heath, L. C. (1978) 'Financial Reporting and the Evaluation of Solvency', *Accounting Research Monograph No. 3*, AICPA.

Hovey, D. F. (1986) 'Memo to FASB: A Cash Flow Statement Suggestion', *Management Accounting (US)*, 63–67.

Ijiri, Y. (May 1978) 'Cash Flow and its Structure', *Journal of Accounting, Auditing and Finance*, 331–348.

Largay, J. A. and Stickney, C. P. (July–August 1980) 'Cash Flows, Ratio Analysis and the W.T. Grant Company Bankruptcy', *Financial Analysts Journal*, 51–54.

Lawson, G. H. (Fall 1980) 'The Measurement of Corporate Profitability on a Cash Flow Basis', *International Journal of Accounting*, 11–46.

Lee, T. (June 1982) 'Laker Airways – The Cash Flow Truth', *Accountancy*, 115–116.

Lee, T. (April 1992) 'Making Cash Flow Statements Useful', *Accountancy*, 35.

Livnat, J. and Zarowin, P. (1990) 'The Incremental Information Content of Cash Flow Components', *Journal of Accounting and Economics*, 13, 25–46.

Murphy, R. (1991) 'Warning: ED-54 Could Damage Your Health', *Accountancy Journal*, 26.

Neill, J. Y. D., Schaefer, T. F., Brahnson, P. R. and Bradbury, M. E. (1991) 'The Usefulness of Cash Flow Data: A Review and Synthesis', *Journal of Accounting Literature*, 10, 117–150.

Percy, M. and Stokes, D. J. (May 1992) 'Further Evidence on Empirical Relationships Between Earnings and Cash Flows', *Accounting and Finance*, 27–49.

Rayburn, J. (1986) 'The Association of Operating Cash Flow and Accruals with Security Returns', *Journal of Accounting Research*, Supplement 112–133.

Sharma, D. and Robb, A. (April 1991) 'Operating Cash Flows – A Classification Problem', *Accountants Journal*, 25–32.

Singleton-Green, B. (November 1991) 'Cash Flow Statements: The Winners and The Losers', *Accountancy*, 22.

Sondhi, A. C., Sorter, G. H., Ross, V. C. and While, G. I. (November–December 1988), 'Cash Flow Redefined: FAS-95 and Security Analysis', *Financial Analysts Journal*, 19–20.

Whiteman, A., Newby, S. (April 1989) 'The Impact of SSAP-10 on Financial Institutions', *Accountants Journal*, 27–31.

Wilson, G. P. (July 1986) 'The Relative Information Content of Accruals and Cash Flows: Combined Evidence at the Earnings Announcement', *Journal of Accounting Research*, 165–203.

Wilson, G. P. (April 1987) 'The Incremental Information Content of the Accrual and Funds Components of Earnings After Controlling for Earnings', *The Accounting Review*, 293–322.

Zega, C. A. (1988) 'The New Statement of Cash Flows', *Management Accounting (US)*, 54–59.

QUESTIONS

1 Dowds and Blake identify a number of differences in the rules on the preparation of the cash flow statement in four different countries. List these differences, rank them in order of importance, and explain the reasons for your ranking.

21

THE CLASSIFICATION OF LEASES BY LESSEES IN THE UNITED STATES AND THE NETHERLANDS:

A Comparative Study

Ruud G. A. Vergoossen

1. INTRODUCTION

The reporting of lease agreements in the annual reports of both the lessor and the lessee is determined by the nature of the agreement. Within this framework, one can differentiate between operating and capital leases.

Capital leasing can be regarded as a mode of financing assets. For example, consider a lease agreement that is non-cancelable for a period which equals its estimated economic life. At the end of this period, the lessee becomes the owner of the underlying asset. In return for this the lessor receives payments which covers the total sum of the investment, the interest charged and a reasonable profit. Executory costs such as servicing, cost of insurance and taxes are to be paid by the lessee. This case implies that the lessee is liable to changes in value of the leased asset. Therefore, the leased asset should be accounted for on the lessee's balance sheet as the acquisition of an asset and the incurrence of an obligation. The depreciation on the leased asset would be deducted in the income statement. Periodically, the sum for the repayment of debt is deducted from the amount accounted for the lease obligation on the balance sheet to determine its value. The interest payments are deducted on the income statement.

From International Journal of Accounting (Vol 27 1992) pp 241–254.
Reprinted by permission of the University of Illinois.

An operating lease is actually a kind of service accorded to the lessee by the lessor. For example, consider a lease contract that can be cancelled at any moment by the lessee. In addition, all executory costs are assumed by the lessor. At the time of termination or cancellation of the agreement, the leased asset must be returned to the lessor. The lease payments are set at a level to cover the estimated depreciation charge, a provision for interest and profit, and the executory costs. In this case, the leased asset is capitalized by the lessor, as the economic risk lies with him or her. The lessee, on the other hand, accounts for the lease payments as expense in his or her income statement.

The above examples of capital and operating leases are the two ends or extremes of a wide spectrum which incorporates many hybrid forms. It is not always easy to ascertain whether the lease under consideration is a capital or operating lease, because these hybrid forms are often a combination of both capital and operating leases. The classification of the lease contract could be of great importance to the lessee, as this could affect the decision to capitalize leases or not, thereby influencing the solvency and profitability of the company as presented on its balance sheet. Capitalization leads to lower solvency and profitability ratios in comparison with an off-balance sheet treatment. Lessees are generally of the view that the non-capitalization of leases does not affect their ability to raise capital as compared with capitalization.[1]

The determination of the nature of a lease contract in the United States is made by testing the terms of the agreement according to four well-defined criteria stipulated by the Financial Accounting Standards Board (FASB). This is contrary to the approach which has been adopted in the Netherlands. As per the Dutch Annual Reporting Guidelines (*Richtlijnen voor de jaarverslaggeving*), the nature of a lease contract is deduced from the terms of the contract as a whole. No specific criteria have been established concerning the manner in which this should be done. In contrast to the lease classification system in the United States, the system in the Netherlands is similar to a black box. The Netherlands could open that black box through the adoption of a lease classification system as in the United States. In this paper, we discuss and draw comparisons between both systems of lease classification in considerable detail. On the basis of this comparative study, we suggest which system should be preferred in the Netherlands.

In section 2 of this paper we deal with the classification of lease agreements in the United States from the point of view of the lessee. Furthermore, in section 3 we discuss different amendments and interpretations of the US regulations concerning lease classification. Section 4 describes the situation as of today in the Netherlands. In section 5, both classification systems are compared. Finally, in section 6 it is suggested which system should be preferred in the Netherlands.

2. CLASSIFICATION OF LEASES IN THE UNITED STATES

In the United States, FASB Statement No. 13, 'Accounting for Leases', and its amendments and interpretations establish standards on the financial accounting and reporting for leases by lessees and lessors. Since the issuance of this statement in 1976, nine statements have been added to the list which contain amendments concerning SFAS 13, the last of them being SFAS 98, which became effective in mid-1988. Besides these nine statements, six interpretations have been issued by the FASB which clarify certain provisions of SFAS 13 in great detail.

The classification of lease contracts from the standpoint of the lessee is based on paragraph 7 in SFAS 13. A lease meeting one or more of the following criteria is to be classified as a capital lease by the lessee:

1 The lease transfers ownership of the property to the lessee by the end of the lease term.
2 The lease contains a bargain purchase option.
3 The lease term is equal to 75 percent or more of the estimated economic life of the leased property.
4 The present value at the beginning of the lease term of the minimum lease payments, excluding that portion of the payments representing executory costs such as insurance, maintenance, and taxes to be paid by the lessor, including any profit thereon, equals or exceeds 90 percent of the excess of the fair value of the leased property to the lessor at the inception of the lease over any related investment tax credit retained by the lessor and expected to be realized by him (the so-called 90 percent recovery test).

The last two criteria are not applicable when the beginning of the lease term falls within the last 25 percent period of the total estimated economic life of the leased property.

A lease which does not meet the above criteria is to be classified as an operating lease from the lessee's perspective. This means that the lessee need not capitalize the lease. But for operating leases having (remaining) non-cancelable lease terms in excess of one year, information of the future obligations must be disclosed in the lessee's financial statements.

Inconsistencies and differences of opinion with respect to lease classification played an important role in developing the criteria. This is recorded in paragraph 62 as follows: 'The Board believes that this Statement removes most, if not all, of the conceptual differences in lease classification as between lessors and lessees and that it provides criteria for such classification that are more explicit and less susceptible to varied interpretation than those in previous literature.'

Clearly, in the United States, the four above-mentioned criteria determine the nature of the lease from the point of view of the lessee. However,

Coughlan[2] has demonstrated that a lease that meets criterion 1 or 2 must also meet the 90 percent recovery test (criterion 4). Further he showed that almost all leases meeting criterion 3 meet criterion 4. According to Coughlan, criteria 1, 2 and 3 are therefore redundant and should be eliminated *for the sake of simplicity*. The assumption that the 90 percent recovery test is sufficient to determine the nature of the lease contract would seem to be correct. However, as shown in the next section, this does not simplify matters concerning lease classification, as the 90 percent recovery test has its own drawbacks.

3. AMENDMENTS AND INTERPRETATIONS OF SFAS 13

To determine whether the lease meets the 90 percent recovery test, the following variables play an important part:

1 the fair value of the leased property at the inception of the lease;
2 the minimum lease payments;
3 the lease term; and
4 the discount rate.

Since SFAS 13 became effective, the meaning of each of these variables has been changed or further clarified by amendments and interpretations. In this section we will discuss the three amendments, two interpretations and one exposure draft which have been issued by the FASB concerning the meaning of these variables. The other amendments and interpretations concern, among other things, lessor-accounting, sale-and-leaseback and subleasing. Therefore, we will not discuss these latter amendments and interpretations any further.

The Fair Value of the Leased Property at the Inception of the Lease

With respect to this variable, problems may arise when the leased property is part of a larger whole, for example, when an office or a floor of a building is leased. The fair value of the leased property is defined as the price for which the property could be sold in an arm's-length transaction between unrelated parties. If it is not possible to determine the fair value in this (objective) way, the lessee shall classify the lease according to the 75 percent criterion only using the estimated economic life of the building in which the leased premises are located. Because many lessees asserted that objective estimates of the leased property's fair value were not possible and the estimated economic life was determined in such a way that the 75 percent test was not met, the FASB issued Interpretation No. 24, 'Leases Involving Only Part of a Building.' It includes the provision that if there are no sales of property similar to the leased property, to estimate the leased property's fair value, other evidence may provide a basis for an objective determination of fair value, for example an independent appraisal of the leased property or estimated replacement cost information.

The Minimum Lease Payments

In addition to fixed rentals, many leases contain contingent rentals which depend on sales volume in the leased facility, an interest rate such as the prime rate, or an index such as a construction cost index. SFAS 13 provides that contingent rentals, from the lessee's point of view, are to be charged to expense as incurred and not considered part of the minimum lease payments for the purpose of performing the 90 percent recovery test. However, in accounting practice diverse ways of determining contingent rentals had developed. As a consequence, similar leases were classified as a capital lease by one lessee and as an operating lease by another lessee. Consequently, the FASB issued SFAS 29, 'Determining Contingent Rentals.' It includes the provision that only amounts based on measurable factors existing at the inception of the lease should be considered part of the minimum lease payments. Thus lease payments that depend on a factor directly related to the future use of the leased property, such as machine hours of use during the lease term, are contingent rentals. On the contrary, lease payments based on an index or interest rate existing at the inception of the lease are part of the minimum lease payments. However, any increases or decreases in lease payments that result from subsequent changes in the index or rate are contingent rentals.

In performing the 90 percent recovery test, a lessee is required to include, in the determination of minimum lease payments, guarantees of the residual value of leased property at expiration of the lease. Interpretation No. 19, 'Lessee Guarantee of the Residual Value of Leased Property', clarifies whether certain kinds of lease provisions constitute a guarantee by the lessee of the residual value.

The Lease Term

The classification of a lease is determined at its inception date. SFAS 13 provides that the inception date is the date of the lease agreement or commitment, if earlier. However, it mentioned one exception to this rule. If the property covered by the lease had yet to be constructed or had not been acquired by the lessor at that date, the inception of the lease should be the date that the construction of the property was completed or that the property was acquired by the lessor. But if the fair value of the leased asset increased during the construction period, it was possible that the present value of the minimum lease payments at the beginning of the lease term could be more than 90 percent of the estimated fair value of the leased asset at the earlier agreement date but less than 90 percent of the fair value of the leased asset at the later date on which construction was completed. Thus, the application of the 90 percent recovery criterion at the date of completion of construction could lead to the classification of a capital lease as an operating lease. To avoid this result, the FASB amended SFAS 13. According to SFAS 23, 'Inception of the Lease', the classification of a lease should *always* be determined at the date of agreement or commitment, if earlier.

In SFAS 98, 'Definition of the Lease Term',[3] the FASB further elaborated the definition of the lease term because of the diversity of interpretations of the definition used in accounting practice.

The Discount Rate

For the computation of the present value of the minimum lease payments the next two discount rates are distinguished:

1 the lessee's incremental borrowing rate: the rate that, at the inception of the lease, the lessee would have incurred to borrow over a similar term the funds necessary to purchase the leased asset;
2 the interest rate implicit in the lease: the discount rate that, when applied to the minimum lease payments, excluding that portion of the payments representing executory costs to be paid by the lessor, together with any profit thereon, and the unguaranteed residual value accruing to the benefit of the lessor, causes the aggregate present value at the beginning of the lease term to be equal to the fair value of the leased property to the lessor at the inception of the lease, minus any investment tax credit retained by the lessor and expected to be realized by him.

The lessee must apply the lower of the two rates. In case the lessee is not able to determine the implicit interest rate of the lease, then SFAS 13 states that the incremental borrowing rate should be applied. As early as 1978, the FASB issued an exposure draft called 'Lessee's Use of the Interest Rate Implicit in the Lease' to counter the misappropriate use of the discount rate as a means to influence the classification of leases. The exposure draft states that the lessee should use an *estimate* of the interest rate implicit in the lease if the implicit rate computed by the lessor cannot be ascertained and classification as a capital lease does not result through the application of the criteria 1, 2 or 3 or through the use of the lessee's incremental borrowing rate. But up till now the exposure draft has not been translated into a statement.

As shown in this section, problems arising in accounting practice have led to adjustments of the criteria for the classification of leases by lessees. This process of adjustment can be visualized as represented in Fig. 1.

The cause of the continuing adjustments is the use of arbitrary criteria (especially the 90 percent recovery test) which contain subjective elements

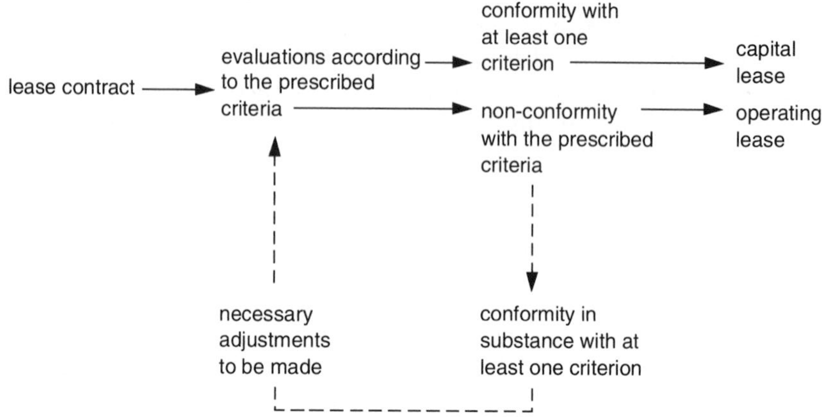

Figure 1 Evaluation of the terms of the lease contract as per the prescribed criteria. (The dotted lines indicate the way in which the adjustments of the criteria take place.)

such as the economic life of the leased asset, the fair value of the leased asset at the inception of the lease, the minimum lease payments, the lease term, and the discount rate in a situation where the lessee is not indifferent to the way leases are classified. In that case, the subjective elements can be manipulated by the lessee in order to influence the lease classification. The conclusion drawn by Dieter[4] puts the above-mentioned dilemma into perspective when he states: 'While arbitrary rules may work when the objectives are at the extremes of available options, they rarely work if the position sought is on middle ground.'

4. CLASSIFICATION OF LEASES IN THE NETHERLANDS

In the Netherlands, the Civil Code contains most of the legal framework for financial reporting by companies.[5] The most important section of the Act is section 362.1. It states among other things: 'The annual accounts shall, in accordance with accounting principles acceptable in the social and economic environment, furnish such insight as to enable a sound judgment to be formed regarding the financial position and results of the legal entity and – to the extent that the nature of annual accounts so permits – regarding its solvency and liquidity.' The rules of the Act are often vague. Concerning lease classification there are no specific rules. The words 'lease' or 'leasing' are not even mentioned in the Act. But it is evident from the explanatory memorandum to section 366 of the Act, that property should not be capitalized by the company that is the legal owner but instead by the company that bears the economic risks.

In the Netherlands, the sections of the Act are interpreted by the Council for Annual Reporting (*Raad voor de Jaarverslaggeving*). The Council is comprised of representatives of Dutch employers' organizations, users of financial statements and the Netherlands Institute of Registered Auditors (*Nederlands Instituut van Registeraccountants, or NIVRA*). It reviews the accounting principles adopted by companies, and decides on the acceptability of these practices within the framework of the Act. It should be noted, however, that the Annual Reporting Guidelines (*Richtlijnen voor de jaarverslaggeving*) determined by the Council are intended to have an impact on accounting practice. It is neither mandatory for companies to follow these guidelines nor obligatory for auditors to qualify their reports if the guidelines are not followed. The guidelines of the Council can best be described as authoritative opinions of an influential private group.

With respect to leasing Guideline 1.05, 'Criteria for the inclusion and disclosure of information', paragraphs 121 to 127 are of importance. Paragraph 121 states that a distinction is made between capital leases and operating leases. A capital lease is described as, in essence, a form of finance, in which the legal ownership of the assets generally remains with the lessor, the economic risks being borne entirely or almost entirely by the lessee (paragraph 122). In the case of an operating lease, the lessee benefits from the use of an asset but the economic risks remain entirely or almost entirely with the lessor. The lessor usually takes care of the maintenance of the leased asset and also arranges for its replacement in the event of temporary failure (paragraph 123).

Concerning the classification of lease agreements, paragraph 124 states that the nature of any specific contract will have to be deduced from the terms of the contract as a whole. If it is evident from the terms of the contract as such that the contract involves a capital lease, the leased asset should be capitalized by the lessee. In the balance sheet of the lessee or in the notes, it should be mentioned that the lessee is the economic but not the legal owner of the leased asset (paragraph 125). Further, this paragraph mentions three examples of the terms of a contract whereby in principle the economic ownership rests with the lessee:

1 The lessee is entitled to purchase the asset at a price which is substantially below its market value during or immediately after the period of expiration of the lease contract.
2 The lessee has committed itself for a period of approximately the same duration as the economic life of the asset.
3 The lessee has committed itself for a shorter period than the economic life of the asset but in addition has been given an option to lease the asset

at a considerably lower rental for the ensuing period up to approximately the end of the economic life of the asset.

The examples cannot be compared to the criteria for classification of leases as used in the United States because contracts that do not include one of the examples could nonetheless also be classified as a capital lease. That is to say, that the examples are not the only prerequisites for classification of leases into capital leases. Paragraph 126 pertains to operating leases. This paragraph mentions that an operating lease can never give rise to the leased property being capitalized by the lessee. But where the lessee has entered into commitments involving substantial sums of money for rather long periods, this fact should be disclosed in the notes. This paragraph is a result of section 381 of the Act. This section states that important off-balance sheet liabilities should be disclosed in the notes.

As mentioned above, the company that bears the economic risks is the economic owner of the leased asset. The guidelines do not state any quantifiable criteria for assessing which party in the lease agreement mainly bears the burden of the economic risks. In the Netherlands, each contract has to be judged on its own merits. Paragraph 125 gives only three examples of situations whereby the economic risks rest mainly with the lessee. The Dutch lease classification system may be visualized as shown in Fig. 2.

5. COMPARISON OF THE CLASSIFICATION SYSTEMS

Both in the United States and in the Netherlands, lease classification clearly has its roots in economic theory. Stated differently, the criterion for the capitalization of leases, in the United States and the Netherlands is the economic ownership of the leased asset. The Netherlands has a broad set of guidelines whereby each lease contract is judged on its own merits. On the other hand, in the United States the classification of leases is achieved by applying strict rules that have been given by the FASB. This implies that every lease contract has to be examined in the light of the four criteria.

The objective of accounting rules is the adequate reporting of the financial

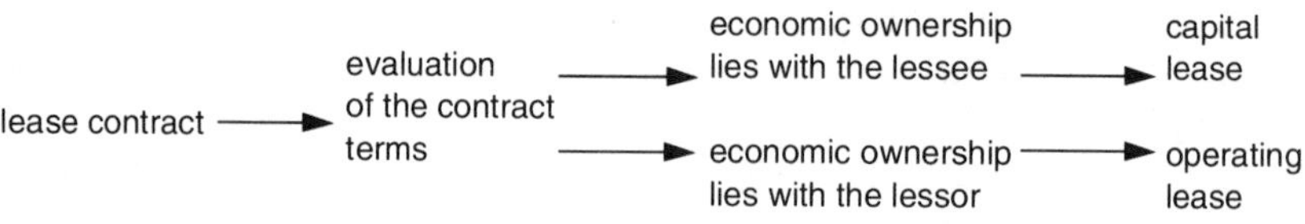

Figure 2 Evaluation of the terms of the lease contract as a whole.

position and the results of operations of an entity. The question that we must ask ourselves is to what extent accounting rules, whether they are broadly formulated or detailed, determine the quality of financial reporting.

The FASB, in its Statement of Financial Accounting Concepts No. 2 (SFAC 2), summarizes a number of qualitative characteristics that should apply to accounting information. The overriding criterion that was applied by the FASB, when formulating the qualitative characteristics of the accounting information, was its usefulness to users such as shareholders, bankers and financial analysts. The qualitative characteristics are as follows:

1 understandability;
2 relevance;
3 reliability; and
4 comparability.

Before applying these qualitative characteristics, the accounting information must pass two litmus tests: it should satisfy a materiality threshold, and the benefits of the accounting information should exceed its costs. The above-mentioned qualitative characteristics can be interpreted in varying degrees depending on the context in which they are used, since clear-cut definitions that apply to all situations do not exist.

Understandability and relevance of accounting information can be eliminated as qualitative characteristics in the case of lease classification, as the latter does not influence them. This is in contrast to the two other qualitative characteristics, namely reliability and comparability of accounting information. The FASB distinguishes three elements of reliability, as follows:

1 verifiability;
2 neutrality; and
3 representational faithfulness.

In accounting practice it is difficult to apply these elements strictly, as there is a certain level of interaction between them. The three elements can be related to the classification of leases as follows:

1 Verifiability in the context of lease classification means that, when using the same information and measurement standards, different parties should arrive at the same classification of the lease contract.
2 Neutrality suggests that the system of lease classification should not be used as an instrument in the service of any vested or particular interests.
3 Representational faithfulness implies that the way leases are classified should present a clear picture, i.e. the information provided on leases should agree with what it is meant to represent. Stated differently, substance should always be preferred over form.

Comparability applied in this context means that the reporting of lease contracts in financial statements of companies should be of such a nature that one is able to compare the lease activities of different companies with each other. Since the nature of the lease contract determines the manner by which it is accounted for in financial statements, comparability is influenced by the system of lease classification.

In general, unambiguous and flexible rules enhance the reliability and comparability of information. But on the whole this is largely a difficult task, as one possible attribute often rules out the other. One can see this happening both in the United States and the Netherlands.

The Dutch accounting rules are flexible; hence there is no necessity to resort to creative accounting such as presenting capital leases as operating leases since the distinction between the two types of leases is drawn on a case-by-case basis. This leads to the situation that it is very often not possible to classify lease contracts unambiguously, the reason being that differences in interpretation or judgment lead to different classifications of similar lease contracts. This can result not only in a loss of comparability between companies but it can also affect the verifiability and neutrality adversely. An example of this ambiguity is that a difference of opinion could arise between the management of the company and the external auditor with respect to the classification of a certain lease contract. This could lead to a situation whereby the external auditor might, for commercial reasons, agree in principle to an incorrect lease classification adopted by the company to satisfy the management. Thus the lease classification becomes an instrument in the hands of the management for the purposes of manipulation to achieve desired results. As observed earlier, non-capitalization of leases leads to a better presentation of solvency and profitability of the company.

The process by which leases are classified in the Netherlands appears like a black box. On the other hand, stringent accounting rules have been laid down in the United States to classify leases in a rather unambiguous manner. This enhances the comparability and the verifiability/neutrality of the accounting information concerning leases. In contrast to the Council for Annual Reporting, the FASB determines whether substantially all the benefits and risks of ownership have been transferred to the lessee. As we have seen earlier, this does not lead to *complete* unambiguity because the evaluation criteria are both incomplete and subject to various interpretations (see SFAS 98 and Interpretation No. 19). In comparison to those in the Netherlands, the American accounting rules are *relatively* unambiguous and rather inflexible. The result is that lessees try to circumvent these criteria to prevent the capitalization of leases. This makes it necessary to redefine the underlying variables of the 90 percent recovery test constantly (see SFAS 23, SFAS 29, Interpretation No. 24 and the above-mentioned exposure draft). This inflexibility endangers the important accounting principle of substance over form. Such is not the case in the Netherlands, where formal evaluation criteria for the classification of leases are non-existent.

We could conclude from the foregoing discussion that comparability between the lease activities of different companies is much greater in the United States than in the Netherlands. However, one should also consider that a lack of representational faithfulness can affect the comparability of the information concerning leases adversely. The reliability of the information as a whole is endangered by both countries' systems of classification as the elements of verifiability and neutrality are threatened according to the Dutch system, while representational faithfulness suffers in the American system. The preceding can be summarized as shown in Table 1.

6. A 'REBUTTABLE PRESUMPTION OF A CAPITAL LEASE'

The question yet to be answered is: should the Netherlands adopt a system of accounting rules concerning lease classification as in the United States? In our opinion, it should not, despite the two plus signs and one plus/minus sign for the American system against only one plus sign for the Dutch system (see Table 1). A broad set of guidelines underlying the system of lease classification should be preferred because it offers a great amount of flexibility. In general, rules should account for all possible situations, thereby enhancing the principle of substance over form. As seen above, amendments have not been necessary because of the fact that arbitrary classification criteria are used, but are instead the result of the use of ambiguous variables that underlie these classification criteria. Therefore, as long as it is impossible to define these variables unambiguously, our preference in principle lies with a system of lease classification as in the Netherlands. Furthermore, we consider the time and energy spent in amending and applying a still more complex set of rules and regulations as a waste of resources that occurs as a direct result of the inflexibility incorporated within the American system.

This, however, does not imply that the Dutch system of lease classification is perfect. According to us, there is still room for improvement, especially in the field of additional information furnished by the company in the notes to their financial statements. More attention should be given to this aspect because of the general character of the guidelines concerning

Table 1 An overview

Qualitative characteristics	*The US system*	*The Dutch system*
Reliability:		
Verifiability	+	–
Neutrality	+	–
Representational faithfulness	–	+
Comparability	+/–	–

+: better than in the other country –: worse than in the other country.

lease classification which could affect the verifiability and neutrality of the information presented about leases, for example, making it compulsory for lessees to state the reasons why leases have not been capitalized in the financial statements. Stated differently, there should be a 'rebuttable presumption of a capital lease.' Under this approach, all leases should be assumed to be capital leases unless there are specific reasons to assume the contrary. Considering the fact that the lessee in general does not wish to capitalize leases, a 'rebuttable presumption of a capital lease' would be superior to a 'rebuttable presumption of an operating lease.' When a lease is treated as operating in the lessee's financial statements, the justification should be stated explicitly in the footnotes. This would improve the insight into the process whereby lease classification takes place in the Netherlands, thereby to a certain extent getting rid of its black box character. This system has some clear-cut advantages. First, it enhances neutrality as it makes it more difficult for the company to use the lease classification system as an instrument to manipulate and therefore to achieve certain desired outcomes. Second, the possibility that the external auditor could be placed in a rather ambivalent position would be greatly reduced, thus improving the verifiability of the lease classification. Third, this would provide greater insight into the manner by which leases are classified, thereby enhancing the comparability of lease activities between companies. However, it should be noted that one should not lose sight of the element of materiality during this process. A description of the manner in which lease contracts are classified by the lessee could lead to a certain amount of self regulation by which accounting standards develop in congruence with the 'accounting principles acceptable in the social and economic environment.' This is in contrast to the situation currently prevalent in the United States where amendments lag behind the developments that have taken place within the accounting practice.

Our choice for a revised Dutch system is more than a choice between Scylla and Charybdis. We have to admit that our choice has a so-called cultural background too. In the Netherlands, the *insight* into the financial position and results of a certain company provided by its financial statements plays an important role, whereas in the United States the *comparability* between companies is of importance. When reviewing one's own system, an author should evaluate the systems of others. Unfortunately, the American system does not contribute to a better insight into the financial position and results of a company. That insight is considered to be more important in the Netherlands than comparability is evident from the comments of the Council for Annual Reporting[6] on exposure draft 32 of the International Accounting Standards Committee: 'E 32 is aimed at comparability. However, the primary requisite is the good insight which annual accounts ought to give into the financial position and results of the enterprise concerned. Comparability of annual accounts of different enterprises is in principle not an aim in itself . . . The objective of comparability may come into conflict with the objective of a good insight into a reporting enterprise. In the cases where the two objectives lead to different bases to be applied for the valuation of assets and liabilities and the determination of income, according to the views held in the Netherlands the choice should be made for the basis which in the first place best meets the objective of good insight, even if the requirement of comparability is thereby not primarily fulfilled.'

NOTES

1 Abdel-khalik et al. (1981) found that a majority of companies surveyed were structuring the terms of lease contracts to avoid capitalization. During the course of that study, bankers were asked to give their opinion concerning two identical companies. The researchers showed them condensed financial statements of two identical companies, differing only in their method of accounting for leases. Almost 40 percent of the bankers considered the company that did not capitalize its leases more profitable, and about 50 percent considered the two companies equal. More than 25 percent of the bankers indicated that the company that kept leases off the balance sheet had a better debt-paying ability. But a comparable study done by Wilkins and Zimmer (1983) concluded that bankers could not be misled by the manner in which capital leases were accounted for in the financial statements of the lessee. According to them, the reasons why bankers were not misled was the fact that explicit guidelines for the treatment of capital leases were used to analyze the loan applicants' financial statements, as well as the attention given to lease accounting alternatives and lease financing in the professional and internal bank literature.

2 J. W. Coughlan, 'Regulation, rents and residuals; The FASB statement on leases is unnecessarily complex and has several major flaws as well,' *The Journal of Accountancy* (February 1980), 58–66.

3 The complete title of SFAS 98 is: 'Accounting for Leases: Sale-Leaseback Transactions Involving Real Estate, Sales-Type Leases of Real Estate, Definition of the Lease Term, Initial Direct Costs of Direct Financing Leases.'

4 R. Dieter, 'Is Lessee Accounting Working?' *The CPA Journal* (August 1979), 13–19.

5 From now on, we shall refer to the part of the Civil Code which deals with financial reporting by companies as 'the Act.'

6 Raad voor de Jaarverslaggeving, 'Commentaar op ED 32 "Comparability of Financial Statements",' *De Accountant* (October 1989), 71–73.

BIBLIOGRAPHY

Abdel-khalik, A. Rashad et al. (1981) *The Economic Effects on Lessees of FASB Statement No. 13, Accounting for Leases*. Stamford, CT: FASB.

Beckman, H. (1982/2) 'Financiële leasing in de jaarrekening van lessees.' *Bedrijkskunde*, 99–109.

Beckman, H. 'Economische beschikkingsmacht: Grondslag voor vermogensverantwoording en winstneming.' *Maandblad voor Accountancy en Bedrijfshuishoudkunde*, July/August 1988, 325–341.

Beckman, H. and A. W. A. Joosen. (1980) *Leasing van roerenden onroerend goed*. Leiden: Stenfert Kroese.

Beckman, H. and O. M. Volgenant jr. (ed.). *Documentatie rond de jaarrekening*. Deventer: Kluwer, August 1988.

Coughlan, J. W. , 'Regulation, rents and residuals; The FASB statement on leases is unnecessarily complex and has several major flaws as well.' *The Journal of Accountancy*, February 1980, 58–66.

Dieter, R. 'Is Lessee Accounting Working?' *The CPA Journal*, August 1979, 13–19.

Financial Accounting Standards Board. *Statement of Financial Accounting Concepts Nos. 1, 2*. Stamford, CT: FASB.

Financial Accounting Standards Board. *Statement of Financial Accounting Standards Nos. 13, 17, 22, 23, 26, 27, 28, 29, 91, 98*. Stamford, CT: FASB.

Financial Accounting Standards Board. *FASB Interpretation Nos. 19, 21, 23, 24, 26, 27*. Stamford, CT: FASB.

Financial Accounting Standards Board. *Proposed Statement of Financial Accounting Standards: Lessee's Use of the Interest Rate Implicit in the Lease*. Stamford, CT: FASB, 1978.

Raad voor de Jaarverslaggeving. *Richtlijnen voor de jaarverslaggeving*. Deventer: Kluwer, June 1988.

Raad voor de Jaarverslaggeving. 'Commentaar op ED 32 "Comparability of Financial Statements".' *De Accountant*, October 1989, 71–73.

The Review Committee (under chairmanship of R. Dearing). *The Making of Accounting Standards*. London: The Institute of Chartered Accountants in England and Wales, 1988.

Wilkins, T. and I. Zimmer. 'The Effect of Leasing and Different Methods of Accounting for Leases on Credit Evaluations.' *The Accounting Review*, October 1983, 749–764.

QUESTIONS

1 Discuss the contrast between the US and the Dutch systems of accounting regulation revealed in this article.

22

EUROPEAN UNIFICATION, ACCOUNTING HARMONIZATION, AND SOCIAL DISCLOSURES

Martin Freedman and A. J. Stagliano

The European Community (EC) has been attempting to narrow the differences in financial statement reporting of companies in member nations. Both the fourth and the eighth directives have been promulgated to help with this endeavor. With the time set for EC unification at hand, there is some question as to how successful these nations will be in achieving uniformity of financial statement reporting.

One source of difference that is wholly ignored by the directives is the area of social reporting. Only the politically unacceptable Vredeling Proposal has dealt with information generation of this type. These disclosures, which include information of companies' relationships with the broad range of stakeholders, tend to be voluntary statements that vary not only among countries but also within countries.

A number of studies have shown that information provided by social disclosures is useful for stakeholders. Unfortunately, a potential consequence of the EC's disregard for these disclosures may be a variation of Gresham's law. That is, firms that do not disclose will serve as the model for future disclosure (or, poor disclosing drives out good disclosing).

In this study, a comparative analysis is made of the current level of social disclosure within and between companies of each of the 12 member EC nations. Financial reports are reviewed to highlight the similarities and differences in social disclosures based on content analysis. Included as part of this analysis are possible future scenarios for social reporting in a unified EC.

From International Journal of Accounting (Vol 27 1992) pp 112–122.
Reprinted by permission of the University of Illinois.

The paper is structured as follows: first, a review of pertinent social reporting literature is presented; second, the methodology used to analyze the disclosures is explained; third, the results are presented and analyzed; finally, alternative scenarios are provided and a conclusion is drawn.

SELECTIVE OVERVIEW OF THE LITERATURE

The literature on social disclosure tends to focus on two issues: (1) why companies choose to make these disclosures: and (2) whether anybody uses the information for decision-making. A good portion of the literature on the reasons for making these disclosures was summarized by Ullmann.[1] The conclusion drawn there was that the reasons for making social disclosures have not as yet been demonstrated satisfactorily. Guthrie and Parker[2] provide two competing hypotheses as to the justification for making social disclosures. The 'user utility model' is based on the demands of stakeholders. That is, corporate interest groups demand certain information and, based on the corporate perception of the demand for the information, the appropriate social disclosures are provided. Unfortunately, this hypothesis fails to explain why large companies from the same industry that operate in the same country make differential social disclosures. Is there any great difference, for example, between the stakeholders of EXXON and Texaco?

The second hypothesis proposed by Guthrie and Parker is termed a 'political economy.' According to these authors, accounting reports serve as social, political, and economic documents. Rather than reacting to the pressure to provide information applied by special interest groups, corporations produce information that serves corporate political and ideological goals. Thus, social disclosures can be perceived as furthering the self-interest of the entity, as Macintosh[3] and Cooper and Sherer[4] have argued similarly in discussing social disclosure production. Since corporations have various agendas, ideologies, and goals, the political economy hypothesis does explain differential disclosures by companies in the same industry facing the same constituencies.

It is probable that there is no single motivation for making social disclosures. Social disclosure, for the most part, is a function of the attitude of top management towards its stakeholders. Whether there is an economic motivation for the disclosure (as some of the studies that Ullmann cites claim), a reaction to user needs (as proposed by Guthrie and Parker), or a political motivation (as suggested by Arnold[5]), is probably a consequence of each management's particular perception of the world it faces.

The problem as far as social disclosures made by EC companies is that, if in the move towards uniformity of financial reports firms from a majority of the countries do not perceive a need to make these disclosures, the reporting technique may become extinct. Since demand to produce these disclosures may no longer be driven by national stakeholder groups or perceived reactions to regulators because of the diffusion caused by the larger reporting community, corporations may elect not to disclose.

The lesson learned from the aborted attempt by the EC's European Commission for Social Affairs and Employment to strengthen disclosure regarding multinational corporate undertakings is worth reviewing in this regard. As the analysis by DeVos[6] has made abundantly clear, internal and/or nationalistic influences are difficult to overcome in developing community-wide directives with respect to social affairs. The relatively mild disclosure proposals contained in the Vredeling Initiative were shelved for pure political reasons – without consideration of either corporate or workers' views.

There are a number of studies that document the use made of social disclosures by financial statement readers in making decisions. Studies include those by Belkaoui.[7] Anderson and Frankle.[8] Jaggi and Freedman[9] and Shane and Spicer.[10] However, all of these studies focus on only one constituent group-investors. That investors are a source of demand for social disclosures certainly makes it easier to justify including these disclosures in financial reports. The problem is that some of the disclosures have important implications for other stakeholders, and, since a demand has not been documented, these disclosures may not be made. As an example, employees form another constituent group for which the demand has been demonstrated (see, for example, Schreuder,[11] Brockhoff,[12] and Dierkes,[13]). Some EC countries have reacted to this demand (notwithstanding the Vredeling Proposal defeat). Cooperative management efforts by labor and owners are fairly common in Belgium, France, and Germany.

It would not be expected that reporting to a community of 12 nations instead of one will reduce the demand of either investors or employees for social information. Still, there is uncertainty as to the actual impact of EC unification on disclosure. It is possible that demand for this information from these groups may remain the same, but that the company, in the guise of improving the uniformity of disclosure with other EC companies, may choose to eliminate social disclosures. However, it is more probable that companies will continue to disclose at least as much social information as they have in the past. Therefore, it is useful to view, in a comparative framework, the baseline for member countries' social reporting.

METHODOLOGY

An analysis was made of the annual reports from companies in each of the 12 EC member nations. A sample of firms was chosen from companies included in *Moody's International*. Since manufacturing firms are most likely to have problems with pollution, product safety, and occupational safety and health (three of the major categories of social disclosure), the sample was based on selecting at least three manufacturing firms from each country. When *Moody's* included more than three manufacturing firms for a given country, the firms were selected randomly. When there were three or fewer, all firms were chosen. Unfortunately, Luxembourg had only service industries reported; three banks were chosen.

Twenty-four companies responded to a request for annual reports and any special reports that are made publicly available (including the French *Bilan Social*). The final sample included at least two annual reports from each country except Portugal, Luxembourg, and Greece, which had one each.

Table 1 shows a classification of the firms by industry. The resulting sample contains 23 firms from manufacturing industries that are all prone to having problems with pollution, occupational safety and health, product safety, and energy conservation.

Social Disclosure Content Analysis

Based on the method of content analysis developed by Freedman and Wasley[14] to analyze social disclosure of US firms, a seven category content analysis was utilized for this study. These categories are:

1 community involvement (e.g., charitable contributions);
2 environmental protection (pollution disclosures);
3 consumer relations;
4 human resources;
5 energy conservation;
6 product safety;
7 occupational safety and health;

For each category of social disclosure, the content of that disclosure is analyzed using a four element index that attempts to assess the quality of the disclosure. These four elements are:

Table 1 Industries included in the study

Industry	*Number*
Oil	10
Pulp and paper	1
Autos	3
Chemicals	4
Tobacco	1
Heavy equipment	1
Cement	1
Metals and glass	2
Banks	1
Total	24

1 time frame (past, present, or future);
2 effect (significant or not);
3 monetary versus non-monetary;
4 reference to specific action, person, event, or place.

This method of content analysis focuses on each statement based on what is included in the statement rather than how much is said. Counting the number of lines or words included in the social disclosure does not convey the importance of the disclosure. The critical attribute is the meaning of the words. In that regard, the social disclosures were scored by assigning a single point to each disclosure. If the report commentary involved future implications, or the disclosure was monetary, two points were given.

Research Questions

The small sample size (given the relatively large number of companies) greatly limits the empirical analysis. However, it is possible to draw some broad conclusions despite this limitation. There are two hypothesized expectations formulated for this study that deal with the differences in social disclosure. These are:

H_1: There is no difference in the level of social disclosure among companies from the 12 member nations of the EC.

H_2: There is no difference in the level of social disclosure made by companies within each EC member country.

If the null hypotheses are not confirmed, this implies that social disclosure is a function of both the headquarters country and the management of the company.

RESULTS AND ANALYSIS

Of the seven categories of social disclosure, the firms included in this study provided disclosures about only four.

Table 2 indicates that there are differences in social disclosures made by companies from different countries. The differences are in both the total amount of disclosure and in the category of disclosure.

Overall, sample firms in France, Germany, the Netherlands, and the UK disclose the most social information. Denmark, Ireland, and Luxembourg companies disclosed no social information (it is to be remembered that the Luxembourg sample element is a banking institution). Based on the literature, for the most part, this is not a surprising result. The only surprise is that the Danish companies made no social disclosures, since Denmark has a reputation of encouraging social disclosure. However, since both companies are oil refineries, it is possible that the CEOs of these companies are not enthusiastic about social disclosure. Again, this may simply be a result of the small sample available for analysis.

The results by category of social disclosure are interesting. The UK seems to dominate disclosure concerning community involvement. However, this is because regulations require that charitable donations and political contributions be disclosed. Companies from Belgium, Italy, the Netherlands, and Spain all make voluntary disclosures of their charitable activities. Sample companies from Germany and France made no disclosures concerning community involvement.

Pollution disclosures are dominated by companies from Germany, with companies from the Netherlands and Belgium also making significant disclosures. These disclosures are all voluntary and many of the disclosures include information of actual pollution emissions. In the USA pollution information is a required disclosure in the annual report (Form 10-K) that is filed with the Securities and Exchange Commission. However, few firms, if any, disclose the actual amount of pollution emissions. Overall, the level of pollution disclosure made by the EC companies is much lower than companies from comparable industries in the USA. Since the companies included in the sample are all from industries that are major contributors to pollution in Europe (except for the Luxembourg bank), it is surprising that companies from Denmark, France, Ireland, and Italy do not disclose anything about their relationship with the environment.

The category of human resources disclosures also shows significant differences across countries. France dominates this disclosure category, with companies from Germany and the Netherlands making significant disclosures. As was the case with community involvement, the domination of France is due to regulations. French companies of a certain size are

Table 2 Average disclosure of country

Category of disclosure	*Community involvement*	*Pollution*	*Human resources*	*Occupational safety and health*	*Total*
Belgium	1.5	7	3	2	13.5
Denmark	0	0	0	0	0
France	0	0	30	30	60
Germany	0	10	18	4	32
Greece	0	4	5	4	13
Ireland	0	0	0	0	0
Italy	1.5	0	2.5	0	4
Luxembourg	0	0	0	0	0
Netherlands	2	7	15	3.5	27.5
Portugal	0	4	2	0	6
Spain	6.3	1.7	4.7	0.7	13.4
UK	12.7	2.3	5.3	5.6	25.9
Total	24	36	85.5	49.8	195.3

required to publish a *Bilan Social*, which is a social report of the firm's relationship with it, employees. As a matter of fact, except for the social report, French firms made no other social disclosures. Belgian companies, too, are well known for their strong participative workers councils from which much information impacting the consultative rights of employees flow. Disclosures made by companies from Germany and the Netherlands were voluntary, as were all the other disclosures in this category. Except for companies from Denmark, Ireland, and Luxembourg, some disclosure was made by companies from all the countries in the EC.

The last category deals with occupational safety and health disclosures. These disclosures are also included in the *Bilan Social*, so French firms once again dominate. Disclosures in this category include both good and bad news. That is, firms report not only their decrease in accident and death rates, but also the number of accidents and fatalities in a given year. Voluntary reporting of these disclosures was done by firms from Germany, Greece, the United Kingdom, the Netherlands, and Belgium. With the possible exception of the Luxembourg bank, all the sample companies potentially have occupational safety and health problems. Voluntary disclosure of this major aspect of management-employee relations appears to be quite limited. In a society where co-determination is common, this lack of disclosure is quite surprising.

To some, corporate social disclosures are a means of communicating social reality. Voluntary production of this reflective viewpoint of management is more likely to occur when widely shared social priorities exist in the localized environment. Stakeholders, for example, may act as if such information (even if it has a propagandist or public relations 'flavor')

Table 3 Average voluntary disclosure by country

Category of disclosure	*Community involvement*	*Pollution*	*Human resources*	*Occupational Safety and health*	*Total*
Belgium	1.5	7	3	2	13.5
Denmark	0	0	0	0	0
France	0	0	0	0	0
Germany	0	10	18	4	32
Greece	0	4	5	4	13
Ireland	0	0	0	0	0
Italy	1.5	0	2.5	0	0
Luxembourg	0	0	0	0	0
Netherlands	2	7	15	3.5	27.5
Portugal	0	4	2	0	6
Spain	6.3	1.7	4.7	.7	13.4
UK	0	2.3	5.3	5.6	13.2
Total	11.3	36	55.5	19.8	122.6

should flow from the firm. Furthermore, voluntary social disclosures may be forthcoming as a responsive pressure from certain constituencies and as a proactive strike to avoid further regulation of the disclosure function.

Table 3 provides information of voluntary disclosures alone. It is apparent from examining the table that there are four tiers of social disclosures on a country basis. Germany and the Netherlands make the most voluntary disclosures. Belgium, Greece, Spain, and the UK are on the next level. Portugal and Italy are on the third tier. Sample companies from Denmark, France, Ireland, and Luxembourg made no voluntary disclosures.

There are differences in social disclosures not only between countries but also within countries. Table 4 provides the within-country comparisons. Of the nine countries with multiple companies in the same sample, four show significant within-group disclosure differences. Companies from the Netherlands and Belgium have the most pronounced differences, with those from Spain and Italy also showing major differences. The two countries with mandated disclosure requirements (France and the UK) show very little difference in the amount or category of disclosure. German companies, which dominate voluntary disclosure, show no variation in overall disclosure but a significant difference in disclosure by category.

DISCUSSION AND CONCLUSION

The lack of consistency in social disclosure either between countries or within countries is not surprising. Since only France and the UK have mandated social disclosure requirements, companies from the ten other EC nations make these disclosures voluntarily. Based on the literature, it is apparent that there is no single reason why companies choose to disclose social information. It is also apparent that when disclosure is mandated the level of disclosure increases.

In attempting to bring uniformity to financial reporting by EC companies, the EC can enact requirements for social reporting that either enhance this reporting, maintain the status quo, or eliminate it. Mandated disclosures from France and the UK might be required of all the EC companies. In that case, existing national requirements would become the model for European reporting. Another way of enhancing social disclosure is by implementing the German model (developed by Dierkes) that Deutsche Shell has utilized in its social report.[15]

The EC can also choose to ignore social reporting and allow both France and the UK to continue to 'force' companies from these countries to make required disclosures. Under this scenario, it is probable that the level of social reporting will continue to be inconsistent both between and within countries. However, it is also possible that companies making voluntary social disclosures will continue to do so. Since there is a demonstrated demand for social information, maintaining the status quo is not the best

Table 4 Disclosure by company and country

Category of disclosure	*Community involvement*	*Pollution*	*Human resources*	*Occupational Safety and health*	*Total*
Belgium					
MHO	0	0	2	0	2
Petrofina	3	14	4	4	25
Denmark					
OK	0	0	0	0	0
Texaco	0	0	0	0	0
France					
Total	0	0	30	30	60
ELF Aquitaine	0	0	30	30	60
Renault	0	0	30	30	60
Germany					
Daimler Benz	0	2	28	2	32
Hoechst	0	18	8	6	32
Ireland					
Seafield	0	0	0	0	0
PJ Carroll	0	0	0	0	0
Italy					
Fiat	3	0	5	0	8
Montedison	0	0	0	0	0
Netherlands					
Royal Dutch Petroleum	4	0	0	0	4
DSN	0	14	30	7	51
Spain					
Finanzanto	0	0	5	0	5
Repsol	4	5	5	0	14
Petrofina	15	0	4	2	21
UK					
British Petroleum	9	2	6	4	21
Pilkington	14	0	5	5	24
ICI	15	5	5	8	33

situation, especially since the inconsistencies make it difficult to complete intercompany comparisons.

A third possible scenario is that the EC can ask both France and the UK to eliminate their mandated disclosures. This would send a signal to the other countries that social reporting is being discouraged. A decrease in the level of social disclosure might be expected to occur. This, though, is not a probable outcome. The French mandated disclosures fit nicely with the model of co-determination that most of the other EC nations have developed with their employees. Therefore, it would appear to be an anti-labor move to force French companies to stop reporting on relationships with their employees. Still, initiatives to enhance worker informedness, like the Vredeling Proposal, have not fared well.

A 'unified' EC can lead (maybe not without difficulty) to more uniform standards for disclosure of the social impacts of economic activity. There is ample historical evidence for a movement towards homogeneity of accounting recording and reporting. When the need has arisen for more consistent financial data outputs (so that intercompany comparisons can be made), the accounting establishment has responded appropriately. But it is inappropriate to expect uniformity of social disclosure without a broader agreement on the underlying purpose that is to be served by reporting on the non-market impacts (i.e., social costs and benefits, negative outputs, production process externalities, and the like) of corporate behavior. There remains today an obvious need for development and acceptance of a transcendent ideology of social reporting.

The empirical evidence developed in this paper from a small sampling of EC annual reports demonstrates that national-level regulation of the reporting function will easily elicit disclosure. In fact, as others have previously noted, without mandated disclosure little social reporting of consequence and substance would be produced voluntarily. Such regulation, though, might be considered simply a parochial manifestation of the particular culture norms, national priorities, or other artifacts of the country involved. Some supra-national goal for this type of disclosure is needed if a rational system of social reporting is to evolve. Even an EC-mandated requirement will necessitate a more fundamental explication of the usefulness of these disclosures to the companies, their stakeholders, and the population at large.

In general, accounting has supported a positivist view of society that is associated with both capitalistic production schema and marginalist or incrementalist economic theories. Capturing a contemporary world view that expresses societal ideologies *can* be a goal in the reporting model. Accounting reports can be seen as phenomena that are reflective of social values in addition to financial and economic metrics alone. Such a transcendent purpose or ideology will be required if social reporting is to have its appropriate place in the soon to be rationalized EC accounting system for reporting on the operations of companies in the unified member countries.

Whether social disclosure is considered to be a reactive or preventative response to governmental or social pressures (this might be seen as a user-utility approach) or an active tool for furthering the private interests of the disclosing entities (i.e., accounting used as a private policy instrument), agreement must be reached as to the purpose to be served by the exercise of disclosure itself. Further, little will be gained if a 'generally accepted' standard for social disclosure is promulgated (whether privately or publicly developed and/or enforced) unless the normal characteristics of financial data (e.g., timeliness, consistency, verifiability, reliability, and so forth) are present. It is clear that mandated disclosures will be produced.

The issue for all involved to grapple with is whether the disclosure mechanism will have the expected or desired effect on the behavior of both the producers and users of the data. Generating data in search of a use would appear to be a counterproductive application of scarce resources.

The current state of discontinuity, inconsistency, and non-comparability in EC social disclosure certainly requires attention as the movement toward unification of the European trading partners continues. There is a risk that without active attention the EC will gravitate toward the position of the member country with the least disclosure. Ignoring the social accounting/disclosure issue while dealing with other matters related to financial reporting is an inappropriate response on the part of the unification planners and architects. Notwithstanding the importance and immediacy of need in handling the rationalization of numerous different systems and standards, it would appear to be far more efficient to face the social disclosure problem now as part of the broader accounting directives.

Accounting numbers and accounting reports are not neutral. They are intended to, and in fact do, convey information and affect behavior. As the data developed in this paper show, cross-national differences exist. Reaching consensus as to the type and amount of social information that ought to be produced will be easier if done now while the whole unified recording-reporting system is being developed. If the elusive promise of international harmonization of accounting standards is to be actualized, the EC can take the lead by providing direction on putting in place a broadly conceived financial *and* social accounting system, one that is truly reflective of the societal values involved. Coalescing to a position acceptable to all the countries in Europe should provide a model for moving the rest of the world's economically developed states to a global standard. Agreement on the purposefulness of social disclosures is the first important step needed.

NOTES

1 Arieh Ullmann, 'Data in Search of A Theory: A Critical Examination of the Relationship Among Social Performance. Social Disclosure and Economic Performance of U.S. Firms,' *Academy of Management Review* (July 1985) 540–557.

2 James Guthrie and Lee Parker, 'Corporate Disclosure Practice: A Comparative International Analysis.' *Advances in Public Interest Accounting* (1990), 159–176.

3 Norman Macintosh, 'Annual Reports in an Ideological Role: A Critical Theory Analysis,' in *Critical Accounts*, edited by D. Cooper and T. Hopper (MacMillan: London, 1990), 153–172.

4 David Cooper and M. Sherer, 'The Value of Corporate Accounting Reports: Arguments for a Political Economy of Accounting.' *Accounting Organizations and Society* (1984) 207–232.

5 Patricia J. Arnold, 'The State and Political Theory in Corporate Social Disclosure Research: A Response to Guthrie and Parker,' *Advances in Public Interest Accounting* (1990) 177–182.

6 Tom DeVos, *Multinational Corporations in Democratic Host Countries: U.S. Multinationals and the Vredeling Proposal* (Brookfield VT 1989).

Part IV

MANAGERIAL ISSUES IN INTERNATIONAL ACCOUNTING

In this section we consider both the accounting issues that arrive in the context of managing a multinational enterprise and international comparative management accounting.

The setting of transfer prices across national boundaries is a major issue for the Multi National Enterprise (MNE) Al-Eryani, Alam and Akhter (1990) report on a study of the practices of US based MNE's in this field. Abdallah (1989) discusses the behavioural aspects of the issue – a major point in discussions of domestic transfer pricing but one which, in the literature on international transfer pricing, has sometimes been neglected in favour of the fiscal and regulatory effects.

Choi and Czechowicz (1983) explore the issues that the MNE must address in assessing the performance of foreign subsidiaries.

The role of the management accountancy system within companies can vary between countries in the same way as the external reporting requirements. Strange (1992) presents a brief summary of the distinctive features of Management Accounting in Germany.

Given the difficulty of comparing accounts prepared under different national jurisdictions, non-financial performance indicators acquire an increased relevance, as discussed by Mugan (1992).

The challenges of environmental accounting are too urgent for the traditional leisurely response of accounting development to social needs. The sharing of experience across national boundaries is one way to expedite the process, and the paper by Blokdijk & Drieehuizen (1992) shares the Dutch experience in this area.

Termes i Angles (1991) discusses the impact of accounting reforms inspired by the EC on local government in Spain.

Finally, Japan offers a distinct challenge to accountants in that the accounting figures have a different significance to that found in the West. Suzaki & Wright (1985) found that accounting measures were less significant in the prediction of corporate bankruptcy than other 'social' measures.

23

TRANSFER PRICING DETERMINANTS OF U.S. MULTINATIONALS

Mohammad F. Al-Eryani, Pervaiz Alam and Syed H. Akhter

In order to successfully compete in the global market, U.S. multinationals use control and evaluation systems for monitoring the performance of their divisions abroad. A multinational corporation also deals with the complexities of cultural and political differences, tax regulations, import-export restrictions, controls on the transfer of funds, and various other restrictions designed by host countries to protect their national economic interests. The challenge for multinationals is to design a transfer pricing strategy which appropriately rewards the management of the unit(s) abroad and also addresses the various legal, cultural, and economic restrictions of the host countries.

International transfer pricing strategies can be classified into two groups: market based and nonmarket based. Market-based transfer pricing uses the prevailing market price for exchanging products within the corporate family. As these prices are market determined, they are considered to be objective and not subject to manipulation by the selling unit. Consequently, the use of a market-based transfer pricing strategy encourages the selling unit(s) to be efficient in order to sell at market prices and also minimizes conflict between divisions over the selection of a fair transfer price. Nonmarket-based pricing includes a wide array of transfer pricing methods, including negotiated prices, cost-based prices, mathematically programmed prices, and dual prices. Arguments for using nonmarket-based transfer pricing strategies by multinationals are based on tax differentials among countries, restrictions on repatriation of funds, import duties, price controls,

From Journal of International Business Studies (3rd Quarter 1990) pp 409–425.
Reprinted with permission from Journal of International Business Studies.

and political instability (see Shulman [1967, 1969]; Burns [1980]). The purpose of this study is to examine the influence of environmental and firm-specific variables on the selection of international transfer pricing strategies by U.S. multinationals. To determine the factors influencing the selection of transfer pricing strategies, the analysis was conducted in two stages. First, thirty-four environmental variables relevant to international transfer pricing were factor analyzed to determine factor scores. Second, the factor scores were used as input to a probit model.[1]

REVIEW OF THE RELEVANT LITERATURE

Theoretical Research

Three different theoretical frameworks (economic, mathematical programming, and behavioral) have been developed to explain transfer pricing strategies. Hirshleifer [1956], in a study of the economic model, argued that if the intermediate market is competitive, the transfer price should be the market price. If the intermediate market is imperfectly competitive, he argued, then the transfer price should be the marginal manufacturing cost. The mathematical programming model, however, posits that the transfer price of the intermediate product should be equal to the opportunity cost of producing the product [Abdel-khalik and Lusk 1974].

Both the economic and mathematical programming approaches place high priority on production efficiency, cost minimization, and profit maximization. However, they tend to ignore the human dimension in transfer pricing decisions. Behavioral models have been developed to incorporate the human dimension in the transfer pricing model. Rather than relying on cost structures and market forces for determining transfer price, the behavioral model recommends the use of negotiated transfer pricing for achieving organizational goals. Watson and Baumler [1975] demonstrated that successful firms handle intra-departmental conflicts through negotiated transfer prices. Acklesburg and Yukl [1979] suggested that negotiated transfer prices can result in better relations and cooperation among divisions.

Empirical Research

Empirical research on international transfer pricing has focused on the following issues: (1) the determination of transfer prices, (2) the transfer pricing behavior of multinationals in different countries, and (3) the examination of the influence of different factors, both at home and in the host country, on the selection of transfer pricing strategies.

With respect to the determination of transfer prices, Business International Corporation [1965] reported that U.S. multinationals mostly determined transfer prices based either on local production cost plus fixed markup, or production cost of the most efficient manufacturing unit in the corporate group plus fixed markup, regardless of individual plant costs. Greene and Duerr [1970], however, found that most U.S. corporations established transfer prices based either on a cost plus or on a negotiated basis.

With regard to the transfer pricing behavior of corporations from different countries, Arpan [1971] found that non-U.S. multinationals mostly used market pricing to price intra-company transfers. Tang [1979], however, found that production cost plus markup was the most popular international transfer pricing method among both U.S. and Japanese companies.

With reference to the examination of the influence of different factors on the selection of transfer pricing strategies, a considerable body of literature exists. Shulman [1969], when discussing the influence of different environmental variables on transfer pricing strategies, suggested that companies could circumvent profit repatriation restrictions by charging a higher price for imports from the parent or related companies. Similarly, lower prices could be charged to circumvent high import duties in host countries. Lecraw [1985] reported that multinationals systematically used non-market-based transfer prices to reduce custom duties and taxes, and to circumvent government price and capital-profit remittance controls.

Recently, Benvignati [1985] found that advertising expenditures, the magnitude of a company's foreign transfers, and the number of countries where a multinational operates were significant determinants of a non-market-based transfer pricing strategy. However, she also found that large firms and those with a large number of foreign subsidiaries showed a greater preference for market-based transfer pricing.

Prior research also suggests that governmental policies and regulations encourage multinationals to engage in transfer pricing manipulation more often in less developed countries than in more developed countries. For example, Plasschaert [1985] noted that transfer pricing manipulation is more widespread in less developed countries (LDCs) than in more developed countries (MDCs) because the governments of LDCs are poorly equipped, compared to MDCs, to understand or to monitor the intricacies of international transfer pricing. Brean [1979] also argued that LDCs are more vulnerable to transfer pricing manipulation because of the greater ignorance of LDCs on matters of international transfer pricing and the inadequacy of LDCs' institutions when dealing with multinationals on various international transfer pricing issues.

The examination of the existing literature shows that, except for Benvignati [1985] and Lecraw [1985], none of the prior studies has directly addressed the issue of the determinants of market-based versus non-market-based transfer pricing in a multivariate framework. Using mainly firm-specific variables, Benvignati reported a fairly high multicollinearity among some of the independent variables used for regression analysis and obtained an *R*-square of only 0.077. Lecraw's sample was confined to subsidiaries of multinationals in only four Asian countries. The present study improves on the Benvignati and Lecraw studies by using (1) both environmental and firm-specific variables, and (2) a sample which includes multinationals operating in MDCs and LDCs.

RESEARCH METHOD

Research Hypotheses

Legal Hypothesis

The laws and regulations of host countries – for example, antitrust and anti-dumping legislation, tax and custom regulations, and financial reporting requirements – influence the pricing of intra-company shipments. For instance, multinationals may underprice the intra-company sale of intermediate products to foreign affiliates to drive their competition out of the market. To thwart the attempts of multinationals to lessen competition, antitrust authorities in host countries enact antitrust legislation to make price discrimination, predatory pricing, and dumping practices illegal. For example, in Canada, Section 32 of the Combines Investigation Act prohibits agreements between related firms which unreasonably increase prices. Transfer prices are controlled in the Federal Republic of Germany under Section 22 of the 1957 Act Against Restraints of Competition; in Brazil, under Law No. 4137 of September, 1962; and in Pakistan, by the Monopolies and Restrictive Trade Practices Ordinance No. V of 1970 (see Greenhill & Herbolzheimer [1981]).

The use of market-based transfer pricing prevents the accusation of transfer pricing manipulation and avoids legal complications. Therefore, the following hypothesis is proposed:

The Legal Hypothesis

> The more important the legal variable to multinationals, the greater the use of market-based transfer pricing by multinationals.

Size Hypothesis

Most existing research on the transfer pricing practices of large firms indicates that large firms use different pricing strategies for intra-company exchanges. Earlier research [Robbins and Stobaugh 1973] presented evidence that big companies normally use standard markups to achieve uniform policies. Similarly, Arpan [1972–1973] argued that the larger the parent firm, the more likely it is to use a cost-oriented (nonmarket) pricing system.

In contrast to these earlier studies, more recent research indicates that larger firms use market-based transfer pricing strategies. For example, Yunker [1982] claimed that large firms tend to use market-based transfer pricing because of environmental variability and worldwide sales. The use of market-based transfer pricing by large firms is also supported by Benvignati [1985] who argued that larger companies are more likely to use market-based transfer pricing methods because their size makes them more visible to government authorities. Thus, the following hypothesis is proposed:

The Size Hypothesis

The larger the multinational, the more likely it is that it will use a market-based transfer pricing strategy.

Political-Social Hypothesis

Political factors (e.g., expropriation, nationalization, civil wars, political turmoil) and social factors (e.g., class conflicts, ethnic conflict) may play a crucial role in motivating multinationals to practice transfer pricing manipulations. Shulman [1967] argued that U.S. multinationals operating in countries with unstable political environments place greater importance on the political and social environment in the host countries. Therefore, we argue that multinationals in such environments will be less likely to employ market-based transfer pricing methods in order to hedge against political and social uncertainties. The following hypothesis is proposed:

The Political-Social Hypothesis

The more unstable the political and social environment, the less likely it is that multinationals will use market-based transfer pricing strategies.

External Economic Hypothesis

Incentives to use nonmarket-based transfer pricing may arise from market imperfections caused by government regulations. These imperfections may occur because of exchange controls, price controls, import restrictions, import quotas, and inflation. Exchange controls make the repatriation of profits from the subsidiaries to the home office difficult; price controls prevent market mechanisms from determining the transfer price; import restrictions in host countries artificially raise prices; and inflation erodes real profit. All these restrictions may encourage the use of nonmarket-based pricing. For instance, if inflation in host countries is higher than in a multinational's home country, the multinational may be tempted to overprice so that its share of real profit from foreign subsidiaries is maintained. Hence, we argue that the more stringent the economic restrictions imposed by host governments, the more likely it is that U.S. multinationals will use nonmarket-based transfer prices to circumvent these restrictions. Thus, the following hypothesis is proposed:

The External Economic Hypothesis

> The stricter the external economic restrictions, the less likely it is that a multinational will use a market-based transfer pricing strategy.

Internal Economic Hypothesis

The internal economic variable relates to firm-specific conditions. These include conditions such as market share of foreign affiliates, competitive position of foreign affiliates, and performance evaluation of foreign affiliates. We argue that all these internal economic conditions affect intracompany transfers. However, the direction of the sign of the internal economic variable is indeterminable because there may be competing practices involved. For example, some multinationals may underprice (or use a nonmarket method) to enlarge the market share of a foreign subsidiary and others may want to use market-based pricing to fairly assess the performance of foreign affiliates. Therefore, we propose the following hypothesis:

The Internal Economic Hypothesis

> Multinational firms are less likely to use market-based transfer pricing when internal economic conditions require underpricing.

LDC Hypothesis

Prior research [Brean 1979; Plasschaert 1985] demonstrates that LDCs are more vulnerable to transfer pricing manipulation than MDCs. Furthermore, as LDCs typically do not have well-developed financial or product markets, there are fewer suppliers of foreign made, better quality products. Often, in such markets, multinationals do not face much competition from local producers or other foreign suppliers, resulting in an oligopolistic or a monopolistic position for the multinationals. Thus, market forces would not be the driving factor in establishing transfer prices.

Other reasons why multinationals may use nonmarket pricing in LDCs are (1) to show lower profits in order to resist trade union pressures, and (2) to assist local affiliates in their early stages of operations through under-invoicing. Hence, the following hypothesis is proposed:

The LDC Hypothesis

> The larger the number of affiliates of a U.S. multinational operating in less developed countries, the less likely it is that a market-based transfer pricing strategy will be employed.

Data Collection

The present study is limited to U.S.-based multinationals having affiliates engaged in the manufacturing and marketing of consumer and industrial goods. For the purpose of this study, MDCs and LDCs are those countries that fit the classification adopted by the United Nations [1985]. Specifically, MDCs include Australia, Canada, Japan, New Zealand, South Africa, U.S.A., and countries in Southern Europe and Western Europe (excluding Cyprus, Malta, and Yugoslavia). LDCs include countries in Latin America and the Caribbean, Africa (other than South Africa), Asia (excluding Japan), Cyprus, Malta, and Yugoslavia.

Data regarding transfer pricing policies were obtained from U.S. multinationals by means of a questionnaire. The first mailing and the follow-up mailing were sent to participating corporations on March 30 and April 15, 1987, respectively.[2] Both *Fortune* directories of the 500 largest and the second 500 largest U.S. companies were used to select a sample of U.S. multinationals. Large companies were used to ensure an adequate number of companies doing business either in MDCs or LDCs, or both. *Angel's Directory*, which provides information on whether or not U.S. multinationals own affiliates in MDCs and/or LDCs, was utilized to classify the 1,000 companies listed in the *Fortune* directories into groups operating primarily in MDCs or primarily in LDCs. A company which owned affiliates in both MDCs and LDCs was included in the MDCs group if more than 50% of its affiliates were located in MDCs. Similarly, if more than 50% of its affiliates were located in LDCs, it was included in the LDCs group.[3] Using this approach, 791 U.S. multinationals were selected to comprise the sample. Of these, 417 were classified as operating primarily in MDCs and 374 as operating primarily in LDCs. Dun and Bradstreet's *Billion Dollar Directory* was used to identify the names and addresses of controllers, treasurers, financial vice presidents, and vice presidents for international operations responsible for international transfer pricing policies. The data collection instrument was pretested on a sample of 30 companies from each of the MDCs and LDCs groups before the general mailing.

The overall response rate was 21% on 791 questionnaires mailed. Of the 417 U.S. multinationals operating primarily in MDCs, 76 usable responses were received, a response rate of 18%. Of the 374 U.S. multinationals operating primarily in LDCs, 88 usable responses were received, yielding a response rate of 24%.[4] We thus had a sample of 164 firms for analysis and interpretation. Table 1 gives the distribution of the sample size by worldwide sales. The table indicates that about 40% of the firms operating in MDCs have worldwide sales of over a billion dollars; for firms operating in LDCs, 47% of the corporations had sales of over a billion dollars. Thus, over 40% of the firms in our sample were relatively large firms with worldwide sales of over a billion dollars.

Questionnaire and Measurement Issues

The primary data concerning general company characteristics, environmental determinants, and transfer pricing methods were obtained by means of a questionnaire. Since there are no universally acceptable set of transfer pricing determinants, multiple indicators were used to capture the key factors. Based on prior research, 34 environmental determinants were selected in designing the data collection instrument. A 5-point scale was used by the responding U.S. multinationals to rate the 34 economic, behavioral, legal, political, and social environmental determinants of international transfer pricing and the 15 transfer pricing methods identified from prior research.[5] The presence of bias from responses received from the first mailing versus responses received from the second mailing was tested using Kendall's tau and Pearson correlation. Results show that the initial and follow up responses were significantly correlated (*Tau* = 0.8610, $P<0.0001$; Pearson = 0.9626, $P<0.0001$).

Factor Analysis

Factor analysis was used to identify the key determinants of transfer pricing. Principal axis analysis with varimax rotation was used to extract

Table 1 U.S. multinational corporations classified by value of worldwide sales in 1986 for the sample firms

Worldwide Sales (in millions)	*Corporations Operating in MDCs*		*Corporations Operating in LDCs*		*Total*	
Less than $50	0	(0.0%)	6	(6.9%)	6	(3.7%)
$50–$100	4	(5.5%)	7	(8.0%)	11	(6.7%)
100–200	7	(9.2%)	9	(10.3%)	16	(9.8%)
200–300	12	(15.8%)	5	(5.7%)	17	(10.4%)
300–500	5	(6.6%)	14	(16.1%)	19	(11.7%)
500–1000	17	(22.4%)	5	(5.7%)	22	(13.5%)
More than $1000	31	(40.8%)	41	(47.1%)	72	(44.2%)
Valid responses	76	(100.0%)	87	(100.0%)	163	(100.0%)
No response	0		1		1	
Total responses	76		88		164	

MDCs = more developed countries
LDCs = less developed countries

factors. This method of factor analysis is appropriate for exploring the underlying dimensions of a construct. It is based on the conservative method of estimating communality by using the squared multiple correlation in the diagonal of the correlation matrix (see Harman [1976]). Prior to the analysis, two factoring criteria were established: (1) to define a factor as having at least three items with loadings of 0.50 or greater, and (2) to select the minimum number of independent factors which explain as much of the common variance as possible in the final solution. Reliabilities of the items defining the final factor solution were estimated using Cronbach's alpha coefficient (see Nunnally [1967]). Table 2 gives the four significant factors and the items with loadings of 0.50 or greater. These four factors explain 54% of the variance and are labeled as the political and social factor, the external economic factor, the internal economic factor, and the legal factor.

Probit Model

In addition to the four factors extracted through factor analysis, two other variables were added to the probit model: the country variable and the size of the company. The country variable is a dummy variable, assigned a value of one ('1') if the majority of the firm's foreign affiliates were located in LDCs and zero ('0') if the majority were in MDCs. The size variable is based on worldwide sales of multinationals in U.S. dollars. The dichotomous dependent variable was coded one ('1') for companies employing market-based methods and a zero ('0') for companies using nonmarket methods.[6]

Following Vancil [1979], Table 3 was prepared portraying the number and percent of firms using nonmarket- versus market-based methods of transfer pricing classified by MDCs versus LDCs. Note that, among non-market-based methods, actual unit full cost plus fixed markup, standard unit full cost plus fixed markup, and negotiated pricing techniques were most widely used in both MDCs and LDCs. Also, none of the respondent firms used actual unit variable cost or marginal costs in transferring goods to either MDCs or LDCs. Our findings are consistent with Vancil's results. He also found that negotiated pricing is widely used but variable or marginal costing is used on a limited basis. Table 3 shows that 65% of respondents used nonmarket-based transfer pricing methods and 35% used market-based methods for the combined groups; approximately similar values are noted for MDCs and LDCs groups, separately.

Most respondents in our study indicated that they used both market- and nonmarket-based transfer pricing methods. However, the frequency of use varied. Firms which used market-based transfer pricing methods more frequently than nonmarket-based methods were classified into a market-based transfer pricing group. Similarly, firms with greater use of nonmarket-based methods were grouped into a nonmarket-based transfer pricing category. Twenty-two cases could not be classified into either of these groups and were excluded from the probit model. This reduced our sample from 164 to 148 firms, with 60 cases in the market-based group and 88 cases in the nonmarket-based group.

The probit model was developed using maximum likelihood estimation technique. Maximum likelihood estimators are consistent, asymptotically efficient, and have a known sampling distribution. The model used in this study is expressed as follows:

$$TPM = \beta_0 + \beta_1\, LEGAL + \beta_2\, SIZE + \beta_3\, POLS + \beta_4\, EXECON + \beta_5\, INTECON + \beta_6\, LDC$$

where:

TPM	= Transfer pricing method; '1' if prices are market based, '0' if nonmarket based;
LEGAL	= Legal factor as described in Table 2;
SIZE	= Worldwide sales in U.S. dollars provided by respondent firms;
POLS	= Political-social factor as described in Table 2;
EXECON	= External economic factor as described in Table 2;
INTECON	= Internal economic factor as described in Table 2; and
LDC	= A dummy variable where a value of '1' is assigned for LDCs and of '0' for MDCs.

ANALYSIS AND INTERPRETATION

The results of the probit model are summarized in Table 4.[7] The table shows that the model has an *R*-square of 0.506 and an overall predictive accuracy of 65.5%.[8] Further, the model classified market-based transfer pricing methods with 75.9% accuracy and nonmarket-based transfer pricing methods with 56.2% accuracy.[9] Of the six variables used in the probit model, the legal variable and the size variable are statistically significant. This suggests that the legal environment and the size of the firm are the most important variables in determining which international transfer pricing strategy will be employed by U.S. multinationals. Although the remaining variables were statistically insignificant, the direction of each relationship was as predicted.

Test of Legal Hypothesis

Table 2 shows that the following items loaded on the legal factor (arranged in descending order of factor loading): (i) compliance with U.S. tax regulations; (ii) compliance with tax and customs regulations of host countries; (iii) compliance with financial reporting rules and requirements; and (iv) compliance with antitrust and antidumping legislation of host countries.

Generally, the factor loadings for these items are strong, ranging from 0.63 to 0.89. Further, Table 4 shows that the *LEGAL* variable is statistically significant at the 0.05 level and positively related to market-based transfer prices. This implies that multinationals use market-based transfer pricing to comply with the laws and regulations of their home as well as host countries. The use of nonmarket-based pricing is avoided because it may lead to charges of price fixing, tax avoidance, and other similar violations.

Test of Size Hypothesis

Table 4 shows that the *SIZE* variable,[10] as predicted, is positively and significantly (at the 0.025 level) related to market-based transfer pricing. This indicates that the larger the size of a firm the more likely it is to use market-based transfer pricing.

Our results differ from early research [Arpan 1972–1973; Robbins and Stobaugh 1973] which presented evidence that larger multinationals tend to use nonmarket-based transfer pricing methods. Rather, our results support Yunker's [1982] arguments that large firms use market-based transfer pricing because of environmental variability and worldwide sales and Benvignati's [1985] conclusions that large firms use market-based transfer pricing because they are more visible.

Test of Political-Social Hypothesis

Table 2 shows that the following four items loaded most heavily on the *POLS* factor (arranged in descending order of factor loading): (i) racial policies of host countries; (ii) civil wars in host countries; (iii) religious conflicts in host countries; and (iv) human rights violations by host governments. The factor loading for all these items are very strong, ranging from 0.85 to 0.89. When the *POLS* factor is used in the probit model, it is found to be negative as predicted (see Table 4) but statistically insignificant. Thus, we cannot conclude that adverse political and social conditions in host countries require multinational firms to rely on nonmarket-based transfer prices.

Test of External Economic Hypothesis

Table 2 shows that the following four items loaded most heavily on the *EXECON* factor (arranged in descending order of factor loading): (i) existence of exchange controls; (ii) existence of price controls; (iii) restrictions on imports imposed by host governments; and (iv) minimization of adverse impact of inflation in host countries. Table 4 indicates that the *EXECON* variable, while statistically insignificant, was negatively related, as predicted. Therefore, although multinationals may rely more on non-

Table 2 Rotated factor loadings environmental factors and their determinants

Environmental Factors and their Determinants		*Factor*** *Loading*	*Communality*	*Eigenvalue*
I.	*Legal Factor*			1.679 (0.860)*
1.	Compliance with U.S. tax regulations	0.890	0.799	
2.	Compliance with tax and customs regulations of host countries	0.846	0.744	
3.	Compliance with financial reporting rules and requirements	0.638	0.439	
4.	Compliance with antitrust and anti-dumping legislation of host countries	0.631	0.467	
II.	*Political & Social Factor*			11.164 (0.951)*
1.	Racial policies of host countries	0.892	0.836	
2.	Civil wars in host countries	0.863	0.851	
3.	Religious conflicts in host countries	0.854	0.810	
4.	Human rights violations by host governments	0.852	0.793	
III.	*External Economic Factor*			3.406 (0.859)*
1.	Existence of exchange controls	0.750	0.675	
2.	Existence of price controls	0.714	0.675	
3.	Restrictions on imports imposed by host governments	0.653	0.545	
4.	Minimization of adverse impact of inflation in host countries	0.579	0.444	
IV.	*Internal Economic Factor*			2.026 (0.799)*
1.	Increased market share of foreign affiliates	0.805	0.691	
2.	Strengthened competitive position of foreign affiliates	0.798	0.673	
3.	Performance evaluation of foreign affiliates	0.697	0.536	

market-based transfer pricing strategies in order to circumvent stringent economic restrictions which hinder the free flow of funds between countries, we could not find statistical support for this contention.

Test of Internal Economic Hypothesis

Table 2 shows that the following three items loaded most heavily on the *INTECON* factor (arranged in descending order of factor loading): i) increased market share of foreign affiliates; ii) strengthened competitive position of foreign affiliates; and iii) performance evaluation of foreign

Table 3 Frequency of use of international transfer pricing methods by respondent firms

	MDCs		*LDCs*		*TOTAL*	
	#	%	#	%	#	%
Nonmarket Based Methods						
Actual unit full cost	4	4	4	5	8	5
Actual unit full cost plus fixed markup	15	15	11	15	26	15
Actual unit variable cost	0	0	0	0	0	0
Standard unit variable cost plus fixed markup	3	3	2	3	5	3
Standard unit full cost plus fixed markup	15	16	10	13	25	15
Standard unit full cost	5	5	0	0	5	3
Standard unit variable cost	1	1	0	0	1	0
Standard unit variable cost plus fixed markup	5	5	4	5	9	5
Marginal cost	0	0	0	0	0	0
Opportunity cost	2	2	0	0	2	1
Negotiated price	13	13	12	16	25	15
Mathematical programming	1	1	3	4	4	2
Dual pricing	1	1	1	1	2	1
Total nonmarket based	65	66	47	62	112	65
Market Based Methods						
Prevailing market price	17	18	12	16	29	17
Adjusted market price	15	16	16	22	31	18
Total market based	32	34	28	38	60	35
Total number of firms	97	100	75	100	172	100

Note: Total number of responses exceeds 76 firms in the MDC group because some firms identified the use of more than one transfer pricing method. On the other hand, the total number of responses for the LDC group is less than 88 because some firms did not identify the transfer pricing method they used for multinational transfers.
MDCs = more developed countries
LDCs = less developed countries

affiliates. As discussed previously in the hypothesis section, we could not predict the sign of the *INTECON* coefficient because of competing implications on transfer pricing of the *INTECON* variable. Table 4 shows that the *INTECON* variable is statistically insignificant and the sign of the coefficient is positive. Thus, neither can we conclude that multinationals use market-based transfer pricing for performance evaluation of foreign affiliates nor could we argue that they use nonmarket-based transfer pricing to enlarge the market share of foreign affiliates.

Test of LDC Hypothesis

Less developed countries impose various restrictions on multinationals out of concern that multinationals manipulate transfer prices. Brean [1979]

Table 4 Probit estimates of the relationship between transfer pricing strategies and environmental and firm-specific variables
($TPM = \beta_0 + \beta_1\ LEGAL + \beta_2\ SIZE + \beta_3\ POLS + \beta_4\ EXECON + \beta_5\ INTECON + \beta_6\ LDC$)

Variable	*Regression Coefficient*	*Standard Error*	*Asymptotic t-value*	*Predicted Sign*
Intercept	4.4442	0.2481	17.9134***	
Legal	0.1841	0.1144	1.6093*	+
Size	0.0006	0.0003	1.9726**	+
Political & Social (POLS)	–0.0024	0.1084	–0.0218	–
External economic (EXECON)	–0.0624	0.1148	–0.5441	–
Internal economic (INTECON)	0.0049	0.1166	0.0419	?
LDC	–0.0482	0.2115	–0.2276	–
Pearson goodness-of-fit chi square		= 145.422		
Degrees of freedom		= 141.000		
Probability		= 0.382		
R-square		= 0.506		
Percent Correctly Classified:				
Market based method		75.9%		
Nonmarket based method		56.2%		
Overall		65.5%		

* Significant at the 0.05 level
** Significant at the 0.025 level
*** Significant at the 0.0001 level

argued that such restrictions result from ignorance of the LDCs with respect to transfer pricing methods. Further, the less developed product markets in such economies do not provide opportunities for market forces to establish transfer prices. Thus, we expected that U.S. multinationals would employ nonmarket-based transfer pricing strategies on intra-company shipments. Table 4 shows that the LDC variable, as predicted, is negatively associated with market-based transfer pricing methods; however, it is statistically insignificant. Therefore, we cannot conclude that the level of development of a country in which a foreign affiliate is located is a significant factor in a multinational's decision to use a market-based transfer pricing strategy.

SUMMARY AND CONCLUSIONS

The purpose of this study was to find the determinants of the international transfer pricing strategies of U.S.-based multinationals. The findings show that the legal and size variables are significantly associated with the use of market-based transfer pricing strategies. These results suggest that legal considerations such as compliance with tax and custom regulations, anti-dumping and antitrust legislations, and financial reporting rules of host countries are influential in the use of market-based transfer pricing. However, the economic restrictions such as exchange controls, price controls, and restrictions on imports, political-social conditions, and the extent of economic development in host countries are either unimportant or are secondary determinants of a market-based transfer pricing strategy.

The results also suggest that U.S. multinationals closely abide by U.S. tax regulations. Treasury Regulation 1.482 prescribes the following transfer pricing methods: the uncontrolled price method, the resale method, the cost plus method, and some other appropriate method when none of the methods described above are applicable. The evidence of this study shows that cost plus and market-based pricing were the most popular methods used both in MDCs and LDCs.

Furthermore, our findings are consistent with prior studies. For instance, our analysis supports one of Arpan's [1972–1973] conclusions 'that there is no universally optimal system of international intra-corporate pricing' (p. 110). We found that most firms in our sample were using both market-based and nonmarket-based pricing. We find that, similar to Yunker's [1982] results, there is no strong positive and significant association between performance evaluation and market-based transfer pricing. It appears that multinationals adjust their performance evaluation policies to the transfer pricing method used.

This study also sheds some light on transfer pricing theories. Our analysis supports the economic theory of transfer pricing which argues that, in imperfectly competitive markets, management will use nonmarket-based transfer prices. Perfect competition is not commonly seen in practice and, therefore, it is not surprising to see that many of the respondent firms reported the use of nonmarket-based transfer pricing. We also found support for the behavioral theory of transfer pricing. The data suggests that nearly 15% of our sample firms used negotiated transfer pricing methods. However, the results do not show the popular use of mathematical programming models.

Finally, the findings of this study are useful for practitioners who may be interested in identifying critical variables for designing a transfer pricing strategy. The significance of the legal and size variables rather than other factors in determining the choice of a market-based transfer pricing strategy suggests that legal rather than economic or social constraints play an important role in the selection of transfer pricing strategies. Future research could examine whether industry and product differences result in different transfer pricing strategies, and the reasons for such differences which do exist. One could also examine reasons why U.S.-based multinationals tend to use nonmarket-based transfer pricing more frequently than market-based transfer pricing as compared to multinationals based in foreign countries.

NOTES

1 Probit analysis was used because of the dichotomous dependent variable (market- versus nonmarket-based transfer pricing). Probit utilizes the ordinality of the dependent variable which may not be the case for logit when the dependent variable is dichotomous. However, logit was also used to test whether the results were sensitive to the statistical procedure. The signs and the significance levels of all coefficients were quite similar to the probit results.

2 A pilot study was conducted in early February 1987 on a sample of thirty corporations. Results indicated that respondents did not have any difficulty in completing the questionnaire.

3 Firms were categorized as operating primarily in MDCs versus LDCs based on the number of affiliates because of the nonavailability of data on total assets or total revenues by country of operation. Consequently, we could not test our model at different levels of involvement (measured by total assets or total revenues) of a multinational in a host country.

4 The overall response rate was not the desirable 30%; however, we believe it is not so low as to be a cause of serious concern. Prior studies have also reported response rates below 30%. For example, Imhoff [1988] had a response rate of 9.4% and Eichenseher and Shields [1983] reported a response rate of 24%.

5 A copy of the questionnaire is available from the second author upon request.

6 We first attempted to use ordinary least squares regression (OLS) with 'percent of times market based methods used' as the dependent variable. However, this variable could not be used as a dependent variable because it was bimodal, suggesting that OLS would be inappropriate. Therefore, we decided to use the probit model.

7 With any set of related data, there is a possibility that the independent variables are correlated to the point that they cause significant multicollinearity. Multicollinearity can affect the signs of probit coefficients; however, unlike regression analysis, multicollinearity has no effect on testing the significance of individual variables in probit equations. In probit analysis, the standard errors of coefficients are not used to perform the likelihood tests [Grablowsky and Talley 1981]. The correlations between the independent variables of the model used in this study were generally low.

8 McKelvey and Zavonia [1975] describe the probit generated *R*-square as an indication of how well the data fit the underlying theoretical distribution. However, they caution that this measure is not strictly similar to the OLS generated *R*-square.

9 Classification rate is affected to some extent by the measurement error in dependent and independent variables.

10 The size variable was treated as a continuous variable because of the nonavailability of data on assets or sales by country of operation. Therefore, we could not test the association of the transfer pricing methods with the size of operation in each of the host countries.

REFERENCES

Abdel-khalik, A. R., Lusk, E. J. (1974) Transfer pricing – A synthesis. *Accounting Review*, January: 8–23.

Ackelsberg, R., Yukl, G. (1979) Negotiated transfer pricing and conflict resolution in organization. *Decision Sciences*, July: 387–98.

Angel's directory. (1984) *Directory of American firms operating in foreign countries*. New York: World Trade Academy Press.

Arpan, J. S. (1971) *International intracorporate pricing: Non-American systems and views*. New York: Praeger Publishers.

Arpan, J. S. (1972–1973) Multinational firm pricing in international markets. *Sloan Management Review*, Winter: 1–9.

Benvignati, A. M. (1985) An empirical investigation of international transfer pricing by U.S. manufacturing firms. In A. M. Rugman & L. Eden, eds., *Multinationals and transfer pricing*, New York: St Martin's Press.

Brean, D. J. (1979) Multinational firms, transfer pricing, and the tax policy of less developed countries. *Malayan Economic Review*, 24, October: 34–45.

Burns, J. O. (1980) Transfer pricing decisions of U.S. multinational corporations. *Journal of International Business Studies*, Fall: 23–39.

Business International Corporation (BIC). (1965) *Solving international pricing problems*. New York: BIC.

Dun and Bradstreet. (1986) *The billion dollar directory: America's corporate families*. Parsippany, NJ: Dun and Bradstreet.

Eichenseher, J. W., Shields, D. (1983) The correlates of CPA-firm change for publicly-held corporations. *Auditing: A Journal of Theory and Practice*, Spring: 23–37.

Fortune. (1982) *The Fortune directory of the second 500 largest U.S. industrial corporations*, June: 178–99.

Fortune. (1986) *The Fortune directory of the 500 largest U.S. industrial corporations*, April: 182–201.

Grablowshky, B. J., Talley, W. K. (1981) Probit and discriminant functions for classifying credit applications: A comparison. *Journal of Economics & Business*, 3: 254–61.

Greene, J., Duerr, M. G. (1970) *Intercompany transactions in the multinational firm*. New York, NY: Conference Board.

Greenhill, C. R., Herbolzheimer, E. O. (1981) Control of transfer prices in international transactions: The restrictive business practices approach. In R. Murray, ed., *Multinationals beyond the market*, 185–94. New York: John Wiley and Sons.

Hair, J. F., Anderson, R. E., Tathan, R. L., Grablowsky, B. J. (1979) *Multivariate data analysis*. Tulsa, OK: PPC Company.

Harman, H. H. (1976) *Modern factor analysis*. Chicago: University of Chicago Press.

Hirshleifer, J. (1956) On the economics of transfer pricing. *Journal of Business*, July: 172–84.

Imhoff, E. A. (1988) A comparison of analysts' accounting quality judgements among CPA firms' clients. *Auditing: A Journal of Practice & Theory*, Spring: 182–91.

Lecraw, D. J. (1985) Some evidence on transfer pricing by multinational corporations. In A. M. Rugman and L. Eden, eds., *Multinationals and transfer pricing*. New York: St Martin's Press.

McKelvey, R. D., Zavonia, W. (1975) A statistical model for the analysis of ordinal level dependent variables. *Journal of Mathematical Sociology*, 1: 103–20.

Nunnally, J. C. (1967) *Psychometric theory*. New York: McGraw-Hill Co.

Plasschaert, S. R. F. (1985) Transfer pricing problems in developing countries. In A. M. Rugman, and L. Eden, eds., *Multinationals and transfer pricing*, 247–66. New York: St Martin's Press.

Robbins, S. M., Stobaugh, R. B. (1973) *Money in the multinational enterprise: A study of financial policy*. New York: Basic Books, Inc.

Shulman, J. (1967) When the transfer price is wrong – By design. *Columbia Journal of World Business*, May–June: 69–76.

Shulman, J. (1969) Transfer pricing in multinational firms. *European Business*, January: 46–54.

Tang, R. Y. W. (1979) *Transfer pricing practices in the United States and Japan*. New York: Praeger Publishers.

Treasury Regulations 1.482-2(e) (ii, iii). (1987) *Standard Federal Tax Reports*, vol. 5, 36, 371. Chicago: Commerce Clearing House.

United Nations. (1985) *Transnational corporations in world development: Third survey.* New York: Centre on Transnational Corporations.

Vancil, R. F. (1979). *Decentralization: Management ambiguity.* Homewood, IL: Dow Jones-Irwin.

Watson, D. J. H., Baumler, J. V. (1975) Transfer pricing: A behavioral context. *Accounting Review*, July: 466–74.

Yunker, P. J. (1982). *Transfer pricing and performance evaluation in multinational corporations: A survey study.* New York: Praeger Publishers.

QUESTIONS

1 On the basis of the evidence in this article, prepare a brief for the board of a multi-national enterprise on the factors to consider when setting transfer prices.

24

HOW TO MOTIVATE AND EVALUATE MANAGERS WITH INTERNATIONAL TRANSFER PRICING SYSTEMS

Wagdy M. Abdallah

Theoretically, MNEs have the ability to use its international transfer pricing policies to maximize their global profits. Practically, it is the toughest pricing problem and it is more complicated than developing domestic transfer pricing policies.

An MNE has to manage its production and marketing policies in a world characterized by different international tax rates, different foreign exchange rates, different governmental regulations, currency manipulation, and other economic and social problems. Such market characteristics create high transaction costs for an MNE when using its regular marketing policies. It is important for them to create an internal market if they want to avoid these problems and any costs associated with them.[1] Allocation of resources among domestic and foreign subsidiaries requires the central management of an MNE to set up to the appropriate transfer price to achieve certain objectives.

Central top-management at the home country and subsidiary managers, both domestic and foreign, must understand the objectives for using transfer pricing policies within their organization. Those objectives are usually interrelated, top management and managers need to understand how they can affect each other.[2]

An International Transfer Pricing system should achieve two different groups of objectives, the first group includes: (a) the consistency with the

From Management International Review 1989 Vol 29 Pt 1 pp 65–71.
Reprinted by permission of Management International Review.

system of performance evaluation, (b) motivation of subsidiary managers, and (c) achievement of goal congruence. The second group includes: (a) reduction of income taxes, (b) reduction of tariffs on imports and exports, (c) minimization of foreign exchange risks, (d) avoidance of conflict with host governments, (e) management of cash flows, and (f) competition in the international markets. This paper will discuss only the first group of objectives.

An international transfer pricing system cannot achieve its full potential until it is integrated with other management control systems such as performance evaluation systems and reward (or motivation) systems.

MNEs set up their international transfer pricing policies at the central (or top) management level to facilitate cash movements where currency restrictions exist and to minimize taxes. It is more likely that a conflict between international transfer pricing techniques and performance evaluation measurement is to be existed, and, in general, transfer pricing policies are not complementary to the profit center concept.

The purpose of this paper is threefold: (a) identify, at the international level, different objectives of establishing transfer pricing systems; especially performance evaluation, motivation, and goal congruence, (b) to investigate how MNEs can achieve these objectives under their international transfer pricing systems, and (c) to point out significant problems MNEs might face when they try to achieve these objectives.

PERFORMANCE EVALUATION

The 1972 Committee on International Accounting of the American Accounting Association indicated that the traditional profit center concept for performance evaluation is inappropriate for MNEs because there is no clear distinction between operating subdivisions of MNEs. With integrated, centrally coordinated operations, foreign subsidiary management does not have authority for major decisions which affect its reported profits.[3] The 1973 Committee on International Accounting of the American Accounting Association agrees with the previously reported conclusions, and adds that the differences between countries such as social, economic, political, legal, and educational differences, have a considerable effect on manager performance. In conclusion, the Committee believes there is a need for further research to introduce additional elements into traditional management accounting evaluation techniques.[4]

In evaluating the performance of the foreign subsidiary, it is appropriate to evaluate its contribution to the objectives and goals of the whole MNE. It is also important to evaluate the contribution of foreign subsidiary managers to the performance of the MNE. Solomons has stated, 'in the absence of evidence to the contrary, the presumption is that the success of one implies the success of the other. But circumstances outside a manager's control may dictate success or failure of the venture'[5]

The headquarters enforce a specific transfer price to be used by its own subsidiaries to achieve certain objectives such as domestic and foreign income tax minimization, foreign exchange risk reduction, and foreign exchange control avoidance among others. To achieve the above objectives, international transfer pricing may result in showing higher artificial profits of foreign subsidiaries, while others may show much lower artificial profits.

A foreign subsidiary manager may have the operations of his area being evaluated as if it were a completely autonomous and independent subsidiary. They may have the greatest degree of freedom in making decisions related to the short-run. However, they have lesser degree of freedom in making decisions directly affecting other foreign subsidiaries and the globe.

With the frequent fluctuations of currency values combined with the floating exchange rates system, MNEs face the problem of distorted performance measurements of their domestic and foreign subsidiaries as profit centers.[6]

Performance of foreign subsidiaries in U.S.-based MNEs is usually evaluated on the basis of reports stated in U.S.-dollars. However, as the exchange rates fluctuate, performance evaluation of subsidiaries is not an easy task to be done. Using transfer pricing as a basis for performance evaluation under the floating exchange rates system makes it much more complicated problem because international transfer prices are not usually adjusted for any fluctuations in currency exchange rates.[7]

At Honeywell Inc., Malmstrom implemented a simple solution for this problem. His technique is called 'dollar indexing'. This technique is used to have the same impact as local currency invoicing including two basic objectives: (a) to allow realistic or undistorted performance evaluation, and (b) to reflect the real economic cost of the product transferred.[8]

Malmstrom used an indexed formula for US-dollar transfer prices as shown below:

$$\mathrm{NTR} = \mathrm{OTP} \times \frac{CER}{PER}$$

where:
NTP = New transfer price
OTP = Old transfer price
CER = Current exchange rate
PER = Planned exchange rate

Using this formula will result in applying a uniform transfer price for all goods transferred out of the same subsidiary.

For illustration, let us assume that subsidiary (A) in the U.K. transferred 16,000 units of its products at an established transferred price, by the parent

US-based MNE, $5.00 per unit to another foreign subsidiary (B) in the Switzerland, owned by the same MNE. The foreign exchange rates were £1.00 = $1.63 and Swiss Frank 1.00 = $1.49 respectively. As can be seen in Table 1, subsidiary (A) achieves a net income of $6,700 or £4,010 (in the U.K. currency), while subsidiary (B) achieves a net income of $37,000 or 24,832 in Swiss franks.

If we assume that the U.S. dollar was depreciated against both of the British and the Swiss currencies to £1.00 = $2.188 and SF 1 = $2.00 respectively, the income statements for both subsidiaries and the MNE measured in US dollars and local currencies are shown in Table 2.

Since the transfer price ($5.00 per unit) was set centrally by the US-based MNE, the operating results of the U.K. subsidiary would show net loss of $18,394 or £8,407, while the swis subsidiary would achieve net income of $77,046 or 38,523 SF because of the devaluation of the US dollar in the international markets as can be seen in Table 2.

The effect of using the $5.00 as a transfer price for international operations when there is devaluation in the parent's currency resulted in switching the operating results of the selling subsidiary from net income of 8% of sales to a net loss of 23% of sales. On the other hand, the operating results of the buying subsidiary would be in the opposite direction by switching from net income of 19% to a higher net income of 30%. That is, this transaction did not only transfer goods from the U.K. subsidiary to the swiss subsidiary but also transferred $25,094 ($6,700 + $18,394) of profits and a translation gains of $14,952, with a total of $40,042. In this case, the MNE as a whole would show a $14,952 higher than before because of the translation gains resulting from the devaluation of the US dollar.

For performance evaluation purposes, the manager of the British subsidiary was negatively affected by the change in the exchange rate and the

Table 1 The effect of transfer pricing on performance evaluation

	Subsidiary (A) (Seller)		*Subsidiary (B) (Buyer)*		*The Global Income Statement*
	USD	*UK*	*USD*	*SF*	*USD*
Sales					
16,000 @ $5.00	$80,000	£49,080			
16,000 @ $12.00			$192,000	SF 128,859	$192,000
Less CGS	(68,000)	41,718	(80,000)	(53,691)	(68,000)
Gross Profits	12,000	7,262	112,000	75,168	124,000
Less S & A Expenses	(5,300)	(3,252)	(75,000)	(50,336)	(80,300)
Net Income Before Taxes	6,700	4,010	37,000	24,832	43,700
Net Income as a Percentage of Sales	8%	8%	19%	19%	22.8%

Table 2 The effect of transfer prices with changes in foreign exchange rates on performance evaluation

	Subsidiary (A) (Seller)		*Subsidiary (B) (Buyer)*		*The Global Income Statement*
	USD	*UK*	*USD*	*SF*	*USD*
Sales					
16,00 @ $5.00	$80,000	£36,563	$257,718	SF 128,859	$257,718
Less CGS	(91,279)	(41,718)	(80,000)	(40,000)	(91,279)
Gross Profits	(11,279)	(5,155)	177,718	88,859	166,439
Less S & A Expenses	(7,115)	(3,252)	(100,672)	(50,336)	(107,787)
Net Income Before Taxes	(18,394)	(8,407)	77,046	38,523	58,652
Net Income as a Percentage of Sales	(23%)	(23%)	30%	30%	22.8%

imposed transfer price. While the Swiss subsidiary's manager did not do nothing more than before to show a 30% net income (which is 11% higher than before the change occurred).

Using the indexed formula for US-dollar transfer prices, suggested by Malmstrom, the adjusted transfer price would be:

$$\text{NTR} = \text{OTP} \times \frac{CER}{PER}$$

$$\text{NTR} = \$5.00 \times \frac{£2.188}{£1.630} = \$6.71$$

or

$$\text{NTR} = \$5.00 \times \frac{SF2.00}{SF1.49} = \$6.71$$

Table 3 shows the effect of transfer prices adjusted for changes in exchange rates. The new transfer price is $6.71, which is higher than the old one. For subsidiary A and B, the net income percentage as related to sales is the same as before any changes in the exchange rate, and both of them have the same measured performance as before. For the MNE, it has higher global profits with the dollar devaluation by $14,952 which is a translation gain. However, the translation gains were divided between the two subsidiaries as $2,266 to the U.K. subsidiary and $12,686 to the Swiss subsidiary.

The Swiss subsidiary has received $12,686 out of total translation gains of $14,952, while the British subsidiary has received $2,266 only due to how much was the US dollar devaluated in relation to the local currency. In other words, Malmstrom's system does not work as it should be as to the net income in dollars even though the ratios are the same as before, therefore, it still gives distorted financial results because of the foreign currency fluctuations.

Table 3 The effect of transfer prices adjusted for changes in exchange rates

	Subsidiary (A)		*Subsidiary (B)*		*The Global Results*
	USD	*UK*	*USD*	*SF*	*USD*
Sales					
(16,00 @ $6.71)	$107,360	£49,068	$257,718	SF 128,859	$257,718
Less CGS	(91,279)	(41,718)	(107,360)	(53,691)	(91,279)
Gross Profits	16,081	7,350	150,358	75,168	166,439
Less S & A Expenses	(7,115)	(3,253)	(100,672)	(50,336)	(107,787)
Net Income	8,966	4,098	49,686	24,832	58,652
Net Income as a Percentage of Sales	8%	8%	19%	19%	22.8%

Exchange Rates: £1.00 = $2.199 USD
SF 1.00 = $2.00 USD
The New Transfer Price (Adjusted for Foreign Currency Fluctuations) = $6.71

MOTIVATION

Motivation is considered as one of the important objectives of setting an international transfer pricing policies for domestic and foreign subsidiaries. Subsidiary managers need to be motivated to maximize (or increase) their divisional profits and transfer, in and out of their areas of responsibility within the MNE, their products or services at an appropriate transfer prices. Transfer prices, in this case, can be used to motivate subsidiary managers to achieve their divisional goals (by maximizing their divisional profits) and at the same time achieving their MNEs goals (by maximizing the global profits).

However, the more the autonomy subsidiary managers have to decide on their transfer pricing to achieve their divisional profits, more conflict may exist between achieving both MNE's and divisional profits. Also conflicts may arise between different objectives of using transfer pricing policies.

Higher transfer pricing for intracompany sales may help a subsidiary manager to show higher profits and be more motivated by doing his best efforts to achieve MNE's goal. However, if the tax rate of the foreign country where that subsidiary located is very high, the global profits will be deteriorated, and a conflict of goal congruence exists between divisional and global goals.

For an international transfer pricing system to be a motivator, it must be tied to performance of subsidiary managers. In doing so, an international transfer price as to be used as a measure of performance must meet the following four criteria:[9]

1 It must be a result of the manager's behavior.
2 It must include all the actions that need to be performed.

3 It must be accepted by subsidiary managers as valid measure of their performance.
4 It must include attainable goals for subsidiary managers.

Now, does the transfer pricing system reflect all the actions which should be performed by the foreign subsidiary manager in selling his products to another subsidiary? In other words, does the transfer price measure completely the foreign subsidiary manager's performance? Certainly, the answer is no, because a foreign subsidiary manager does not have control over the fluctuations of the exchange rate of the foreign currency of the country in which he is doing business. He can easily achieve translation gains or losses to be included in his performance report because of political legal, economic, or social factors over which he does not have any degree of control. His profits can go up or down because of sudden increase in inflation rates and/or commodity or stock prices, and; consequently, the outcome will be an increase or decrease in the market price, when it is used as a transfer price.

MNEs must analyze the potential impact of using transfer pricing system as a motivator on foreign subsidiary managers' behavior. Actions or decisions, which are made by managers to improve their performance, can have a negative effect on the global goals or profits of the MNE as a whole.

GOAL CONGRUENCE

Goal congruence is existed when the goals of subsidiary managers in the MNE are, so far as feasible, consistent with the global goals of the MNE. In establishing an ITP policies, top management would like to motivate subsidiary managers to achieve their divisional goals by contributing toward the achievement of their MNE's goals.

It is almost impossible to achieve perfect congruence between subsidiary managers' goals and MNE's goals. However, at least the ITP policies should not motivate subsidiary managers to make decisions which may be in conflict with the MNE's goals.

Motivation and goal congruence are important factors in designing ITP systems. If a MNE desires to have their subsidiary managers to be strongly motivated toward achieving congruent goals, it is necessary to consider the effect of the transfer pricing on their divisional profitability or performance. However, if there is a conflict between subsidiary managers' goals and the global goals, it may be preferable to have as little motivation and autonomy of subsidiary managers as possible.

Generally, an ITP system should be designed in such a way that a foreign or domestic subsidiary manager is motivated to make decisions which are in the best interest of the MNE as a whole. When subsidiary managers increase their divisional profits and at the same time increase the global profits, then subsidiary managers are in the MNE interest if the

ITP system does not mislead managers about what the MNE interests really are.

However, both subsidiary managers and central management must be aware that their divisional net income (or contribution) as measured under this ITP system are inherently imperfect, and the limited usefulness of that performance measure is further complicated by the existence of common resources used with the MNE.

SUMMARY AND CONCLUSION

This paper identified and discussed three different objectives of establishing an international transfer pricing policy. They are: (1) performance evaluation, (2) motivation, and (3) goal congruence.

Whenever performance evaluation systems are combined with the fluctuation in foreign exchange rates, transfer pricing policies will lead to presenting misleading and imperfect financial measures of performance. Malmstrom's system (dollar indexing technique) has been believed to give distorted financial results for performance evaluation.

Achieving motivation, goal congruence, and autonomy of foreign subsidiaries and their managers are always leading to conflicting results with performance evaluation, reduction of income taxes, reduction of tariffs, and avoidance of foreign exchange risks. Whenever international transfer pricing objectives lead to conflicting consequences, MNEs are enforced to trade-off between achieving different objectives and must accept less global profits when one objective has a priority over others especially for achieving long run objectives.

In designing an international transfer pricing policy, accounting literature does not provide MNEs with any unique technique or model to help them to arrive at the appropriate transfer price. Therefore, MNEs are in urgent need for a practical and objective technique or model, which can avoid conflicts between different objectives of the system, and, at the same time, achieve the global goals of MNEs to continue in doing their international business under different political, economic, and social environmental variables.

NOTES

1 Rugman, Alan M. 'Internationalization Theory and Corporate International Finance,' *California Management Review*, (Winter, 1980) p. 76.
2 Knowles, Lynette L. and Ike Mathur, 'International Transfer Pricing Objectives,' *Managerial Finance*, Vol. II (1985), p. 12.
3 *'An Introduction to Financial Control and Reporting in Multinational Enterprises'* (Austin: Bureau of Business Research, The University of Austin, 1973), pp. 71–73.
4 American Accounting Association, 'Report of the Committee on International Accounting,' *The Accounting Review*, 49 (1974), Supplement, pp. 252–257.

5 Solomons, David, *'Divisional Performance, Measurement and Control'* (Illinois: Richard D. Irwin Inc., 1976, p. 59).
6 Malmstrom, Duance, 'Accommodating Exchange Rate Fluctuations in Intercompany Pricing and Invoicing,' *Management Accounting* (September 1977), p. 25.
7 Benke Ralph L., Jr. and James Don Edwards, *'Transfer Pricing Techniques and Uses'* (New York: National Association of Accountants, 1980, p. 118).
8 Ibid., p. 25.
9 Lawler, Edward E. *'Motivation in Work Organizations'* (California: Wadsworth Publishing Company, Inc., 1973, p. 133).

QUESTIONS

1 Compare and contrast the issues raised by Abdallah in this article with those raised by Al-Eryani et al in the previous article.

25

ASSESSING FOREIGN SUBSIDIARY PERFORMANCE

A multinational comparison

F. D. S. Choi and I. J. Czechowicz

Evaluation of subsidiary performance remains as much of an art as it is a science, and the complexity increases when operations are located abroad. Performance evaluation of foreign operations must take into account such complicating factors as currency volatility, foreign inflation, interest rate differentials, and sovereign risk. Unless these factors are appropriately considered, headquarters may receive a distorted picture of foreign results, use inappropriate standards to assess performance, and encourage overseas managers to take actions not in line with overall corporate goals. A direct consequence, conceivably, is reduced corporate efficiency and international competitiveness.

Until recently, foreign operations comprised but a small part of US companies' total operations. It is not unusual then for many US-based companies to regard the American market to be their primary concern with overseas operations viewed as export markets for excess domestic production or technology already exploited in the US. In contrast, many European-based multinationals, such as those in Sweden and Switzerland, operate almost entirely outside their national boundaries with their principal revenue sources derived multinationally. With international business operations comprising an ever increasing share of US corporate activities, the comparison of US performance evaluation systems with their European counterparts appears timely.[1] Useful insights may be achieved when domestic practices are viewed from an international perspective.

From Management International Review 1983 Vol 23 Pt 4 pp 14–25.
Reprinted by permission of Management International Review.

SCOPE AND METHOD

This study covers corporations based in the U.S. and Europe. Overseas operations considered are those with profit responsibility, i.e., individual branches, subsidiaries, countries, regions, product lines, or a combination of these. Although the study emphasizes how firms measure the financial performance of overseas operating *units*, performance appraisals of foreign managers is also assessed. All too often, a single evaluation measure includes both managerial and unit performance evaluations when it is inappropriate to do so. The study is concerned only with ongoing firms and is limited to manufacturing entities.

Information for the study was obtained from several sources. A questionnaire provided the foundation.[2] It was supplemented with personal and telephone interviews as well as executive roundtables. 300 questionnaires were sent to the world's leading multinationals and 88 responses were received. Of these, 64 came from US-based MNCs; 24 from non-US MNCs domiciled principally in the UK, Sweden, Switzerland, and a small group of other countries.

Financial executives of 20 firms were interviewed, including 10 US-based and 10 non-US based MNCs. Telephone interviews were conducted with 10 more US firms and a total of 50 US-based corporations participated in three separate roundtable discussions.

OBJECTIVES AND ORGANIZATIONAL CONSIDERATIONS

Both US and foreign multinationals establish foreign operations largely for strategic considerations, the most common of which are to penetrate foreign markets, diversify business risk, and maximize long-term profits. Strategic considerations notwithstanding, both respondent groups indicated that the primary purpose of a performance evaluation system for foreign operations is to insure adequate profitability. Most firms surveyed also rated the ability to identify possible problems (deviations from plan) and facilitate resource allocation decisions as important objectives. Evaluating the subsidiary manager was considered to be of secondary importance. This does not mean the performance evaluation system does not play a role in evaluating foreign managers. The profitability of a foreign unit appears to be an important ingredient in managerial evaluation.

To the extent that adequate profitability incorporates the strategic nature of foreign operations, objectives of multinational performance evaluation systems appear congruous with overall corporate objectives. To the extent that the profitability criterion focuses solely on short-term profitability, foreign performance measures may produce misleading control signals.

Most firms tend to view their foreign operations as part of an integrated system. On the whole, however, non-US companies allow their foreign operations a greater degree of local autonomy in terms of organization than do US companies. This difference in operating style explains, in some measure, differences observed with regard to the measurement of performance.

PERFORMANCE CRITERIA

An ideal measure of the true economic performance of a foreign subsidiary is to compare the profitability of the entire corporation with and without that unit. This is difficult, if not impossible, to accomplish operationally particularly when there are many interrelated subsidiaries in the multinational network. As a practical alternative, multinational companies rely on multiple criteria, as no single criterion can capture every aspect of foreign performance.

In practice, financial criteria tend to dominate performance evaluation systems (see Table I). Both US and non-US MNCs indicate that the most important financial criterion used to evaluate the performance of overseas units is budget compared to actual profit followed by return on investment. Also considered somewhat important are budget compared to actual sales, return on sales, return on assets, budget compared to actual return on investment, and operating cash flows. With regard to the latter, however, US-based multinationals tend to emphasize the importance of cash flows to the parent, whereas non-US multinationals express a preference for cash flows to the foreign subsidiary, indicating a more local perspective. Both groups attached little importance to such yardsticks as return on equity, contribution to earnings, budget compared to return on equity, and residual income.

Despite difficulties in measurement, some nonfinancial criteria are considered important in multinational performance evaluation systems (see Table II). For the sample respondents, market share was considered most important. Also important were productivity improvement, relationships with host governments, quality control, employee development and safety. Responses in this regard were similar for both US and non-US firms. Research and development activities and community service were deemed less important by both respondent groups.

A particularly noteworthy study finding was the similarity in criteria employed by both US and foreign multinationals in evaluating the performance of the foreign unit as well as that of its manager (Table I). The similarity extended to both financial and non-financial criteria, as well as domestic and foreign operations. Although many companies are aware of the importance of evaluating the manager somewhat differently than the unit (either subjectively or otherwise), for many companies this distinction is apparently blurred. That is to say, the same measurements, calculated in the same way, are used to evaluate the performance of the unit and its manager. However, additional judgemental factors tend to come into play when evaluating the manager.

Despite the similarities in performance criteria employed internationally, measures of these criteria varied. Whereas US companies were divided over using pretax or aftertax numbers in computing ROI and ROA ratios, non-US companies generally opted for pretax calculations. US multinationals are also split over deducting headquarters expenses and foreign exchange adjustments from the reports of foreign subsidiaries. Non-US MNCs tend not to include them. The rationale many companies gave as to why certain expenses were not included in their evaluations was that these were matters over which the manager often did not have control. Other companies argued that some expenses could not be attributed to a particular unit.

Table 1 Financial criteria used to evaluate performance of overseas unit and subsidiary manager

Items	*US MNCs* N = 64 *avg**		*Non-US MNCs* N = 24 *avg**		*Total Responses* N = 88 *avg**	
	Unit	*Manager*	*Unit*	*Manager*	*Unit*	*Manager*
Return on Investment	1.8	2.2	2.1	2.2	1.9	2.2
Return on equity	3.0	3.0	2.9	3.0	3.0	3.0
Return on assets	2.3	2.3	2.2	2.4	2.3	2.3
Return on sales	2.2	2.1	1.9	2.1	2.1	2.1
Contribution to earnings per share	2.8	3.2	3.5	3.4	3.0	3.2
Operating cash flow to subsidiary	2.5	2.7	2.2	2.5	2.4	2.7
Operating cash flow to parent	2.3	2.8	2.5	2.6	2.3	2.7
Residual income	3.4	3.3	3.4	3.2	3.4	3.3
Budget compared to actual sale	2.0	1.6	1.9	1.8	1.9	1.7
Budget compared to actual profit	1.5	1.4	1.4	1.3	1.5	1.3
Budget compared to actual return on investment	2.3	2.4	2.4	2.5	2.3	2.4
Budget compared to actual return on assets	2.6	2.7	2.7	2.2	2.7	2.5
Budget compared to actual return on equity	3.1	2.9	3.2	3.1	3.1	3.0

* 1 = most important
2 = important
3 = less important
4 = not used

Table 2 Nonfinancial criteria used to evaluate performance of overseas unit and subsidiary manager

Items	*US MNCs N = 64 avg**		*Non-US MNCs N = 24 avg**		*Total Responses N = 88 avg**	
	Unit	*Manager*	*Unit*	*Manager*	*Unit*	*Manager*
Increasing market share	1.8	1.5	1.7	1.6	1.8	1.5
Quality control	2.2	1.9	2.4	2.0	2.3	1.9
Cooperation with parent company and other affiliates	2.4	2.0	2.5	2.1	2.4	2.0
Relationship with host country government	2.1	1.8	2.4	1.9	2.1	1.9
Environment compliance	2.4	2.3	2.5	2.4	2.4	2.3
Employee development	2.4	2.0	2.4	2.2	2.4	2.0
Labor turnover	2.7	2.5	2.8	2.7	2.8	2.6
Research and development in foreign unit	3.1	3.2	2.8	2.7	3.0	3.1
Productivity improvement	2.2	2.1	1.7	1.6	2.0	2.0
Employee safety	2.4	2.2	2.2	2.3	2.4	2.2
Community service	2.9	2.8	2.8	2.5	2.9	2.7

* 1 = very important
2 = important
3 = less important
4 = not important

CURRENCY VOLATILITY

Foreign operations may be evaluated in terms of the foreign currency or parent-country currency. Both currency perspectives yield consistent performance measures when exchange rates are relatively stable. When exchange rates are volatile, the currency framework employed can have a significant impact on the assessment of both unit as well as managerial performance.

When asked which currency perspective they employ for performance evaluation purposes, most US companies surveyed adhered to a parent-currency perspective. This is partially reflected in the currency translation method employed for internal reporting purposes (the temporal method per FAS No. 8) as well as the US dollar denomination of foreign operations: performance statistics.

In contrast, non-US multinationals generally prefer a local currency perspective when evaluating both the foreign unit and its manager. Although non-US MNCs also employ the same translation method internally and externally, most employ the current rate method which is consistent with a local currency perspective.

Both US and non-US multinationals were consistent in their treatment of foreign exchange gains and losses. Here a distinction is drawn between transaction gains or losses (i.e., those stemming from a change in exchange rates between the reporting currency and the currency in which a foreign currency transaction is denominated) and translation gains and losses (i.e., those resulting from the process of translating foreign currency financial statements to their reporting currency equivalents).

Transaction gains and losses were generally included in the performance measures of both the foreign unit and its manager. For both respondent groups, holding the unit manager accountable for transaction gains and losses was generally consistent with the authority granted for hedging this form of exchange rate risk.

Principal differences between US and foreign multinationals center on the treatment of translation adjustments. US companies tend to include translation gains and losses primarily in the performance measures of the foreign unit (56%) and corporate treasury (56%). A significant minority (38%), however, also hold foreign managers accountable for this item. Non-US MNCs, on the other hand, generally absolve the unit and manager from accountability for such exchange adjustments, placing such responsibility higher up the corporate ladder. A possible explanation, cited earlier, is the preference among non-US firms for a local currency perspective. Another may relate to the fact that most non-US respondents do not have to immediately recognize translation gains and losses in income for external reporting purposes.

In the case of US companies, responsibility for translation gains and losses is reportedly designed to instill an exchange rate consciousness among foreign managers. During our interviews, many executives voiced a keen sensitivity to the perceived reaction of the US capital markets to reported earnings translated under FAS No. 8. Since managers perceive themselves as being evaluated according to this accounting standard, so should the units and managers giving rise to such adjustments. In some instances, responsibility for translation gains and losses were not always commensurate with hedging authority, this responsibility being partly shared with corporate headquarters.

Foreign exchange rates enter the budgetary-control process when local operating budgets are translated to the currency equivalents of the parent company. Rates used in translating beginning of period targets may vary from those used to monitor actual end of period results. Different exchange rate combinations to set budgets and track performance give rise to differing managerial responses. Thus, the use of projected rates to translate capital budgets encourage local managers to adjust their business and financial decisions (e.g., local pricing, currency denomination of export sales, national sources of input etc.) in anticipation of expected exchange rate movements. Translating actual results using the same projected rate shields foreign managers from unexpected rate changes during the period;

tracking actual performance using the year-end rate includes unexpected rate changes in the performance measures of the local manager prompting local hedging actions that may or may not be optimal from the corporate point of view.

Our survey results indicate that the majority of firms, both US and non-US, use a projected exchange rate to establish budgets and end of period rates to track performance. In most instances, however, variances due to the use of these different exchange rates are seldom held against either the unit or manager as they are regarded as forecasting errors. Those that do hold subsidiary managers accountable for these variances feel that local managers possess the authority and tools to achieve their targeted results.

It is noteworthy that some firms feel that the variance between budgeted and actual exchange rates is meaningless in interpreting the impact of exchange rate movements on performance.

PERFORMANCE EFFECTS OF FAS NO. 52

Responding to criticism of its controversial FAS No. 8, on accounting for foreign currency translation and transactions, the FASB has recently issued FAS No. 52. Among other things, this new currency pronouncement enables multinationals reporting to US shareholders to (1) replace the temporal method of foreign currency translation with the current rate method (foreign currency financial statements translated at the exchange rate prevailing as of the financial statement date) and (2) reflect translation gains and losses in a special section of Stockholders' Equity as opposed to including them in current income.

How will FAS No. 52 affect the performance evaluation systems of US-based MNCs? While it is too early to say, some tentative judgements are offered based on recent follow-up interviews with US respondents to the present study.[3]

Perhaps the most significant impact of switching from FAS No. 8 to FAS No. 52 is the removal of translation gains and losses from the income statement into equity. FAS No. 52 will have little if any impact on companies originally adhering to FAS No. 8 which did not hold their foreign operations responsible for these gains and losses. Those companies which did hold their foreign managers accountable for foreign currency translation adjustments will likely reconsider their policy, save those which choose to retain the dollar as their functional currency and thus remain on FAS No. 8. According to a financial executive of a major food products company, FAS No. 52 will make the company's foreign operations more competitive internationally.

Translating local currency financial statements at the current rate provides dollar statements that are similar to their local currency counterparts (i.e., relationships existing in local currency are preserved as local currency balances are simply multiplied by a constant). Accordingly, some companies feel that FAS No. 52 will make it easier for local management to understand their evaluations as it provides an evaluation that parallels the local perspective of the foreign operation. Headquarters management will likewise review foreign subsidiary performance from the perspective of the foreign manager as the foreign currency is retained as the unit of measure. In doing so, FAS No. 52 will simplify the performance evaluation process.

INFLATION AND PERFORMANCE EVALUATION

Economists often assume an inverse relationship between a country's internal inflation rate and the external value of its currency. If as is often the case, exchange rates lag local price changes, an internal evaluation system should provide information on the effects of both inflation and exchange rate changes. Inflation accounting can be a useful technique for minimizing the distortive effects of local inflation on measures of performance such as understated values of a foreign operations' investment base, overstated earnings, overstated ROI's, and non-comparable performance measures both within and between countries as performance measures are not adjusted for changes in the general purchasing power of the monetary unit.

Companies participating in our study were asked whether they formally incorporate inflation adjustments into their performance evaluation systems, particularly in high inflationary economies. The overwhelming response from US multinationals was that they do not.[4] Even in Brazil, for instance, where government-supplied indexes are available for revaluing assets and inflation are made for local reporting purposes, most of the US companies surveyed continue to utilize historical cost in assessing the performance of their Brazilian operations.

One reason for some US firms' reluctance to use inflation accounting for internal management purposes is that they are not convinced the stock market will evaluate them or inflation-adjusted numbers.

When US firms do make internal adjustments for inflation, the process has been largely confined to budgeting. As with foreign exchange adjustments, such companies incorporate an anticipated inflation rate in setting the budget and then use the actual rate at the period's end to monitor performance.

The absence of inflation adjustments, aside from selling prices and certain cost adjustments in budgeting, does not mean that US managers are unaware of the potential benefits of a more comprehensive treatment of inflation. On the contrary, interviews revealed a growing awareness that inflation accounting provides the most realistic input into the total evaluation process.

In contrast to US MNCs, many non-US multinationals, particularly those based in the UK and Sweden, responded positively to questions on inflation accounting. The concensus among European multinationals is that inflation adjustments – no matter how crude – provide more useful measures of performance than do unadjusted cost figures.

The majority of non-US respondents adjust their foreign units, assets for inflation and base depreciation and cost of goods sold on the restated amounts. These firms generally feel that foreign statements should first be restated for local inflation and then translated into the parent-company currency.

INTEREST COSTS

Owing to differential interest rates between the parent and host countries, interest costs are frequently a significant expense component for foreign operations. A majority of both US and non-US multinationals deduct interest expense when measuring foreign operations. Companies not doing so argue that these costs were often not controllable by the foreign manager. As an example, corporate headquarters frequently determines the level of foreign borrowings for exchange risk protection, as a hedge against political risk, or to fund sister operations. However, some firms feel that the manager should not be relieved of all responsibility as the cost of resources under his control are very real and should not be ignored. One approach to this dilemma, which surfaced during our interviews, was the use of a common debt-equity ratio throughout the multinational corporate system. Under this method, local managers are charged an imputed local interest credit or debit which is a function of the difference between its debt to equity ratio and the corporate-wide norm and the level of its net operating assets. In addition to making the manager aware of his effective local interest costs, this approach encourages him to manage his local currency net assets efficiently as the interest charge varies directly with the level of resources employed.

Our respondents were also asked to indicate whether they allocate to foreign operations the cost of corporate funds used, whether debt or equity, and what methods they use to compute this cost.

Half of the companies, both US and non-US, indicated that they do not charge their subsidiaries for use of corporate funds. Among those respondents who did charge for such use, the local interest rate was the most popular choice as 1) local banking sources are increasingly relied on to finance short-term needs, 2) it is difficult to calculate a single interest cost statistic for worldwide use, and 3) the local interest rate is a means of measuring the manager's performance using local criteria.

Again, interviews unveiled a novel approach to enhancing management's understanding of the interest cost of financing local working capital even though the funds may not be secured locally. A form of responsibility allocation, the 'capital charge' approach imputes the opportunity cost of net working capital under the foreign manager's control. The charge equals the cost of local borrowings times the sum of accounts receivable and inventory less accounts payable, all in local currency.

In addition to encouraging the local manager to minimize his inflation and foreign exchange exposure in net working capital, the capital charge also helps to separate treasury's responsibility from that of the foreign operating manager. Under this approach, the subsidiary's budget includes a capital charge based on an agreed interest rate at the beginning of the year. Treasury provides the subsidiary with the capital needed at an agreed interest rate for the year. Any variance in the volume of the capital needed is the responsibility of the operating manager, while any rate variance is treasury's responsibility. Treasury is then measured by the difference between the rate it committed to finance the foreign operation and the actual cost of funds.

COUNTRY RISK

Another issue involved in setting performance standards for foreign operations is whether and how country risk should be incorporated. If one accepts the premise that higher levels of risk should be offset by higher levels of return, it is reasonable to expect higher profitability from operations in riskier countries.

To determine how MNCs account for risk when evaluating foreign operations, financial executives were asked to indicate which of the following applied in their companies:

- Country risk is not formally considered in performance evaluation
- A higher rate of return is required for high-risk countries.
- Country risk is incorporated into budget projections.

Most firms, both US and foreign, indicated that, country risk is not formally considered in performance evaluation. Companies that do consider country risk (approximately 40% in both cases) either require a higher rate of return for high-risk countries, or incorporate country risk into budget projections. Thus, while most firms expect a higher rate of return from a riskier country when making initial investment decisions, fewer do so when evaluating subsequent performance. There appears to be considerable inconsistency between the standards set for investment decisions and those used in performance evaluation.

One reason given for the discrepancy was that companies do not wish to 'penalize' a manager in a risky country by requiring that he provide a higher rate of return than a manager in a 'safe' country. They felt it might have a detrimental effect on his morale, particularly since political risk is not under his control. Another reason was that once a foreign investment is made, management may no longer have the flexibility to require a higher rate of return as compensation for risk.

While many companies feel it is difficult to come up with a reasonable means of incorporating country risk into performance evaluation, some firms are attempting to make the link. They admit that determining premiums for country risk is a subjective process, but agree it should be done.

MANAGEMENT CONSIDERATIONS

Following is a list of considerations worth pondering. As individual company circumstances differ, these comments, stemming from our comparative survey, are offered in generalized fashion.

(1) Short-term vs long-term performance

Given the strategic nature of many overseas operations, companies need to tailor their performance evaluation measures more closely to the specific role of the foreign unit in the total corporate scheme. Concomitantly, companies should assure that longer-term or strategic objectives are not sacrificed because of foreign managers' preoccupations with short-term results.[5] This can be accomplished by conforming short-term performance goals and related management incentive schemes to the company's strategic plans.

(2) Nonfinancial measures

Since accounting numbers provide, as best, crude approximations of enterprise performance, they should be supplemented as much as possible with nonfinancial measures of performance. Nonfinancial measures are useful, not only in reinforcing quantitative performance statistics, but also in capturing dimensions of performance related to longer-run strategic considerations. In foreign operations, nonfinancial performance measurements are often as important as financial measurements. It is difficult, obviously, to ascertain the relative importance that should be attached to nonfinancial considerations, but some firms have found ways to make this dimension of performance evaluation more systematic.

(3) Unit vs manager

In measuring performance, a clear distinction should be made between evaluation of the unit and of the manager. A foreign unit should be held accountable for items that are clear attributable to it; a manager should be held accountable only for items over which he has control.

(4) Exchange rates

Translation gains and losses: If as many economists and financial executives contend, such gains and losses are merely 'bookkeeping fictions,' they should not be included in the evaluation of a unit or that of its manager. However, if top management believes that these gains and losses are 'real' or are perceived by the market to be 'real', it would be consistent to include them when evaluating a unit. Whether they should be included in managerial evaluation depends on the extent to which the manager is given the hedging tools and authority to protect against these losses.

Transaction gains and losses: These are real and should be considered in performance evaluation. An exception may be made when evaluating the local manager for transaction gains and losses that do not stem from operational requirements. For example, corporate treasury might use intercompany trade as a financing or hedging vehicle. Intercompany transaction gains and losses stemming from such circumstances may be eliminated in managerial evaluation.

Exchange rates in budgeting and tracking. The use of projected rates in budgeting is recommended because it allows management to adjust operating or financial decisions in anticipation of exchange rate changes (e.g. raising prices, changing sources of input or currencies of denomination for export sales). In order to prevent biases from entering the system, companies might use an objective measure such as the forward rate, when available, in arriving at a projected rate.

The use of projected rates for tracking managerial performance is recommended when a manager cannot react quickly to unexpected exchange rate changes by raising his selling prices or cutting his costs. The same perspective is maintained if different rates are used in budgeting and tracking (budget at projected, track at actual) if the variance due to changes in the rate of exchange is set aside when evaluating a manager. This maintains a local-currency perspective. Indeed, assessment of managerial performance in local-currency terms could be practised to a greater extent than is currently the case.

On the other hand, when the local manager has flexibility, and the absence of fierce competition permits a quick rise in prices (and naturally in countries without price controls), performance should be tracked at the actual rate of exchange.

The economic impact changes in the rate of exchange have on performance is more profound than can be discerned through simple accounting measures. For example, a change in exchange rates may unfavorably affect local selling prices and the volume of sales, the effect of which is not captured by a simple variance analysis of exchange rate changes. To assess the impact of inflation and currency volatility and gauge their ability to react to these factors, companies need to analyze their competitive position in the market and the economic impact of these factors on their costs and revenues vis-a-vis their competitors. This more complex approach appears to be more meaningful for purposes of evaluating performance and determining appropriate responses than accounting measures of exchange gains and losses.

(5) Inflation

To be truly meaningful, performance statistics should incorporate the effects of local inflation. Inflation-adjusted numbers provide more realistic measures of performance and lead to more equitable resource-allocation decisions both within a country and between countries. The practices of European-based MNCs in this regard suggest that the benefits of accounting for inflation exceed the costs of doing so and indeed, that such adjustments are feasible. When translating inflation-adjusted foreign-currency results to their home-currency equivalent, use of the current rate method is recommended. Incorporating local inflation in performance measures also makes comparisons of units in different countries and at different times more valid. The evaluation system should be designed to allow management to assess separately the impact of local inflation, currency changes and operational improvements.

The US Financial Accounting Standards Board is currently in the process of conforming the reporting requirements of FASB No. 33, *Financial Reporting and Changing Prices* with the changes in the method of foreign currency translation set out in FASB Statement No. 52, *Foreign Currency Translation*.[6] The final methodology that will emerge is not yet clear. However, to the extent that internal reporting systems are influenced by external reporting rules, it is highly likely that US MNCs will move to embrace inflation adjusted numbers in their performance evaluation of foreign operations.[7]

(6) External reporting bias

Internal performance evaluation systems should emphasize organizational objectives rather than external reporting standards; i.e. management must carefully discern the extent to which external accounting rules are consistent with operating realities. For example, evidence suggests that the stock market 'discounts for' (removes the impact of) translation gains and losses. In such a case, emphasis on external accounting-based performance measures applied internally will not necessarily improve the market value of a company's shares in the long run.

(7) Country risk

Country risk often can and frequently should be taken into account in evaluating performance. Higher rates of return can be required from affiliates in riskier countries. While a truly objective and quantifiable method for making such adjustments is not presently available, the use of a systematic method to arrive at a subjective risk premium or hurdle rate can be a practical approach.

CONCLUSION

To conclude, there appears to be a number of areas of multinational performance evaluation in which improvement is possible. Nevertheless, the success of any evaluation system ultimately lies in the judgment management brings to bear on interpreting foreign operating results. Given the complexities involved, it is probably impossible to develop an evaluation system that is a complete and accurate reflection of the true economic performance of a foreign operation.

NOTES

1 This article is based on a recent research study conducted by Business International Corporation, *Assessing Foreign Subsidiary Performance: Systems and Practices of Leading Multinational Companies* of which the authors were the principal investigators.
2 We wish to thank Professor V. Bavishi of the University of Connecticut for his help in reviewing the questionnaire and tabulating the questionnaire responses.
3 Business International, *New Directions in Managing Currency Risk: Changing Corporate Strategies and Systems Under FAS No. 52* (NY: Author, 1983).
4 Many surveyed companies, particularly US MNCs, did not answer most of the questions on inflation giving as their reason that they did not make inflation adjustments for inflation purposes.
5 For example see Robert H. Hayes and William J. Abernathy, 'Managing Our Way to Economic Decline,' *Harvard Business Review*, July – August, 1980.
6 For example see Proposed Statement of Financial Accounting Standards, 'Financial Reporting and Changing Prices: Foreign Currency Translation' (Stamford, Connecticut: FASB, December 22, 1981).
7 Further evidence of this trend is contained in Cornelius J. Casey and Michael J. Sandretto, 'Internal Uses of Accounting for Inflation,' *Harvard Business Review*, November – December, 1981.

QUESTIONS

1 This article offers a number of examples of different approaches to assessing foreign subsidiary performance when US and European multi-nationals are compared. Summarise these, with a discussion of why they may arise.

26

GERMAN MANAGEMENT ACCOUNTING

Nicholas Strange

If we are largely what we eat and drink, so large companies are often what their accounting systems have encouraged them to become. Cultural influences are crucial to both. British and German management accounting are at least as different as roast beef and *Sauerbraten*; yet our knowledge of management accounting in our greatest trading partner is almost non-existent.

As our recent survey of 25 medium to large engineering companies in Britain and Germany shows, there are significant – and disquieting – differences in the goals of the management accounting systems, in the way, and by whom, the systems are designed, in the ways they are used and in the accuracy and relevance of the information produced.

The differences start at the top with system goals. Over 80 per cent of senior British managers (and 15 out of 16 financial managers) chose 'maximising the long-term value of the company' over 'giving a true and fair view of its financial situation' as the goal of management accounts. No mean goal. Even if this may sometimes be the accountancy version of political correctness, it contrasts strongly with Germany, where views are roughly evenly split. Questioned in more detail, British managers saw performance evaluation and the motivation of efficiency improvement as very important system goals while they came almost bottom of the German list.

Those designing and maintaining the systems to achieve these goals also differ. A recent survey showed that a fifth of all job vacancy advertisements for financial controllers in Germany specify an engineering degree. We found in engineering companies in Germany that all those responsible for the management accounting systems were business economics graduates

From Management Accounting (October 1992) p46.
Reprinted by permission of the Chartered Institute of Management Accountants.

(amongst other qualifications) while in Britain only a third had such a relevant degree. On the other hand, all such managers in Britain were qualified accountants. In Germany, whose accountancy profession is less than a third the size relative to population, none were *Wirtschaftsprüfer* (chartered accountants).

The way management uses accounting systems shows that the purely financial performance of the company matters more, to more people extending further down the hierarchy in Britain than Germany. This is not least because German bonus schemes are often based on task completion or, at the highest levels, on absolute profit whereas in Britain some sort of capital productivity base is used down to surprisingly low levels. German and British main boards have similar 'top four' performance measures, sharing an overwhelming interest in ROCE, though German boards are cooler about EPS and cashflow. But one level lower ROCE drops to seventh place in Germany and to 12th place two levels below main board. Indeed, at this level, no profitability measures reach the top four in Germany whereas ROCE and cashflow still rule in Britain.

Use of productivity measures underlines these differences. German management at all levels is significantly more interested in personnel and fixed asset productivity than British management. The British obsession is current asset productivity, presumably because of its potential for rapid change.

But it is in the structure and content of management accounts that the basic philosophical divide between the two cultures finds its clearest and most practical expression. Technical influences on the willingness to invest are particularly interesting because of suggestions in the press that German industry has privileged access to cheap capital.

Whether or not German companies pay less for capital, it is almost certain that German management accounts make new investment in productive capacity *seem* more attractive than under otherwise identical conditions in Britain. There are two main technical reasons for this. Three quarters of German engineering companies use replacement values in their management accounts and in more than half the companies surveyed these values are depreciated on a notational basis often far below zero value. Thus the sort of senior manager who must be the champion of, say, new production technology can often argue in Germany that replacing obsolescent plant will barely cause depreciation to rise although the financial accounts show the plant to be fully depreciated.

But is this not precisely the vulgar error that DCF investment appraisal techniques avoid? At this point the accounting focus blurs and sociology intrudes. In both Britain and Germany (where we found them less used) DCF calculations support funding applications on their way up the hierarchy. But applications are initially launched because of their positive impact on expected profit under the existing rules of the management accounting system. If, as in Germany, the comparison base is depressed by replacement values and notional depreciation and the financial goal is absolute profit or profit as a percentage of sales, the propensity to apply for investment funds is correspondingly higher than in Britain with historic, financial values and capital productivity goals. In other words, at a crucial stage in investment decision-making, German management accounting in some respects 'simulates' a lower cost of capital.

We also found in Germany a much stronger influence of strategic considerations in investment appraisal. Historically, German industry has found that technical product or production excellence usually leads to adequate profit. Once the strategic decision has been taken to excel in particular areas there is often very little attempt to justify individual re-equipment decisions in terms of capital productivity.

There are other areas in which German management accounting has long practised some form of what the profession is still only discussing in Britain.

For example, the fine detail and strong emphasis on causation of German cost centre hierarchies in both direct and indirect areas have, since the 1930s, brought most of the advantages of ABC. Flexible budgets, though not so called even in translation, are commonplace in Germany. In industrial companies, the very structure of the profit and loss statement, by being based on cost of goods produced rather than CGS, allows a simpler link to budgeting and monthly control. Multi-level contribution hierarchies no longer tied to fixed versus variable costs seem to offer a useful weapon against bureaucracy in the age of the fixed cost. Inflation accounting has been in place for more than 50 years.

On the other hand, once understood, there is much to raise a critical British eyebrow in other areas of German management accounting. For example, the bridge back from notional operating profit to the published profit and loss statement, often a multiple of the final profit figure, is usually opaque.

The European Community already requires increasing harmonisation of financial accounting. While harmonisation is entirely inappropriate to management accounts, we surely remain ignorant of our neighbours' practices at our peril. The comparison between Britain and Germany strongly suggests that management accounting can be a formidable competitive weapon in its own right.

QUESTIONS

1 Summarise the key features of German management accounting as perceived by Strange.

27

EXPLORING THE EFFECT OF NON-FINANCIAL INDICATORS ON RETURN ON INVESTMENT IN MULTINATIONAL COMPANIES

Can Şimga Muğan

INTRODUCTION

The domain of business performance covers concepts from financial performance to various dimensions of organizational performance. Financial performance is based on the assumption that financial indicators reflect the attainment of the economic goals of a firm. Return on investment (ROI) is generally accepted as the main indicator of financial performance domain. The next domain covers both financial and operational performance which is mostly reflected in recent strategy research.[1] The broadest domain is the organizational effectiveness which envelopes financial, operational and social aspects of business performance.

This study develops a performance evaluation model which explores the association between non-financial indicators of performance and ROI of both US and non-US multinational firms. It also attempts to uncover the temporal association between the financial and non-financial indicators, that determine whether lagged non-financial indicators provide a better explanation of the variance in ROI than contemporaneous factors utilizing publicly available financial and non-financial data.

The presentation of the paper consists of two main sections. The first part

From International Journal of Accounting (Vol 27 1992) pp 123–136.
Reprinted by permission of the University of Illinois.

reviews the performance measures and presents the development of the basic performance model employed in the analysis. In the second section, methodological issues and the statistical model are discussed and the results are presented.

PERFORMANCE MEASURES

In the 1960s profit seemed to be the most popular financial measure;[2,3] in the 1980's however, ROI has become just as, if not more, important as a measure of performance.[4]

The current view in strategic management literature reflects that 'market' or 'value-based' measures are more appropriate than accounting based measures.[5–7] However, these indicators are basically financial in nature and consequently suffer from being subject to monetary fluctuations which may distort their short as well as long-term usefulness.[8–12] In a multinational setting the existence of different accounting systems and regulations contribute to the reduction in usefulness of financial indicators. Furthermore, problems of financial statement translations, setting transfer prices, and rules governing earnings transfer from host country to home country enhance the difficulties.

COMPREHENSIVE PERFORMANCE MODEL

In strategy research and theory, as illustrated in Figure 1, the performance of a business unit is based on several activities. Fig. 1 indicates how the major activities of a firm could be pictured together. The inputs of the system (functional area activities) are processed within the strategic business unit (SBU – firm); and the outputs of the 'black box' (SBU) are revealed through the key indicators.

Although the relevance of any non-financial criterion depends on its ultimate impact on the financial outcome, it is possible that certain non-

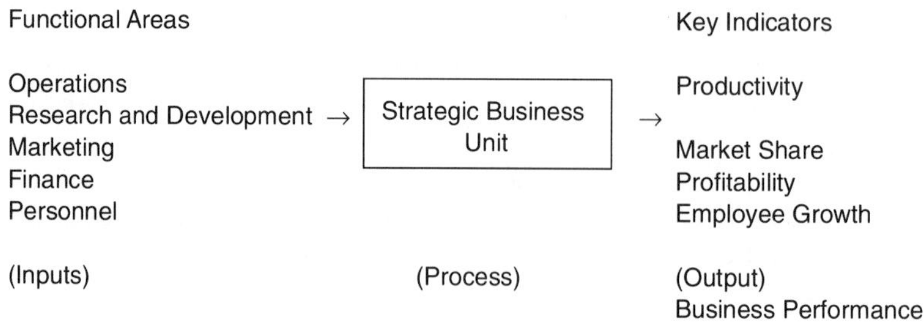

Figure 1. Strategic areas and key indicators. Adapted from I. Jauch and R. Osborn, 'Toward an Integrated Theory of Strategy.' *Academy of Management Review* (6, no. 3, 1981), 493.

financial criteria could indicate the trend in the overall business performance earlier than the financial criteria. This possibility finds its roots in the belief that the impact of some of the activities, such as marketing and product innovations, will be felt in the future.[13–16] Thus, by focusing only on the financial aspects, some of the information is inevitably lost.

In this study a statistical model relating three non-financial indicators which are considered as the representatives of the functional areas, i.e., manufacturing, marketing, and administration to financial area, is developed. The model can be represented in general terms as follows:

$$\text{ROI} = f(X_1, X_2, X_3)$$

where ROI = return on investment,
X_1 = total factor productivity growth (TPI),
X_2 = market share growth (MSI),
X_3 = growth in the number of employees (CNE).

Total Factor Productivity Growth (TPI)

In most enterprises a positive association between long-term productivity gains and profitability increases is normally expected.[17] Regarding the relationship between financial and productivity ratios, Kendrick (1961)[18] states that intercompany comparisons of total factor productivity indices might reveal unfavorable trends sooner than would the profit and loss statements and thus provide management with ways that can improve technological performance of the business. However, he warns against using productivity indices as 'all purpose' indices and suggests using them in conjunction with other measures to assess progress in the broader realms of social and economic efficiency as contrasted with the narrower realm of technological efficiency.[19] The same view is also supported by other researchers.[20,21] The growth rate of total factor productivity provides information of the changes in the production efficiency in addition to the points mentioned above.[22]

Total factor productivity indices can be calculated using Laspeyres, Paasche, or Divisia methods. The former indices are calculated by using base year prices as weights. Consequently, depending on the base year, they suffer from under- or over-estimating the total change. Selection of the base year will be especially difficult for multinationals because of the dynamic nature of the environment they operate in. On the other hand, the weights in Divisia indices are assigned according to the respective shares of inputs (outputs) in total costs (total sales revenue) in two consecutive years.[23–25] This procedure is dynamic enough in nature to facilitate a 'truer' comparison of different years. Hence in this study, Divisia index numbers are used to estimate the total factor productivity growth index (TPI).[26]

$$\frac{\text{TPI}_t}{\text{TPI}_{t-1}} = \frac{\P_j(Y_{j,t}/Y_{j,t-1})^{½(\beta_{j,t}+\beta_{j,t-1})}}{\P_j(X_{i,t}/X_{i,t-1})^{½(\alpha_{i,t}+\alpha_{i,t-1})}}$$

where $Y_{j,t}$ = sale of product j in period t,
$\beta_{j,t}$ = share of product$j$ in total sales in period t,
$X_{i,t}$ = cost in input i in period t,
$a_{i,t}$ = share of cost of input i in total costs in period t,
i_1 = cost of goods sold,
i_2 = capital inputs (includes amortized research and development costs).

Market Share Growth Index (MSI)

The relationship between market share and ROI has been addressed by many strategy researchers. Most of the findings display a positive association between ROI and market share.[21–32] A study on corporate strategy shows that although the relationship between return on equity and market share is positive at the industry level, among more homogeneous firms the association is negative. The authors tie this result mainly to profit/market share trade-off in the short run and, as a consequence of market share growth, increased production facilities in the long run, especially at the national firms level.[33] This finding also supports the expectation that market share would provide an indication of long-run performance of a firm.

A study on the determinants of profitability for the firms in the United States, Europe, Canada, and Great Britain indicates that market share and quality have the highest positive correlation with profitability.[34] However, in the literature in addition to positive association between market share and ROI a negative association is also observed.[35]

A market share growth index (MSI) is employed as the second non-financial performance indicator because of its demonstrated importance and association with ROI. This variable is calculated as follows:

$$\text{MSI}_{j,t} = \Sigma_i\, a_{i,j,t}{}^*\text{PSC}_{i,j,t} - \text{CEX}_{i,t})$$

where $\text{MSI}_{j,t}$ = weighted market share growth for firm j between periods t and $t-1$,
$a_{i,j,t}$ = weights assigned to different products or product lines (i) as their share of the sales for firm j in period t,
$\text{PSC}_{i,j,t}$ = ratio of the sale of a product or group of products (i) for firm j in period t to the sale of the same product (i) in period $t-1$,
$\text{CEX}_{i,j,t}$ = ratio of global sales of product (i) in period t to global sale of the same product in period $t-1$.

The market for a multinational company is the world market, which is defined as the global market of a product or a product line in this study. It is believed that this index reflects how well the firm is performing in comparison to the world development in a specific market (i) during a period (t).

Change in the Number of Employees (CNE)

As suggested by the AAA Committee Report (1971)[36] on non-financial indicators of performance, the growth of the number of employees is used as the third indicator as a representative of the administrative functions. Since the focus is on managerial control, it appears necessary to include a variable which is mostly under the control of the management. In times of financial or operational difficulties the first resource that is reduced is the labor-force. In times of increasing demand, on the other hand, to meet the new demand level, especially in the short run, capacity utilization is boosted via an increase in the labor-force.

In a study to determine strategic postures, it is found that an excess or shortage of personnel ranks among the higher strategic disadvantages (3.58 out 5) over the period 1930–1974.[37] Therefore, inclusion of this variable is supported from the strategic planning perspective as well.

To avoid possible size effects, percentage change in the number of employees (CNE) from the previous year is used as the third non-financial index.

RESEARCH DESIGN AND EMPIRICAL QUESTIONS

In this study, the general proposition is to determine the temporal validity of non-financial indicators as shown by their explanatory power to depict the variance in ROI. Based on earlier discussions, it is expected that all non-financial variables will be positively correlated with ROI when a lag is introduced. However, contemporaneous association between market share and ROI could be positive or negative.

Data Collection and Sample Selection

Data for this research were gathered from Compustat II tapes (Industrial Segment, Geographic Area, Business Segments and Annual Industrial) for US multinational companies (USMNEs), and from annual reports of non-US multinational companies (NUSMNEs), and World Trade Statistics of the United Nations.[38]

Compustat II tapes were screened to ensure that:

1 the companies are multinational companies engaged in manufacturing only with operations at least in two or more countries (620 companies);

2 the company data met the data requirements of the research, i.e., to consistently provide data on research and development expenses and on product sales (150 companies); and
3 the product mix was relatively similar during the period under study (1980–1984) (88 companies).

Annual reports of NUSMNEs were obtained from a private collection at the New York University Accounting Department and from CIFAR (Center for International Financial Analysis and Research,Princeton, New Jersey), and the companies themselves. Altogether, 52 annual reports of NUSMNEs were collected.

After the screening process, 88 USMNEs and a total of 14 MNEs from Japan, France and Germany were included in the study. The main business segments (product lines) were obtained from Compustat Industrial Segment Tape '84 for USMNEs, and from the annual reports of foreign multinationals. Four-digit SSIC codes were matched with the United Nation's three- or six-digit STIC codes, depending on the specificity of the product, to determine the movement in the global sales of a product line.[39] Since world sales figures were not available, and because production figures were incomplete, export figures were used as surrogates.[40]

Simple statistics of the independent variables (TPI, CNE, MSI) and dependent variable (ROI) were examined to provide an overall picture. Table 1 summarizes the means and variances of the variables for USMNEs and NUSMNEs.

Examination of Table 1 reveals that average ROI of NUSMNEs is considerably lower than that of USMNEs in the 1980–1981 period; however, in later periods average ROIs of both groups are not very different. The results also reveal that while NUSMNEs had relatively stable return rates, USMNEs experienced fluctuating return rates. This finding could indicate the emphasis placed by management during the above period to long-term results in NUSMNEs and to short-term profitability in USMNEs, which would lead to different strategies manifesting unstable return rates.

Table 1 Means and variances of dependent and independent variables[a]

VAR	*1984*		*1983*		*1982*		*1981*		*1980*	
	U	N	U	N	U	N	U	N	U	N
ROI	.10	.09	.07	.08	.08	.08	.12	.09	.13	.09
	(.005)	(.002)	(.008)	(.001)	(.006)	(.002)	(.005)	(.003)	(.006)	(.002)
TPI	1.02	.94	.97	.95	.94	.94	.97	.97	–	–
	(.01)	(.003)	(.004)	(.003)	(.006)	(.005)	(.004)	(.007)	–	–
CNE	–.02	.02	.02	.00	–.10	.02	–.02	.05	–	–
	(.14)	(.006)	(.02)	(.003)	(.02)	(.003)	(.10)	(.01)	–	–
MST	.12	.04	.04	.08	.002	.17	.10	.14	–	–
	(.03)	(.01)	(.02)	(.01)	(.02)	(.005)	(.09)	(.04)	–	–

[a] U = US; n = 88. N = Non-US; n = 14.

On the other hand, although the average TPI was similar for both groups in 1981 and 1982, during 1983 and 1984 USMNEs enjoyed a higher productivity growth rate. This growth was also observed in domestic production in the United States (147.6 in 1983 and 163.4 in 1984).[41] This finding might be a reflection of productivity awareness of the US companies in recent years.

However, CNE seems to be quite different between the two sets of companies. This finding could be the outcome of labor policies and the prevailing economic conditions in different countries. Earlier in the paper it was stated that an excess or shortage of personnel is regarded as one of the major strategic disadvantages. Especially during times of recession, an excess personnel seems to carry higher weight than a shortage.[42] If trends in TPI and CNE are examined, it is observed that they change similarly. This finding supports the above position.

The development of MSI is also interesting. Although in the 1981–1983 period NUSMNEs perform better, in 1984 USMNEs realize a higher average, although the net exports are negative for the United States.[43] This finding might be a result of the effect of the trade regulations among nations as well as the changes in trade policies of USMNEs and intrafirm imports and exports, and their strategies in product diversification.

Regression Analyses and Results

A cross-sectional linear multiple regression technique is employed to determine the contemporaneous and lagged relationship between the independent variables (TPI, CNE, MSI) and the dependent variable ROI. The following regression models are tested to investigate the temporal association. The models are run for the combined sample of 102 companies as well as for USMNEs. The regression results obtained from the combined sample are presented following the model specifications.[44]

Model 1: Contemporaneous Model

To determine the contemporaneous relation among the variables, ROI_t is regressed on TPI_t, CNE_t, and MSI_t. This model is run for each year separately (1981–1984) to observe the relationship over the period based on sample companies (102).

$$ROI_t = b_0 + b_1\,TPI_t + b_2\,CNE_t + b_3\,MSI_t + e \text{ (error term)}$$

As presented in Table 2, there is a low but significant relationship (0.25 in 1982) between the non-financial indicators and ROI during 1981–1983 period. However, 1984 data do not display any relationship. This finding could be taken as an indication of the change in strategic planning perspectives, i.e., more long-term profitability-oriented decisions were made in 1983 and 1984.

TPI and especially CNE are the significant variables. As expected CNE and ROI are positively related. Especially in 1982, CNE has the highest coefficient value. This is the year when ROI and CNE values dropped considerably from their previous year levels. However, MSI does not enter the model as one of the significant variables, although the association is positive as observed in most of the earlier research.

Model 2: One-Year Lag Model

In this and the following models lagged relationships are explored. Due to the long-term nature of the independent variables and the conceptualized relationship between each independent variable and ROI, it is expected that these models will perform better than the first one to explain the variance in ROI. It is believed that the production plans are made earlier according to the anticipated demand which is reflected in the sales estimates. Thus, it is expected that growth in market share and change in the number of employees will affect ROI the following year. This model is run for 1982, 1983, and 1984 for 102 companies:

$$ROI_t = b_0 + b_1\ TPL_{t}-1 + b_2\ CNE_{t}-1 + b_3\ MSI_{t}-1 + e$$

This model yields more information than Model 1, as evidenced by the adjusted R^2 values, particularly in 1983 ($R^2 = 0.43$).

In this model, TPI and CNE especially have a significant effect on ROI the following year. As expected, the association between these variables and ROI is positive. This finding conforms to the belief that companies will enjoy higher returns during the following period due to changes in demand and related production adjustment.

Table 2 Results of contemporaneous model

Dependent variable = ROI_t

Var.	*Exp sign*	*1981 (n = 101) Coeff.*	*t*	*1982 (n = 100) Coeff.*	*t*	*1983 (n = 102) Coeff.*	*t*	*1984 (n = 100) Coeff.*	*t*
inter		.0456	.407	−.0453	−.522	−.2439	− 1.899	.0767	.973
TPI_t	+	.0725	.623	.1482	1.596[c]	.3263	2.350[a]	.0286	.358
CNE_t	+	.1845	2.914[a]	.1935	3.054[a]	.1134	1.734[b]	.0074	.397
MSI_t		.0561	1.110	.0953	1.516	.1004	1.590	−.0243	.587
Model F		4.997		12.058		9.236		1.53	
d.f.$(m; e)$		(3; 97)		(3; 96)		(3; 98)		(3; 96)	
Prob. of signif.		<.003		<.0001		<.0208		<.9243	
R^2		.1339		.2716		.2204		.005	
Adjusted R^2		.1071		.2491		.1965		.000	

[a] Statistically significant at $\alpha = .01$, one-tail.
[b] Statistically significant at $\alpha = .05$, one-tail.
[c] Statistically significant at $\alpha = .10$, one-tail.

Table 3 Results of one-year lag model

Dependent variable = ROIt							
		1982		*1983*		*1984*	
	Exp.	*(n = 100)*		*(n = 102)*		*(n = 100)*	
Var.	*sign*	*Coeff.*	*t*	*Coeff.*	*t*	*Coeff.*	*t*
inter		–.2136	–2.431[a]	–.3295	–3.366[a]	.0774	1.039
TPI_{t-1}	+	.3107	3.342[a]	.4374	4.385[a]	.0134	.179
CNE_{t-1}	+	.2169	3.696[a]	.2832	4.902	.1819	3.142[a]
MSI_{t-1}	+	.0132	0.549	.0865	1.631[c]	.1239	2.605[a]
Model F		7.107		25.394		10.497	
d.f.(*m*; *e*)		(3; 96)		(3; 98)		(3; 96)	
Prob. of signif.		<.0003		<.0001		<.0001	
R^2		.1787		.4424		.2451	
Adjusted R^2		.1381		.4250		.2217	

[a] Statistically significant at $\alpha = .01$, one-tail.
[b] Statistically significant at $\alpha = .05$, one-tail.
[c] Statistically significant at $\alpha = .10$, one-tail.

Model 3: Two-Year Lag Model

In order to examine the association involving longer lags, this and the following models are tested. It is believed that when longer lag periods are involved, the temporal interaction among the independent variables will help to improve the information provided by the non-financial indicators:

$$ROI_t = b_0 + b_1\, TPL_{t-1} + b_2\, CNE_{t-2} + b_3\, MSI_{t-2} + e$$

Contrary to expectations, this model did not perform as well as Model 2 in 1983, although there is a slight increase in 1984. However, it still performs better than the contemporaneous model. Although the coefficients are not as large as the ones observed in the previous model, again TPI and CNE

Table 4 Results of two-year lag model

Dependent variable = ROI.t					
		1983		*1984*	
	Exp	*(n = 102)*		*(n = 100)*	
var.	*sign*	*Coeff.*	*t*	*Coeff.*	*t*
inter		–.1981	–2.131[b]	–.1892	–2.017[b]
TPI_{t-1}	+	.2864	2.912[a]	.3155	3.229[a]
CNE_{t-2}	+	.1159	1.807[b]	.2338	4.110[a]
MSI_{t-2}	+	.0227	.892	.0219	.428
Model F		3.69		14.76	
d.f.(*m*; *e*)		(3; 98)		(3; 96)	
Prob. of signif.		<.0145		<.0001	
R^2		.1025		.3112	
Adjusted R^2		.0747		.2901	

[a] Statistically significant at $\alpha = .01$, one-tail.
[b] Statistically significant at $\alpha = .05$, one-tail.

are the most significant variables. This observation could lead us to believe that in a manufacturing MNE indicators that reflect the production and personnel functional areas occupy the central position in determination of a strategy to reach higher ROI in the following two periods under the given demand conditions.

Model 4: Lagged Interdependencies Model

To examine one of the possible combined lag effects among the independent variables, the following model is developed:

$$ROI_t = b_0 + b_1\ TPL_{t-1} + b_2\ CNE_{t-2} + b_3\ MSI_{t-1} + e$$

The results of this model show that although the observed R^2 values are lower for 1983, most independent variables exhibit significant effects in explaining the variance in ROI.

Although the association between the independent variables and ROI is still positive, this model does not outperform Model 3.

Model 5: Three-Year Lag Model

For 1984 only, it was possible to try a three-year lag model. The rationale for the design of the model lies in the belief that demand expectation occupies a central role in the long-term planning process. Therefore, MSI is lagged by three years. If we can conceptualize that CNE could be a surrogate measure for the capacity utilization, the next step following the planning would be capacity adjustment which will affect the productivity growth (TPI) in the following period. Thus the following model is formed:

Table 5 Results of lagged interdependencies model

Dependent variable = ROI_t

Var.	*Exp. sign*	*1983 (n = 102) Coeff.*	*t*	*1984 (n = 100) Coeff.*	*t*
inter		–.5120	–4.565[a]	–.0203	.277
TPI_t	+	.5961	5.136[a]	.0929	1.239
CNE_{t-2}	+	.1438	2.369[a]	.2344	4.618[a]
MSI_{t-1}	+	.2002	4.048[a]	.0992	2.327[a]
Model F		16.16		13.47	
d.f.(m; e)		(3; 98)		(3; 96)	
Prob. of signif.		<.0001		<.0001	
R^2		.3310		.2919	
Adjusted R^2		.3105		.2702	

[a] Statistically significant at α = .01, one-tail.
[b] Statistically significant at α = .05, one-tail.
[c] Statistically significant at α = .10, one-tail.

$$ROI_t = b_0 + b_1\,TPL_{t-1} + b_2\,CNE_{t-2} + b_3\,MSI_{t-3} + e$$

In 1984, this model outperformed the others, with an R^2 of 32% ($p \geq .0001$). All variables (TPI, CNE, and MSI) enter the picture as significant variables. An MNE which innovates a product especially in fast developing industries, e.g., electronics, might enjoy the outcome in the following year or the year after. A study on intrafirm trade provides yet another explanation. In 1984, it is found that 16.2% total US imports were from manufacturing USMNEs; and the foreign affiliates of these companies shifted the focus of their sales in approximately the same period and, while their sales in the local markets fell, sales to their US parents increased (from 8% to 12% of their sales in 1984). During the same period, exports of US companies increased at a higher rate (30.8% in 1984).[45] This finding also explains the higher increase in MSI of USMNEs relative to NUSMNEs in 1984.

DISCUSSION OF RESULTS

The results of the models demonstrate the existence of an association between ROI and non-financial indicators when publicly available data are utilized. Although a contemporaneous association during the period 1981–1983 is observed, 1984 does not follow the same pattern. On the other hand, the results obtained for the USMNEs show a stronger relation than the whole sample (Table 7). At this point, based on limited observation we could possible state that while there seems to be a shift to more long-term planning in USMNEs, it seems that NUSMNEs are shifting to short-term profitability-oriented decisions.

The results of Models 4 and 5 support the expectation that lagged models perform better than contemporaneous ones in providing information of the

Table 6 Results of three-year lag model

Dependent variable = ROI_t			
		1984	
	Exp.	*(n = 100)*	
Var.	*sign*	*Coeff.*	*t*
inter		–.1924	–2.087[a]
TPI_{t-1}	+	.3174	3.364[a]
CNE_{t-2}	+	.2465	5.515[a]
MSI_{t-3}	+	.0277	1.424[c]
Model F		15.651	
d.f.(*m*; *e*)		(3; 96)	
Prob. of signif.		<.0001	
R^2		.3239	
Adjusted R^2		.3032	

[a] Statistically significant at $\alpha = .01$, one-tail.
[b] Statistically significant at $\alpha = .05$, one-tail.
[c] Statistically significant at $\alpha = .10$, one-tail.

Table 7 Comparative R^2 values (adjusted)

	USMNEs				*Entire Sample*			
	1981	*1982*	*1983*	*1984*	*1981*	*1982*	*1983*	*1984*
model								
1	.14	.19	.22	.00	.11	.25	.20	.00
2		.17	.44	.16		.14	.43	.22
3			.09	.36			.08	.29
4			.37	.33			.31	.27
5				.36				.30

variance in ROI. Thus, this finding would support the view that non-financial indicators reflect the changes in performance of an enterprise earlier than the financial indicators.

Except for 1984, when longer lag period(s) are introduced, R^2 values tend to decrease in USMNEs. We should remember that although the results are obtained in 1984, the decisions leading to those are taken in 1983 and possibly in 1982. This might suggest the view that the perceptions of the foreign operations changed from 1980 to 1984. A survey of multinational company practices of subsidiary evaluation[46] and colloquium presentations of company practices on performance evaluation strengthen the same view.[47] Development of the intrafirm trade also provides an indication of the globalization of the production network to take advantage of economies of scale and national differences.[48]

Although the importance of lag is demonstrated through the models, especially for USMNEs, no single model has been detected as the best one for the years and sample companies in the study. However, we could say that Model 4, in which CNE and MSI are lagged by two periods, performs better than the other ones in general. Therefore, we could possibly state that the employee turnover and market share growth indices are the leading indicators.

Table 8 summarizes the direction of association between the independent variables and ROI for each year and models for USMNEs and the entire sample.

The results reported in Table 8 indicate that in most models non-financial indicators are positively related to ROI as expected. It might have been expected that all MNEs display similar strategies; however, the results of the analyses suggest that cultural and economic differences affect the management of MNEs even at the global level as depicted by the differences in R^2 values and the significant variables.

CONCLUSION AND DIRECTION FOR FURTHER RESEARCH

As the main conclusion we can state that although a specific model of association cannot be defined clearly, the importance of non-financial

Table 8 Significant variables and direction of association

USMNEs

	1981			*1982*			*1983*			*1984*		
Mod./var.	*TPI*	*CNE*	*MSI*	*TPI*	*CNE*	*MSI*	*TPI*	*CNE*	*MSI*	*TPI*	*CNE*	*MSI*
1	+	+[a]	+	+	+[a]	+[c]	+[a]	+[c]	+[c]	+	+	–
2				+[a]	+[a]	+	+[a]	+[a]	+[b]	+	+[c]	+[a]
3							+[a]	+[a]	+	+[a]	+[a]	+
4							+[a]	+[a]	+[a]	+	+[a]	+[b]
5										+[a]	+[a]	+[c]

Entire sample

	1981			*1982*			*1983*			*1984*		
Mod./.var	*TPI*	*CNE*	*MSI*	*TPI*	*CNE*	*MSI*	*TPI*	*CNE*	*MSI*	*TPI*	*CNE*	*MSI*
1	+	+[a]	+	+[c]	+[a]	+[c]	+[a]	+[b]	+[c]	+	+	–
2				+[a]	+[a]	+	+[a]	+[a]	+[b]	+	+[a]	+[a]
3							+[b]	+[b]	+	+[a]	+[a]	+
4							+[a]	+[a]	+[a]	+[c]	+[a]	+[a]
5										+[a]	+[a]	+[c]

[a] Statistically significant at $\alpha = .01$, one-tail.
[b] Statistically significant at $\alpha = .05$, one-tail.
[c] Statistically significant at $\alpha = .10$, one-tail.

indicators of performance is demonstrated, especially employee and productivity growth for USMNEs. The performance of the lagged models support the belief that non-financial indicators do signal the financial future performance of a company. The results of Model 4 show that market share growth and employee growth are the leading indicators whose outcome is felt in total productivity growth and ROI in later periods.

Therefore, to appraise and predict the overall performance of a company, it is necessary to develop a model which takes functional areas, such as production, financing, and administration and the culture(s) in which the company operates, into consideration. This model can be developed for both short- and long-term purposes. Consequently, it will be possible to make or modify the plans to reach the predesignated financial goals by the help of leading non-financial indicators. Thus, further research, probably case studies, combining accounting data and strategic planning goals of firms in a way to facilitate decision making of outside parties will improve our understanding of multinational companies.

NOTES

1 N. Venkatraman and V. Ramanujam, 'Measurement of Business Performance in Strategy Research: A Comparison of Approaches.' *Academy of Management Journal* (October, 1986), 801–814.
2 D. E. Hawkins, 'Controlling Foreign Operations.' *Financial Executive* (February 1965), 25–32.

3 J. J. Mauriel, 'Evaluation and Control of Overseas Operations.' *Management Accounting* (May 1969), 35–39, 52.

4 V. Govindarajan, and A.K. Gupta, 'Linking Control Systems to Business Strategy: Impact on Performance.' *Accounting Organizations and Society* (10, No. 1, 1985), 51–66.

5 R. J. Kudla, 'The Effects of Strategic Planning on Common Stock Returns.' *Academy of Management Journal* (23, No. 5, 1980), 30.

6 J. B. Kusewitt, Jr., 'An Exploratory Study of Strategic Factors Relating to Performance.' *Strategic Management Journal* (April–June, 1985), 151–169.

7 C. A. Montgomery, A. R. Thomas and R. Kamath, 'Divestiture Market Valuation and Strategy.' *Academy of Management Journal*, (27, 1984), 830–840.

8 D. Solomons, *Divisional Performance Management and Control* (Homewood, IL: Richard D. Irwin, 1965).

9 J. J. Mauriel, and R. N. Anthony, 'Misevaluation of Investment Center Performance.' *Harvard Business Review* (March–April, 1966), 98–105.

10 J. Dearden, 'The Case Against ROI Control.' *Harvard Business Review* (May–June, 1969) 124–135.

11 E. V. McIntyre, 'Interaction Effects of Inflation Accounting Models and Accounting Techniques.' *Accounting Review*, (July 1982), 607–617.

12 R. B. Kaplan, 'Management Accounting and Manufacturing: The Lost Connection.' Working Paper, Pittsburg. PA: Carnegie-Mellon University (October 1982) and 'The Evolution of Management Accounting.' *Accounting Review* (July 1984), 390–419.

13 T. Schneeweis, 'Determinants of Profitability: An International Perspective.' *Management International Review* (23, No. 2, 1983), 13–21.

14 C. R. Anderson, C. P. Zeithaml, 'Stage of the Product Life Cycle, Business Strategy and Business Performance,' *Academy of Management Journal* (27, No. 1, 1984), 5–24.

15 S. Eilon, *The Art of Reckoning* (London: Academic Press). 1984).

16 V. Prabhu, and M. Baker, *Improving Business Performance* (London: McGraw Hill, 1986).

17 E. F. Sudit, *Productivity Based Management* (Boston: Kluwer-Nijhoff, 1984).

18 J. W. Kendrick, *Productivity Trends in the United States*, National Bureau of Economic Research (Princeton, NJ: Princeton University Press, 1961).

19 J. W. Kendrick, *Improving Company Productivity: Handbook with Case Studies* (Baltimore, MD: Johns Hopkins University Press, 1984).

20 B. Gold, *Foundations of Productivity Analysis: Guides to Economic Theory and Managerial Control (University of Pittsburgh Press, 1955) and Explorations in Managerial Economics* (Great Britain: Basic Books, 1971) and 'Technology, Productivity and Economic Analysis.' *OMEGA* (1, No. 1, 1971).

21 S. Eilon, 'Some Useful Ratios in Evaluating Performance.' *OMEGA* (7, No. 2, 1978), 166–68.

22 D. W. Jorgenson, and Z. Griliches, 'The Explanation of Productivity Change.' *Review of Economic Studies* (XXIV, No. 99, 1967), 250–270.

23 L. Christensen, and D. W. Jorgenson, 'U.S. Real Product and Real Factor Input: 1929–67.' *Review of Income and Wealth* (16, No. 1, 1981), 19–50.

24 C. R. Hulten, 'Divisia Index Numbers.' *Econometrica* (41, 1973), 1017–1026.

25 E. F. Sudit, (1984) *loc. cit.*

26 All monetary data are expressed and entered into calculations in home currency to avoid the problems of currency translation.

27 B. T. Gale, 'Market Share and Rate of Return.' *Review of Economics and Statistics* (November 1972).

28 B. Branch, 'The Impact of Operating Decisions on ROI Dynamics.' *Financial Management* (Winter 1978), 54–60.

29 R. D. Buzzell, B. T. Gale, and R. G. M. Sultan, 'Market Share, Profitability and Business Strategy.' Working Paper, Cambridge, MA: Marketing Science Institute, (August 1974).

30 S. P. Douglas, and C. S. Craig, 'Examining Performance of U.S. Multinationals in Foreign Markets.' Journal of International Business Studies (Winter 1983), 51–62.

31 D. J. LeCraw, 'Performance of Transnational Corporations in Less Developed Countries.' *Journal of International Business Studies,* (Spring/Summer 1983), 15–33.

32 C. R. Anderson, and C.P. Zeithaml, (1984), *loc. cit.*

33 D. Schendel, and R. Patton, 'A Simultaneous Equation Model of Corporate Strategy.' *Management Science* (24, No. 15, 1978), 1611–1621.

34 T. Schneeweis, (1983). *Ioc. cit.*

35 B. A. Kirchoff, and J. J. Kirchoff, 'Empirical Assessment of the Strategy/Tactics Dilemma.' *Proceedings of Academy of Management 40th Annual Meeting* (1980), 7–11.

36 American Accounting Association, 'Report of the Committee on Non-Financial Measures of Effectiveness.' *Accounting Review*,(46, Suppl., 1971).

37 W. F. Glueck, *Business Policy and Strategic Management*, 3d edn., (New York: McGraw Hill, 1980).

38 *1984 International Trade Statistics Yearbook, Vol. II, Trade by Commodity* (New York: United Nations 1986).

39 Standard International Trade Classification, Revision 2, Series M No. 34 Rev. 2 New York: United Nations, 1975).

40 *Industrial Statistics Yearbook 1983, Vol. II. Commodity Production Statistics, 1974–1983* (New York: United Nations, 1985) and *Industrial Structure Statistics 1984* (Paris: OECD, 1986).

41 Chase Econometrics, December 1984.

42 W. F. Glueck (1980, p. 194) *loc. cit.*

43 Chase Econometrics, 1984.

44 Regression models, statistical and diagnostic analyses are carried out by utilizing SAS (Statistical Analysis System) version 5.08 software package, available from University of Illinois at Urbana-Champaign.

45 J. S. Little 'The Impact of Intra-firm Trade Flows.' *Economic Impact*,(No. 1, 1988), 48–52.

46 I. J. Czechowicz, F. D. S. Choi and V. Bavishi, *Assessing Foreign Subsidiary Performance Systems and Practices of Leading Multinational Companies* (New York: Business International, 1982).

47 P. H. Holzer and H. M. Schoenfeld (eds.), *Managerial Accounting* (Berlin: Walter de Gruyter, 1986).

48 J. S. Little, (1988) *loc. cit.*

QUESTIONS

1 Discuss the advantages and disadvantages of non-financial indicators compared to financial indicators of company performance.

28

THE ENVIRONMENT AND THE AUDIT PROFESSION

A Dutch research study

J. H. Blokdijk and F. Drieënhuizen

The environment has been a subject of growing public concern in the Netherlands, as in neighbouring countries, in recent years. Although the public debate is still in full swing, a study group at the Limperg Institute has investigated the consequences of environmental problems for the audit profession. It has published its findings in *Milieu en accountant* (The Environment and the Audit Profession).[1] This article considers a number of the study's most important findings.

In a speech made to auditors several years ago, the Dutch Minister for Housing, Physical Planning and the Environment (VROM) stressed that auditors could make a key contribution to environmental management. He even went so far as to say that Dutch legislation on annual reports would eventually have to be amended so as to account for the necessity and financial consequences of cleaning up polluted industrial sites. He was referring in part to studies carried out by employers' organizations on the possibilities of internal environmental management systems.

These and other examples illustrate that the audit profession cannot ignore the issue of environmental management. However, there is confusion as to the scope and implications of the views expressed. There are also widely differing opinions on the terminology used, such as environmental accountant and environmental auditor.

Questions raised by auditors include:

- is environmental auditing the domain of the traditional independent auditor?

From European Accounting Review 1992, 1, 437–443. Reprinted by permission of European Accounting Review.

- how can a registration system be set up to record pollutants, and what are the permissible tolerances for such records?
- can a financial auditor issue an opinion on a company's environmental report?

To answer such questions, we first examined how environmental problems affect the accountant in his position as an adviser and auditor. We then considered the contribution auditors can make to controlling and solving environmental problems where possible. In addition to studying the available literature, fact-finding interviews were held with members of government and industry and with advisers from related disciplines.

In a National Environmental Policy Plan, the Dutch government recommends the introduction of internal environmental management systems at companies. The State is taking action to recover clean-up costs from polluters and important legislative and regulatory amendments are being passed. A draft EC regulation that will allow voluntary participation by industrial sector companies in an 'Eco-audit scheme' is also under consideration.

The EC's draft proposal on the Eco-audit scheme defines an environmental management system as 'the organisational structure, responsibilities, practices, procedures, processes and resources for implementing environmental management'. Environmental management systems should be an integral part of a company's general management system and accounting organization. It is concluded that the auditor, with his knowledge and experience in the field of accounting organization and internal control structures, can make a meaningful contribution to the design of environmental management systems. Since a good accounting system cannot be established without reference to a company's transactions, in this case the environmental aspects of its operations, the auditor should also be involved in setting up a system of internal environmental management measures and the related input and output of information.

The accounting techniques and internal control procedures currently available are adequate for use in environmental management systems, but their application requires changes in emphasis. In particular, more attention will have to be focused on three areas: the basic recording of environmentally hazardous substances as and when they occur (pollutant records): the internal procedures governing the storage and processing of hazardous substances; and the feasibility of segregating duties wherever possible.

SPECIFIC ACCOUNTING SYSTEM REQUIREMENTS

A company's accounting system is designed partly to safeguard its assets, such as goods, securities, receivables and cash. The accounting records show which assets are owned by the company, so that they can be made readily available (logistical information) and so that their physical presence can be verified (accounting information). In addition, it is designed to provide reliable management information so that the company can be managed as effectively as possible.

Environmental management, however, introduces a new dimension. Environmental pollution is caused by the release of hazardous substances during the production process. These substances must be stored temporarily and/or rendered harmless, which usually involves additional costs. These substances are not assets in the traditional sense of the word. On the contrary, they have no value and are in fact involving the company in additional costs. Traditionally accounting systems and related internal control structures implemented at many businesses are not designed for controlling these substances with their 'negative value'. The methods must therefore be adapted. This is technically possible but would require a shift in emphasis towards, for example, specific on-site observations, stock counts of hazardous waste products, coherence tests to very strict tolerance levels and the like. The segregation of duties would perhaps be of less benefit because hazardous waste is not an economically desirable product. The natural conflict of interests, based on the positive value of goods, is lacking. To remedy this problem, internal responsibilities and duties regarding the environmental impact of hazardous activities and their registration should be clearly defined. It is important that the officials involved are aware that they will be held accountable for the incomplete registration of environmental hazards. Internal procedures and regulations should provide sufficient safeguards for the complete registration of environmentally hazardous substances, including waste, at all stages of the production process. The choice of waste transport company and final waste processing company is also an important area of accountability.

At any rate, hazardous substances should be recorded wherever possible; without adequate and systematic records, there will be no source of reliable information, and so no way of determining whether the substances have been fully and properly rendered harmless.

POLLUTANT RECORDS AND THE HAZARDOUS SUBSTANCE RECONCILIATIONS

The possibilities of recording hazardous substances depend on the business involved and the extent to which quantitative relationships exist between the production of desirable goods and the use of certain raw materials and consumables which may be environmentally hazardous. It is important that all businesses involved set up a registration system to record pollutants. If information on the production process is sufficiently reliable, and provided reliable standards are available, additionally 'hazardous substance reconciliations' (HSRs) may be drawn up to verify the reliability of pollutant records.

The term HSR indicates that in these circumstances a reconciliation can be made between the input of certain raw materials and consumables on the one hand and the output of goods produced and resultant waste flows on the other. For the reconciliation to balance, the precise relationships within the production process should be known and subject to relatively tight tolerances. If, however, the reconciliation does not balance, there may have been a loss of potentially hazardous substances during the production process. It is not necessary for an HSR to account for *all* the products used in the production process. HSR is a generic term; practice, however, requires a product-specific approach. In the chemicals industry, for example, the production of sulphuric acid could be reconciled by measuring the sulphur content of raw materials and that of finished products. In this case the emission of sulphur dioxide can be calculated. Any discrepancy in the reconciliation would mean there had been a loss from the system and thus a release of hazardous substances (SO_2) into the environment.

The reconciliation between the consumption of raw materials and consumables and the production of waste would never be perfect: conversion factors in the production process may vary slightly depending on circumstances; temperature, humidity and the like can result in discrepancies. Although it may be impossible to detect small, accidental emissions, the reconciliation would disclose all significant discrepancies. An HSR would therefore be an important tool to help ensure the reliability of information on hazardous waste.

Often, in practice, there are only weak quantitative relationships between the production of desirable goods and the use of certain raw materials or consumables which may be environmentally hazardous. For example, it is often difficult to calculate precisely the amount of lubricants, solvents, cleaning agents and other hazardous substances used in some production processes. In these situations it is not possible to draw up an HSR and other procedures become the more important. The reliability of the information in pollutant records can be increased if adequate attention is paid to the segregation of duties and resultant procedures. More so than in the past, it will be necessary to keep hazardous products in separate stores so that their issue and use can be recorded. This segregates the duties of purchaser, storekeeper and user of such substances. The reliability of the user records can then be checked by means of stock counts. The registration of substances used and environmentally hazardous waste flows may also be verified in this manner.

It will be clear that environmental problems cannot be controlled within companies unless adequate pollutant records are kept. At present, though, such records are far from readily available and solutions have to be found for practical problems concerning measurement and analysis; for example, the problem of measurement where there are chemical reactions. The solutions will have to be based primarily on the objectives of the records, taking into account their cost and benefits.

Pollutant records in general, and especially the HSR, provide the information needed to determine that all environmental costs incurred in the current accounting period have been included in the annual accounts, thus increasing their reliability and completeness.

Lastly, it cannot be denied that these measures may involve additional costs. If they can mitigate environmental problems, however, it is realistic to assume that the company will benefit in the longer term.

ACCOUNTING AND REPORTING IMPACTS

Environmental problems have a significant impact on annual accounts, an area in which the auditor is directly involved. Annual accounts should properly and fully account for the damage a company causes to the environment during the year, so as to give a fair view of the company's financial position and results. This fair view should also reflect environmental costs incurred in the past but not previously reported. Where necessary, and where quantifiable, the balance sheet should include a provision for the expected cost of cleaning up polluted soil or similar environmental problems. It has to be recognized that quantifying a provision for environmental costs would at first often pose serious practical problems. The user of the annual accounts should be aware that the tolerance allowed for a provision for environmental risks would generally have to be wide. This makes appropriate notes all the more important. Environmental costs are often so great, in fact, that they should be disclosed in the report of the directors. Studies show that this is increasingly the case.

Having to report and account for the financial consequences of environmental damage makes entrepreneurs more than a little concerned about the continuity of their business. Published statements by the Government Prosecutor, recently confirmed by a Ministry of Finance resolution, show that such concern may be unfounded since in certain circumstances the Dutch government will allow companies to repay it for soil decontamination work in instalments. The ministerial resolution will allow some tax relief for environmental costs incurred in the past in that they may be charged evenly to taxable income over a number of years by means of an equalization account.

AUDITING IMPACTS

Environmental problems also have an effect on the tools available for an audit. In co-operation with three large Dutch audit firms, a new tool has been developed: an environmental checklist for annual accounts. The checklist is intended to facilitate risk analyses of environmental hazards and their financial consequences. It can be used in combination with pollutant records and the HSR to determine the completeness of waste flows. Other important sources of information for the auditor include soil decontamination plans drawn up by provincial authorities, industrial documentation and external research reports. If there are no strict standards to measure environmentally hazardous waste, however, the auditor has to depend primarily on reviewing and testing procedures and checking related records on the environmental management system.

Materiality or tolerance is a key item in auditing. The tolerance allowed in an audit of certain substances should be related to their potential impact. Practice has shown that the environmental impact of small quantities of some hazardous substances (chemicals) is many times their own value. In setting the materiality of an audit, the auditor should be thoroughly aware of such dangers.

ENVIRONMENTAL REPORTS AND ENVIRONMENTAL AUDITS

There are various schools of thought at present on the desirability of producing environmental reports for third parties. Many people find compulsory external reporting unacceptable. The problem requires a co-ordinated study drawing on various disciplines, although it should be realized that final decisions will be determined by political considerations.

The verification of environmental reports may be important, especially when the information is intended for use outside the company. The verification should be made by a specially trained environmental auditor rather than a financial auditor. The Limperg Institute's study group has drawn up a profile of a member of this new profession. An environmental auditor should be well versed in the design of accounting systems and internal controls, including the methods and techniques used to measure and verify variables (the basic principles of financial auditing). The financial audit profession can make a meaningful contribution to the training of environmental auditors. The working relationship between the financial and the environmental auditor would be similar to that between the auditor and the actuary in the audit of an insurance company's pension fund.

SUMMARY

The environment is a very relevant topic to the financial audit profession. It has many features in common with every aspect of the auditor's expertise. The financial audit profession can make an important contribution to the training of environmental auditors and to the implementations of environmental audits. Further study in this field is necessary and obviously requires an interdisciplinary approach. The Limperg Institute intends to initiate such a study at an international level.

29

MUNICIPAL ACCOUNTING IN SPAIN

Ferran Termes i Anglés

The 1978 constitution opened up a new era for the State of Spain, bringing to an end 40 years of dictatorship.

The Constitution created a new form of State, called the State of the Autonomies. This is a hybrid, somewhere between a far-reaching federal system and one that is simply decentralized. The new system includes both those communities that had historically laid claim to such autonomy and those that had never even considered the idea.

In terms of public administration, the State of the Autonomies is established on three levels: central administration; autonomous administration; and local administration. The functions of each of these three levels are clearly defined in the Constitution, which guarantees the institutional autonomy of the municipalities and grants them legal status, thus breaking with their traditional position which, in reality, had made them subordinate to the central administration.

The 1978 Constitution also definitively breaks with the centralist model, of French origin, creating an intermediate administrative level with a wide territorial, historical and cultural scope. This is the level of the Autonomous Communities which, in a way, are responsible for the financial and administrative direction of the municipalities in their respective territorial areas.

The areas of municipal competence are very extensive and are defined by the law which establishes the basis on which local authority systems are run.

The areas include:

- security in public places;
- traffic control;

From Public Finance and Accountancy (14 June 1991) pp. 6–7.
Reprinted by permission from the Charted Institute of Public Finance and Accountancy.

- civil protection and fire fighting;
- town planning and discipline, parks, gardens and road repairs;
- historical-artistic heritage;
- public health protection;
- primary health care;
- cemeteries;
- social services;
- water and power supplies, refuse collection, street cleaning operations, collection and treatment of waste products, drainage and sewage systems and the treatment of waste water;
- public transport;
- cultural and sports activities and facilities; and
- the creation, construction and maintenance of educational facilities.

When the nature of the service or the size of the municipality makes it impossible for the municipality to supply the service, it may call for the respective Autonomous Community to exempt it from its obligation. The Autonomous Community will then be responsible for supplying the service.

ACCOUNTING SYSTEM

Up until the 1990 tax year the municipalities were only bound by law to use the classic budgetary accounting system, based on the cash principle.

More specifically, the municipalities were only obliged to keep revenue and expense budgets, a record of no budgetary operations, a treasury book and an equity account. Obviously, in itself, such information does not give a full enough knowledge of the financial position of the municipality nor does it permit costs to be calculated making it impossible to audit the level of performance of the services supplied.

In July 1990, the Spanish Treasury passed a series of provisions relating to the standards and principles of local administration and a General Accounting Plan, with a simplified version for municipalities of less than 5,000 new law established a set of public accounting objectives for municipalities which were now required:

(a) to establish the balance sheets of the local entity, clearly stating the composition changes in any position of its equity;
(b) to determine its economic equity results;
(c) to determine its analytical results, clearly stating the cost and level of performance of the services supplied;
(d) to record the execution of the general budgets of the municipality, providing evidence of budgetary results;
(e) to make it possible to exercise legal, financial and efficiency controls;

(f) to make it possible to keep an inventory of and control over tangible and intangible fixed assets and investments and debts and
(g) to generally supply all the information and data required for decision making, for the preparation of public sector financial accounts and for the statistics required by the Spanish Treasury Department.

The regulations also specify the documents and books that the local corporations should keep, the way certain accounts provided in the plan should operate and the information that should be given to third parties.

It is compulsory for the municipalities of over 5,000 inhabitants to adhere

Table 1 Main accounts in the General Accounting Plan

Group 1. Basic finance
Capital
Results pending application
Capital grants received
Loans/debentures
Loans received from the public sector
Long-term loans received from sources other than the public sector
Long-term guarantees and deposits received
Group 2. Fixed assets
Tangible fixed assets
Intangible fixed assets
Investment in infrastructure and in general use goods
Public sector investments (treasury bonds, etc)
Permanent investments (shares, etc)
Guarantees and deposits made (deposits made by the entity)
Capitalised costs
Depreciation of fixed assets (to receive the annual depreciation charges and accumulate them)
Group 3. Inventories
Group 4. Creditors and debtors
Creditors
Rebates payable
Debtors
Public entities
Accruals and prepayments
Provisions
Group 5. Financial accounts
Loans received and other private sector debts
Other non-budgetary creditors
Guarantees and deposits received
Short-term investments
Guarantees and deposits made
Items pending application
Other non-budgetary debtors
Cash and banks
Bridging accounts
Group 6. Purchases and expenses
Personnel expenses
Interest expense (interest, commissions, etc)
Levies payable by the entity
Third party work and supplies
Social services
Operating grants
Current asset transfers
Capital transfers
Depreciation charges
Group 7. Sales and revenues
Sales
Property and company income
Levies linked to production
Current income and equity taxes
Current asset transfers
Capital taxes
Other earnings
Group 8. Results
Current results for the year
Extraordinary results
Security portfolio results
Modification of duties and levies from prior years
Results for the year
Group 0. Budgetary and memoranda accounts
Current year – Budgetary control
Prior years – Budgetary control
Guarantees
Securities in deposit
Control of receipts and securities.
Collectors.

to the General Accounting Plan from the 1991 tax year onwards, while for the smaller municipalities the requirement is more flexible.

The outline of the General Accounting Plan contains the main accounts listed in Table 1, each of which breaks down into a multitude of sub-accounts, which, for the sake of brevity, we have not included.

CONTROLS

The financial and legal control of the local authorities is performed on two levels: internal control (*intervención*) and external control (through a National Audit Office – *Tribunal de Cuentas* – and seven Regional general auditors).

Interventión is a body of civil servants responsible for the internal control of the municipalities. The training and qualification of these civil servants is the responsibility of the Ministry of Public Administration. Vacancies are filled by way of a direct agreement between the local authorities and the *Interventor*.

The purpose of such supervision is to control all local entity action which gives rise to the recognition or settlement of duties, levies or economic costs and any income or payments that may be made. It also exercises financial and efficiency controls, through audit procedures carried out in accordance with the regulations concerning public sector auditing standards.

The *interventor* issues reports to the municipality.

External control is a function of the National Audit Office and the Regional general auditors. Although the law provides for the co-ordination of the two organisations, to avoid the duplication of the work done, the municipalities are bound to render account to both organisations, even though the Regional general auditors only perform financial, legal and performance controls while the National Audit Office also covers the opening of procedures for cases of legal accounting liability.

QUESTIONS

1 Identify the separate areas of responsibility of the internal control and external control function in municipal accounting in Spain.

30

FINANCIAL STRUCTURE AND BANKRUPTCY RISK IN JAPANESE COMPANIES

Sadahiko Suzuki and Richard W. Wright

INTRODUCTION

As the world's financial markets become more internationalized, the capital markets and corporations of Japan assume an increasingly important role. But financial practices and institutional relationships unique to Japan pose major obstacles to the foreigner's understanding.

Of particular concern to lenders and investors abroad in the extremely high financial leverage of Japanese companies. By measures of financial soundness traditionally used in western countries, risk exposures almost inconceivable elsewhere prevail in Japanese business finance. It is common, for example, for borrowed funds to exceed owners' equity by a multiple of five or six times.[1] Figure 1 illustrates the declining trend of equity ratios (equity/total assets) among listed Japanese companies since the end of World War II. Table 1 contrasts Japanese equity ratios with those of other industrialized nations.[2] Similarly high risk complexions are suggested by other financial statement measures such as interest coverage and cash flow coverage.

The article seeks (1) to interpret to non-Japanese the nature and significance of financial risk in Japanese companies; and (2) to provide empirical evidence on the types of variables that best indicate bankruptcy risk, with particular attention to the relative importance of financial structure versus institutional relationships at financially critical moments.

From Journal of International Business Studies (Spring 1985) pp 97–110.
Reprinted with permission from Journal of International Business Studies.

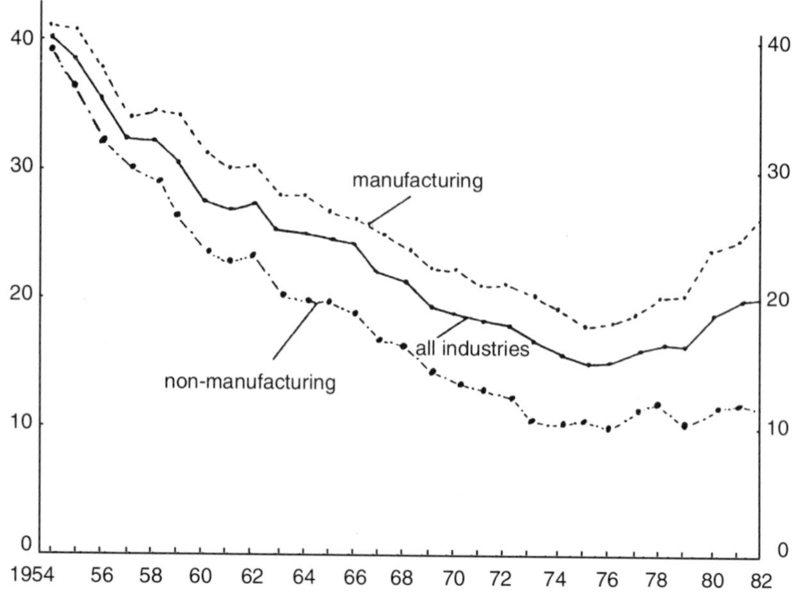

Figure 1 Average equity ratios of major Japanese companies
Source: Ministry of International Trade and Industry, Wakeguni Kigyono Keiei Bunksei (Analysis of Japanese Corporation), 1981.
Note: Equity ratio = Equity ÷ total assets

FINANCIAL STRUCTURE INFLUENCES

Accounting Biases

In part, Japanese equity ratios appear lower than those in other countries because of accounting practices unique to Japan. The most serious abberation is 'hidden assets,' caused by carrying fixed assets and equity at book value rather than at replacement or market values. The problem exists in any country that has experienced rapid inflation without a corresponding revaluation of assets; but the distortions are particularly severe in Japan because of the spectacular increases in real estate values.[3] A case in point was the recent sale of an obsolete factory in Tokyo by a major electronics firm for nearly 150 times its book value.

Equity ratios also appear lower in Japan because of the extensive use of special reserve allowances for retirement, investment losses, exchange gains and losses, etc., to normalize net earnings. Often considered part of owners' equity in other countries, such allowances are recorded as liabilities in Japan. Further distortions in comparative equity ratios result from:

Table 1 Equity ratios by country

Country	*1977*	*1978*
Japan (103 firms average)	21.77%	22.86%
United States (177 firms average)	49.92	49.40
Canada (15 firms average)	46.59	45.13
United Kingdom (38 firms average)	42.05	41.87
West Germany (25 firms average)	28.59	28.92
France (21 firms average)	24.99	26.80
Italy (7 firms average)	22.90	26.31
Netherlands (3 firms average)	40.17	40.18
Belgium (3 firms average)	30.55	30.81
Switzerland (6 firms average)	49.68	50.88
Sweden (11 firms average)	25.69	25.66

Source: Ministry of International Trade and Industry, *Sekui no Kigyo no Keiel Brunseki* (International Comparison of Management), 1980, pp. 84–87.
Note: Weighted averages

different depreciation rules in Japan; the less frequent use of leasing; and different accounting treatments of finance subsidiaries and production payment financing.

Adjusting for such accounting differences will narrow the difference in apparent capital ratios between most Japanese companies and western companies.[4] Even adjusted reports, however, still indicate much riskier financial structures in Japan than elsewhere. Explaining this difference requires an understanding of the financing practices of Japanese companies and of the lending policies of Japanese banks.

Why Companies Borrow So Heavily

A basic feature of Japanese business has been its objective of growth. Particularly in the 1950s and 1960s, Japanese managers believed that massive investment in expanding size and output would contribute to higher cash inflows in the future. But it was difficult for companies seeking to maintain their market share to accumulate sufficient capital out of earnings, even with full retention of profits. Thus, increasing dependence on external funds was inevitable.[5]

In choosing among the various sources of external funds (borrowing, bonds, stocks), tax deductibility of interest favored unquestionably debt financing. But the strong Japanese bias toward debt is not explained sufficiently by taxes, because roughly comparable tax burdens in other countries have not led to a comparable corporate financing decision.

More important, according to financial managers interviewed in the present study, was the unique stock issue system prevalent in Japan during most of the post-war growth period and continuing, to a limited extent, today. Under this system, all stocks were issued at par value (generally Y 50 per share) regardless of market prices. Larger companies were expected to pay a dividend of 10–15 percent of par value to maintain a respectable corporate image. Thus, corporate financial managers seeking low-dividend-burden funds were constrained by the traditional practice of stock issue at par.

Even for those large firms that began, in the 1970s, to issue stocks at or near market value, the explicit cost of equity funds, as viewed by management, remained high. Under a voluntary rule enforced by the major securities companies, issuing companies were required to return all of the premium between par and issue price to the shareholders in the form of free distribution of shares, over a period of five years. These free shares were distributed not only to new shareholders but also to existing shareholders. By increasing the dividend burden in the future, the practice of free distribution of shares negated most of the additional benefit of market-price issues in the long run. The rule discriminated particularly against highly capitalized companies that already had a large number of outstanding shares.

New rules[6] governing stock issues and dividend payments introduced in September 1980, have added new flexibility to equity issues in Japan, and equity ratios in Japanese industry are likely to rise slowly over time.[7] But the historical need of Japanese companies for major external financing, combined with numerous regulations making frequent use of the equity markets difficult and costly, help to explain why Japanese companies have turned largely to the most convenient and abundant source: bank funds.

Why Banks Lend So Much

The desire of Japanese companies to raise vast amounts of funds from borrowed sources is facilitated by the unique lending practices of the commercial banks.[8] The arms-length, competitive principles of North American and European-style banking do not exist in Japan's clannish, cooperative business society. The *zaibatsu* holding companies that controlled large clusters of firms were broken up at the end of World War II; but the largest banks have, in effect, replaced them in their function as leaders of 'groups,' a role that calls for ties and capabilities not ordinarily associated with the concept of commercial banking. Thus, banks in Japan are much more closely involved with their borrowers over the long run than are commercial banks elsewhere.[9] Lending, while ostensibly short term, is rolled over automatically to create long-term financing; banks continue lending in times of financial adversity for a borrower; loans are almost never recalled. The closeness of the lending relationship itself is reinforced by the banks' major holdings of bonds and common stock of the companies to which they lend. It is also common for the banks to send officers directly into the top management of corporate borrowers in financial difficulty.

Thus, commercial bank lending in Japan involves a much deeper and more intimate identification with borrowers than it does elsewhere. Bank officers interviewed in the present study stressed strongly the quality of the borrowing firm's management over such considerations as growth potential and cash flows as influences on their lending policies. Particularly in the case in which a borrowing company belongs to the same group of firms as its main bank, the bank's lending decisions are determined not so much by the financial position of the company itself as by its strategic position and importance to the whole family of firms.

The willingness of the commercial banks to lend very large amounts to corporate borrowers is facilitated by the Bank of Japan, which allows Japanese banks to have exceedingly high loan-out ratios (often in excess of 1:1) through 'overloans.' Confronted during much of the postwar period with a demand for funds which they have not been able to satisfy from their deposits, the commercial banks have had heavy recourse to non-deposit sources of funds, such as the rediscount window of the Bank of Japan and the call money market in which other financial institutions place their surplus funds. The major commercial banks remain in almost constant debt to the central bank.[10] Whereas such a chronic overloan position of commercial banks would seem financially precarious in other countries, the Bank of Japan has made it clear in word and deed that it stands fully behind the banks, and the major commercial banks know that they can rely on the central bank to tide them over any liquidity crisis.

Thus, ultimately, there is the Government of Japan in a highly involved role. As a Brookings Institute study concluded:

> Japan is largely free from the belief that business failures constitute a desirable process because they eliminate the inefficient, at least among large firms. In Japan the firm is regarded as a national asset. Because most firms have received large amounts of development assistance from the government, and because they assume large social functions in lifetime employment, government will do what it can to help a large firm in difficulty, and its instruments of action are many, particularly in the working through commercial banks.[11]

THE NATURE OF FINANCIAL RISK

In the context of these unique interrelationships among companies, banks and government, several observations central to a foreigner's understanding of corporate financial risk in Japan may be stated.

1. *The individual company cannot be viewed realistically as an independent financial entity in Japan as it can in the U.S.*

The intimate relations between companies and banks, and among companies of the same industrial group, enable Japanese firms to safely maintain financial structures that would be almost impossibly risky in an isolated firm. In case of temporary financial adversity, the Japanese company can rely usually on help from other institutions. The lead bank may help directly, and it can help indirectly by arranging loans from other banks. Firms that are customers or suppliers within the group can help by promoting sales of the product, by paying their bills more promptly or by postponing their demands for payment, by discriminatory pricing, or even by providing management assistance. While the Japanese company may be independent in a legal sense, its financial risk situation is more closely akin to a corporate division of a highly diversified conglomerate. The financial strength of the company may be evaluated realistically only in the context of its position in the larger industrial group.[12]

2. Much of what Americans would consider equity risk is borne by the commercial banks in Japan.

Generally, one of the usually numerous banks from which large Japanese corporations borrow is regarded as the 'main' bank. A company entering into a main bank relationship yields an extraordinary amount of power to the bank. The bank, in effect, exercises a tacit veto power over the financial decisions of the firm. It may also inject its executives directly into the senior management of the firm.

In return, the main bank assumes an even greater responsibility than the others with respect to the borrower. The bank, in effect, guarantees the long-term viability of the company by continuing to provide financing in times of adversity or even, in extreme situations, by engineering a merger or takeover by another firm. In the unusual event of a bank-supported firm being forced into default or bankruptcy, other creditors can expect their claims to effectively though not legally outrank those of the main bank. In a notable example, Kojin Corporation went into bankruptcy several years after its main bank relationship with Dai-Ichi Kangyo Bank deteriorated. Nevertheless, since Kojin had borrowed widely while a full main-bank relationship *had* existed, Dai-Ichi Kangyo undertook voluntarily to repay Kojin's other creditors and absorb losses itself, thus fulfilling the implicit obligations of main bank support and avoiding damage to the bank's prestige.

3. The distinction between debt and equity is much less clear in Japan than in the U.S.

Debt in Japan contains many characteristics that foreigners commonly associate with equity: credit, in the form of bank loans, provides the major financial base of the firm; creditors have a flexible-return obligation in that banks allow their corporate customers to defer interest and principal payments and to reduce compensating balances during financial adversity; the time horizon of the creditors' involvement with the company is infinite, as loans are invariably rolled over; and the creditors, especially the main bank, may actively influence management policy by exercising an implicit veto power over financial decisions or by direct participation in the firm's management.

Common stock, on the other hand, possesses many characteristics that foreigners associate with credit: the stockholders provide a relatively small portion of the firm's total financing; they hold a reasonably fixed return obligation, as dividend payout is traditionally a fixed percentage of the par value of the stock and is rarely changed; and the stockholders usually exercise negligible influence on management. It was suggested by one Japanese securities analyst interviewed in the present study that foreigners will get a more realistic picture of a Japanese company's financial position by reversing the labels: calling equity debt, and debt equity. While exaggerated, this suggestion nevertheless underscores the importance of the foreigner understanding that characteristics of debt and equity are far more intermingled in Japan than they are elsewhere.

EMPIRICAL TEST

Conceptual Basis

Early research by Altman and others[13] emphasized the value of accounting information in forecasting defaults. But given the mixed nature of debt and equity claims in Japan, the unique relationships among companies of the same industrial group, and the quasi-equity nature of main-bank lending, bankruptcy risk in large Japanese companies may be much lower than traditional financial measures suggest. Leverage that would appear dangerously high in a western company may, to a large extent, be offset by the implicit support of other companies, of commercial banks and ultimately of the Japanese Government. Financial accounting criteria appropriate for measuring bankruptcy risk in other countries thus, may be much less relevant in Japan.

More recent studies by Stonehill et al., Wright and Suzuki, and Nikkei Business[14] suggest a variety of institutional relationships that may be decisive in determining the long-run viability of Japanese companies. The present study tests the hypothesis that indicators of the firm's social importance and of the strength of its main-bank relationship are more reliable than accounting ratios as measures of bankruptcy risk in financially troubled Japanese companies.

Methodology

Two sets of Japanese companies were identified for analysis in the present study:

Set A consists of 18 firms listed on Japanese stock exchanges that went bankrupt or filed for reorganization during the period 1974–78. The post-1973 oil shock depression period was chosen because it was a time of severe financial difficulty for many Japanese firms, when the nature of bankruptcy risk became clearer than in other periods. The firms *of Set A* comprise a 100-percent sample.

Set B consists of 34 listed firms that experienced financial adversity during the same period, but which received extraordinary rescue financing from private banks. Rescue financing is defined here as consisting of any of the following bank actions, separately or in combination:

- lowering of interest rates below previous or commercially prevailing levels;
- deferment of interest payments;
- deferment of principal payments;
- cancellation of interest and/or principal payments.

Set B consists of companies that, it may reasonably be presumed, would have gone into bankruptcy or reorganization had it not been for the extraordinary bank rescue operations. Although the information is not conclusive, the authors believe that the firms of *Set B* comprise of a near-100-per cent sample.

What characteristics distinguish those financially troubled firms that actually went bankrupt, from those that did not? Regression analysis was performed on the two sets of firms, using the following variables:

A. *Traditional Financial Accounting Measures:*

1 Equity ratio (percent): (share capital + retained earnings) ÷ total assets.
2 Interest coverage (percent): (operating profit + dividends and interest received) ÷ interest paid.
3 Cash flow coverage (percent): (after-tax profit + depreciation — increase in working capital (excluding bank borrowing)) ÷ short-term borrowing and current maturities of long-term debt.

B. *'Social Importance' Measures*

4 Annual sales volume (value): Because of the great reliance of Japanese companies on trade financing with extended terms, collapse of a major Japanese firm may trigger widespread bankruptcies among smaller firms.
5 Number of employees (number): The lifetime employment prevailing in large Japanese companies reduces vastly the mobility of labor; collapse of a major company, therefore, may create severe employee relocation problems.

C. *Strength of Main-Bank Relationship Measures:*

6 Size of main bank's loans to company (value): indicates the magnitude of the main bank's commitment or loss potential.
7 Share of main bank's lending in company's total borrowing (percent): indicates importance of the main-bank relationship.
8 Share of main-bank holdings of company's common stock (percent): indicates importance of the main-bank relationship.
9 Change in ranking of main bank's lending position during prior three years (yes or no): indicates stability of the main bank relationship; change in ranking may signal a deteriorating relationship leading to withdrawal of main-bank support.
10 Existence of main-bank personnel in senior management of the company (yes or no): indicates closeness of the main-bank relationship and commitment of the main bank to the long-term viability of the company; also may indicate more direct access to and careful scrutiny of the company's financial operations and controls by main bank.

Data analysis consisted of applying the Mann–Whitney U-test for differences between two independent groups to variables 1–8; and the Chi-square test to variables 9 and 10. In applying multiple regressions, the latter two were treated as dummy variables with values of 0 (no) or 1 (yes). The dependent variable, Y, was assigned a value of 0 for bankrupt firms and 1 for rescued firms.

RESULTS AND DISCUSSION

Individual Variables

The Mann-Whitney U-test results reveal that *none* of the first three variables, representing traditional accounting ratios, were statistically significant in distinguishing between the two sets of firms, even at the 10 percent confidence level. The results fail to support a hypothesis that the traditional accounting risk measures tested here usefully discriminate between those troubled firms that went bankrupt and those which did not.

Variables 4 and 5, on the other hand, representing measures of the social importance of the firms, were both shown to have a significant ability to distinguish between the two groups of companies – sales volume (variable 4) at the 1 percent level, and number of employees (variable 5) at the 5 percent level. These results support the hypothesis that social importance indicators are significant in identifying bankruptcy risk in Japanese companies.

Of the five variables related to the main-bank relationship, the amount of lending (variable 6) and the proportion of the main bank's holding of common stock (variable 8) were shown by the Mann-Whitney U-test to be significantly at the 1 percent level, while the presence of bank personnel in the company's senior management (variable 10) was found significant at the 1 percent level by chi-square analysis. Stability of the main bank relationship (variable 9), also tested by chi-square, was significant at the 5 percent level. The share of main bank lending in the company's total borrowing (variable 7) was found to be not significant, even at the 10 percent level. Thus, four of the five measures of the main bank relationship were seen to be statistically significant in distinguishing between those financially troubled companies that went bankrupt and those that did not.

Packages of Variables

The results described above indicate the power of individual variables to distinguish between individual firms of the two sample groups. Additional analysis was performed on the distinguishing power of packages of variables. To examine the predictive power of traditional financial statement data, equity ratios (x_1), interest coverages (x_2), and cash coverages (x_3) were combined into a 'financial ratio package.' The results of their multiple regression is as follows:

$$y = 0.653 - \underset{(0.667)}{0.049\,x_1} + \underset{(0.047)}{0.030x_2} - \underset{(0.148)}{0.010x_3} \qquad R^2 = 0.010$$

Figures in parentheses show t-values. The scatter diagram for this analysis is shown as Figure 2. The horizontal axis shows y-values. If the two groups were perfectly separated, y-values for the bankrupt firms would tend toward 0, and those of the rescued firms toward 1. As seen in Figure 2, y-values of both groups scatter around similar values, indicating that the financial ratio package cannot distinguish between the two groups. Application of the Mann-Whitney U-test on the composite y-values fails to show a statistically significant difference between the two groups, even at the 10 percent level.

To examine the power of the social importance indicators, sales volume (x_4) and number of employees (x_5) were combined into a 'social importance package.' The multiple regression for this package is as follows:

The scatter diagram is shown in Figure 3. It is obvious from the diagram that the overlapping of y-values is much less than with the previous package. Differences between the two sets of y-values are shown to be significant at the 1 percent level, both by the Mann-Whitney U-test and by the chi-square test.

Finally, a 'main-bank relation package' was formed, using the size of the main bank's loans to the company (x_6), share of the main bank's lending in the company's total borrowing (x_7), share of the main bank's holdings of the company's common stock (x_8), changes in the ranking of the main

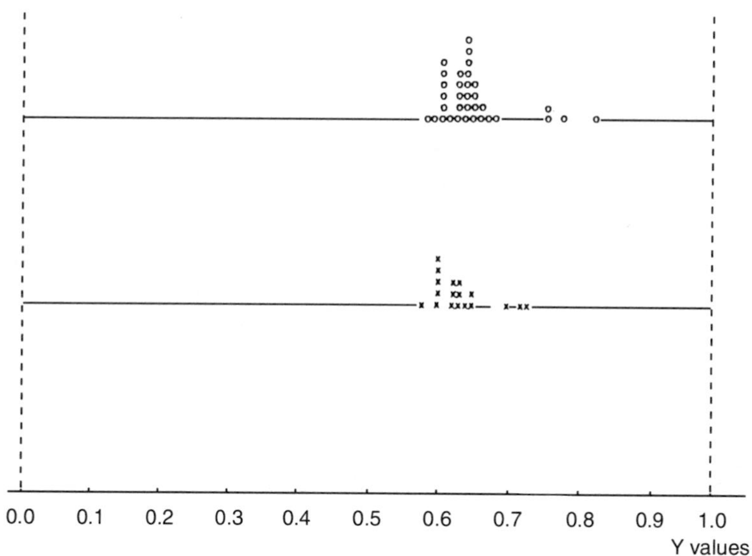

Figure 2 Scatter diagram using financial accounting variables
Note: 0's represent rescued firms, X's represent failed firms

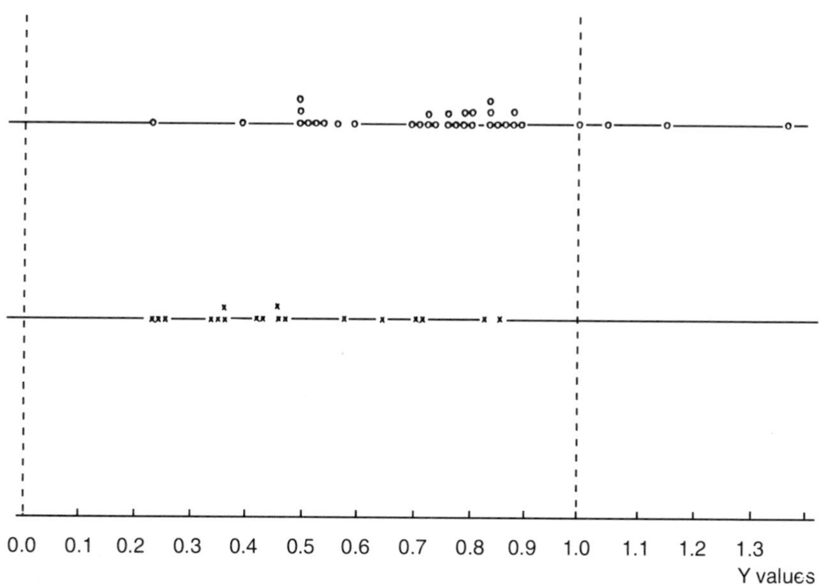

Figure 3 Scatter diagram using social importance variables
Note: 0's represent rescued firms, X's represent failed firms

bank's lending position (x_9), and existence of main-bank personnel in the senior management of the company (x_{10}). The result of the multiple regression is as follows:

$$y = 0.399 + 1.031\,x_4 - 0.047x_7 + 0.061x_8 + 0.170x_9 + 0.187x_{10} \quad R^2 = 0.44$$
$$(2.568) \quad (0.511) \quad (0.505) \quad (1.259) \quad (1.116)$$

The scatter diagram is shown as Figure 4. The distinguishing power of this package appears from the diagram to be similar to that of the social importance package, and clearly much greater than that of the financial accounting ratio package. The differences are shown to be significant at the 1 percent level by both the Mann-Whitney U-test and the chi-square test.

Least-Classification Errors Package

Finally, regression analysis was performed to calculate the 'best fit' package of variables which would minimize the total number of classification errors. With the cut-off point of y-values at 0.5, the following equation produced the minimum error:

$$y = 0.512 + 0.191\,x_4 - 0.550x_5 + 1.231x_6 + 0.034\!-_8 + 0.198x_{10} \quad R^2 = 0.44$$
$$(0.920) \quad (1.146) \quad (2.579) \quad (0.280) \quad (1.170)$$

The best-fit equation retains five of the ten independent variables originally tested. All three of the financial accounting measures (Variables 1, 2 and 3) drop out from the best-fit equation, consistent with the expectations dis-

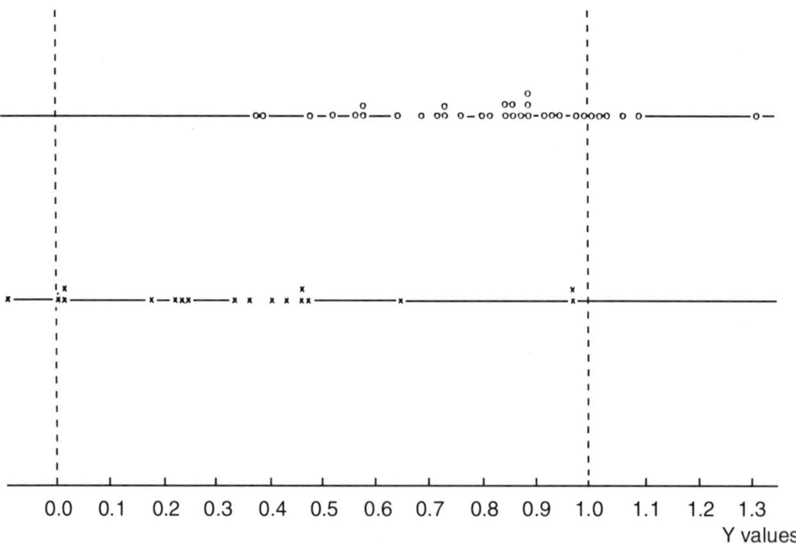

Figure 4 Scatter diagram using main bank relation variables

cussed earlier. A possible explanation for the dropout of Variable 7 (share of the main bank's lending in the company's total borrowing) may be the tendency for the main-bank loans to constitute a smaller proportion of total borrowing in large companies than in small ones, as large companies have transactions with a greater number of banks. The main bank's position may rest more on the ranking of its lending rather than on the proportion of total lending it provides. The dropping of variable 9 (change in the ranking of the main bank's lending position) may be due to the fact that many of the firms that actually went bankrupt (*Set A*) had not experienced such a change during the preceding three years. This least-classification-error formula may be useful in suggesting directions for future research.

SUMMARY AND CONCLUSIONS

This article has explored some of the unique interrelationships among companies, banks and government that characterize the financial environment of Japan. Three conditions were identified as central to a foreigner's understanding of financial risk in Japanese companies: the mixed nature of debt and equity claims; the special relationships among companies of the same industrial group; and the quasi-equity nature of main-bank lending. Given these conditions, bankruptcy risk in large Japanese companies is probably much less than traditional Western accounting measures suggest. The true riskiness of a Japanese company may ultimately be determined more by its social importance and the strength of its institutional relationships than by financial conditions reflected in its accounting statements.[15]

Empirical testing was performed to determine which types of measures most accurately indicate bankruptcy risk in Japan. Independent variables representing traditional financial accounting ratios, the firm's social importance, and the strength of its main-bank relationship were regressed against two sets of financially troubled Japanese firms. The results revealed that the financial accounting variables were not significant in distinguishing between those financially troubled companies which went bankrupt and those that did not. In contrast, both of the social importance measures and three of the five bank relationship measures were shown to be highly significant.

The results suggest that the extraordinary rescue operations performed by Japanese banks may be a significant intervening factor between financial adversity and bankruptcy in Japanese companies. U.S.-style bankruptcy models tend to assume a neutral role of banks: sufficient deterioration in the financial condition of a company may lead directly to bankruptcy. But in Japan, there is a tradition of commercial banks intervening to rescue major corporate borrowers who in other environments might go bankrupt, both to protect their loans and on behalf of the other members of their industrial groups and of Japanese society in general. While traditional indicators such as worsening cash flow, falling profits, or increasing debt may help to identify those Japanese companies heading toward financial difficulty, they are not decisive in predicting which of them will actually go bankrupt. Other measures, reflecting the firm's social importance and the strength of its main-bank relationship, seem at least as important as accounting information in determining which of the financially troubled companies will actually go bankrupt.

NOTES

1 Not all Japanese firms, of course, have low equity ratios. Some companies (e.g., Kyoto Ceramics, Toyota, Taisho Pharmaceuticals), do not have significant borrowings. But these firms are rare and do not represent Japanese companies in general.

2 For more detailed comparative analysis, see Arthur Stonehill, Theo Beckhuisen and Richard Wright, 'Financial Goals and Debt Ratio Determinants: A Survey of Practice in Five Countries,' *Financial Management*, Autumn 1975, pp. 27–41. Also, N. Toy, A. Stonehill, L. Remmers, R., Wright and T. Beckhuisen, 'A Comparative International Study of Growth, Profitability, and Risk as Determinants of Corporate Debt Ratios, in the Manufacturing Sector,' *Journal of Financial and Quantitative Analysis*, November 1974, pp. 875–886.

3 A recent study estimated the average inflation-adjusted value of the total assets of 823 companies listed on the Tokyo Stock Exchange at about 1.4 times their book value. Inflation-adjusted value as a multiple of book value was 1.0 times for inventories, 1.3 times for depreciable assets, and 11.3 times for land, for the period 1965–1978. Keimei Wakasugi, 'Infure de Yugamu Kigyo Zaimu' (Corporate Finance Distorted by Inflation), *Nippon Keizai Shinbun*, August 30, 1980, p. 12.

4 International Business Information, Inc., *Japanese Corporate Finance 1977–1980* (London: The Financial Times Limited, 1977), See Also Masaki Takenka, ed., *Shian Sahiyoka*(Asset Revaluation), November 1974; and Robert J. Ballon, *Financial Reporting in Japanese Companies*, (Tokyo: Sophia University Press, 1972), pp. 183–270.

5 Tachi and Komiya proposed in the early 1960s a 'high economic growth hypothesis,' in which they claimed that high economic growth, combined with 'ready fund availability at banks,' was the major factor behind lower equity ratios in Japan. R. Tachi and R. Komiya, 'Kigyokinu to Keizaischicho' (Corporate Finance and Economic Growth), in *Keizai Seisaku no Riron* (The Theory of Economic Policies), Tokyo: Keiso Shobo, 1964, pp. 258–270. A more recent study by Yamaichi Securities Research Institute also confirmed a high economic growth rate as the major determinant of low equity ratios. If the growth rate had been half the actual rate in 1955–74, equity ratios would have improved to 30–35 percent, depending on assumptions, against the actual average ratio of 18.3 percent. Yamaichi Securities Co., 'Jikonshihon Hiritsu Teika no Genin o Saguru' (Examination of Reasons for a Decline in Equity Ratios), *Shoken Gepo*, August 1976, pp. 4–54.

6 The following is a translated excerpt of the new rules set by underwriting managers of 12 large securities firms effective September 16, 1980:
(a) When issuing stocks at market price, the issuing company must promise

its shareholders to maintain a certain dividend payout ratio for a specific period after the issue of stock, and to distribute to shareholders specified portion of earnings to maintain the promised payout ratio. When the issuing company cannot distribute earnings on the basis of the constant dividend payout formula, it must make a free distribution of stock out of its premiums received at the time of issue (capital surplus), at the end of each accounting period.

(b) The issuing company must publicly announce its formula for the distribution of earnings.

(c) The underwriter(s) must make every effort to ensure, in each accounting period, that the issuing company distributes earnings to shareholders in accordance with the promised formula.

(d) The underwriter(s) must examine past performance of the issuing company with respect to the distribution of earnings following previous issues of stock and convertible debentures.

(e) The underwriter(s) must exercise caution in underwriting issues of stock and convertible debentures, and must delay its underwriting until it judges that the satisfactory amount of earnings can be distributed:

(i) when the issuing company did not in the past observe the promise regarding the distribution of earnings, or

(ii) when there is no effective increase in distribution of earnings as compared with the level at the time of the previous issue of stocks.

7 Although a few large companies have accomplished substantial borrowing reductions, overall debt ratios have shown only slight improvement, 'Japan's Firms Relying Less on Borrowing,' *The Asian Wall Street Journal*, September 17, 1982, p. 1; also 'Japan Firms Turning from Bank Loans,' *The Asian Wall Street Journal*, January 12, 1982, p. 3.

8 Seven trust banks and three long-term credit banks also play an important role in long-term financing. For a discussion of the changing role of foreign commercial banks in Japan, see Neil Osborn, 'How Foreign Banks Took Their Lumps in Japan,' *Institutional Investor*, July 1981, pp. 80–88.

9 Andreas K. Prindl, *Japanese Finance: A Guide to Banking in Japan* (New York: John Wiley & Sons, 1981).

10 For an excellent discussion, see Hugh Patrick and Henry Rosovsky, eds., *Asia's New Giant* (Washington: The Brookings Institution, 1976), especially Chapter 4, 'Banking and Finance,' by Henry C. Wallich and Mable I. Wallich.

11 Patrick and Rosovsky, *Asia's New Giant*, p. 274. This applies mainly to the large companies of Japan. The rate of bankruptcies among smaller Japanese companies has been rising through the 1970s and early '80s.

12 C. D. Elston, 'The Financing of Japanese Industry,' *Bank of England Quarterly Bulletin*, December 1981, pp. 510–518. A detailed analysis of each of Japan's industrial groups is contained in Dodwell Management Consultants, *Japan's Industrial Groups*, published periodically.

13 Edward I. Altman, *Corporate Bankruptcy in America* (Lexington, Mass.: Heath Lexington Books, 1971). See also Kichinosuke Takahasi, et al., 'Zaimushohyo ni Arawareta Tosanakigyo no Tokucho' (Some Financial Statement Characteristics of Failed Companies), *Keio Business Forum*, Vol. 1, No. 1 (April 1979), pp. 40–64; also Keiichi Kubuta, 'Bankruptcy Prediction Model: An Alternative to Altman's Model,' *The Journal of Musashi University*, September 1979, pp. 61–85.

14 A. Stonehill, T. Beckhuisen and R. Wright, 'Financial Goals and Debt Ratio Determinants,' *op. cit.*; R. Wright and S. Suzuki, 'Debt Ratios and the Nature of Financial Risk,' *Keio Business Forum*, No. 20 (Summer 1977), pp. 52–70; 'Ginko ga Kaisha Sasaeru Kaisha' (The Companies Banks Abandon and the Companies Banks Support), *Nikkei Business*, September 12, 1977, pp. 36–45.

15 The practice of rescuing companies for social or institutional reasons is, of course, not unique to Japan. In countries such as Germany, where financial institutions may be simultaneously both creditors and major shareholders, financial structure does not have the same significance as when debt holders and equity holders are completely separate. But the strength of the Japanese banks' rescue efforts is clearly disproportionate to their shareholdings. Unlike Germany, for example, where banks frequently hold controlling shares of their major corporate clients (see, for example, *Der Spiegel*, No. 20, 1981, p. 57), Japanese banks are precluded by law from holding more than 5 percent of the shares of any corporation. Shareholdings by Japanese banks are regarded more as a symbolic indicator of long-term support for their corporate borrowers than as a direct source of influence or control. Thus, the commitment of Japanese banks toward their corporate clients appears to derive much more from their role as major creditors than from their relatively insignificant ownership positions.

QUESTIONS

1 What are the implications of this study for the analysis of Japanese company accounts by western analysis.

Part V

INTERNATIONAL FINANCIAL MARKETS AND INTERNATIONAL FINANCIAL ANALYSIS

In this section we consider some evidence on how accounts are used by the international financial markets.

We have already seen, above, the assertion that different accounting practices in different countries impede the work of the financial analyst. A short paper from the Economist (1992) shows how one firm of analysts estimates the effect of these variations.

Two papers report experiences of trying to cope with diversity of national accounting practices when analysing accounts:

(i) White (1984) explored the proposition that UK and US companies appeared low geared compared to companies from France, Germany and Japan. He found that a large part of the apparent difference was attributable to different bases of accounting.
(ii) In a major comparative study of US, Japanese and Korean companies, Choi, Hino, Min, Nam, Ujiee, and Stonehill (1983) found that it was necessary to explore both accounting and cultural variations to make a meaningful comparison.

Adhikari, Coffman, and Tondkar (1991) report on the practical issues that arise from seeking an international stock market listing.

31

ALL THE WORLD'S A RATIO

The boom in international portfolio investment is stimulating new ways of comparing stockmarkets

Daunting in one country, investors' difficulties in valuing companies multiply abroad. In theory, investors buy equity to have a share in companies' earnings. Companies either pass these on directly in the form of dividends; or, if firms retain earnings to invest in new projects, shareholders take their rewards indirectly in the form of capital gains. The challenge for investors is to judge what firms are really earning.

Even within the accounting rules of one country, companies find plenty of ways to adjust their earnings up or down–which is why both America and Britain have tightened their rules recently. International comparisons are even harder. Untroubled by the threat of takeover, German and Japanese companies tend to understate profits and so escape taxes; British and American firms are sufficiently nervous of their shareholders to prefer the opposite approach. Some recent work by Smithers & Co, a London research boutique, attempts to tackle these distortions.

Andrew Smithers begins this labour with Japan. Despite the recent fall in Tokyo's market, investors are still willing to pay much more for a given stream of Japanese earnings than for the same stream in other big economies: Tokyo's market sells on a price/earnings ratio of 36.7, compared with 25.6 for Wall Street's S&P industrial index and 15.5 for London's FT-A 500 index. The most obvious justification is that Japanese earnings are expected to grow faster than those of other companies, so bringing temporarily high ratios down. Yet the p/e ratios still seem astronomical: the growth in

From The Economist (22 February 1992) p 94.

Japan's corporate earnings, though high, has been less remarkable than the growth of its economy.

Mr Smithers sets out to explain Japan's p/e ratios by adjusting them for the effect of cross-shareholdings. On his reckoning, 45% of the shares in Tokyo's market are beneficially owned by another quoted company. To own the entire market, therefore, an investor needs only to buy 55% of it: Tokyo is really 45% cheaper than its market capitalisation.

This affects Japan's p/e ratios, because the overstatement of the market's price is not matched by an equivalent overstatement of earnings. As in most countries, Japanese companies do not consolidate earnings of subsidiaries of which they own less than 20%. Mr Smithers therefore calculates that Tokyo's true p/e is 57% of the stated one.

This adjustment helps make Japanese p/e ratios comparable with those of other markets. To build on this start, Mr Smithers considers the different accounting procedures by which firms calculate their profits. One big variable is the rate at which capital is depreciated. Many German firms write off their capital quickly, during which time their profits are misleadingly small; subsequently they are artificially inflated. In America and Britain firms tend to mislead in the opposite direction.

To get round these problems, Mr Smithers turns to national accounts. These show rates of capital consumption: for Japan it is around 14.5% of GDP, for America it is 10.5%. These numbers reflect unquoted companies as well as quoted ones; but at least national statisticians are impartial. Besides, national accounts reduce the distortions of inflation. They record the cost of replacing exhausted capital, whereas company accounts amortise the original cost of installing it. Company practice therefore conceals the weakness of firms in high-inflation countries, whose replacement cost of capital rises faster than that of their low-inflation rivals.

Inflation also bedevils international comparison by boosting the value of inventories (stocks). Companies often enter such boosts as profit. Yet the cost of replacing stocks rises too, so these 'profits' are illusory. Since inflation varies across countries, this artificial boost varies as well. But national accounts quantify stock appreciation, so Mr Smithers is able to measure this distortion.

Taking capital depreciation and stock appreciation together, Mr Smithers arrives at a factor by which company earnings should be adjusted to make them comparable from country to country. In Germany no adjustment is needed. In Britain, by contrast, reported profits should be multiplied by a factor of 0.75, because of inventive accountants and a history of inflation.

The last step towards internationally comparable ratios is to reflect economic cycles. Investors naturally pay more for shares at the start of a recovery, when they expect company earnings to grow faster. Mr Smithers adjusts the profits of companies in each market to compensate for this cyclical bias.

The results are summarised in Table 1. They make the discrepancies be-

Table 1 International price/earnings ratios

	Published P/E 18th Feb 1992	*Cyclically adjusted P/E (A)*	*Ratio of true* to published profits (B)*	*Fully adjusted P/Es (A)/(B)*
Japan**	36.7	37.3	1.69‡	22.1
United States†	25.6	20.4	0.77	26.5
Britain††	15.5	14.7	0.75	19.6
France**	11.2	12.2	0.84	14.5
Germany**	15.9	19.1	1.00	19.1

* Calculated from most recent national accounts ** Datastream total market indices † S&P Industrial Index ‡FT-A 500 index ‡Includes the effect of cross-shareholdings
Source: Smithers & Co.

tween market valuations look less alarming: the ratio between the highest and lowest p/e comes down by nearly half. They also make most markets look overvalued. Investors have historically expected total real returns of 6% a year from equities. Since returns, whether derived from dividends or capital gains, stem from earnings, investors should expect earnings per share to be 6% of the share's value too. That implies a p/e of 16.7. On this measure, France is the only big market that looks worth buying.

FUTURE LABOURS

Mr Smithers admits that his work is unfinished. It is not just Japan's market that is inflated by cross-holdings; Germany's is probably 20–25% smaller than it appears to be. German p/e multiples may be less distorted, partly because subsidiaries' earnings are more often consolidated, and partly because Germany's modest dividend payouts are nonetheless more generous than Japan's minuscule ones. The bigger the dividend, the more the double counting of market price that results from cross-shareholdings is matched by double counting of earnings, since dividends boost the parent company's revenues.

As long as the Smithers recalculation is incomplete, most investment managers will carry on happily without him. County Natwest Investment Management, for example, says it prefers history to comparison: the past behaviour of a market illuminates its future more than cross-border accounting. Yet investors are growing more international, markets more intertwined. Increasingly, genuine differences in p/e ratios will be seized upon by arbitragers. There should be plenty of appetite for theories that distinguish genuine differences from accounting ones.

QUESTIONS

1 This article takes an unusual route to demonstrate the lack of uniformity in national accounting practices. Compare the differences identified in this article with those identified by two other approaches.

32

INTERNATIONAL DIFFERENCES IN GEARING

How important are they?

Bob White

INTRODUCTION

It is a continual source of controversy that capital gearing – defined here as the proportion of a company's total assets financed by borrowing – is lower in the United Kingdom than in a number of other countries. It is sometimes blamed for the relative stagnation of industry in the United Kingdom. Some commentators believe that UK companies would choose to borrow more than they do but that they are restricted from doing so by their banks.

H. Lever and G. Edwards, for example, in their series 'Banking on Britain', which was featured in the *Sunday Times* in November and December 1980, believed that the gearing ratio is 'an index to describe and document this hidden dynamic behind Britain's decline'. Other authors have shown similar concern. J. M. Samuels, R. E. V. Groves and C. S. Goddard in their book, Company Finance in Europe, argued in 1975 that higher gearing would benefit UK industry because it would reduce the cost of capital; the presumption was that debt is cheaper than equity. But these authors maintained that to enable companies to have higher gearing ratios banks would need to lend more freely and that companies themselves would have to accept a greater involvement by banks in their affairs.[1]

Certain studies, however, have reached different conclusions. The National Economic Development Office attempted in the mid-1970s to estimate industry's average cost of capital in a number of countries. No relationship was found between reported gearing ratios and these cost-of-capital estimates. As regards the banks being too cautious, the Confedera-

From the National Westminster Bank Quarterly Review (November 1984) pp 14–25.
Reprinted with permission from the National Westminster Bank.

tion of British Industry in its evidence to the Wilson Committee[2] in 1977 argued that most UK companies choose their gearing ratio for themselves; it is not something that is imposed on them from outside. Finally, D. N. Vittas and R. V. Brown writing in 1982 on behalf of the banks underlined the measurement problems that exist when gearing ratios are compared internationally.[3] The same authors also questioned the relationship between economic growth and reported gearing in the 1970s in the world's major economies.

The objective of this article, prompted by these arguments, is to evaluate the variations in capital gearing that exist between France, West Germany, Japan, the United Kingdom and the United States. But first the measurement problems involved in making the international comparisons are examined since these act to exaggerate the true differences.

MEASUREMENT PROBLEMS

Table 1 shows capital gearing ratios which have been estimated from the balance sheets of non-financial companies in the five countries being considered. Some of the more obvious measurement problems which can occur when comparing these ratios internationally are overcome in this Table. Provisions, for example, are counted as equity. Certain provisions – such as those for deferred taxation – may be more genuinely viewed as liabilities than others. But for comparative purposes, adopting this approach avoids inconsistencies caused by differences between countries in the extent to which provisions for different purposes are made. Japanese companies, in particular, are allowed to deduct from taxable earnings a large number of reserves for special purposes such as inventory price fluctuations, doubtful receivables, development costs and so on. There is an incentive for Japanese companies to make these provisions since they reduce the corporate tax burden. The effect of this, since they tend generally to be recorded as long-term liabilities, is to understate the true equity of Japanese companies.

Table 1 also adjusts for the fact that official German accounts add the depreciation reserves of companies to liabilities instead of deducting them from assets. Gearing in Germany without this correction and leaving provisions as a liability would be about 80 per cent. Finally, Table 1 includes all forms of borrowing, including trade credit. This acknowledges the substitutability of different classes and maturities of debt. By contrast, some studies of gearing have only included long-term debt in the numerator of the ratio. However, this raises definitional problems as regards what constitutes short- and long-term debt. Definitions vary substantially between countries. Moreover, debt which is technically short-term is often in practice used to finance long-term projects.

Unfortunately, there are still a number of remaining inconsistencies in

Table 1 Capital gearing ratios of companies calculated from reported data[1]

	1970	*1975*	*1980*	*1981*
France	65	70	70	72
Germany	63	63	64	65
Japan	84	85	84	83
United Kingdom	52	51	49	49
United States	44	37	37	38

Note: [1] Total borrowing as a percentage of total assets.
Source: OECD, 'Non-financial Enterprises Financial Statements', *Financial Statistics Part 3.*

Table 1. For France, Germany and Japan, the accounts from which the gearing ratios are calculated are not consolidated for groups of companies. Therefore reported gearing in these countries is inflated by intercompany indebtedness by a greater amount than in the United Kingdom and the United States where consolidated accounts are used. And the ratios obscure distributional patterns of gearing between companies in different countries. In the United States and United Kingdom small companies have much higher gearing relative to large ones. In the United Kingdom, the gearing ratio of small firms is approaching 80 per cent (according to the HMSO 'Business Monitor MA3 – Company Finance', Fourteenth issue, 1983). The differences in gearing ratios in Table 1 may also be influenced by the varying degrees of public ownership of industry between the countries concerned.

Much more significant than these problems, however, is that published balance sheets normally understate the underlying value of companies and therefore overstate the gearing ratios calculated from them. Although this is a universal problem, it is more serious in some countries than in others. In France and the United Kingdom the problem is less acute because land and buildings are periodically revalued. But in Japan, Germany and the United States, all assets are valued on the basis of historical costs.

Another difficulty with Table 1 is that assets which are financed through leasing contracts are not normally capitalized in company balance sheets. The only exception to this is in the United States where capitalization of finance leases is required. UK companies are to be treated in the same way under the new accounting standard SSAP21. But at present their reported gearing ratios remain misleading. The proportion of total UK corporate investment financed by this method has been around 9 per cent in recent years, twice as much as in Japan and France and nine times the figure for Germany.

Leasing is an alternative to conventional borrowing and has many of the same benefits. Lessors can take advantage of capital allowances against corporation tax when they invest in assets which they then lease out. In the United Kingdom over 80 per cent of this tax saving is generally reckoned to have been passed on to the lessee in recent years. Moreover, the overall tax benefit from leasing has been higher in the United Kingdom than in other countries because of the unusually generous capital allowances available against corporation tax. This has been very important to the many UK companies which have accumulated an overhang of tax allowances which they cannot use.

Finally, the gearing ratios reported in Table I are swollen to varying degrees by companies acting, in effect, as financial intermediaries especially in providing and receiving trade credit. Japanese companies, for examples, have a particularly high level of trade creditor and debtor balances. One way of adjusting for this difficulty would be to deduct trade creditors from both the numerator and the denominator of the gearing ratio. But, as explained earlier, equally misleading data could result by stripping out one form of liability which is to a large extent substitutable for another. The impact on reported gearing ratios of companies acting as financial intermediaries can be judged from Table II. It shows the proportion of total company assets in each country accounted for by financial assets. Comparing this with Table I it can be seen that the countries with relatively high reported gearing ratios are, as might be expected, also those with a higher reported proportion of financial assets to total assets.

All these arguments suggest that variations between countries in gearing ratios calculated from reported company balance sheets are significantly greater than the true effective gearing. This conclusion is borne out by several studies which have recalculated the gearing ratios of companies in Japan and the United States, applying more realistic values either by using stockmarket valuations or by making direct estimations.[4] Most studies suggest that, in reality, Japanese gearing ratios should be, at most, between 60 and 70 per cent in Table I and that the US ones are nearer to 30 per cent. So although the range of gearing over the five countries concerned is almost 50 percentage points in Table I, the true range is nearer to 35, at a conservative guess, with the United Kingdom somewhere in the middle. And the difference in reported gearing between Germany and the United Kingdom is almost certainly even less in reality than is shown in Table I as UK companies use more finance leasing than German companies and periodically revalue some of their assets while German

Table 2 Companies' financial assets as a percentage of their total assets

	1970	*1975*	*1980*	*1981*
France	46	44	47	48
Germany	38	39	42	42
Japan	59	58	58	58
United Kingdom	34	33	35	36
United States	30	27	27	26

Source: OECD, 'Non-financial Enterprises Financial Statements', *Financial Statistics Part 3*.

companies do not. For this latter reason, effective gearing in Japan and France is probably also similar.

UNDERDEVELOPED EQUITY MARKETS

Having examined these measurement problems, we now assess the significance of the remaining differences in gearing between the countries being considered. Where there is a choice between alternative types of company finance this involves evaluating the major benefits and costs of gearing from the point of view of companies in each of the countries concerned. However, this approach is less useful when applied to countries with poorly developed equity markets in which companies may find it very difficult or even impossible to issue shares on a significant scale. In these circumstances, relatively high gearing may be the only way companies can obtain the finance they require. This has tended to be the case in France, Germany and Japan which all have bank-oriented financial systems.

Governments in Japan and France, by providing incentives, have deliberately harnessed the banking system as the major provider of company finance. They have thereby maintained a greater control over resource allocation and industrial expansion because of the close dialogue that exists between banks and governments in these countries. In Germany, the dominance of the banks emerged due to gaps in the provision of equity finance. Now banks in Germany have a considerable influence over the way companies are financed because of their entrenched position.

In the United Kingdom and the United States, equity as well as loan markets are well developed. There is therefore more choice available to companies as to how they finance themselves. Evaluating whether gearing is too low in these countries then involves judging how close it seems to be to the optimum in terms of the benefits and costs and not how it compares with other countries. The major factors, which may influence this optimum in the countries we are considering, are discussed below.

CONCENTRATION OF OWNERSHIP AND CONTROL

One advantage in borrowing is that it allows companies to raise funds without diluting their ownership and control by issuing shares to outsiders. However, the impact of this advantage is probably weaker in countries like the United States and the United Kingdom where equity is a more common type of finance and therefore where ownership is already fairly widely dispersed. In bank-oriented countries ownership of companies tends to be more highly concentrated, even among larger enterprises. It is likely that the impact of dilution from new share issues is given more consideration by companies in these countries when financing decisions are being made.

INFLATION

Another influence often considered important to the company's gearing decision is inflation. This is because inflation causes the real value of a sum borrowed to diminish over time and because it can reduce the real rate of interest paid on loans. If the burden of debt is eased in this way it may encourage companies to have higher gearing levels but the effect on the financial policies of the company is by no means clear-cut. If inflation is fully anticipated by the lender then, it is incorporated into the rate of interest on the loan. In this case inflation may be harmful to firms with high gearing. A premium for inflation on interest rates means that a term loan has, in effect, to be paid off more quickly than would have been the case if there had been no inflation. This has an adverse effect on company cash flow especially when inflation is high. Looking at the five countries being considered, there does not appear to be any obvious link between their inflation and gearing ratios. However, inflation in the United Kingdom – which has been higher during the 1970s than in any of the other countries – may have tended to lessen the attractiveness of gearing.

TAX SAVINGS

One of the major benefits attributed to gearing is that it can reduce the tax burden on companies because interest payments on debt are deductible against corporation tax. However, this benefit varies according to the nature of the tax system in operation. In all of the countries we are considering, except the United States, some of the corporation tax paid by companies is offset, or imputed, against the shareholder's own income tax liability on their dividends. Under an imputation system therefore, tax savings from gearing occur only in so far as corporation tax imposes a burden on profits over and above the burden of income tax. This depends, on the degree of imputation allowed and, since there is no tax offset to shareholders in respect of retained earnings, on company dividend policy. Under a classical system of corporation tax, as in the case of the United States, no imputation is allowed, so the corporation tax savings from gearing are less ambiguous.

The beneficial effect of the deductibility of interest payments against corporation tax under either system is diminished, or even reversed, if lenders are subject to high marginal rates of income tax. Providing investors in different income tax brackets have a degree of choice between types of investment, some investor segmentation by tax bracket should develop, taxpayers subject to high marginal rates tending to prefer equity, others preferring debt. But this effect will be complicated by the desire of investors in all tax brackets to diversify their investments.

Finally, the use of gearing as a tax saving device is limited by the taxable capacity of companies. Taxable capacity is restricted by levels of company profitability and the extent of other deductions allowable for corporation tax purposes, such as capital allowances. Companies that have exhausted their taxable capacity derive no tax benefit from increasing their gearing. Given the uncertain nature of future profitability, the risk of tax exhaustion also therefore tends to influence the company's gearing decision.

One way of putting a value on the further tax savings available to companies from higher gearing in each of the countries being considered is to measure the effective rate at which companies pay 'mainstream' corporation tax. This is the total corporation tax paid by companies minus any tax credits imputed against the shareholders' tax liability on their dividends. However, it is to be stressed that this is very much a maximum figure of the tax savings available from higher gearing in each country. In reality, the savings could be less depending on the marginal rates of tax being paid by lenders. Moreover, under an imputation system, companies can also reduce their mainstream corporation tax by increasing their dividend pay-out ratio.

A recent study by the Institute for Fiscal Studies measured effective mainstream corporation tax rates since 1965 for the countries that we are considering.[5] These are given in Table III. The table shows that the maximum tax savings available from additional gearing in countries with relatively low gearing ratios, such as the United States and the United Kingdom, are not necessarily correspondingly higher than those available in countries with reportedly high gearing. In 1980, UK companies had the least to gain of all, in terms of mainstream corporation tax savings, by refinancing their assets with a higher gearing ratio, in spite of their gearing ratios being low by comparison. In the United States, even though rates of mainstream corporation tax were higher in most years than in the other countries, an increase in the gearing ratio by say 20 percentage points would have reduced this rate virtually to zero. Effective gearing in the United States would still then only have been around the ratio prevailing in Germany.

Table 3 Effective average rates of mainstream corporation tax[1]

	1965	*1970*	*1975*	*1980*
France	6.4	8.1	8.6	10.5
Germany	9.0	7.3	7.3	9.7
Japan	9.3	10.7	12.6	17.8
United Kingdom	10.7	19.2	10.1	9.2
United States	16.6	20.3	17.5	17.8

Note: [1] Mainstream corporation tax as a percentage of the gross operating surplus of companies on a national accounts basis (Certain additional taxes on corporations have been included such as local taxes in Germany and the US Federal minimum tax.)
Source: J Kay and J Sen, 'The Comparative Burden of Business Taxation', *Institute for Fiscal Studies, Working Paper 45*, 1983.

These results reflect the way the impact of other tax allowances and imputation vary between countries as well as the different levels of company profitability. Statutory rates of corporation tax in the countries concerned have, in fact, been reasonably similar. As far as the United Kingdom is concerned, since the early 1970s the effective average rate of mainstream corporation tax has fallen substantially because of the reliefs and allowances against tax that were introduced during that period together with the introduction of imputation. Until the March 1984 budget, when extensive changes to UK corporation tax were announced, the main ones were a 100 per cent offset in the first year on plant and machinery, 75 per cent on the cost of constructing industrial buildings and full relief for increases in stock values caused by inflation. Not only have these allowances been higher in the United Kingdom than in the other countries being considered, but the ability of companies to offset tax losses (incurred when profits have been insufficient to absorb fully any allowances available) against profits earned in past and future years is also more generous in the United Kingdom, though the United States is fairly liberal in this regard as well.

The impact of these tax allowances in the United Kingdom has meant that the problem for a growing number of companies has not been one of how to reduce their tax burden but one of how to take full advantage of the available allowances. The 1982 Green Paper on UK corporation tax estimated this to be the case for 60 per cent of companies. It reckoned the tax overhang (unused tax allowances) of UK companies to be around £30 billion and to be growing annually by some £5 billion. Following the March 1984 budget, the major UK corporation tax allowances responsible for this situation are now being phased out. But it is unlikely that this will make gearing any more attractive to UK companies. The statutory rate of corporation tax is also being reduced, eventually to 35 per cent. Since basic income tax rates seem likely to remain at about 30 per cent, the high degree of imputation will ensure that the tax benefits from gearing remain small.

THE COST-OF-CAPITAL

Finally, gearing is thought to benefit companies because loans, having a prior claim over a company's assets, can, up to a point, be raised more cheaply than equity irrespective of any tax advantage. Although higher gearing makes shareholders' returns more risky, this may not at first be reflected in a fully compensating higher required return on equity because of the different levels of willingness to take risks among investors. The company is catering for investors of different tastes and by so doing is reducing the cost of capital. However, there are severe limitations to this argument because of the problems of bankruptcy and agency costs.

BANKRUPTCY

The prior claim which creditors have on the company extends to the possibility of the company being liquidated if it cannot honour its debt commitments as a going concern. Liquidation is costly to shareholders. There are legal and administrative expenses and assets tend to be sold-off at discounted prices. As gearing increases, so does the risk that liquidation will occur. Moreover, because liquidation costs are a charge on the company's assets, they affect the degree to which those assets can provide security. Therefore they influence the terms on which loans are supplied. As an alternative to liquidation, in most countries insolvency laws provide to a greater or lesser extent for companies to be reorganized to continue in business on a sounder footing. However, since re-organization in many cases can lead to the value of creditors' claims on the company being reduced, this is a major concern of lenders and also has to be taken into account when loan terms are first agreed.

Finally, the risk of bankruptcy even if it does not eventually occur, usually affects adversely a company's performance and its own share rating. This makes it difficult for the company to strengthen its position whether by undertaking new investment or by raising equity in order to repay debt.

It is the problem of bankruptcy which makes the ratio of interest payments on a company's borrowing to its gross earnings, known as the income gearing ratio, a major influence on capital gearing decisions and on assessments of credit risk by lenders. Income gearing varies from country to country not simply because of variations in capital gearing but due to differences in interest rates and profitability. Some have argued, for example, that companies in other European countries have been able, in the past, to borrow more than those in the United Kingdom because they have been more profitable and because they have had more access to subsidized and guaranteed loans.[6] In other words, the pressure on income gearing for a given level of capital gearing has been less than in the United Kingdom. And it was income gearing on which the CBI placed a particular emphasis as a determinant of UK industry's choice of capital gearing in its evidence to the Wilson Committee, mentioned earlier.

AGENCY COSTS

The cost-of-capital advantage to gearing is further weakened by the fact that, in spite of their prior claim over the company, lenders are at a disadvantage because of the fundamental conflict of interest that exists between them and the shareholders. And the prime responsibility of company management is to shareholders, not to creditors. In addition to this moral hazard there is the prospect of the company unwittingly conducting its business in a way which could damage the possibility of the loan contract being honoured.

Insolvency law can only provide limited protection for the lender against these risks. Therefore they have to be taken into account when the cost of a loan is negotiated. Lenders may, in addition, attempt to monitor the company or foster closer relations with it. But this must also be paid for by the company. All these costs are referred to in academic literature as agency costs. This is because the company in many senses is acting as an agent for the lender. It takes decisions which affect the lender's welfare. Agency costs are incurred both to help ensure that this agency relationship works properly and to compensate for the fact that it may not.

It should be emphasized that agency costs are not peculiar to loan finance. They are also relevant when companies issue shares to investors who have no control over the business except their vote. Shareholders not directly involved in the day-to-day running of their companies face the risk that management may not act in their best interest either. This risk, or the cost of monitoring management in order to avoid it, will similarly be reflected in the minimum return required by shareholders. The agency costs of equity are therefore relevant to the gearing decision as well.

EVALUATING AGENCY COSTS IN DIFFERENT COUNTRIES

In the United States and United Kingdom, where markets are well-developed in both equity and loan finance, it is reasonable to suppose that the agency costs of equity are lower than those of debt, given the responsibility of company management to its shareholders. In France, Germany and Japan, on the other hand, where equity markets are poorly developed, the agency costs of equity are almost certainly higher than those in the United Kingdom and the United States. Disclosure requirements in the Japanese equity market are particularly poor. But the machinery of communication that exists in the US and UK equity markets are lacking in all three of the bank-oriented economies we are concerned with. The higher agency costs associated with equity in these countries are therefore likely to enhance the cost-of-capital advantage of gearing.

Reinforcing this tendency is the fact that in France, Germany and Japan, because of their bank orientation, relations between banks and industry are particularly close. Lead-banks co-ordinating all the financial needs of companies are a common feature in all three countries. In France, banks also employ industrial experts and in Germany they have supervisory company board seats. In Germany and Japan staff exchanges occur between banks and industry. Banks' relations with industry in Japan are further enhanced by the important role played by banks in the industrial groupings.[7]

These close bank-company relations in France, Germany and Japan have partly developed out of necessity because bank borrowing is so prominent.

They have evolved in response to companies facing up to the agency costs associated with high gearing. Although there is a cost to sustaining such relationships, now that their tradition is firmly established and the machinery and techniques highly developed, the agency costs of debt are probably lower in these countries than in the United Kingdom and the United States where borrowing has traditionally been a more of a secondary source of industrial finance.

One might reasonably ask why the agency costs of borrowing in the United Kingdom cannot also be lower through closer bank-company relations. Even though it has been argued that such relations have received a greater stimulus for development in bank-oriented economies, does that rule out initiatives for closer relations in the United Kingdom? Samuels, Groves and Goddard, it will be remembered, argued that UK companies would not only get the cost-of-capital advantages of gearing if companies allowed banks a greater involvement in their affairs.

The greater the involvement in recent years by UK banks in the provision of medium- and long-term company finance, partly resulting from the decline of the corporate bond market in the 1970s, has in fact spurred the development of closer bank-company relations. This has allowed lending to be extended on better terms than would otherwise have been the case. But involvement by UK banks in company affairs has not developed to the same extent as in the bank-oriented systems, largely perhaps because of the absence of lead-banks. Intense competition among banks in the United Kingdom – with the benefits this undoubtedly offers to companies – seems to militate against lead banking. Moreover, because the benefits of gearing do not seem as large in the United Kingdom as in France, Germany and Japan, the willingness by companies to enter into closer relations with their banks is probably less.

It should finally be emphasized that the cost of gearing in terms of more volatile earnings to shareholders and the risk of insolvency has stimulated much of the well-documented encouragement that is currently being given in France, Germany and Japan for a greater use of equity finance by companies in these countries. Closer relations between banks and industry have not therefore stemmed the perceived need for more efficient markets in risk capital in bank-oriented economies.

CONCLUSIONS

The following conclusions may be drawn from the above assessment of international differences in gearing:

- Due to measurement problems, effective differences in gearing ratios between the five countries which have been considered are much smaller than one is led to believe from looking at reported data.

- Gearing ratios in France, Germany and Japan are heavily circumscribed. Underdeveloped equity markets mean that relatively high gearing is often the only way companies can obtain the finance they require in these countries.
- In the United States and the United Kingdom, notorious for their relatively low reported gearing ratios, alternatives to borrowing are much more readily available. Companies in these countries are therefore more able to choose between alternative types of finance according to their relative benefits and costs without this placing a constraint on their overall funding.
- Having evaluated the benefits and costs of gearing as they apply in the countries under consideration, it seems that concern expressed in certain quarters over relatively low gearing in the United Kingdom and the United States is unfounded. The gearing ratios in these countries seems closer to an optimum which balances out these benefits and costs.

NOTES

1 Similar arguments were also advanced by Yao-Su Hu, 'National Attitudes and the Financing of Industry', published by Political and Economic Planning in 1975.

2 See 'Evidence on the Financing of Industry and Trade' produced by the *Committee to Review the Functioning of Financial Institutions* (Wilson Committee) Vol 2, HMSO, 1977.

3 D. N. Vittas and R. V. Brown, 'Bank Lending and Industrial (Investment – A Response to Recent Criticisms:', Banking Information Service, March 1982.

4 For Japan, they include an official Japanese survey in the 1960s, another by the Yamaichi Securities Company in 1974 and a paper by I. Kuroda and Y. Oritani, 'A Reexamination of the Unique Features of Japan's Corporate Financial Structure', *Japanese Economic Studies*, Vol. 8, no. 4., Summer 1980 which covered US companies as well. Gearing ratios of US companies were re-estimated also by R. H. Gordon and B. G. Malkiel, 'Corporation Finance', in Aaron and Pechman (Eds), *How Taxes Affect Economic Behaviour*, Brookings Institution, 1981.

5 J. Kay and J. Sen. 'The Comparative Burden of Business Taxation', *Institute for Fiscal Studies, Working Paper 45*, 1983.

6 This point, for example, was made in a report by Finance for Industry, 'The Capital Structure of Industry in Europe,' 1981.

7 An examination of banks' relations with industry in France, Germany and Japan has recently been carried out by D. N. Vittas, 'Banks' Relations with Industry', CLCB Research Group, January 1983, unpublished.

ACKNOWLEDGEMENT

This article has benefited from discussions within the banking system and elsewhere for which the author is grateful. In particular the author wishes to thank Paul Tillett, Dimitri Vittas and David Gowland for their helpful comments.

QUESTIONS

1 Analyse:

(a) The variations in national accounting practice that gave rise to a misleading picture of gearing levels.

(b) The other varying factors in national cultural and economic patterns that also made such comparisons misleading.

33

ANALYZING FOREIGN FINANCIAL STATEMENTS

The use and misuse of international ratio analysis

Frederick D. S. Choi, Hisaaki Hino, Sang Kee Min, Sang Oh Nam, Junichi Ujiie, and Arthur I. Stonehill

INTRODUCTION

Since the removal of the interest equalization tax in 1974, the U.S. domestic long-term securities market once again presents a viable alternative to foreign firms who wish to sell dollar-denominated securities abroad. At the same time, U.S. investors have become increasingly aware of the potential benefits of holding internationally diversified portfolios of securities.[1] Nevertheless, capital market barriers in the U.S. and other international markets prevent as free an international flow of portfolio investment as might be desirable from a welfare-theoretic viewpoint.[2] Within the U.S. domestic securities market, foreign firms perceive several major hurdles that can be surmounted only with considerable expense and elapsed time. Notwithstanding foreign exchange risk, SEC regulations, and, to a much lesser extent, stock exchange listing requirements, impose significant barriers.[3] Even if foreign firms can live with these regulatory barriers, they face an investor population that is relatively unsophisticated when it comes to interpreting foreign financial statements. Financial ratios, which may be appropriate measures of financial risk (leverage and liquidity), efficiency, and profitability for U.S. firms, are often misused when applied to foreign firms,[4] partly because of explainable differences in accounting principles. A more serious problem, however, is that even when ratios are based on

From Journal of International Business Studies (Spring/Summer 1983) pp 113–131.

U.S. GAAP they may be misinterpreted because the investor does not understand a particular foreign environment that influences all financial ratios in that environment.

In a previous study,[5] in-depth interviews with industrial corporations, professional accounting firms, securities firms, and governmental agencies were undertaken to elicit perceived U.S. SEC and stock exchange barriers to foreign borrowers. These perceptions were then compared to the reality of regulatory barriers discerned from official SEC, NYSE, and ASE news releases, official documents, internal memoranda, public addresses, and conference proceedings. Findings indicate that many of the perceived stock exchange listing and SEC disclosure barriers are myths because of inaccurate perceptions or accommodations contained in recent modifications of SEC registration requirements.

The purpose of this paper is to analyze the problem of misuse of international ratio analysis with the hope that investors, securities analysts, and regulatory authorities will become more aware of the pitfalls. With a better understanding of foreign accounting and environmental differences, the U.S. securities market could provide investors with an increased supply of investment grade foreign securities for purposes of international portfolio diversification. In return, foreign firms should be able to lower their cost of capital through the greater availability of long-term funds in the U.S. domestic market, a supply which far exceeds that available if these firms were limited to using their home capital markets supplemented by the Eurobond market. In addition, many foreign multinational firms are forced by exchange restrictions at home to finance their worldwide activities in capital markets and foreign currencies outside their home markets, whether or not that strategy changes their cost of capital.[6] Apart from financial considerations, foreign firms are often motivated to sell, or at least list, securities in the U.S. in order to enhance corporate visibility and product identification in the U.S. market.[7]

Despite perceived regulatory, accounting, and investor-understanding barriers, several foreign firms have indeed registered their securities with the SEC, sold securities to U.S. investors through a public offering, and listed their securities on one of the major stock exchanges.[8] During 1980, for example, there were 36 foreign firms listed on the New York Stock Exchange, representing about 3 percent of the total number of firms listed. Of these, however, only 14 were firms domiciled outside North America; and of these 5 were from Great Britain, 3 from the Netherlands, 4 from Japan, and 1 each from South Africa and the Philippines. Only 8 foreign firms domiciled outside North America were listed on the American Stock Exchange. Of these, 4 were from the Philippines, 3 from Israel, and 1 from South Africa. An additional 53 foreign firms were being traded over-the-counter in ADR form with a NASDAQ listing. None of these had gone through the full SEC registration process and therefore were not eligible to sell new securities or list on an organized exchange in the U.S.

METHODOLOGY

Although the problems of SEC disclosure requirements and stock exchange listing requirements probably affect most foreign firms in a similar manner, the problem of misinterpretation of the risk and return characteristics of foreign industrial firms varies according to their country of origin. For example, financial reporting and disclosure practices in Canadian and British firms are similar enough to corresponding U.S. practices to suggest that misinterpretation on those counts is generally minor.[9] By contrast, financial reporting and disclosure practices in many nonwestern and developing countries are so different from U.S. practices that misinterpretation is highly likely.[9] Because it would be an immense task to identify the reporting and disclosure barriers faced by potential capital-seekers from every country, the authors have chosen initially to research in depth only the problems faced by a representative sample of Japanese and Korean firms which would be qualified a priori to sell or list securities in the U.S.[10, 11] The accounting and interpretation barriers faced by these sample firms are representative of the types of problems faced by firms domiciled outside countries in which accounting principles and financial ratio norms are similar to those of the U.S. system (for example: Great Britain, Canada, and the Philippines).

The representative sample of 10 Japanese and 8 Korean firms was studied through a combination of personal visits on site in Japan and Korea during 1978–1979, and by financial statement analysis based on data for the period 1976–1978. Appendix A identifies the sample firms and their U.S. counterparts for comparison purposes. Appendix B identifies the firms and organizations that were visited and interviewed on site.

In order to investigate possible misinterpretation by the U.S. investment community, the unadjusted financial statements of the 18 Japanese and Korean sample firms were subjected to a rigorous financial ratio analysis. The objective was to compare their accounting-based liquidity, leverage, efficiency, and profitability ratios during the period 1976–1978 with a sample of matched U.S. firms. Appendix C contains an explanation of the ratios employed.[12; 13]

An attempt to restate the unadjusted Japanese and Korean financial statements to U.S. GAAP in hopes of discerning the degree to which differences in ratios might be explained by differences in accounting principles was only partially successful. Nevertheless, significant differences between Japanese, Korean, and U.S. financial ratios remained despite these adjustments. The authors therefore investigated those environmental considerations, other than accounting, that might explain the observed differences.

INTERNATIONAL RATIO ANALYSIS

An initial comparison of the aggregate financial ratios of manufacturing enterprises in Japan and Korea with those in the U.S. reveals striking differences. As can be seen in Table 1 (top section), Japanese and Korean companies generally appear less liquid, solvent, efficient, or profitable than their U.S. counterparts. An analysis of industries likely to seek U.S. financing reveals similar ratio patterns (Table 1); however, there are some exceptions, such as, inventory turnover and return on equity ratios in the chemical and transportation industries, respectively.

To minimize the effects of industry, size, and other extraneous influences on the ratio differences observed, the authors examined the unadjusted financial ratios of the sample of Japanese and Korean enterprises, which were previously deemed most inclined to raise funds in the U.S. domestic capital market.[14] Their risk and return ratios were compared with a sample of matched U.S. companies, the results of which are disclosed in Tables 2 and 3.[15]

For each comparison, absolute paired-ratio differences are followed by percentage differences. Bracketed entries indicate that the foreign ratios in question were greater than comparable U.S. ratios, and conversely. Because of small sample sizes, several of the observed ratio differences (no dagger-†) were not statistically significant (t-test); however, with the exception of the efficiency ratios, most ratio differences observed were consistent with the initial comparisons (Table 1).

While sampled Japanese and Korean companies again appear more risky and less profitable than their U.S. counterparts, ratios of the 2 former groups are based on foreign as opposed to U.S. accounting principles. To minimize the apples and oranges problem, an attempt was made to conform Japanese and Korean financial statements to U.S. GAAP. No significant difficulties were encountered in the case of Japan. Secondary financial statements for the sample of Japanese companies were obtained through the cooperation of the Nomura Securities Co., Ltd. These statements are original Japanese financials in which language, currency, and accounting principles have been restated for U.S. audiences-of-interest. In all cases, auditor opinions appearing in these secondary statements were rendered by major U.S. international accounting firms.

Adjusted ratio differences between Japanese and U.S. companies reflecting common accounting measurement rules appear in Table 4. A comparison between adjusted and unadjusted data (Tables 2 and 4) suggests that accounting restatements do have some effects on paired-ratio differences. In most instances, however, these effects are not appreciable because sig-

Table 1 Mean differences in aggregate financial ratios U.S.* Japan** Korea*** (unadjusted)

Enterprise Category	*Current Ratio*	*Quick Ratio*	*Debt Ratio*	*Times Int. Earned*	*Invty T/O*	*Avg. Coll. Period*	*F/A T/O*	*T/A T/O*	*Profit Margin*	*Return on T/A*	*Return on N/W*
All Manufacturing											
Japan (976)	1.15	.80	.84	1.60	5.00	86	3.10	.93	.013	.012	.071
Korea (354)	1.13	.46	.78	1.80	6.60	33	2.80	1.20	.023	.028	.131
U.S. (902)	1.94	1.10	.47	6.50	6.80	43	3.90	1.40	.054	.074	.139
Diff. (U.S.-Japan)	40%	26%	(77%)	75%	26%	(102%)	22%	32%	26%	84%	49%
Diff. (U.S.-Korea)	42%	58%	(66%)	73%	2%	24%	29%	9%	57%	62%	6%
Chemicals											
Japan (129)	1.30	.99	.79	1.80	7.10	88	2.80	.90	.015	.014	.065
Korea (54)	1.40	.70	.59	2.40	7.10	33	1.60	.90	.044	.040	.100
U.S. (n.a.)	2.20	1.30	.45	6.50	6.50	50	2.80	1.10	.073	.081	.148
Diff. (U.S.-Japan)	42%	22%	(74%)	72%	(8%)	(75%)	0%	19%	79%	83%	56%
Diff. (U.S.-Korea)	36%	45%	(31%)	62%	(9%)	34%	44%	19%	39%	50%	32%
Textiles											
Japan (81)	1.00	.77	.81	1.10	6.20	66	3.50	.92	.003	.003	.017
Korea (34)	1.00	.37	.83	1.30	4.90	30	2.20	1.00	.010	.011	.064
U.S. (n.a.)	2.30	1.20	.48	4.30	6.50	48	5.80	1.80	.027	.049	.094
Diff. (U.S.-Japan)	55%	38%	(70%)	74%	5%	(39%)	40%	50%	87%	93%	82%
Diff. (U.S.-Korea)	55%	70%	(74%)	70%	24%	36%	63%	44%	62%	78%	32%
Transportation											
Japan (85)	1.20	.86	.83	1.90	3.90	116	4.50	.90	.017	.015	.092
Korea (14)	.95	.40	.91	1.90	18.60	18	1.10	.80	.026	.021	.221
U.S.	1.60	.74	.52	8.70	5.60	31	6.50	1.60	.049	.078	.161
Diff. (U.S.-Japan)	21%	(16%)	(61%)	78%	28%	278%	30%	44%	65%	80%	43%
Diff. (U.S.-Korea)	40%	46%	(75%)	77%	(234%)	40%	84%	50%	47%	73%	(37%)

Source: * U.S. Federal Trade Commission.
Source: ** Bank of Japan.
Source: *** Bank of Korea.
(Parentheses indicate foreign ratios greater than U.S. ratios.)

Table 2 Mean paired differences in selected ratios: U.S./Japan (unadjusted)

Matched Pairs	*Current Ratio*	*Quick Ratio*	*Debt Ratio*	*Times Int. Earned*	*Invty T/O*	*Avg. Coll. Period*	*F/A T/O*	*T/A T/O*	*Profit Margin*	*Return on T/A*	*Return on N/W*
Xerox – Ricoh	.49	.49	(.10)	1.30	(7.50)	(15)	(2.30)	(.36)	.045	.033	.042
	26%	33%	(19%)	15%	(272%)	(28%)	(106%)	(36%)	56%	40%	25%
Polaroid – Cannon	1.90	1.10	(.41)	29.70	(2.70)	44	2.10	0	.041	.041	(.017)
	57%	50%	(173%)	83%	(69%)	49%	45%	0	48%	46%	(15%)
Kodak – Fuji Photo	1.10	.83	(.34)	2.10	1.30	(10)	(.35)	(.09)	.072	.067	.028
	42%	50%	(125%)	93%	24%	(16%)	(15%)	(9%)	60%	56%	17%
Zenith – Sony	.92	.13	(.07)	(1.30)	(.30)	(14)	4.40	.88	(.037)	(.023)	(.056)
	38%	11%	(15%)	(16%)	(5%)	(33%)	57%	45%	(186%)	(60%)	(84%)
RCA – Matsushita	.36	.21	.13	(.35)	(8.40)	(5)	(.48)	(.07)	(.006)	.005	.057
	21%	16%	20%	(6%)	(133%)	(8%)	(17%)	(5%)	(15%)	10%	35%
GE – Hitachi	.22	.09	(.21)	7.30	1.90	(31)	1.60	.31	.037	.055	.084
	15%	10%	(37%)	71%	27%	(51%)	33%	24%	61%	70%	46%
AMC – Honda	.09	(.20)	.02	(2.40)	(4.30)	(.40)	6.40	.75	(.021)	(.034)	(.104)
	7%	(35%)	3%	(179%)	(59%)	(1%)	65%	31%	(2957%)	(8600%)	(1526%)
Caterpillar – Komatsu	1.10	(.01)	(.27)	6.70	.70	(126)	.87	.76	.031	.077	.091
	46%	(1%)	(58%)	69%	15%	(312%)	29%	56%	40%	74%	47%
Penney – Ito Yokada	.79	(.02)	(.16)	1.30	(9.60)	16	4.10	.17	.012	.029	.024
	45%	(4%)	(33%)	27%	(152%)	74%	56%	7%	42%	46%	19%
ITT-Mitsui	.37	(28)	(.36)	2.30	(36.40%)	(23)	(8.50)	(1.20)	.042	.045	.038
	25%	(37%)	(61%)	68%	(706%)	(37%)	(293%)	(112%)	99%	99%	34%
Average Mean Differences	.73	.23	(.18)	11.70	(5.70)	(16.40)	.78	.15	.023	.029	.019
	35%	21%	(58%)	23%	(133%)	(36%)	(15%)	1%	42%*	38%*	12%*
Significance Level (t-test)	3.70 †	18.30%	1.00% †	30.00%	20%	30%	60%	58.20%	11.20% †	8.70% †	37%

* Excludes AMC – Honda percentage difference.

Table 3 Mean paired differences in selected ratios: U.S./Korea (unadjusted)

Matched Pairs	*Current Ratio*	*Quick Ratio*	*Debt Ratio*	*Times Int. Earned*	*Invty T/O*	*Avg. Coll. Period*	*F/A T/O*	*T/A T/O*	*Profit Margin*	*Return on T/A*	*Return on N/W*
Thiokol – Samsung	.98	.62	(.41)	11.50	(2.40)	–	(21.40)	(1.00)	.041	.056	(.051)
	49%	47%	(85%)	90%	(28%)	–	(507%)	(68%)	82%	74%	(35%)
Whittaker – Daewoo	.85	.18	(.11)	1.60	(1.70)	–	(18.00)	.21	(.016)	(.015)	(.119)
	45%	20%	(16%)	39%	(38%)	–	(240%)	14%	(63%)	(38%)	(1.04%)
Trinity – Hyundai	1.40	.70	(.11)	.93	(131.60)	–	(1045)	(9.80)	.054	.079	.129
	47%	34%	(24%)	6%	(1460%)	–	(13,500%)	(486%)	91%	66%	56%
Zurn – Int'l Trading	1.20	.69	(.19)	4.70	(3.30)	–	(1.90)	(.39)	.012	.007	(.069)
	55%	54%	(34%)	66%	(61%)	–	(31%)	(26%)	33%	14%	(55%)
Standex – Lucky	2.40	1.00	(.25)	2.70	(4.40)	–	1.90	.05	.002	.003	(.093)
	73%	71%	(53%)	47%	(99%)	–	38%	3%	4%	6%	(83%)
EG&G – HyoSung	1.60	1.00	(.44)	19.10	(1.10)	–	(28.90)	.66	.032	.094	.093
	64%	60%	(98%)	92%	10%	–	(166%)	23%	87%	90%	48%
Republic – Ssan Yong	.95	.39	(.32)	3.10	(5.10)	–	(22.80)	(.24)	.023	.039	(.031)
	47%	34%	(56%)	64%	(79%)	–	(415%)	(13%)	73%	69%	(24%)
Athlone – Sun Kyong	1.30	.38	(.21)	2.40	(3.70)	–	(1.50)	(.43)	.036	.047	.059
	61%	42%	(30%)	65%	(77%)	–	(29%)	(31%)	82%	76%	30%
Average Mean Differences	1.30	.63	(.25)	5.80	(5.80)*	–	(13.20)*	(1.60)	.023	.079	.01
	55%	45%	(50%)	59%	(56%)*		(193%)*	(14%)	49%	45%	21%
Significance Level (t-test)	4.30% †	4.30% †	4.70% †	19.90% †	32%		35.2%	34%	9.40% †	1.00% †	76%

Source * Excludes Trinity – Hyundai percentage differences.
Source: —Insufficient data provided.

nificant ratio differences remain. For those who wish to examine the specific effects of accounting differences on specific ratio differences – a task which is beyond the scope of this paper and one that is ultimately company specific – the authors have prepared an accounting principles matrix detailing major differences between U.S., Japanese, and Korean principles. (See Appendix D.)[16]

Korean restatements, however, proved troublesome. To begin, consolidation of group accounts, taken for granted in the United States, is rarely practiced in Korea. To date, only 2 major companies have attempted such restatements, namely, Daewoo and Samsung. Even here, group statements prepared by Samsung represent 'combined' rather than 'consolidated' statements. In the latter case, intercompany transactions and intercompany profits are eliminated upon consolidation with a separate accounting for minority interests (standard practice in the U.S.).[17]

In addition to different ownership and control patterns,[18] which, among other things, make identifying a group's parent extremely difficult, accounting principles of consolidation are neither well formulated nor understood in Korea.[19] Accordingly, companies are granted considerable leeway in structuring consolidated accounts. Under these circumstances, combined rather than consolidated statements proved the only feasible and least controversial alternative in providing an overall glimpse of a group's financial status. Combined statements incorporating the major subsidiaries and affiliates of the sample group companies were therefore prepared.[20]

In most instances, individual company accounts comprising the group were combined on a line-by-line basis with intercompany transactions eliminated, where disclosed. Because of nondisclosure, elimination of intercompany profits was impossible as was computation of minority interest and reversal of major accounting differences highlighted in Appendix D. Ratio differences based on the combined financial statements are set forth in Table 5. On the basis of these restatement experiences, it appears that minimal corporate financial disclosures, which make it difficult for analysts to reconcile Korean with American accounting principles, will prove to be a major stumbling block to Korean companies in their efforts to gain access to the U.S. capital markets.

ENVIRONMENTAL CONSIDERATIONS

To ascertain whether these financial ratio profiles are truly indicative of what they purport to measure, the authors examined the cultural and institutional dimensions of the Japanese and Korean business environments for possible explanatory variables. Insights obtained from field interviews and literature search are discussed next.[21]

LEVERAGE

The financial statistic that captures the immediate attention of U.S. security analysts is the extremely high leverage of Japanese and Korean firms. In the sample groups, debt ratios averaged 64.3 percent for the Japanese and 78.8 percent for the Koreans. In sharp contrast, average debt ratios for the U.S. control group were only 48.9 percent for Japan and 54.0 percent for Korea. Several reasons seem to account for these glaring differences. Explanations that follow apply to both experimental groups unless otherwise noted.

The lower relative cost of debt that results from the tax deductibility of interest expense is as relevant in Asia as it is in the U.S. Additional considerations, however, characterize the former. In Korea, companies face severe supply constraints when it comes to equity financing. A shallow market and short history of public distribution of shares (since 1973), account for this state. Thus, equity funds are frequently not to be had at any price. Within the framework of corporate borrowing, a decided preference is found in Korea for bank financing owing partially to subsidized interest rates. The magnitude of this subsidy can be gleaned from a comparison of rates charged by commercial banks with those charged in Korea's unregulated curb market which operates outside the official banking system. Rates in the former average 21 percent per year in contrast to 30 to 54 percent per year in the latter.[22]

In Japan, a stock issue system based traditionally on preemptive rights with shares issued at par as opposed to market values figures highly in the lower cost of debt as opposed to equity funds. Dividend rates are typically fixed at 10 to 15 percent of par values (normally $50 per share) and paid whether earned or not – except when in dire financial straits. Even though Japan's larger firms have issued stocks at market, the cost of equity generally remains high. Reflecting the sentiment of their clients, securities companies insist that premiums received from shares sold in excess of par value be returned to shareholders. This takes either the form of higher dividend rates or stock dividends. In either case the cost advantage associated with issuing stock at market value is largely negated.[23]

Whereas cost considerations are not a trivial concern, it appears that in the context of rapid economic growth, characteristic of both the Japanese and Korean economies, the sheer availability of funds to sustain corporate expansion has been of even greater import. Consider, first, the case of Japan. At the end of World War II, Japan was confronted with the enormous task of rebuilding its war-torn economy. With a limited equity market and savings destroyed, government-supported debt financing was the only available source of funds. Encouraged by the government and financed by the Bank of Japan, new enterprise groupings were formed around Japan's major commercial banks. These new *Keiretsu* replaced the former *Zaibatsu*, huge pre-war conglomerates, as the major engines of Japan's post-war economic expansion and the ones most likely to need access to the U.S. securities market[24]. Interdependence was fostered among Keiretsu group companies through financial, commercial, and personal ties. Under such arrangements, the relationships between the borrowing company, related companies, and their bank were very close. Cross shareholdings between borrower, related companies, and the bank were common. Today, their relationship has evolved to the point where a bank would seldom impose financial penalties on delayed interest payments nor call a delinquent loan from a related company; instead, the lending bank would typically postpone interest and principal repayments and, in some instances, even refinance the loan on more liberal terms. It is common practice for the lending bank to install a bank official as president or board member of the troubled company to provide it with helpful managerial assistance[25]. Likewise, related companies would prepay receivables owed to the distressed firm and allow payables by that firm to related companies additional lag time. Additional background on the interrelationships and group strengths posed by the new Keiretsu can be found in Freitas[26], Stonehill *et al.*[27], Patrick and Rosovsky[28], and Wright and Suzuki[29].

Similar considerations apply to Korea with the exception that the government assumes an even larger role in corporate finance. Consider some interview findings. To encourage certain business firms to undertake projects or enter into industries deemed beneficial to national growth and development, the government will grant the firm various tax and trade privileges including special financing. These firms are normally group companies with a general trading company rather than a bank at the core of the association. In the Korean case, owing to the shortage of domestic loanable funds, this financing arrangement, more often than not, assumed the form of foreign currency loans secured by bank guarantees; however, since commercial banks in Korea are effectively owned and controlled by the government, the government, in effect, is the ultimate lender.[30] Because of its interest in the success of the borrower's undertaking, the government would generally do whatever it could to assist the troubled firm – for example, to see to it that the defaulting company is merged with other companies in its group or industry. Another feature of Korean lending practice is that corporate borrowers are not classified into credit risk categories with interest rates scaled accordingly. Rather, the more bank debt a company has, the greater the bank's stake in the success of the enterprise, and the higher the probability that the bank will come to the firm's rescue in times of economic adversity. Thus, rather than being viewed with alarm, high debt ratios in Korea signify a company's close ties with its bank which, in turn, signify a company's favorable association with the government.

With long-term debt assuming the characteristics of preferred stock, interest can be likened to dividends. Accordingly, interest coverage ratios, which are considerably lower in Japan (average 4.7 times) and Korea (averaging 2.6 times) than the U.S. (average 16.5 and 9.4 times for the U.S.-Japan and U.S.-Korea control samples, respectively), are not viewed with much concern. In Japan, business earnings over and above those needed to cover its 'captive' loan charges are of modest perceived benefit to the bank. When a loan is negotiated, a general agreement, seldom disclosed, also stipulates that the company stands ready to provide the lending bank with collateral or guarantors upon the bank's request.[31] Again at the bank's request, borrowing companies must submit their year-end proposed appropriation of income (including dividends) before it can be submitted to shareholders for approval. Compensating balances, though illegal, are customarily insisted upon with 20–50 percent of company borrowings reportedly kept with the bank in the form of time or other deposits[25]. Under these conditions, low interest coverage does not necessarily mirror high default risk.

In Korea, interest coverage ratios also receive little attention. Indeed, the Bank of Korea and Korean Development Bank make no mention of this ratio in their annual reports summarizing financial ratio analyses of Korean enterprises. In evaluating financial risk, greater emphasis is placed on the presence of loan guarantees, the reputation of the company management, and the collateral value of assets. In light of the Korean economy's high growth rate, real asset values have remained consistently high. In an environment of rapid corporate expansion, financial resources acquired to fund new investments are also used customarily to partially service debt.

An insight on how excessive debt financing (according to U.S. standards) has functioned in the past can be gleaned from examining some bankruptcy statistics for both Japan and Korea vis-a-vis the United States. (See Table 6.)

Tabled figures constitute the ratio of number of corporate bankruptcies to total number of corporations in the respective countries. As can be seen, despite high debt and lower interest coverage ratios in Japan and Korea, actual bankruptcy experiences have not exceeded those in the U.S.; indeed, they have actually been lower. It should be noted, in addition, that the foregoing statistics relate to all business corporations in general regardless of size. Interviews suggest that such rates would be significantly lower, if non-existent, for larger companies capable of entering foreign capital markets.

Liquidity

Consistent with the aggregate ratio comparisons (Table 1), liquidity ratios for both samples of Japanese and Korean entities were found to be lower than in the U.S. Environmental considerations account, however, for much of the differential. In Japan, short-term borrowing is actually preferred to long-term debt. From a lender's viewpoint, shorter maturities allow for the

Table 4 Mean paired differences in selected ratios: U.S./Japan (adjusted)

Matched Pairs	*Current Ratio*	*Quick Ratio*	*Debt Ratio*	*Times Int. Earned*	*Invty T/O*	*Avg. Coll. Period*	*F/A T/O*	*T/A T/O*	*Profit Margin*	*Return on T/A*	*Return on N/W*
Xerox – Ricoh	.64	.46	(.16)	1.60	(6.10)	(16)	(3.60)	(.21)	.040	.032	.015
	33%	31%	(32%)	20%	(222%)	(30%)	(169%)	(21%)	50%	39%	97%
Poloroid – Cannon	2.10	1.30	(.51)	32.10	(.30)	2	(.83)	.06	.045	.049	(.042)
	62%	60%	(217%)	90%	(8%)	2%	(17%)	6%	53%	55%	(36%)
Kodak – Fuji Photo	1.00	.79	(.29)	72.20	1.40	(13.60)	(1.10)	.08	.059	.065	.036
	41%	48%	(109%)	92%	25%	(22%)	(48%)	8%	50%	54%	22%
Zenith – Sony	1.10	.42	(.16)	(.75)	1.90	(35)	2.70	1.01	(.038)	(.017)	(.068)
	46%	35%	(37%)	(9%)	35%	(81%)	36%	52%	(191%)	(43%)	(103%)
RCA – Matsushita	.14	.19	.10	(1.60)	(1.10)	3.40	(6.30)	.23	(.002)	.007	.056
	8%	15%	16%	(31%)	(17%)	6%	(222%)	17%	(4%)	14%	35%
GE – Hitachi	.20	.08	(.19)	6.70	2.30	(22)	(.79)	.38	.027	.048	.062
	14%	9%	(34%)	65%	33%	(37%)	(16%)	29%	45%	61%	34%
AMC – Honda	.14	.03	(.08)	(2.40)	2.50	(3)	4.50	.96	(.024)	(.035)	(.142)
	11%	6%	(12%)	(179%)	34%	(12%)	45%	39%	(3400%)	(874%)	(2084%)
Caterpillar – Komatsu	1.30	.21	(.28)	7.20	.99	(72)	(1.20)	.71	.043	.082	.107
	55%	21%	(61%)	75%	21%	(179%)	(39%)	52%	56%	79%	55%
Penney – Ito Yokada	.86	.03	(.16)	.27	(10.60)	16	3.20	.16	.008	.021	.003
	48%	6%	(33%)	6%	(69%)	72%	44%	7%	28%	33%	2%
ITT – Mitsui	.49	(.14)	(.36)	2.40	(21.20)	(25)	(4.00)	(.79)	.042	.044	.084
	33%	(19%)	(16%)	69%	(411%)	(40%)	(134%)	(74%)	99%	97%	75%
Avg. Mean Differences	.80	.34	(.21)	11.80	(3.00)	(16.40)	(.74)	.26	.020	.029	.011
	35%	21%	(58%)	20%	(68%)	(32%)	(52%)	12%	21%*	43%*	10%*
Significance Level (t-test)	4.10% †	8.80% †	3.9% †	19%	27%	12.70% †	52.90%	20%	1.41% †	8.5% †	60%

Source * Excludes AMC – Honda percentage differences.

Table 5 Mean paired differences in selected ratios: U.S./Korea (adjusted)

Matched Pairs	*Current Ratio*	*Quick Ratio*	*Debt Ratio*	*Times Int. Earned*	*Invty T/O*	*Avg. Coll. Period*	*F/A T/O*	*T/A T/O*	*Profit Margin*	*Return on T/A*	*Return on N/W*
Thiokol – Samsung	1.00	.84	(.32)	11.30	1.30	(7)	(.50)	.10	.031	.054	.032
	51%	64%	(67%)	88%	15%	(21%)	(12%)	7%	63%	71%	22%
Whittaker – Daewoo	.70	.25	(.11)	1.70	.40	13	3.80	.71	(.008)	.003	(.048)
	37%	28%	(17%)	42%	8%	23%	51%	47%	(31%)	7%	(41%)
Trinity – Hyundai	1.50	1.30	(.28)	11.70	.50	(29)	4.60	.90	.018	.071	(.144)
	52%	62%	(59%)	73%	5%	(83%)	59%	45%	30%	59%	(62%)
Zurn – Int'l Trading	1.10	.77	(.24)	5.50	(.40)	26	1.70	.40	.014	.029	(.008)
	52%	59%	(42%)	76%	(7%)	40%	27%	27%	39%	53%	(6%)
Standex – Lucky	2.10	.90	(.31)	2.60	(4.40)	7	(1.90)	(.40)	.007	(.001)	(.175)
	65%	64%	(64%)	46%	(97%)	14%	(38%)	(27%)	18%	(2%)	(156%)
EG + G – HyoSung	1.50	1.20	(.33)	19.20	4.60	10	13.70	1.60	.018	.082	.091
	57%	70%	(75%)	93%	40%	21%	79%	57%	48%	78%	47%
Republic – Ssan Yong	.80	.56	(.20)	3.20	(2.30)	32	3.30	.80	0.10	.035	.034
	40%	51%	(35%)	67%	(36%)	57%	60%	44%	32%	61%	26%
Athlone – Sun Kyong	1.10	.41	(.17)	2.50	(1.90)	(9)	2.70	.40	0.29	.046	.083
	52%	45%	(25%)	67%	(39%)	(27%)	53%	28%	64%	74%	42%
Average Mean Difference	1.20	.78	(.24)	7.20	(.27)	5.40	3.40	.56	.015	.039	(.017)
	51%	55%	(48%)	69%	(16%)	3%	35%	28%	33%	50%	16%
Significance Level (t-test)	4.40% †	4.70% †	4.40% †	8.70% †	78.40%	49.20%	15.30% †	10.00% †	7.80% †	6.90% †	65.30%

Table 6 Relative business bankruptcy rates* U.S./Japan/Korea

Year	*U.S.*	*Japan*	*Korea*
1976	.017	.012	.012
1977	.015	.014	.010
1978	.014	.011	.008
1979	.013	.011	.009
1980	.014	.011	.012

Source: Statistics for the U.S. and Japan were adapted from Edward I. Altman, 'Business Failure Models: An International Study' Salomon Brothers Center Occasional Paper in Business and Finance, No. 5, 1982; statistics for Korea: Bank of Korea, *Monthly Economic Statistics*, December 1981.

adjustment of interest rates at frequent intervals to reflect current market rates. From a borrower's perspective, short-term financing is cheaper than long-term loans. Thus, for all practical purposes, short-term debt in Japan is more akin to long-term debt. As a matter of fact, while short-term loans are officially granted for working capital purposes, they are frequently used to finance long-term investment[25].

In Japan the liquidity ratios can also be misleading because companies typically sell their accounts receivable with recourse, thus reducing a current asset without a corresponding balance sheet offset on the current debt side. On the other hand, as pointed out by Freitas[26], the recourse feature is footnoted, if reported at all, as a contingent liability but might be considered as worsening the leverage situation. Another feature of Japanese balance sheets, that can significantly alter liquidity (and leverage) ratios, is the degree to which the typical large marketable securities portfolios are understated compared with market value.

In Korea, extensive use of short-term debt is not so much a matter of choice as it is a necessity. The scarcity of long-term funds leaves companies little choice but to borrow short-term to finance both working capital and long-term needs. Because short-term loans are also customarily rolled over in Korea, the designation 'short-term' is a misnomer. With government ultimately behind the credit, lower current and quick ratios do not necessarily portend lower liquidity.

Efficiency

Turning to activity ratios, Tables 4 and 5 suggest that differences in inventory turnover were not materially different in both Japanese and U.S. samples. Differences between Japanese and U.S. collection periods, however, were more noticeable, with average collection periods significantly higher in Japan than in the U.S. A reason for this, also found in Korea, is that the purchaser seldom pays cash upon receipt of an invoice; instead, the purchaser is customarily given 20 to 30 days in which to make payment.

At that time, a note rather than cash is given with the note's maturity ranging anywhere from 60 to 120 days. The rationale for this practice is easily understood when one views it from the perspective of a country like Korea. Given the scarcity of loanable funds to finance frenetic growth, extended payment terms are a logical means of accommodating the working capital needs of favored customers. In Japan, however, reasons for longer collection periods go deeper and are related to the Japanese tradition of lifetime employment[25]. Thus, during business downturns, repayment extensions are granted to avoid putting the buyer in a financial bind and thereby threatening an otherwise stable employment base. In return, continued future patronage helps assure employment stability for the selling enterprise.

Although differences between U.S. and Korean collection periods were not statistically significant, both Tables 1 and 5 show Korean collection periods to be relatively short. This may be due to the use, even by Korean authorities, of the U.S. formula: *accounts receivable divided by average daily sales equals average collection period*. In light of what has been said about the 2-stage nature of receivables collection, this formula is incorrect. It was learned that even in the modified formula employed in Table 5, adding notes receivable to accounts receivable is incorrect. The recommended formula is:

$$\frac{\text{accounts receivable}}{\text{daily sales}} + \begin{array}{c}\text{average maturity of}\\ \text{notes receivable}\end{array}$$

On this basis, the average collection period of the Korean sample would be about 105 to 110 days. The average maturity of notes receivable, furthermore, can be very flexible in practice. Depending on the degree of general monetary tightness, this figure may also vary between 60 and 180 days. This flexibility is often employed as a liquidity cushion by larger enterprises who are in a better position to negotiate such terms than are smaller competitors.

Differences in asset turnover figures were not significant for the Japan-vs.-U.S. experimental group; however, they were for the Korea-vs.-U.S. group (Tables 4 and 5). Lower asset turnover figures in Korea result, in large measure, from enormous investments by Korean enterprises in plant and equipment. In its quest to accelerate Korea's economic development timetable, the government has encouraged enterprises to expand existing activities and to venture into new and untried fields, such as, heavy chemicals. Much of this investment is very recent with construction in progress tending to be very large. Consequently, current revenues still do not reflect anticipated sales that will come on stream when operations are at expected capacity levels and construction in progress is completed. Revaluation of asset values for inflation is another contributing factor. If we examine the numerator of the asset turnover ratios, we find that sales revenues in Korea tend to be understated relative to those in the United States. This is caused by government price controls, which are imposed on domestic goods to stem local inflation and imposed on exports to penetrate overseas markets while generating foreign exchange to pay for needed imports.

In terms of stage of economic development, Japan is further along the industrialization path than Korea. Japanese investments in fixed assets nevertheless remain high despite relatively rapid allowable depreciation schedules, especially when compared with the U.S. This, in part, accounts for Japan's relatively lower asset turnover figures (Table 2). Moreover, high inventory levels, owing partly to long channels of distribution and to support the Japanese penchant for ever-growing sales, together with large investments in receivables (owing to long collection periods), also give total assets an upward bias.

Profitability

Differences in relative profit margins and return on assets between both experimental and control groups were significant. Here again, one must look to the environment to interpret properly apparent lower profitability of both Japanese and Korean companies.

In Japan, managers are not as concerned with short-run profits as are their U.S. counterparts. One reason is that management security in Japan is higher than in the U.S. Because corporate shares of the sample companies are typically held largely by related commercial banks, trade suppliers, and corporate customers, these 'stable shareholders' are more interested in maintaining and strengthening functional business ties than short-run stock market gains. Accordingly, corporate shares are normally held over long-term horizons regardless of short-term market performance[23].

Embracing sales growth as their primary objective, corporate managers in Japan believe that increased market share will assure profits in the long run. Moreover, growing sales contribute to higher employment and job security and are therefore consistent with the tradition of lifetime employment. With increased sales as a common goal among Japanese enterprises, price competition is severe, which results in low profit margin and profitability statistics. This is especially true of the large companies in the sample who typically sell heavily in extremely competitive export markets.

In Korea, profits figure more highly in management decisions; however, as high-lighted earlier, export pricing policies as well as government controls tend to keep prices and, hence, margins relatively low. High interest costs on debt and depreciation of relatively new assets also exert downward pressures on the bottom line. Lower profits coupled with a large asset base, adjusted periodically to incorporate the effects of inflation, understandably account for the lower profitability ratios observed.

With government ultimately influencing lending, investment, and pricing policies, lower profitability is not necessarily indicative of managerial performance.

CONCLUSIONS

On the basis of these findings, institutional, cultural, political, and tax considerations in Japan and Korea do indeed cause their accounting ratios to differ from U.S. norms without necessarily reflecting better or worse financial risk and return characteristics being measured. In evaluating whether Japanese and Korean firms in reality have access to the U.S. securities market, one should probably assess the degree to which the capital-seeking firm is in a priority industry, an entrenched member of an industrial group, and/or bank-supported. If the answer is yes on all counts, it is likely that its financial risk is in fact much less than might be indicated by financial ratio analysis. In the case of a Korean firm, its financial risk may be further assessed by analyzing the Korean Government's attitude toward growth and the specific firm at the time the firm is seeking capital. Also important, but not covered in this article, is the attitude of the international financial community toward 'country risk' in Korea. At the moment, money lenders believe Korea is nearing its external debt capacity. No similar constraint appears to affect Japanese firms.

A major conclusion of our study is that accounting measurements reflected in corporate financial reports represent, in one sense, merely 'numbers' that have limited meaning and significance in and of themselves. Meaning and significance come from and depend upon an understanding of the environmental context from which the numbers are drawn as well as the relationship between the numbers and the underlying economic phenomena that are the real items of interest.

NOTES

1 Levy, H., and Sarnat, M. 'International Diversification of Investment Portfolios.' *American Economic Review*, September 1970.

2 Cooper, Richard N. 'Towards An International Capital Market?' in *North American and Western European Economic Policies*, edited by Charles P. Kindleberger and Andrew Shofield, reprinted in *International Financial Management: Theory and Application*, edited by Donald R. Lessard. New York: Warren Gorham and Lamont, 1979, pp. 94–95.

3 NYSE. 'Visits with Unlisted Corporations, London, England, September 25–28, 1978.' *Memorandum to Advisory Committee on International Capital Markets*, 2 January 1979.

4 Choi, Frederick D. S. 'Primary-Secondary Reporting: A Cross-Cultural Analysis.' *International Journal of Accounting*, Fall 1980, pp. 84–104.

5 Choi, Frederick; Min, Sang Kee; Nam, Sang Oh; and Stonehill, Arthur. 'Foreign Access to U.S. Securities Markets.' *Journal of the Korean Listed Companies Association*, Spring 1981.

6 Eiteman, David K., and Stonehill, Arthur I. *Multinational Business Finance*, 2nd Reading, MA: Addison-Wesley Publishing Company, 1979, pp. 347–48, 366–68.
7 Schaefer, Jeffrey. *Policies to Increase Foreign Listings on the NYSE*. New York: Report of the Subcommittee on Trading and Listing Foreign Securities to the Advisory Committee on International Capital Markets, October 1975, p. 16.
8 NYSE. Business Research Division, *Foreign Securities Listed*. New York: New York Stock Exchange, July 1980, 8 pp.
9 Fitzgerald, R. D.,; Stickler, A. D.; and Watts, T. R. *International Survey of Accounting Principles and Reporting Practices*. New York: Price Waterhouse International, 1979.
10 International Bank for Reconstruction and Development. *Description of Foreign and International Bonds Publicly-issued in Major Capital Markets*. Updated periodically.
11 Terasawa, Yoshio. 'Another Overseas Record in 1979.' *Euromoney*, March 1979, xix–xxix.
12 Phillips, Jackson. 'Analysis and Rating of Corporate Bonds.' In *Financial Analysts Handbook*, pp. 215–225.
13 Standard and Poor's Corporation. *Standard and Poor's Ratings Guide*. McGraw-Hill, 1979, chapter 17.
14 The authors are grateful for the assistance of the Institutional Research Advisory Department of the Nomura Securities Company, Ltd. and the Korean Listed Companies Association in this regard.
15 In the case of Korea, all of the companies examined were 'General Trading Companies.' These enterprises are multi-industry in nature and specially organized to serve as export windows for Korea's domestic companies lacking expertise in international marketing. U.S. conglomerates, although not a perfect match, were selected as the closest counterpart of these unique organizations.
16 The following methodology was employed in constructing the accounting principles matrix: (1) an item was selected for inclusion if it was deemed to have material valuation or income determination implications for accounting-based ratio analysis; (2) to simplify cross-country analysis, matrix cells contain discrete yes/no responses to signify adherence or non-adherence to U.S. accounting practice; (3) information on differences in national accounting principles was obtained from field interviews with major international accounting firms and secondary source materials (9, 32, 33, 34, 35, 36, 37).
17 ARB No. 51, *Consolidated Financial Statements*.
18 A Korean General Trading Company is generally not legally a holding company; the only legal tie between group members is family owners who simultaneously own stocks of related entities.
19 In the case of Daewoo, consolidation was possible because of the existence of a clearly identified holding company. Its founder and major shareholder, who personally owns less than 5 percent of the company's shares, disclosed his effective ownership control through proxy rights obtained from relatives, friends, and other nominee owners.
20 Annual report data for each major listed affiliate were obtained from files of the Korean Listed Companies Association; for each registered company – fillings with the Korean Securities Supervisory Board; and for each unlisted and unregistered affiliate – data from the Annual Business Statistics Publication of the Korea Productivity Center and *Maell Kyungie Shinmun* (daily newspaper). Because data on unlisted and unregistered companies are often incomplete, the authors were not able to capture all companies in their combination efforts; however, they are confident that most key subsidiaries and affiliated companies were accounted for.

21 Owing to nonreversal of accounting differences in the case of Korea, differential accounting principles must necessarily be included as an environmental variable in the following discussion.

22 One reviewer raised the interesting question of whether 'hidden reserves' (accounting understatement of asset values) might account for seemingly higher Korean debt ratios. Appendix D suggests that this is probably not the case owing to the Korean practice of capitalizing many expenditures and restating asset values for inflation.

23 Barrett, M. Edgar; Price, Lee N.; and Gehrke, Judith Ann. 'Japan: Some Background for Security Analysts.' *Financial Analysts Journal*, January-February 1974, pp. 33–44.

24 Takahashi, Kamekichi. *The Rise and Development of Modern Economy: The Basis of Miraculous Growth*. Tokyo: Jiji Press, 1969, p. 43.

25 Ballon, Robert J.; Tomita, Iwao; and Usami, Hajime. *Financial Reporting in Japan* Tokyo: Kodansha International Ltd., 1978, pp. 44–52.

26 Freitas, Lewis P. 'Views From Abroad: Japan: Analyzing Financial Statements Japan.' *Journal of Accounting, Auditing and Finance*, Fall 1980.

27 Stonehill, Arthur; Remmers, Lee; Beekhuisen, Theo; and Wright, Richard. 'Financial Goals in Debt Ratio Determinants: A Survey of Practice in Five Countries.' *Financial Management*, Autumn 1975, pp. 24–41.

28 Patrick, Hugh, and Rosovsky, Henry, eds. *Asia's New Giant*. Washington, DC: The Brooking's Institute, 1976.

29 Wright, Richard, and Suzuki, Sadahiko, 'Capital Structure and Financial Risk in Japanese Companies.' *Proceedings of the Academy of International Business Asia Pacific Dimensions of International Business*. Honolulu, Hawaii, 18–20 December 1979.

30 The Korean government has recently announced that it will begin to liberalize its control of the banking industry.

31 Under article 4 of the General Banking Agreement (1948), borrowing firms are required to sign a form which allows the bank to demand additional collateral almost without limitation. Although this reduces the firm's financial risk that the bank will call the loan, it increases the risk of bondholders. Thus, there is little interest in the long-term bonds of private firms and Japanese firms would have considerable problems getting an 'A' bond rating from the agencies if they tried to market bonds outside Japan. In practice, of course, the banks would use considerable restraint in invoking Article 4, especially if it jeopardized an international bond issue.

32 Donald R. Lessard. New York: Warren Gorham and Lamont, 1979, pp. 94–95.

33 *Korea*. New York: Coopers and Lybrand, 1981, 44 pp.

34 Peat Marwick Mitchell and Company. *Accounting in Korea*. Seoul: Peat Marwick Mitchell & Co. of Korea, white paper, 1979.

35 Price Waterhouse. *Doing Business in Japan*. New York: Price Waterhouse & Co., October 1975, pp. 95.

36 Samil Accounting Corporation. *Major Differences in Korean and U.S. Accounting Principles and Reporting Standards*. Seoul: Samil Accounting Corporation, white paper, May 1980, pp. 26.

37 Touche Ross International. *Business Study: Japan*. New York: Touche Ross & Co., 1980, pp. 143.

ACKNOWLEDGEMENTS

The authors gratefully acknowledge the financial support of the New York University's Graduate School of Business Administration, the University of Hawaii's Research Council and College of Business Administration Office of Faculty Research, and Korea Listed Companies Association. They also gratefully thank the Nomura Securities Co., Ltd., of Tokyo, and the companies and organizations interviewed in Japan and Korea for contributing their time and data.

QUESTIONS

1 Analyse the types of factor that impede comparison of accounts in different countries as identified in this study, and discuss how each should be tackled.

APPENDIX A

Sample Japanese companies and their U.S. counterparts (1978 Sales in $Millions)

Japanese Companies		*United States Companies*	
Ricoh	$ 724	Xerox	$ 6,018
Cannon	$ 721	Polaroid	$ 1,376
Fuji Photo	$ 1,452	Kodak	$ 7,012
Sony	$ 2,156	Zenith	$ 980
Matsushita	$ 8,411	RCA	$ 6,600
Hitachi	$ 5,859	GE	$19,654
Honda	$ 4,854	AMC	$ 2,585
Komatsu	$ 2,087	Caterpillar	$ 7,219
Ito Yokado	$ 2,571	J. C. Penny	$10,436
Mitsui	$36,495	ITT	$15,314

Sample Korean Companies and Their U.S. Counterparts (1978) Sales in $Millions)

Korean Companies		*United States Companies*	
Ssan Yong Co.	$250	Republic Corp.	$239
Sun Kyong Co.	$347	Athlone Industries, Inc.	$264
International Trading Co.	$316	Zurn Industries, Inc.	$260
Hyun Dai Co.	$246	Trinity Industries, Inc.	$239
Hyo Sung Industrial Corp.	$415	EG&G, Inc.	$441
Lucky Co.	$211	Standix International Corp.	$242
Samsung Industrial Co.	$585	Thiokol Corp.	$564
Dae Woo Industrial Co.	$923	Whittaker Corp.	$884

APPENDIX B

Firms and Organizations Visited on Site

Industrial Corporations	
Japan	*Korea*
Fujitsu Ltd. Mitsubishi Corporation Komatsu Ltd. Esso Kagaku	Samsung Industrial Co. Dae Woo Industrial Co.
Professional Accounting Firms	
Japan	*Korea*
Asahi & Co. Coopers & Lybrand	Samil Accounting Corp. Peat, Marwick, Mitchell & Co. SGV Group
Securities Firms	
Japan	*Korea*
The Nomura Securities Co., Ltd.	Korea Merchant Banking Corporation
Government Agencies	
Japan	*Korea*
International Capital Markets Division, Ministry of Finance	Korean Securities Supervision Board

APPENDIX C

Choice of Financial Ratios

The ratios selected for analysis should be the ones most frequently used by investors vestors, security analysts, and bond rating services. The ratios used in Weston and Brigham, *Essentials of Managerial Finance*, latest edition, should suffice for this purpose. They are as follows:

Ratio	Formula	Use
A. Liquidity		
1 current	current assets / current liabilities	Used to analyze the ability to meet short–run debt commitments
2 quick, or acid test	current assets–inventory / current liabilities	
B. Leverage		
3 Debt to total capitalization	Total debt (book value) / Total assets (book value)	Used to analyze the abili to meet long–run debt and fixed charge commitments.
4 Times interest earned	EBIT / Interest Charges	
5 Fixed charge coverage*	EBIT–Fixed charges / Fixed charges	
C. Efficiency (Activity)		
6 Inventory turnover	Cost of goods sold / Average inventory	Used to analyze the 'staleness' of inventory.
7 Average collection period	Receivables / Sales per day	Used to analyze the staleness of receivables.
8 Fixed asset turnover	Sales / Fixed assets	Used to analyze sales efficiency of total assets.
9 Total operating assets turnover	Sales / Total operating assets	Used to analyze sales efficiency of total assets.
D. Profitability		
10 Period margin on sales	Net profit after taxes / Sales	Used to analyze competitive margins.
11 Return on total assets	Net profit after taxes / Total assets	Used to measure profit efficiency to total assets.
12 Return on net worth	Net profit after taxes / Net worth	Used to measure profit efficiency of total stockholders' funds.

* Insufficient data existed to be able to utilize this ratio in any of the analyses.

APPENDIX D

Synthesis of Major Accounting Differences

	U.S.	*Japan*	*Korea*
1. Marketable securities recorded at lower cost or market?	Yes	Yes	No
2. Inventory costed using FIFO?	Yes	No[a]	Yes
3. Inventory valued at lower of cost or market?	Yes	No[b]	No[c]
4. Accounting for long-term investments less than 50% owned: equity method?	Yes	No[d]	No[d]
5. Accounting for long-term investments more than 50% owned: full consolidation?	Yes	Yes	No[d]
6. Minority interest excluded from consolidated income?	Yes	Yes	No
7. Minority interest excluded from consolidated equity?	Yes	Yes	No
8. Deferred taxes recorded when accounting income not equal to taxable income?	Yes	No	No
9. Financial leases capitalized?	Yes	No	No
10. R&D expensed?	Yes	Yes	No[e]
11. Dismissal indemnities accounted for on a pay-as-you -go basis?	Yes	Yes	Yes
12. Full accrual of severance benefits?	Yes	No[f]	No[f]
13. Fixed assets revalued above historical cost.	No	No	Yes[g]
14. Depreciation based on revalued cost?	No	No	Yes
15. Depreciation expense based on straight-line method?	Yes	No[h]	No[h]
16. Excess depreciation permitted?	No	Yes[i]	Yes[j]
17. Pre-operating expenses capitalized?	No	No	Yes
18. Prior period adjustments limited to correction of errors?	Yes	Yes	No[k]
19. Tax deferred reserves permitted?	No	Yes[l]	Yes[l]
20. Foreign currency financial statements translated using temporal method?	Yes	No[m]	No[m]
21. Translation gains/losses reflected in current income?	Yes	Yes	Yes
22. Unsettled foreign currency transactions translated at current rate?	Yes	No[n]	Yes
23. Exchange gains and losses on unsettled transactions reflected in current income?	Yes	No[o]	No[o]
24. Accounting principles consistently followed?	Yes	No[p]	Yes

NOTES: [a] average cost methods; [b] cost; [c] while Korean firms are permitted to follow the lower of cost or market rule they rarely do; [d] cost method; [e] capitalized and amortized over a 3-year period; [f] limited to 50 percent of estimated liability (based on voluntary separation); [g] fixed assets may be revalued whenever the wholesale price index increases by more than 25 percent since the last revaluation; [h] double declining balance method; [i] for equipment deemed in the national interest; [j] for equipment in special industries; [k] prior period adjustments, regardless of the nature, are included in the income statement as 'extraordinary items' and are a major source of income smoothing; [l] reversal of these reserves also permits income smoothing opportunities; [m] current rate method; [n] only short-term payable and receivables; [o] only on short-term losses; [p] loose compliance.

34

GOING GLOBAL

A Toronto-to-Tokyo guide to the intricacies of foreign stock listings

*Ajay Adhikari, Edward N. Coffman and Rasoul H. Tondkar**

No single event demonstrated the interdependence of the world's major stock exchanges more than 'Black Monday,' the Oct. 19, 1987 stock market crash. That event, and its aftermath, produced a 22.6% decline in the Dow Jones Industrial Average and sent stock prices plummeting around the world in a matter of days. Most analysts agreed that Black Monday proved one fundamental point – the trend toward globalization was more or less complete.

Such integration between exchanges presents new opportunities for companies in search of an international orientation, but it also places new demands on market participants and regulators. The dynamic nature of the global equity market poses challenges for accountants as well. As cross-border investment grows[1], accountants are increasingly asked to assist investors, underwriters and regulators. Only accountants with a well-developed knowledge of foreign accounting practices can help interpret and analyse the financial statements prepared under various generally accepted accounting principles (GAAP).

But accountants face even greater challenges: They must not only follow accounting developments in different countries, but also keep abreast of the many initiatives designed to harmonize accounting disclosure and reporting requirements that are issued by international and regional organizations such as the International Accounting Standards Committee (IASC), the International Organization of Securities Commissions (IOSCO) and the European Community (EC).

From CA magazine (July 1991) pp 24–31.
Reprinted with permission from CA magazine.
Published by the Canadian Institute of Chartered Accountants, Toronto, Canada.

Other challenges come from the international tax arena, where new developments can occasionally pose a serious threat to security investments in stocks and bonds. Eurobonds issued by US multinationals before 1984, for example, lost 15% of their value after the US government decided to revoke its income tax treaty with the Netherlands Antilles on June 29, 1987.

Nonetheless, more and more companies around the world want to list their shares on foreign stock exchanges. A recent survey of global money managers, securities traders and chief financial officers revealed that international securities sales and trading are expected to grow rapidly over the next five years.[2] The increase can be attributed, at least in part, to the deregulatory initiatives implemented by host governments in their respective financial markets and to the belief that the benefits from foreign listing outweigh the costs.

But what *are* the benefits and the costs? We'd like to present the pros and cons of such listings and highlight the major filing requirements of six stock exchanges – New York, Toronto, Tokyo, London, Frankfurt and Paris. We focus on these exchanges because in terms of market turnover (volume of buying and selling), the New York and Toronto exchanges are the most active in North America: the London, Frankfurt and Paris exchanges are the most active in Europe: and the Tokyo Stock Exchange is the most active in Asia.

Companies seek a foreign listing for a variety of strategic, commercial or financial reasons. Large companies based in countries with small markets where equity securities are not actively traded often find it less expensive and easier to raise equity financing elsewhere. Swedish multinationals like Ericsson, Electrolux and Swedish Match offer a good case in point. These companies have listed their shares on such broad-based equity markets as the London and New York stock exchanges because their domestic market isn't large enough to support their needs. Ericsson recently sold 14 million shares in the United States at the same time it sold 17 million shares in Sweden. The market turnover of Ericsson's shares on the New York Stock Exchange was 350,000 to 400,000 shares a day compared to only 20,000 shares on the Stockholm Stock Exchange.[3]

Another incentive for multinationals to list outside their country of origin is the possibility of global 24-hour trading. The desire to create a 24-hour market for their shares has led many multinationals to list on at least the New York, London and Tokyo exchanges – the primary centres for around-the-clock trading.

Broad exposure in international capital markets provides flexibility when raising capital. One of the latest developments in this area is the increase in corporate issues of nonvoting stock, which enables a company to raise new capital without dilution of control. Another popular financial instrument is the equity-related bond, which possesses features of both bonds and stock and often holds an advantage over pure equity in terms of its attractiveness to investors and lower cost to issuers.

Investors' perceptions also play a part in a company's decision to list on a particular stock exchange. Technology firms frequently list their equity securities on foreign stock exchanges in the belief that their product is appreciated more outside the country. In that case, listing on foreign exchanges would allow a company's stock to be sold in the most favourable market at the time.

A foreign listing, besides raising capital, can help a company build name recognition, brand loyalty and an international reputation. Walt Disney Company, in an effort to finance its European operations (Euro Disneyland) and gain international exposure, issued its stock on five European exchanges in 1989. Foreign listing can also help generate employee and customer loyalty on a worldwide basis.

Issuing shares in foreign markets helps to broaden the shareholder base, which may serve as both a defensive and an offensive mechanism in takeover bids. On the one hand, it may be difficult for a predator company to launch a takeover of a company whose shares are held in different countries. On the other hand, a company that has a substantial presence in foreign countries can more easily mount its own takeover and merger bids through stock swaps.

Even after considering advantages like the ones just mentioned, however, many companies choose to stay put. A foreign listing can be both costly and time-consuming without offering any immediate benefits. One disadvantage of raising equity capital abroad is the potential for shares issued in foreign markets to flow back to the issuer's domestic market soon after they're released, thus depressing the stock's price in the domestic market. Companies usually have to commit themselves to some research and a strong promotional campaign before issuing foreign stock in order to develop loyal shareholders – one way of preventing the flow back.

Because accounting and taxation laws differ from one country to the next, the tax and income consequences of corporate decisions must be taken into account for each country in which the company is listed. In 1984, for example, Swiss and US shareholders of Bowater Industries, a British multinational, were less than ecstatic when shares of the corporation's 'demerged' North American subsidiary were classified as income by their respective tax authorities. The decision to distribute shares of the demerged subsidiary was apparently based on demerger legislation in the United Kingdom, which treated the transaction as a tax-free distribution.[4]

Accountants can play a vital role in such decisions. By analysing the tax rules of the various countries in which shareholders are located, they can better advise companies on dividend distribution policies and other actions that affect stockholders.

As with any listing, there are numerous costs associated with initiating and maintaining one on a foreign stock exchange (see Table 1). The normal fees, however, are only a fraction of the total costs. Commissions payable to the bank acting as the shareholder service agent in the foreign country, accountants' and lawyers' fees, the expense of translating annual reports, and the costs of receptions, press conferences and advertising are some of the additional outlays that must be considered. Most of these costs are recurring – they will continue even after the initial listing is granted. Companies with foreign listings must also maintain strong investor relations programs, with the attached expenditures on presentations and road shows.[5]

The different accounting principles used in various countries create major concerns for companies considering foreign listing. Financial information determined under local accounting principles may have to be restated in accordance with those of the country in which a listing is being sought. The treatment of goodwill, for instance, varies among the six exchanges discussed here. In the United States and Canada, it's capitalized and amortized over periods not exceeding 40 years. In the United Kingdom, goodwill is immediately written off against reserves or amortized over its economic life (most companies choose immediate deduction from reserves). In France, goodwill is amortized over its useful life, although in some cases it may be written off immediately against reserves. In Germany, it may be written off against reserves, amortized over four years or amortized over the number of years benefited. Finally, in Japan, immediate expensing of goodwill is encouraged, although it may be capitalized and amortized over five years or less.

Companies must also concern themselves with the differences in listing and filing requirements between stock exchanges around the world. One way to address this challenge is to have accountants within the company familiarize themselves with the requirements of stock markets on which listing is sought. Some accounting firms also specialize in this field. Regardless of the approach, the accountant's role is critical.

Table 1 Listing fees for six exchanges[5]

Stock exchanges	*Initial listing**	*Annual listing**
New York	$36,800 upwards	$14,630 upwards
Toronto	$1,680–$23,000	$2,200–$10,600
Tokyo	$20,000	$1,200 upwards
London (ISE)	$990–$62,500	$910–$16,300
Frankfurt	$272–$27,256	None
Paris	None	None

*Depends on number of shares listed and traded. All figures are expressed in US dollars.

In some instances, governments impose artificial barriers such as foreign exchange controls, deposit requirements and interest equalization taxes to restrict foreign listing and cross-border equity financing. Because of competitive pressures from domestic companies with foreign listings and from other stock markets, many countries have begun to relax such barriers.

NEW YORK STOCK EXCHANGE

The NYSE is one of the leading stock exchanges in the world. Reflecting the stringent accounting standards in the United States, the listing and filing requirements of the NYSE and the Securities and Exchange Commission (SEC) are some of the toughest for foreign companies. This helps to explain why the number of foreign listings on the NYSE is so low; as of Dec. 31, 1989 (the latest figures available), only 86 foreign companies were listed, compared to 599 on the London exchange.[6]

Foreign companies that want to list on the NYSE are required to submit audited annual financial statements for the last three years. These statements can be prepared in accordance with accounting principles of the home country but the results must be reconciled with US GAAP. Foreign companies listed on the NYSE are also required to publish and submit additional information, such as audited consolidated annual statements and interim statements of earnings, within the time periods specified in the regulations.

The SEC, in conjunction with the NYSE, has made a special effort to reduce the onerousness of such requirements. In 1986, responding to foreign companies' complaints, the SEC modified the filing standard that required listed foreign companies to submit interim earnings statements on a quarterly basis. Interim reporting is a new development in many foreign countries; some do not require companies to file interim statements at all. Under the modified standard, the NYSE will accept a foreign company's interim earnings reporting as long as it's consistent with the law and practices of the home country; it will not, however, accept interim reporting on a basis less frequent than semiannual, no matter what the law in the home country. Despite such concessions, the NYSE remains one of the most demanding stock exchanges for foreign companies.

TORONTO STOCK EXCHANGE

The TSE, the biggest stock exchange in Canada, accounts for approximately 75% of the total value of shares traded on the five Canadian exchanges. As of Dec. 31, 1989, the TSE had 68 foreign listings – like the NYSE, an insignificant number when compared to the other exchanges discussed here.

The TSE's listing and filing requirements are largely comparable with the NYSE's. Financial statements submitted by foreign companies can be prepared in accordance with the home country's accounting principles. Companies are required to disclose differences in financial results between home-country and Canadian GAAP, although a reconciliation of the financial results is not required at the time of listing. Once listed, however, if a foreign company wants to issue new securities on the TSE, it must provide a reconciliation of the financial results determined under local accounting principles and the results determined under Canadian GAAP at that time. In the early 1980s, the TSE became one of the few stock exchanges in the world to encourage compliance with the International Accounting Standards (IASs) issued by the International Accounting Standards Committee.

The Toronto Stock Exchange permits a certain latitude in the listing and filing requirements of foreign applicants with exceptional circumstances. For instance, a foreign company listed on another major stock exchange may be allowed to enter into a modified form of the listing agreement whereby it could obtain exemptions from certain requirements of the TSE. Applications for such exemptions are handled on a case-by-case basis.

A new multijurisdictional disclosure system (MJDS) is currently under study by the Ontario Securities Commission, the Commission des valeurs mobilières du Québec, and the US Securities and Exchange Commission. Recognizing the similarity in disclosure and financial reporting practices in Canada and the United States, this proposal is based on the concept of mutual acceptance of the other country's requirements. Under the MJDS, a company registered with the SEC in the United States could fulfil most of the TSE's listing and filing requirements by providing copies of the documents filed with the SEC. The MJDS will also permit the use of a single registration statement for a multijurisdictional security offering by US and Canadian issuers.

TOKYO STOCK EXCHANGE

The TKSE is fast becoming one of the leading stock exchanges in the world. Since 1985, it has made a concentrated effort to attract more foreign listings, with significant results. By the end of 1987, the TKSE had exceeded the NYSE in terms of total market capitalization; $2.7 trillion for the TKSE compared to $2.2 trillion for the NYSE (all figures are quoted in US dollars). And by the end of 1989, the TKSE boasted 116 foreign listings compared to 21 in 1985.

Foreign companies seeking to list on the TKSE have to meet the requirements of the TKSE and Japan's Ministry of Finance before they're admitted. Financial statements for the last five years must be translated into Japanese and the amounts must be presented in the currency of the company's home country along with yen equivalents; a restatement of the financial statements to conform with Japanese GAAP is not required. The foreign company must have at least 1,000 shares in Japan before it can apply for a listing. Given that a company is not authorized to trade its shares before being granted listing status, this requirement seems difficult to fulfil. To meet it, a Japanese sponsor acquires shares on foreign stock exchanges and places them with a sufficient number of investors in Japan.

What this boils down to is that companies seeking a listing on the TKSE must be sponsored by a Japanese securities company. Japan's Big Four – Daiwa, Nikko, Yamaichi and Nomura – actively market their skills in this area. The sponsor plays a key role in the listing process: It prepares all the necessary documents related to the application, and bears the (unspoken) responsibility of thoroughly examining the aspirant's basic qualifications for TKSE listing. As a result, once a formal listing application is made, it's almost certain to be approved. According to *Euromoney Magazine*, not a single foreign application has been turned down.[7]

The TKSE requires companies to file *audited* semi-annual interim reports, a condition unique to the TKSE among the exchanges discussed here. While the Tokyo exchange's requirements may be demanding, they are considered substantially liberalized from those of several years ago. Previously, for instance, all foreign companies listed on the TKSE had to have their audited financial statements reaudited by Japanese auditors. In 1983, partly in response to complaints and a number of 'delistings,' the TKSE abolished its 'double audit' requirement.

Although some differences remain between the TKSE and the North American exchanges (such as the 1,000 shareholders requirement), North American companies seeking a TKSE listing are usually at an advantage because of the familiarity of the Japanese with the former's accounting and auditing standards. As such, the listing process for North American companies is usually more efficient than that for companies from other continents.

EUROPEAN COMMUNITY

As part of its goal to unify capital markets, the EC has issued three directives concerning admission, listing and interim reporting. These directives must be incorporated into member states' national laws, although some latitude is allowed on the timing of incorporation. They are intended to harmonize the listing and filing requirements of EC stock exchanges, a move that has important implications for foreign companies seeking to list on these exchanges. Harmonization would allow simultaneous listings, enabling foreign companies to tap the full potential of Europe's 'single market,' targeted for completion by 1992. All three EC stock exchanges discussed here (London, Frankfurt and Paris) have incorporated the directives.

INTERNATIONAL STOCK EXCHANGE

In recent years, London has strongly asserted its position as an international financial centre. In October 1986, it undertook a major deregulation of its financial markets – quickly nicknamed the 'Big Bang' – which was followed by a name change from the London Stock Exchange to the International Stock Exchange. The ISE had 599 foreign listings as of Dec. 31, 1989, the largest number of foreign listings of any stock exchange in the world.

Although the ISE's listing and filing requirements are complex, it gives special consideration to foreign companies. Such companies are permitted to submit financial statements for only the past three years instead of the five years required of domestic companies. What's more, these companies are not required to restate their financial statements to comply with UK GAAP, although compliance with International Accounting Standards is encouraged. Significant departures or noncompliance with IASs must be disclosed or explained.

The ISE has made a strong commitment to attract and maintain foreign listings. Its strategic location offers a special opportunity for foreign companies in that it bridges the closing time of stock exchanges in the Far East with the opening time of stock exchanges in the United States. The ISE offers a key link in 24-hour global trading.

FRANKFURT STOCK EXCHANGE

The FSE, the largest exchange in Germany, has also maintained a strong international profile. As of Dec. 31, 1989, the FSE had 348 foreign listed companies. The incorporation of the three EC directives concerning securities legislation greatly strengthened the FSE's listing and filing requirements and brought them in line with other EC stock exchanges. A funds statement, for example, was not previously required from companies seeking to list on the FSE; since incorporating the EC's interim reporting directive, the Frankfurt exchange requires it.

Like the ISE, the FSE provides some latitude to foreign companies. Interim reports may be prepared in another language, provided that it's not unusual in the investments field. Foreign companies that want to list on the FSE are required to submit financial statements for the past three years, but need not restate their financial statements to conform with German GAAP.

PARIS STOCK EXCHANGE

Compared to the London and Frankfurt stock exchanges, the PSE is more closely regulated. As on the other two EC exchanges, foreign companies seeking to list on the Paris exchange are required to submit financial

Table 2 Listing and filing requirements of six stock exchanges

Disclosure requirements	*New York*	*Toronto*	*Tokyo*	*London*	*Frankfurt*	*Paris*
General information						
• History of the company	Yes	Yes	Yes	Yes	Yes	Yes
• Outline of business	Yes	Yes	Yes	Yes	Yes	Yes
• Research and development	Yes	No	Yes	Yes	Yes	Yes
• Employee-labour relations	Yes	Yes	Yes	Yes	Yes	Yes
• Capital expenditures	Yes	Yes	Yes	Yes	Yes	Yes
• Corporate social responsibility	Yes	No	Yes	No	No	Yes
• Pending or potential litigation	Yes (Both)	Yes (Both)	Yes (Pending)	Yes (Both)	Yes (Pending)	Yes (Pending)
• Extent of dependence on major customers	Yes	No	Yes	No	No	No
Information on principal contents of each significant contract (not contracts entered into in ordinary course of business)	Yes	Yes	Yes	Yes	No	No
Information on managers and directors						
• Names, salaries, and functional responsibilities of managers	Yes	Yes	Yes (Not salaries)	Yes	Yes	Yes (Not salaries)
• Names, salaries, and major outside affiliations of directors	Yes	Yes	Yes (Not salaries)	Yes (Not salaries)	Yes	Yes (Not salaries)
Information about company capital						
• General information on capitalization	Yes	Yes	Yes	Yes	Yes	Yes
• Statement of changes in share capital in past years	Yes	Yes	Yes	Yes	Yes	Yes
• Number and types of stockholders	Yes	Yes	Yes	Yes	No	Yes
• Names and size of holdings of largest stockholders	Yes	Yes	Yes	Yes	Yes	Yes
• Names and particulars of parties who are seeking to obtain substantial interest in the company	No	No	No	Yes	No	No

• Information on options, warrants and conversion rights outstanding	Yes	Yes	Yes	Yes	Yes	Yes
Financial information						
• Historical summary of important operating and financial data	Yes	Yes	Yes	Yes	Yes	Yes
• Audited financial statements (income statement and balance sheet)	Yes	Yes	Yes	Yes	Yes	Yes
• Statement of sources and application of funds	Yes	Yes	Yes	Yes	Yes	Yes
• Interim reports (Quarterly or semiannually)	Yes (Quarterly)	Yes (Quarterly)	Yes (Semiannual)	Yes (Semiannual)	Yes (Semiannual)	Yes (Semiannual)
• Post-balance-sheet events	Yes	Yes	Yes	Yes	Yes	Yes
• Consolidated statements	Yes	Yes	Yes	Yes	Yes	Yes
• Segment information (Sales or earnings)	Yes (Both)	Yes (Both)	Yes (Sales)	Yes (Sales)	Yes (Sales)	Yes (Sales)
• Pro forma statements where there is major financing, recapitalization, acquisition or reorganization (or where these are under consideration)	Yes	Yes	No	Yes	No	No
Recent development and prospects						
• Any significant information that may affect the market for a company's securities	Yes	Yes	Yes	Yes	Yes	Yes
• Discussion of major factors that will influence next year's results	Yes	Yes	Yes	Yes	Yes	Yes
• Profit forecast	No	Yes	Yes	Yes	No	Yes
Other requirements for foreign companies						
• Differences between accounting principles in country of origin and country in which listing is sought (when former used)	Disclose and reconcile	Disclose (Compliance with IAS is encouraged)	Disclose	Disclose (Compliance with IAS is encouraged)	Additional information required	Additional information required

statements for the past three years; but the PSE's listing and filing requirements are more rigid. Foreign companies' financial statements, submitted as part of the listing requirements, must be translated into French and be understandable to a French reader; an independent auditor is required to verify the translation's 'understandability.' Such a requirement is unique to Paris out of the six exchanges we examined. And that's not all. Foreign companies outside the EC must receive authorization from the French Ministry of Finance and they must be listed on a stock exchange in the domiciled country. (Companies from other EC countries seeking to list on the PSE are exempt from these requirements.)

The French government's effort to internationalize the PSE is reflected in the growing number of foreign companies listed on the exchange: At the end of 1989, 223 foreign companies were listed compared to 166 in 1984. The general financial deregulation of the French capital markets in the 1980s, coupled with the increased privatization of industry, have made it easier and more attractive for foreign companies to list on the Paris exchange.

Because of the opportunities offered by a global marketplace, more and more companies are seeking to list their shares on foreign exchanges. But there are advantages and disadvantages. Benefits such as the reduced cost of capital, flexibility in raising capital and enhanced international image may be offset by the potential flowback of shares to the home market, the different tax regulations of various countries, and differences in accounting principles and listing and filing requirements (see Table 2 for a comparative summary of the listing and filing requirements of the exchanges discussed here). These differences can present challenges for companies desiring a foreign listing – challenges accountants can demystify. One thing is sure: some of the most lucrative benefits attached to this globalization belong to the accounting profession itself.

NOTES

1 According to Frederick D. S. Choi and Richard M. Levich, authors of *The Capital Market Effects of International Accounting Diversity*, at least one equity trade in nine has a foreign investor on the other side.

2 Michael R. Sesit's 'Global sales of securities seen growing' in the *Wall Street Journal*. Nov. 23, 1990, pp. C1, C9.

3 Paul Stonham's *Global Stock Market Reforms*, Gower Publishing, Cambridge, 1987, p. 11.

4 'Tips from a seasoned issuer,' *Euromoney Magazine Supplement*, November 1986, p. 12.

5 Information extracted from F. D. S. Choi's and R. M. Levich's *The Capital Market Effects of International Accounting Diversity*. Dow Jones-Irwin, Homewood, Illinois, 1990, pp. 112–113.

6 All statistics concerning the number of listed companies used here are obtained from *Activities and Statistics 1989 Report*, issued by the International Federation of Stock Exchanges.

7 Norman Sklarewitz's 'Cores for congratulation,' *Euromoney Magazine Supplement*, January 1988, p. 54.

QUESTIONS

1 Discuss the opportunities and risks posed to the accounting profession by the globalisation of capital markets, and suggest how the profession might respond to this.

AUTHOR INDEX

SUBJECT INDEX